Microsoft Office 97 Quic...

tear here

Quick Keys That Work in All Off...

Lose your mouse and use your keyboard to enter common com...

To	Press	To	Press
Select entire document	Ctrl+A	Paste format	Ctrl+Shift+V
Copy selection	Ctrl+C	Paste selection	Ctrl+V
Insert page break	Ctrl+Enter	Cut selection	Ctrl+X
Find text or format	Ctrl+F	Repeat last action	Ctrl+Y
Replace text	Ctrl+H	Undo last action	Ctrl+Z
Insert hyperlink (on a Web page)	Ctrl+K	Delete selection	Delete
Create new file	Ctrl+N	Get help from an Office Assistant	F1
Open file	Ctrl+O	Check spelling	F7
Print file	Ctrl+P	Activate menu bar	F10
Save file	Ctrl+S	Same as File/Save As command	F12
Copy format of the selection	Ctrl+Shift+C	Insert line break	Shift+Enter

Microsoft Powerpoint Keystrokes

PowerPoint shortcut keys vary depending on the selected view. Use this as your guide.

Outline and Slide Views

To	Press	To	Press
Promote a paragraph	Alt+Shift+Left Arrow	Show only level 1 headings	Alt+Shift+1
Demote a paragraph	Alt+Shift+Right Arrow	Show all text and headings	Alt+Shift+A
Move selected paragraphs up	Alt+Shift+Up Arrow	Collapse text below selected heading	Alt+Shift+ – (minus)
Move selected paragraphs down	Alt+Shift+Down Arrow	Show text below selected heading	Alt+Shift+ + (plus)

Slide Show Controls

To	Press	To	Press
Display next slide	Enter	Use original timings during rehearsal	O
Display previous slide	Backspace		
Go to specified slide number	Slide ##+Enter	Change mouse pointer to a pen	Ctrl+P
Start or stop timed slide show	S	Change the pen back into a mouse pointer	Ctrl+A
End slide show	Esc		
Set new timings during rehearsal	T		

Microsoft Word Keystrokes

Word has more shortcut keys than we can list here. But these are the pick of the lot (mostly for formatting text).

To	Press	To	Press
Change font	Ctrl+Shift+F	Make text italic	Ctrl+I
Change font size	Ctrl+Shift+P	Remove text formatting	Ctrl+Shift+Z
Open selected drop-down list	Alt+Down Arrow	Single-space lines	Ctrl+1
Uppercase/lowercase letters	Shift+F3	Double-space lines	Ctrl+2
Make text bold	Ctrl+B	Center paragraph	Ctrl+E
Underline text	Ctrl+U	Move selected text or graphic	F2
Underline text but not spaces between words	Ctrl+Shift+W	Insert an AutoText entry after typing its abbreviation	F3

Microsoft Access Keystokes

Yes, even Access has its own shortcut keys.

To	Press	To	Press
Move to the next field in a form or table	Tab	Delete the current record	Ctrl+ – (minus)
		Save changes to the current record	Shift+Enter
Move to the previous field in a form or table	Shift+Tab	Select the column to the left of the currently selected column in Datasheet view	Shift+Left Arrow
Insert current date	Ctrl+;		
Insert current time	Ctrl+:	Select the column to the right of the currently selected column in Datasheet view	Shift+Right Arrow
Insert a field's default entry	Ctrl+Alt+Spacebar		
Insert the same value as in the previous record	Ctrl+'		
		Open selected drop-down list in a field	Alt+Down Arrow
Add a new record	Ctrl++ (plus)	Change to Form view from Design view	Ctrl+R

Microsoft Outlook Keystrokes

Use the following keystrokes to create new entries in Outlook.

To	Press	To	Press
Create a new mail message	Ctrl+Shift+M	Make a new folder or subfolder	Ctrl+Shift+E
Make a new appointment	Ctrl+Shift+A	Check for new e-mail	F5
Send a meeting request	Ctrl+Shift+Q	Display the Address Book	Ctrl+Shift+B
Add a task to your task list	Ctrl+Shift+K	Find an item	Ctrl+Shift+F
Send a task request	Ctrl+Shift+U	Reply to a selected e-mail message	Ctrl+R
Add a contact to the Address Book	Ctrl+Shift+C	Reply to the sender and all recipients of an e-mail message you received	Ctrl+Shift+R
Record a journal entry	Ctrl+Shift+J		
Post a note to yourself	Ctrl+Shift+N		
Post a description of a discussion	Ctrl+Shift+S	Forward an e-mail message you received	Ctrl+F
Create a new Office document	Ctrl+Shift+H		

Office Assistant Shortcut Keys

When the Office Assistant pops up on your screen and offers to help, use the following keys to control it.

To	Press	To	Press
Select a topic from the list that the Assistant displays	Alt+1, Alt+2…	Display the Assistant	F1
		Display the next tip	Alt+N
Close the Assistant	Esc	Display the previous tip	Alt+B

Microsoft Excel Keystrokes

When you have a lot of entries to type, you don't want to be fumbling with your mouse. Use the following keystrokes instead.

To	Press	To	Press
End an entry you typed	Enter (Or Arrow key)	Select entire column	Ctrl+Spacebar
Cancel an entry you typed	Esc	Select entire row	Shift+Spacebar
Create a new line in a cell	Alt+Enter	Move one screen to the right	Alt+Page Down
Edit a cell entry	F2	Move one screen to the left	Alt+Page Up
Edit a cell note	Shift+F2	Flip to the next worksheet page	Ctrl+Page Down
Fill a cell entry into cells below	Ctrl+D	Flip to the previous worksheet page	Ctrl+Page Up
Fill a cell entry into cells to the right	Ctrl+R	Go to a specific cell or named range	F5
End cell entry and move to the next cell to the right	Tab	Perform all formula calculations	F9

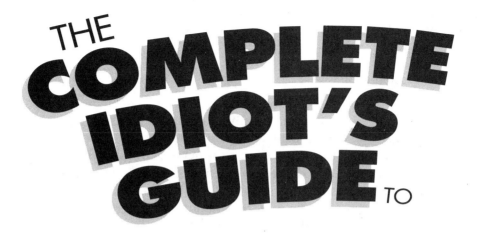

THE COMPLETE IDIOT'S GUIDE TO

Microsoft® Office 97
Professional

by Joe Kraynak and Sherry Kinkoph

A Division of Macmillian Computer Publishing
201 W. 103rd Street, Indianapolis, IN 46290 USA

To my dear friend, Stacey Federhart, who (to the best of my knowledge) has never even touched a stupid old computer, unless you count ATM machines. —Sherry Kinkoph

To Nick and Ali, for helping me keep my mind fresh. —Joe Kraynak

Library of Congress Catalog Card Number: 96-70770

International Standard Book Number: 0-7897-0950-3

99 98   8 7

Interpretation of the printing code: the rightmost double-digit number is the year of the book's first printing; the rightmost single-digit number is the number of the book's printing. For example, a printing code of 97-1 shows that this copy of the book was printed during the first printing of the book in 1997.

Screen reproductions in this book were created by means of the program Collage Complete from Inner Media, Inc, Hollis, NH.

Printed in the United States of America

Publisher
Roland Elgey

Publishing Manager
Lynn E. Zingraf

Editorial Services Director
Elizabeth Keaffaber

Managing Editor
Michael Cunningham

Director of Marketing
Lynn E. Zingraf

Acquisitions Editor
Martha O'Sullivan

Technical Specialist
Nadeem Muhammed

Product Development Specialist
Melanie Palaisa

Technical Editor
Herb Feltner

Production Editor
Audra Gable

Book Designer
Barbara Kordesh

Cover Designer
Dan Armstrong

Production Team
Angela Calvert
Tricia Flodder
William Huys Jr.
Malinda Kuhn
Daniela Raderstorf
Beth Rago
Laure Robinson
Elizabeth San Miguel

Indexer
Chris Barrick
Brad Herriman

We'd Like to Hear from You!

As part of our continuing effort to produce books of the highest possible quality, Que would like to hear your comments. To stay competitive, we *really* want you, as a computer book reader and user, to let us know what you like or dislike most about this book or other Que products.

Although we cannot provide general technical support, we're happy to help you resolve problems you encounter related to our books, disks, or other products. If you need such assistance, please contact our Tech Support department at 800-545-5914 ext. 3833.

To order other Que or Macmillan Computer Publishing books or products, please call our Customer Service department at 800-835-3202 ext. 666.

You can mail comments, ideas, or suggestions for improving future editions to the address below, or send us a fax at (317) 581-4663. For the online inclined, Macmillan Computer Publishing has a forum on CompuServe (type **GO QUEBOOKS** at any prompt) through which our staff and authors are available for questions and comments. The address of our Internet site is **http://www.mcp.com/que** (World Wide Web).

In addition to exploring our forum, please feel free to contact me personally to discuss your opinions of this book: I'm **73353,2061** on CompuServe, and I'm **mpalaisa@que.mcp.com** on the Internet.

Thanks in advance—your comments will help us to continue publishing the best books available on computer topics in today's market.

Melanie Palaisa
Product Development Specialist
Que Corporation
201 W. 103rd Street
Indianapolis, Indiana 46290
USA

Contents at a Glance

Contents

Part 2: Whipping Up Word Documents 37

4 Making and Editing Word Documents 39

5 Giving Your Text a Makeover 57

6 Aligning Text in Tables and Columns 75

14 Giving Your Worksheet a Professional Look 177

15 Graphing Data for Fun and Profit 187

Introduction: Your Office in 1997

Life in the business world used to be easy. If we needed to send a memo, we fired up a word processor, typed the memo, printed it, and distributed it while on the way out to lunch. We used one program at a time (usually WordPerfect or Lotus) to type letters and crunch numbers. When we had a meeting, we would actually meet each other, maybe share a box of donuts and gulp coffee in the early morning. We usually knew what our colleagues looked like, and we knew corporate etiquette (even if we didn't always practice it).

The business world of the '90s is much more complex. Instead of working on our own computers, we are now connected to a global neighborhood of computers. Instead of typing and printing letters, we now tap out e-mail messages. We work from virtual offices, and we have virtual meetings using chat programs, Internet phone applications, and whiteboards. Many of us even have our own Web pages. As for the new etiquette of the virtual world, we are all sort of feeling our way around.

Welcome to Microsoft Office 97!

To master this new age, a simple word processing or spreadsheet application is no longer sufficient. We need a new set of tools. We need a suite of applications that not only work together, but also allow us to collaborate on projects, exchange ideas and information via e-mail, and make our presence known on the Web. We need Microsoft Office 97.

Microsoft Office has served us well for years, allowing us to create and publish letters, memos, brochures, and newsletters; to combine Excel spreadsheets with Word documents; to manage our schedules and documents; to record and manipulate our data; and to create professional slide show presentations.

Office 97 extends the capabilities of its former versions by adding tools that make it even easier to collaborate on projects over a network, take advantage of intranets, exchange e-mail within a company and over the Internet, and publish Web pages. With Office 97 and the right training on how to use its components individually and together, you will be well-equipped to master this age of information and communication.

Welcome to The Complete Idiot's Guide to Microsoft Office 97 Professional

The Complete Idiot's Guide to Microsoft Office 97 Professional is your key to success with Office 97. It explains all about the new versions of the Microsoft Office programs: Word, Excel, PowerPoint, Access, and Outlook—including all the spiffy things you can do with them. This book covers everything from word processing to spreadsheet number crunching, from database management to graphics, from slide shows to appointment books. But that's not all—for a limited time only, we'll tell you how to make the programs work together so you can tackle even bigger tasks. And you'll learn how to unleash these various tools through e-mail and on the Web.

How Is This Book Going to Help?

Basically, this book will help you:

➤ Grasp the basics of Office 97 (and use its Help system when you get into a jam).

➤ Master the ins and outs of using Office 97 to create documents of all kinds, design graphic presentations with pizzazz, make spreadsheets using formulas and functions, keep an electronic calendar, and much more.

➤ Get the most out of Office 97 by using all of the products together. Here you will learn how to transform a Word document into a PowerPoint presentation, drop an Excel spreadsheet or graph into a Word document, or even merge a list of addresses from an Access database into a form letter created in Word.

➤ Communicate more effectively with people in your company and around the world through e-mail. You will learn how to send messages, documents, and files right from the Office 97 applications instead of using a separate e-mail program.

➤ Publish professional-looking pages on the Web. You will learn how to transform Word documents, Excel spreadsheets, and PowerPoint presentations into brilliant Web pages!

How Do You Use This Book?

There's no need to read this book from cover to cover—unless you're just trying to rack up some overtime at work. We know that you probably don't use *all* of the Office products, so we divided the book into the following seven parts to make it easy for you to skip the information you don't need (or so you can read one part each day for a week):

➤ Part 1, "Microsoft Office Over Easy," provides a brief introduction to Office, unveiling the new features, teaching you the basics, and instructing you on how to use the online Help system for more in-depth knowledge.

➤ Part 2, "Whipping Up Word Documents," focuses on Microsoft Word, Office 97's word processing application.

➤ Part 3, "Crunching Numbers with Excel Spreadsheets," gives you the low-down on how to create spreadsheets and graph your data.

➤ Part 4, "Snapping Slide Shows in PowerPoint," teaches you how to dazzle your friends and colleagues with on-screen slide shows, and how to transfer your slide show to overhead transparencies, slides, or paper.

➤ Part 5, "Mastering the Information Age with Access," gives you the database management skills you need to create a database and use it to extract and analyze information.

➤ Part 6, "Looking After Your Life with Outlook," shows you how to use Office 97's brand new application, Outlook, to manage your schedule and your desktop.

➤ Part 7, "Tapping the Office Synergy," shows you how to use the various Office 97 applications together to dynamically share data between applications, to manage your documents, and to use Office 97 effectively on a network or an intranet (an internal internet). As an added bonus, Chapter 31 shows you how to publish on the Web using Office 97.

At the end of the book, you'll find a glossary of all the crazy terms you'll need to know in order to use the programs. And, in case you're upgrading Windows at the same time you're moving up to Office 97, you'll find a Windows 95/Windows NT primer at the back of the book, too. (We placed it at the back, so it wouldn't get in the way for all you Windows experts.)

Wait, There's More

To make this book a little easier to use, we took it upon ourselves to follow a few conventions. Anything you need to type appears in bold, like this:

Type **this entry**

If there's any variable information to be typed, such as your own name or a file name, it appears in italics, like this:

Type *this number*

In addition, you'll find boxed information (like the examples below) scattered throughout the book to help you with terminology, boring technical background, shortcuts, and other tips. You certainly don't have to read these little boxes, although I did work hard putting them together for you. If you want to understand more about a topic, you might find these boxes helpful. But in case you don't, they're sort of tucked out of the way so you can quickly skip them.

Techno Talk

These boxes contain technical twaddle that will make you drowsy. Read them only if you're planning to appear on *Jeopardy!*, the game show for people who wish they'd been born computers. Look to these boxes when you want to find definitions and explanations of technical words and operations.

Check This Out!

Hey, you'll like reading these boxes. They contain tips, tricks, shortcuts, and other suggestions on how you can cheat your computer out of a long, boring procedure. Plus, I'll throw in fascinating tidbits for you, just to keep things exciting.

New! Office 97 To quickly discover the differences between Office 95 and Office 97, scan the margins for this icon. Although this icon won't point out *all* the differences in the new version, it will point out the most innovative and exciting new features.

Web Work! If you see a Techno Talk box that's labeled Web Work!, be ready to learn how to use one of the exciting (not to mention new) Office 97 Web features.

Acknowledgments

Now for the obligatory author-thanks-everyone part of the introduction. Special thanks to Martha O'Sullivan for pulling all the strings that needed to be pulled to make this book a success. Thanks go to Melanie Palaisa for putting her development expertise to good use. Even more special thanks to Audra Gable, who had to read every single word *and* make sure the book made it to the printer on time. Also, extra thanks to our tech editor, Herb Feltner, for double-checking all the geeky stuff. Finally, big thanks to everyone in production who worked on this book to make it look nice.

Trademarks

All terms mentioned in this book that are known to be or are suspected of being trademarks or service marks have been appropriately capitalized. Que Corporation cannot attest to the accuracy of this information. Use of a term in this book should not be regarded as affecting the validity of any trademark or service mark.

Part 1
Microsoft Office Over Easy

When you first drive a new car off the dealer's lot, you usually don't know that much about it. The salesperson takes three minutes out of his busy life to show you how to turn on the lights and the windshield wipers, point out the location of the AM/FM radio, and give you confusing instructions on how to set and cancel cruise control. It takes a couple weeks to find out all the little things, like how to adjust the steering wheel, turn on the A/C, or even pop the hood.

It's the same way with a new program. You need to know what's new about it, why it places that extra toolbar on your desktop (and how to get rid of it), how to use some of the basic controls, and how to navigate its Help system (for when you back yourself into a corner). This part teaches you all that (and a little more)—so you can sit behind the wheel of Office 97 with complete confidence.

"SLOW RESPONSE TIME" INTERVENTION.

What's New in Office 97?

Office 97 has hit the streets, and you're wondering, "What's all the hubbub, bub?" Maybe you are trying to decide whether you should move up to Office 97 or stick with Office 95. Or, perhaps you're an experienced Office 95 user, and you simply need to know what's up with this latest version.

Whatever the case, this chapter shows you the coolest new features and improvements in Office 97 and in the applications that make it up. Here you will learn about the new buttons on the Shortcut bar; the new look and features of Word, Excel, PowerPoint, and Access; why Microsoft dumped Schedule+ in favor of Outlook; and how to use the funky new mouse that may have come bundled with your Office 97 package.

Overall Office 97 New Features

Overall, Office 97 doesn't differ much from its predecessor. After you install it, the Microsoft Office Shortcut bar appears on your Windows desktop whenever you start Windows 95, and the buttons are nearly the same (see the following section for details). The Start, Programs menu still functions as the home base for the Office applications.

When you run any of the Office applications, however, you will notice that they all look a little different from the previous versions. The toolbars don't seem as three-dimensional as they once did. However, whenever you pass the mouse pointer over a toolbar option, the option appears three-dimensional, which helps you determine exactly which button you are about to choose. (This helps prevent you from clicking on the wrong button.) You may also notice that the toolbars contain a couple of unfamiliar buttons for the new Web features.

You will encounter another obvious change in the Office 97 applications whenever you open a menu. To the left of many menu commands, you will now see a button that represents the command graphically.

When you pass the mouse pointer over an option, it appears three-dimensional.

New Web buttons

The Office 97 applications sport an improved look.

Buttons appear next to many menu commands.

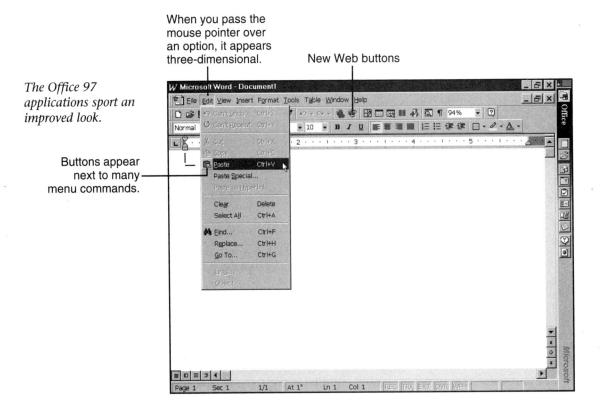

Office 97 ValuPack

Office 97 comes with some additional tools in its ValuPack. The ValuPack includes a copy of Microsoft Internet Explorer to help you get started cruising the Internet, along with some additional document templates, fonts, sounds, and other programs. When you install Office, you'll be given the option of checking out the ValuPack.

New Office Shortcut Bar

The Microsoft Office Shortcut bar isn't a brand new feature; Microsoft introduced it in Office 95. However, Microsoft assigned all the buttons new names and gave them all a new set of clothes so they look a little different. For example, what used to be called the Start a New Document button is now called the New Office Document button (although if you installed Office 97 over Office 95, your Shortcut bar might have *both* buttons).

A couple of less fortunate buttons were bumped off the bar, including the Office Compatible button and the Answer Wizard. These buttons have been replaced by the New Note button (for adding a yellow Post-it note to your screen) and Microsoft Bookshelf Basics (for accessing Microsoft's reference library). You'll learn more about the Shortcut bar in Chapter 2, "10-Minute Office 97 Primer."

New Help with Assistants

 Microsoft has given Office 97 a little taste of BOB, replacing the Answer Wizard with an animated character called Clippit. Whenever you start one of the Office applications, Clippit appears, offering a helpful hand. As you work, Clippit crouches in the corner, and keeps track of what you're doing. When you click on Clippit, he "talks," asking you what you need help with and then displaying a list of tasks you might need to perform. You will learn more about Clippit and some of his colleagues in Chapter 3, "When in Doubt, Ask for Help."

Web Ready, Internet Savvy

If you have used Microsoft's Internet Assistants to transform your documents, spreadsheets, and slide shows into Web documents, you will be happy to hear that Microsoft has built the capabilities of the Internet Assistants into its Office applications. You can now save your Word documents, Excel

Web Work!
Chapter 31, "Creating Your Own Web Pages," shows you how to use Office 97's Web features to convert documents into the HTML format, add links, and use the Web toolbar in the Office applications. Throughout this book, you will find additional Web tips.

spreadsheets, and PowerPoint slide shows as HTML documents. You can then add links and even open Web pages directly from your Office applications.

In addition, the Office 97 applications now offer a Send To option (on the File menu), with which you can send a file via e-mail or fax.

Click here to view Clippit.

Clippit, the Office Assistant, has replaced the Answer Wizard.

Click Clippit when you need help.

Click the Close button to get rid of Clippit.

Beefing Up Your Applications with Add-Ins

The latest craze on the World Wide Web is the *add-in*, a component that gives your application an additional capability. For example, if you are using Internet Explorer 3.0 to navigate the Internet, you can install an add-in called ActiveMovie that plays video clips you might encounter. Microsoft has designed all of its Office applications to use add-ins (developed by Microsoft or third-party developers). After you purchase or download (copy) an add-in, you must install it on your hard drive, and then use the Tools, Add-Ins command to make the add-in available to the Office application. Add-ins typically add a menu command or button to the application.

What's New with Word?

Microsoft knows not to mess with success, and it hasn't given Word a major overhaul. Instead, Microsoft has tweaked the program here and there, taken popular options out of dialog boxes and placed them on menus, and built in a few extra features to enhance its award-winning word processor. You'll learn more about all these features in Parts 2 and 7. Following is a list of many of the changes and additions to Microsoft Word:

➤ **WordMail** allows you to use Word to compose and send e-mail messages. To use this feature, you must have Microsoft Exchange installed (it comes with Windows 95), and you must choose to use Word as your e-mail editor. See Chapter 30, "Using Office on a Network or Intranet."

➤ **Draw Table** (a new option on the Table menu) allows you to use your mouse to drag a table into existence. You can then drag lines to create rows and columns. When you draw a table, another toolbar appears, presenting buttons for coloring cells, styling text, and so on.

➤ **Enhanced grammar checker** can now check your grammar as you type. I have to warn you; this can make you so self-conscious about your writing that you may never be able to write again. The Spelling button in Word 7 is now the Spelling and Grammar button.

➤ **Web toolbar** displays the toolbar for Microsoft's Web browser (Internet Explorer). You can use this toolbar to open a Web page and select from a list of your favorite Web pages. See Chapter 31, "Creating Your Own Web Pages," for details.

➤ **Document Map** (option on View menu and in button bar) splits the window into two panes. The left pane shows an outline of the document; the right pane shows the complete text. This is great for reorganizing a document.

➤ **3D settings** (on the Drawing toolbar) allow you to create cool, three-dimensional text boxes and other shapes that look as though they're floating above the page.

➤ **Comments** (formerly annotations) allow a reviewer to add hidden comments to your text. When you rest the mouse pointer over text that the reviewer has commented on, the comment pops up on your screen.

➤ **Toolbars** have multiplied, and you can now turn them on and off via a submenu (View, Toolbars), instead of using a dialog box. Additional toolbars include AutoText, Picture, Text box, Web, and WordArt.

➤ **Background** (on Format menu) allows you to add a background color and style to your document. This is great for creating Web pages.

➤ **Scanner support** (Insert, Picture, From Scanner) enables you to insert a scanned picture into your document, assuming you have a scanner that supports this feature. (This feature is also available in PowerPoint and Excel.)

You'll see additional tweaks and features as you start working with Word and as you read Part 2, "Whipping Up Word Documents."

Cool New Features in Excel

Just when you thought Excel couldn't get any better, Microsoft enhanced it with several new features and with new approaches to old features. You'll learn the specifics of these improvements in Part 3, "Crunching Numbers with Excel Spreadsheets." The following list provides an overview of the most important changes.

➤ **Conditional Formatting** (Format menu) changes the color of a cell, depending on the value it contains. (Before, you could change the color of the value itself, but you could not change the color of the cell.)

➤ **Insert, Picture** now displays a submenu instead of a dialog box, as you can see in the following figure. The submenu allows you to insert a piece of clip art (from the clip art gallery), a graphics file, AutoShapes, an organizational chart, or a WordArt object, or to scan in a picture (if you have a TWAIN-compatible scanner).

Many Office options have migrated from dialog boxes to submenus.

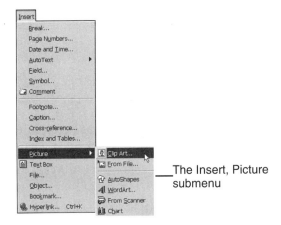

The Insert, Picture submenu

➤ **AutoShapes** (mentioned above) are predrawn objects you can stick in your spreadsheets, such as arrows, boxes, comic strip bubbles, and starbursts.

➤ **Web features** allow you to display a Web toolbar (as in Word) add links to your Excel worksheet, and save the worksheet as an HTML file (a Web page).

➤ **Additional toolbars** include the Control Toolbox (for inserting items such as check boxes), Picture, Reviewing, and WordArt. Now you can turn these toolbars on or off by selecting them from the View, Toolbars submenu. You can turn on additional toolbars by selecting Tools, Customize.

➤ **Page Break Preview** (on the View menu) shrinks the view to show you how your spreadsheet will be divided into pages when printed. You can then reformat the page to avoid funky page breaks.

➤ **Report Manager** allows you to create, save, and manage several versions of the same worksheet so that you can compare the results of two or more scenarios. (This is an add-in program that comes with Office 97.)

PowerPoint Overhauled

None of the other applications in the Office suite have undergone the major restructuring evident in PowerPoint. Most of these changes seem to be inspired by the need to place PowerPoint presentations on the Web and the desire to take more control over presentations. I'll cover PowerPoint in more detail in Part 4.

Although the changes to PowerPoint are too numerous to mention here, the following list highlights the major changes:

➤ **Action Buttons** (Slide Show menu) appear at the bottom of each slide. You can click on a button to display the next or previous slide.

➤ **Action Settings** (Slide Show menu) allow you to insert links to other slides, video clips, animations, pictures, audio recordings, macros, programs, and other objects. A simple mouse click in the right spot plays the associated file.

➤ **Animation Preview** (Slide Show menu) provides additional preview of animation effects in slide show transitions.

➤ **Animated bullets** allow you to create a list of bulleted items that "fly" onto a slide one at a time to "build" the list. This option was available in the previous version of PowerPoint, but it is more easily accessible now through the Slide Show, Preset Animation submenu.

➤ **Common Tasks toolbar** provides buttons for tasks you would frequently perform while creating a slide show: add a new slide, change the slide layout, and apply a design.

➤ **Custom Animation** (Slide Show menu) expands upon the Animation Settings options available in the previous version of PowerPoint, allowing you to add special effects to your slide show, including timing and chart effects.

➤ **Custom Shows** (Slide Show menu) is one of the cooler features. It allows you to create various versions of the same slide show by specifying which slides you want to include in the show. For example, if you were demonstrating supply-side economics at the Republican National Convention, you might want to omit the slides that show the ballooning federal deficit.

➤ **Movies and Sounds submenu** (Insert menu) contains several options for inserting sounds and video clips from either the gallery or from a file. This submenu also includes an option for playing a specific track from an audio CD.

➤ **Record Narration** (Slide Show menu) allows you to play a presentation and do a voice-over as it plays. In previous versions of PowerPoint, you could attach a recording on a slide-by-slide basis (which you can still do in this version).

➤ **Set Up Show** (Slide Show menu) expands the slide show customization options that were available in previous versions of PowerPoint. You can now set up the slide show to run without narration or animation; to have the slides advanced automatically, by a presenter, or by the user; and to omit some slides from the presentation.

➤ **AutoShapes** (same as in Excel) allows you to insert predrawn objects (such as smiley faces, lines, boxes, arrows, and starbursts) on your slides.

PowerPoint's Slide Show menu steals the show.

The Slide Show menu

Access Accessorized

Access (covered in detail in Part 5) has always lagged behind the other applications in keeping up with the times. Maybe it's just getting too close to perfection to warrant changing it. Whatever the case, if you're an experienced Access database user, you will notice only a few changes:

➤ **Tabbed forms** allow you to create multipage forms for entering data into your database. You (or whoever is doing the data entry) can flip pages on the form by clicking through the tabs.

➤ **ActiveX Controls** (Tools menu) allows you to insert ActiveX Controls in your database. ActiveX Controls are enhanced versions of OLE (Object Linking and Embedding) controls. This is a fairly advanced topic that you should pray you never have to get into.

➤ **Delete Column** (Edit menu) and **Insert Column** (Insert menu) allow you to delete or insert an entire field in a table along with all of its entries. To delete or insert columns, you must be working on a table in Datasheet view (View, Datasheet).

➤ **Insert, Control** allows you to insert controls from other applications, including the calendar control, marquee, scroll bar, spin buttons, and tab strip.

➤ **Save to HTML** (File menu) allows you to publish your database on the Web or save it as a Web page.

➤ **Database utilities** allow you to convert your Access database to a different format, repair a damaged database, compact the database, and compile the database application you created (assuming you created a database application).

Good-Bye Schedule , Hello Outlook!

Office 95 offered a personal information manager called Schedule+, which acted as a sort of day planner, providing you with a calendar and an address book. Outlook offers the same tools, but then it goes way beyond Schedule+ by providing e-mail support, a Post-It note utility (I love this feature), links to your favorite Web pages, e-mail addresses for your business and personal contacts, and a whole lot more. You will learn how to tap into all these new features in Part 6, "Looking After Your Life with Outlook."

Outlook's tools

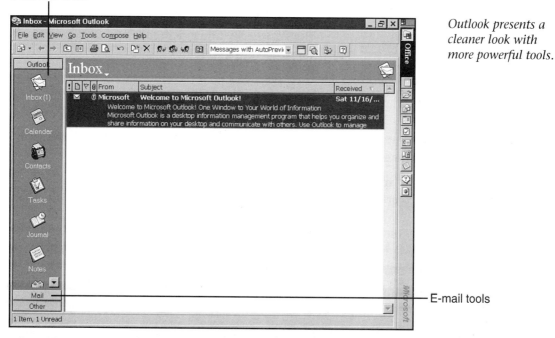

Outlook presents a cleaner look with more powerful tools.

E-mail tools

Building a Better Mousetrap

 As much as Bill Gates wants people to think that Microsoft is no Cracker Jack operation, the Office 97 packaging is strikingly similar to the Cracker Jack box. If you dig down to the bottom of some Office 97 boxes, you will find a free toy: a Microsoft IntelliPoint mouse (called IntelliMouse for short).

Although similar in shape to the standard two-button Microsoft mouse, this mouse has a small gray wheel between the two buttons. Although it gets in your way as you slide your finger from the left to the right, the wheel gives you much more control over scrolling and entering commands, and it is fairly easy to use.

To install the mouse, exit all your applications, shut down Windows, and turn off your computer. Then unplug your old mouse and plug in the new IntelliMouse. Turn everything back on. Insert the floppy disk that came with the mouse, and run the setup program (you can use the **Start**, **Run** command in Windows 95). This installs the mouse driver that gives the wheel the power to operate.

Once you've installed the appropriate driver, you can start using the mouse. The left and right mouse buttons work as they always have, but in applications that support the IntelliMouse (including all the Office 97 applications), you can do two things with the wheel: spin it and click it. What spinning and clicking do depends on the application you're in. For example, in Word, you can use the wheel to scroll more accurately, as described here:

➤ Rotate the wheel forward to scroll up; rotate backward to scroll down.

➤ To pan up or down, click and hold the wheel while moving the mouse pointer in the direction of the text that you want to bring into view.

➤ To autoscroll up or down, click the wheel, and then move the mouse pointer up (to scroll up) or down (to scroll down). Autoscrolling remains on until you click the button again.

➤ To zoom in or out, hold down the **Ctrl** key and rotate the wheel. Rotate forward to zoom in or backward to zoom out.

➤ To expand or collapse headings in Outline or Document Map view, hold down the **Shift** key and rotate the wheel.

To view general Help on how to use the IntelliMouse, open the Windows **Start** menu, point to **Programs**, **Microsoft Input Devices**, and **Mouse**, and then click on **IntelliPoint Online User's Guide**. For specific help on using the IntelliMouse with an application, check that application's Help system. Note that some applications are not designed to use the little gray wheel.

Mouse Options in Windows 95

You can set the IntelliMouse options the same way you set your old mouse options in Windows 95. Display the **Control Panel** and double-click the **Mouse** icon. The Mouse Properties dialog box displays options that allow you to turn on or off the wheel and wheel button. This dialog box also contains several tabs full of options that can keep you busy for days.

The Least You Need to Know

If you look at the bushels of new features described in this chapter, you might find it difficult to remember them all. Keep in mind that Microsoft wants to simplify its products, increase e-mail support, and provide users with tools for publishing on the Web. The Office 97 improvements are signs of those overall strategies:

➤ Office 97 is Web aware. Each Office 97 application has some way of linking to the Web. Most provide tools for transforming your documents into Web pages.

➤ Office 97 offers additional support for e-mail. You can now use Word as your e-mail editor. All the Office 97 applications have a Send To option (on the File menu) that lets you send files via e-mail.

➤ To reduce the number of options you need to select, Microsoft has moved several options from dialog boxes to submenus.

➤ Office 97 replaced the anemic Schedule+ with Outlook, an application that can manage both your life and your e-mail.

➤ The Assistant can help you find help for any task you are trying to perform in any of the Office 97 applications. It replaces the (more complicated) Answer Wizard from the days of Office 95.

➤ The Office 97 applications have a menagerie of new toolbars that place commonly used commands within easy reach.

Chapter 2

10-Minute Office 97 Primer

In This Chapter

➤ Office 97 installation tips

➤ Running the Office 97 applications

➤ Using and configuring the Shortcut bar

➤ Entering commands, displaying toolbars, and performing other basic maneuvers

➤ Saving, opening, and printing files

You're no idiot. You've probably poked around in several Windows applications, and you have a general idea of how they all work. You are quite capable of opening pull-down menus and clicking buttons, and you didn't shell out twenty bucks to be told what you already know. So I'm not going to give you the step-by-boring-step tutorial of Office 97 basics.

Instead, this chapter provides you with a brief overview of the basics (to refresh your memory), as well as some in-depth tips that can help you perform the basics a little faster.

Tips for Installing Office 97

Installing programs in Windows 95 is easy. You stick the first floppy disk or the CD in the drive, open the Windows Control Panel, double-click the **Add/Remove Programs** icon, click the **Install** button, and follow the on-screen instructions. If it were any easier, your boss would replace you with a chimpanzee. However, if you want the installation procedure to go as smoothly as possible, you should do a little preparation first:

➤ Run Windows Explorer and check the amount of free disk space you have on the hard disk to which you are installing Office 97. Explorer displays the free disk space in the status bar. You will need about 100 megabytes of free disk space to install Office 97.

Web Work!
After you install Microsoft Office, you should have an Internet Explorer icon on your Windows desktop. Internet Explorer is Microsoft's Web browser, a program that enables you to navigate the Web. Double-click that icon if you want to install Internet Explorer from the CD ValuePack.

➤ To free up some disk space, open the Recycle Bin, make sure it does not contain any files you may need, and empty it (**File, Empty Recycle Bin**).

➤ To free up more disk space, double-click the **Add/ Remove Programs** icon in the Windows Control Panel, and then use the resulting dialog box to remove any applications you no longer use.

➤ If you can't remove an application through the Add/Remove Programs dialog box, see if the application has an Uninstall or Setup (or similar) icon in its directory. If it does, double-click it. (The application's submenu on the Start, Programs menu may list the Uninstall option.)

➤ You can free up more disk space by using the Start, Find option to hunt for temporary and backup files and deleting them. (Search for ***.tmp** and then ***.bak**.)

➤ If you plan to use Office 97 to send and receive e-mail, install Microsoft Exchange from your Windows 95 CD or floppy disks *before* you install Office 97.

➤ If you want to install only one or two of the Office 97 applications, choose the **Custom Installation** option. Otherwise, choose **Typical**. (If you want to use the Microsoft Office Shortcut Bar, as explained later in this chapter, you may have to choose to install this application later.)

Running Your Office (Applications)

The installation procedure places icons for the Office 97 applications on the Windows **Start**, **Programs** menu. Just click the name of the application you want to run. You can also run some of the applications by using the Microsoft Office Shortcut bar, as explained in the following section.

If you use some of the Office 97 applications frequently, consider placing shortcuts to them on the Windows desktop. Open My Computer or Windows Explorer and change to the folder into which you installed Office 97 (typically C:\Program Files\Microsoft Office). This folder contains icons for all the Office 97 applications you installed. Drag the icon for the desired application onto a blank area of the Windows desktop. This places a copy of the icon on the desktop; double-click the icon to run the application.

Scooting Up to the Shortcut Bar

After you install Office 97, whenever you start Windows, the Microsoft Office Shortcut bar appears on the right side of your screen. This bar contains several buttons designed to help you quickly perform tasks using the Office 97 applications:

New Office Document lets you start creating a document using a template. The application that runs depends on the type of document you choose to create; for instance, if you choose a presentation, PowerPoint runs.

Open Office Document lets you open and start editing a document that has already been created and stored on your computer or on the network.

New Message displays a window you can use to send an e-mail message.

New Appointment lets you add an appointment to your schedule. Outlook will notify you before the scheduled date and time.

New Task displays a dialog box that lets you add a task to your to-do list (as if you didn't have enough to do). Again, this button runs Outlook.

New Contact lets you add a person's name, address, phone number, e-mail address, and all sorts of other information to your address book in Outlook.

New Journal Entry prompts you to enter information about something you have done during the day, about an e-mail message you sent or received, or about anything else you want to record.

New Note sticks an electronic Post-it note on your screen in Outlook.

Microsoft Bookshelf Basics provides options for using the various reference tools on the Bookshelf CD.

Getting Results Book displays an online guide that can help you get the most out of Office 97.

ScreenTip Tip

Most Windows 95 applications offer ScreenTips, little text boxes that pop up and show the name of a button when you rest the mouse pointer on it. To change the name of the button, right-click the button and select **Rename**.

Turning On Other Shortcut Bars

The Shortcut bar initially displays the Office toolbar, which contains buttons mostly for Outlook tasks. You can turn on other toolbars to give you quick access to other files and programs on your computer. To turn a toolbar on or off, right-click in a blank area of the Shortcut bar and select any of the following toolbars:

➤ **Desktop** turns on a toolbar that displays the shortcuts on the Windows desktop.

➤ **Quickshelf** displays buttons for opening Bookshelf's dictionary, thesaurus, and book of quotations, and for searching all the volumes in Bookshelf.

➤ **Favorites** displays icons for Web pages that you added to your list of favorites in Internet Explorer (assuming you cruise the Web with Internet Explorer).

➤ **Programs** turns on the toolbar equivalent of the Windows Start, Programs menu.

➤ **Accessories** displays icons for all the applications on the Start, Programs, Accessories submenu.

Whenever you turn on a toolbar, an icon for that bar appears in the Shortcut bar, and the toolbar's buttons appear. Only one toolbar's buttons are shown at a time. You can display the buttons of another toolbar (assuming you turned it on earlier) by clicking its icon, as shown in the following figure.

Customizing the Shortcut Bar

The first thing you'll probably want to know about the Shortcut bar is how to turn it off. Right-click the title bar (at the top of the Shortcut bar) and click **Exit**. A dialog box appears, asking if you want the Shortcut bar to appear the next time you start Windows. Take your pick: **Yes** or **No**. If you choose No, you can run the Shortcut bar by double-clicking the **Microsoft Office Shortcut Bar** icon in the MSOFFICE folder.

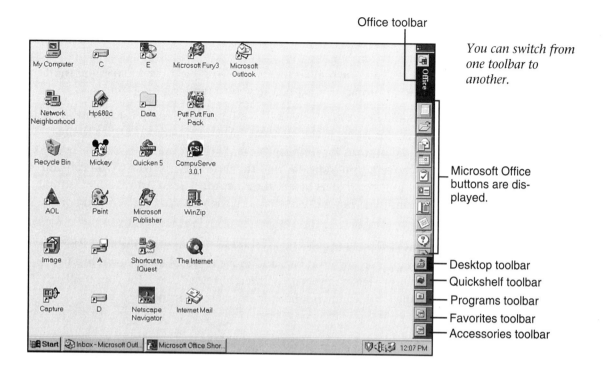

Office toolbar

You can switch from one toolbar to another.

Microsoft Office buttons are displayed.

Desktop toolbar
Quickshelf toolbar
Programs toolbar
Favorites toolbar
Accessories toolbar

If you have a genuine affection for the Shortcut bar and decide to leave it on, you can customize it in all sorts of ways. My favorite option is AutoHide, which tucks the Shortcut bar out of the way as you work in an application. Whenever you need the Shortcut bar, you can slide the mouse pointer over to the right side of the screen to display it. To turn on AutoHide, right-click in a blank area of the Shortcut bar and click **AutoHide**.

You can also move the Shortcut bar. To do so, drag any blank area of the Shortcut bar to the desired position on your screen: left, right, top, bottom, or (to make it most intrusive) smack dab in the middle. When moving the Shortcut bar, keep the following in mind:

➤ If you move the Shortcut bar to the middle of the screen, AutoHide won't work.

➤ If you have AutoHide turned on and you move the Shortcut bar to the top, bottom, or left side of the screen, you must move the mouse pointer to that edge to bring the Shortcut bar into view.

For additional customization options, right-click in a blank area of the Shortcut bar and click **Customize**. The View tab appears up front, giving you options for changing the look and behavior of the Shortcut bar. I'm not going to bore you with all the details. Just be sure that if you have more than one toolbar turned on, you select the toolbar you want to customize from the **Toolbar** drop-down list before you start changing settings.

Another tab that you should check out is the Buttons tab. It contains a list of buttons that you can turn on or off. For example, if you click the **Buttons** tab for the Office toolbar, you can turn on additional buttons for running Word, Excel, PowerPoint, and Access. A check in the box next to a button indicates that the button is turned on. You can add icons for commonly used files or folders by clicking the **Add File** or **Add Folder** button. You can also move buttons by clicking the button and then clicking the **Move** up or down arrow.

As for the other two tabs (Toolbars and Settings), you can ignore them for now. The Toolbars tab lets you create your own toolbars and move toolbars up or down inside the Shortcut bar. The Settings tab lets you specify a different folder to use for your toolbars; if you mess with this setting, Office may not be able to locate your toolbars.

Select a button and click one of these buttons to move it.

You can add or remove buttons from individual toolbars.

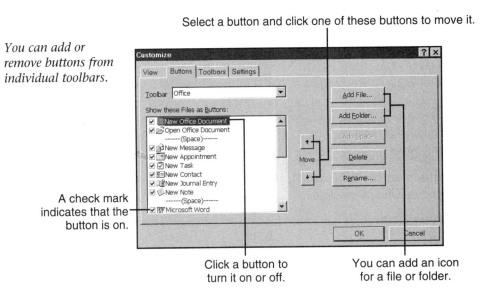

A check mark indicates that the button is on.

Click a button to turn it on or off.

You can add an icon for a file or folder.

Getting Help in Dialog Boxes

Dialog boxes are typically packed with cryptic options. To determine what an option does, right-click its name and select **What's This?**, or click the question mark icon in the upper-right corner of the dialog box and then click the option's name. A small text box appears, describing the option.

Menus, Dialog Boxes, and Other Ways to Talk to Your Applications

If you've worked in any Windows applications, you know your way around menu bars, dialog boxes, and toolbars. If you want something, you just point at it and click the left mouse button. What happens next?

On a menu, if you click an option that's followed by a series of dots (such as the File, Open... command) a dialog box appears, asking for more information. If the option has a check box next to it, clicking the option turns it on or off; a check mark indicates the option is on. If nothing appears before or after the option (check out Edit, Copy, for example), the application automatically executes the command when you select it.

When a dialog box appears, you must supply additional information or at least give your confirmation. Dialog boxes typically offer several ways for you to enter your preferences:

➤ **Tabs** appear when a dialog box has two or more "pages" of options. Click a tab to bring its options to the front.

➤ **Option buttons** let you turn on *only one* option in a list of options. When you click an option, a black dot appears in the circle indicating that it is on.

➤ **Check boxes** let you turn on one or more options in a list of options. Click an option to turn it on (place a check in the box) or to turn it off (remove the check).

➤ **Text boxes** allow you to type an entry, such as a file name.

➤ **Spin boxes** allow you to set a value incrementally by clicking the up or down arrow to the right of the box. In most cases, you can type an entry in the spin box instead of using the arrows.

➤ **Sliders** display a button on a bar. You drag the button to the left or right (or up or down) to enter your setting. Sliders are especially useful as volume controls.

➤ **List boxes** display lists of items (such as type styles) from which you can select.

21

➤ **Drop-down lists** are like list boxes, but the list is hidden (like a pull-down menu). To display the list, click the drop-down arrow button (to the right of the list box).

➤ **Command buttons** let you give your final okay or cancel the dialog box settings. Most dialog boxes contain at least three command buttons: OK, Cancel, and Help.

Dialog boxes ask you to enter additional information.

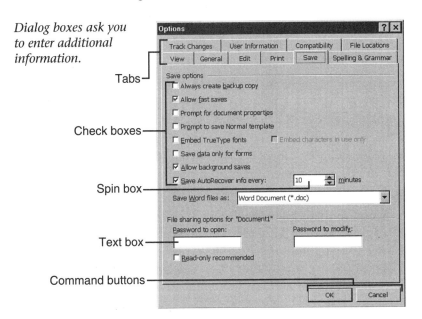

Tabs

Check boxes

Spin box

Text box

Command buttons

Bypassing Menus with Toolbar Buttons

Although the pull-down menu concept is one of the major technological advances of the 20th Century, it's still a little clunky. That's why most applications display toolbars that you can use to bypass the menu commands. Instead of pulling down a menu and selecting a command, you simply click a button.

You don't need instructions on how to click buttons. However, there are a couple tricks for using toolbars that you may not be aware of:

➤ Most applications have more toolbars than they first display. To turn on another toolbar, right-click in a blank area of any toolbar that's displayed, and then select the toolbar you want to turn on.

➤ In Office 97, you can turn on toolbars by selecting them from the View, Toolbars submenu.

➤ At the bottom of the list of toolbars is the Customize option. Click this option to display a dialog box that lets you add, remove, or move buttons on the toolbar. (For details, see the following section.)

Adding and Removing Toolbar Buttons

You can customize the toolbars in any of the Office 97 applications. To do so, first make sure the toolbar you want to customize is displayed. Then open the **View** menu, select **Toolbars**, and click **Customize**. The Customize dialog box has three tabs. The first tab, Toolbars, is the easy one; it allows you to turn a toolbar on or off.

The second tab, Commands, is a little less intuitive. The Commands tab contains two lists. On the left is a list of categories for various types of commands (File, Format, Insert, and so on). When you click a category, the list on the right shows the names of the commands in that category. To add a button for a command to a toolbar, simply drag the command from the list on the right up to the toolbar. To remove a button, drag it off the toolbar to a blank area of the screen.

The third tab, Options, is a fairly easy one. It contains options for making the buttons larger, turning ScreenTips on or off, and displaying shortcut keys in the ScreenTips. One option that may not seem so obvious is Menu animations. It is a drop-down list that allows you to add special effects to the pull-down menus. For example, you can choose Slide to have menus and submenus slide out on the screen when selected.

Drag a command to the toolbar, and a button appears, representing the command.

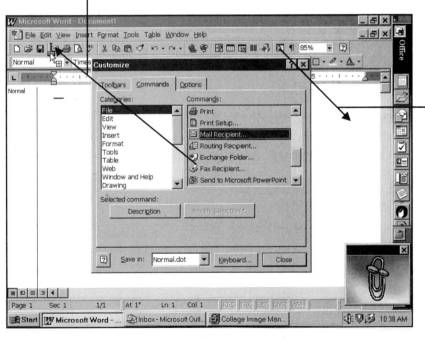

You can easily add or remove buttons from any displayed toolbar.

Drag a button off the toolbar to remove it.

What's with the Keyboard Button?

Click the **Keyboard** button (at the bottom of the Customize dialog box) to call up another dialog box that allows you to assign keystrokes to commands. Select the command to which you want to assign a keystroke, click inside the **Press New Shortcut Key** text box, and press the key combination you want to use (such as **Ctrl+3**). If the keystroke is already being used for another command, a message appears telling you so.

Saving, Naming, and Opening the Files You Create

Windows 95 makes it fairly easy to save, open, and name files. It provides a system of folders and subfolders that help you organize your files, and it allows you to use long file names (up to 255 characters) that include spaces.

The Save Options

By default, all Office applications save files to the My Documents folder and look to that folder whenever you enter the Open command. To use a different folder as the default folder for one of the Office applications, open the Office application's **Tools** menu and select **Options**. Click the **File Locations** tab, click **Documents**, click the **Modify** button, and select the folder you want to use.

To save a file in any of the Office 97 applications, open the **File** menu and select **Save** (or click the **Save** button on the toolbar). The first time you save a file, the application prompts you to name it and specify where you want it stored. Select the folder in which you want to store the file, as shown in the following figure. Type a name for the file in the **File Name** text box. (Don't type a period or a file name extension; the application will add the correct extension.)

You should save your file every ten minutes or so to protect your work in the event of a power outage or system crash. Once you've named a file, saving your changes is easy: just click the **Save** button. Your application remembers the name and location of the file, and saves it automatically.

Select a drive from this list.   Click here to move up one folder.

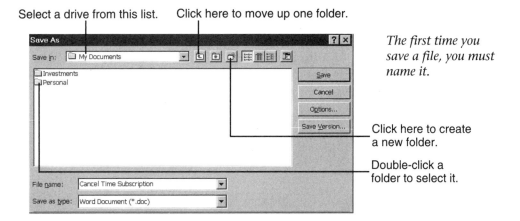

The first time you save a file, you must name it.

Click here to create a new folder.

Double-click a folder to select it.

To work on an existing file, you have to open it in the application you used to create it. You can enter the **File**, **Open** command (or click the **Open** button) and use the Open dialog box to select the file, but there are some easier ways:

➤ The Windows Start, Documents menu contains a list of the 15 documents you've most recently worked on; select the file from this list.

➤ The File menu in the Office application you used to create the file displays the names of the last four files you worked on; select the file from the bottom of the File menu.

➤ Click the **Open Office Document** button in the Shortcut bar, and double-click the name of the file you want to open.

➤ If you edit the document on a regular basis, drag its icon from My Computer or Windows Explorer onto the Microsoft Office Shortcut bar. To open the document, click its icon.

Printing (When You Finally Have Something to Print)

Once you successfully have your printer working with any of your Windows applications, printing is pretty simple. You make sure your printer has plenty of paper and ink or toner, you turn it on, you open your document, and you click the **Print** button. It's easy enough that a child could do it—so watch out!

To take more control of the printing—to print extra copies, print sideways on the page (Landscape mode), collate copies, select a print quality, or enter other settings—you must display the Print dialog box. To do this, open the **File** menu and select **Print** instead of clicking the Print button. You can then use the Print dialog box to enter your preferences.

25

Some Not-So-Basic Mouse Moves

Newer baby books now list mouse skills as a stage of human development that falls somewhere between walking and talking. "Click," "double-click," and "drag" are standard words in any grade-schooler's vocabulary. However, there are some new mouse moves that might confuse even a well-educated adult:

➤ **Right-click pop-up menus.** Sometimes the quickest way to act on existing text is to drag over it (to select it) and then right-click on it to display a menu. Pop-up menus are great because they present options that are used only for the selected text or object.

 ➤ **Right-dragging.** When you right drag, a pop-up menu appears when you release the mouse button. This menu usually provides options for moving the selected object, pasting a copy of it, or (in the new Office 97 applications) creating a *hyperlink* for it.

➤ **Scraps.** You can drag selected text onto a blank area of the Windows desktop to create a *scrap.* You can then drag the scrap into a document to paste it into that document.

➤ **Funky selection moves.** Everyone knows you can drag over text to select it. However, most applications offer additional ways to select with the mouse. For example, in Word, you can double-click a word to select it or triple-click inside a paragraph. I'll point out these special selection techniques in the chapters that deal with the individual applications.

Hyperlink
Hyperlinks are specially formatted icons or bits of text that point to other files. These files may be stored on your hard drive, on the network drive, or on the Internet. When you click a hyperlink, Windows finds and runs the application needed to play the file that the link points to, and then opens the file in that application.

➤ **Selection areas.** Many applications have designated areas of the screen in which you can click to select text. In Word, for instance, if you move the mouse pointer to the left of the document, the arrow changes direction, pointing up and to the right instead of up and left. When the pointer points right, you can click to select a line of text or drag to select multiple lines. In Excel, you can click on a number to the left of a row or on a letter at the top of a column to select the entire row or column.

➤ **Selection boxes.** If you paste pictures or other objects on a page, most applications let you select two or more objects by dragging a box around them.

Dragging and dropping text a long distance in a document was nearly impossible in the Office 95 applications. As you dragged a selection, the page would either sit still or zip by so fast, you couldn't find a place to drop the selection. It's much better now; give it a try. If you still have trouble with it, use the Cut and Copy commands, instead.

The Least You Need to Know

This chapter contains little that you absolutely must know to use Office 97. However, it does offer a bunch of great tips for making the most of it. Here are some of the highlights:

➤ Before you even think of installing Office 97, make sure your hard drive has room for it.

➤ The Microsoft Office Shortcut bar is fully customizable. Right-click it to turn on additional toolbars, to turn on AutoHide, or to select the Customize option.

➤ You can add buttons to any toolbar in any Office application. Right-click in a blank area of the toolbar and click **Customize**.

➤ To quickly open a document you recently worked on, open the **File** menu in the Office application you used to create the file, and select the name of the file.

➤ To quickly print a file (without dealing with dialog box options), click the **Print** button in the application's toolbar.

➤ After selecting text, a picture, or other objects, you can right-click the selection to display a pop-up menu, which should contain the command you're looking for.

27

Chapter 3

When in Doubt, Ask for Help

In This Chapter

➤ Make Clippit hunt down information for you

➤ Turn off Clippit when he starts getting on your nerves

➤ Find a topic in the table of contents

➤ Search an on-screen index of Help topics

Online help systems: you love 'em or you hate 'em. Either they're impossible to find and navigate, or they're like some overzealous philanthropist who just won't leave you alone.

Throughout its development, the Microsoft Help system has tested both extremes. Its early Help systems made it nearly impossible to find specific information. When you finally stumbled across the instructions you needed, you had to shuffle back and forth from the Help window to your application to perform the task.

In an attempt to fix this problem, Microsoft invented the Answer Wizard, a pesky aid who would perform half the steps for you, prompt you to complete the remaining steps, and trip you up all along the way.

In Office 97, Microsoft has finally found a middle ground with the Office Assistant, an animated character who can answer your questions and who knows when to get out of your way.

Meeting Clippit, Your Office Assistant

Whenever you start one of the Office applications, Clippit appears in the lower-right corner of the window giving you an occasional demure wink. As you type, edit, format, and enter commands, this animated paper clip keeps an eye on what you're doing and remains ready to jump in and help.

When you need help, all you have to do is click Clippit, and he (she?) jumps into action, displaying a list of four or five Help topics that pertain to what you are currently doing. For example, if you just entered the File, Print command, Clippit displays topics that deal with printing. At that point, you have the following options:

➤ If the topic you need help with is in the list, click it to display information and instructions for that topic.

➤ If the desired topic is not listed, click **See More** at the bottom of the list to display additional topics.

➤ If Clippit apparently has no idea of the type of help you need, type your question in the text box below the list and click the **Search** button. When you start typing, Clippit whips out a notepad and starts jotting down your question. Clippit returns a list of topics that should answer your question. Click on the desired topic.

Clippit can usually track down the help you need.

If the desired topic appears, click on it.

If the help you need is not listed, type your question here.

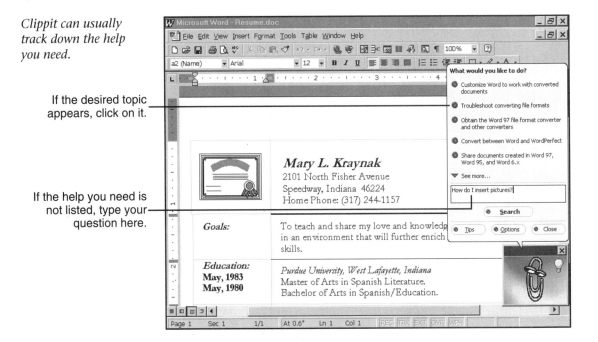

Once you master the basics of finding help with Clippit, you may notice that sometimes Clippit has a light bulb floating above his head. This means that Clippit knows a time-saving tip for the task you're trying to perform. Click the light bulb, and Clippit displays the tip. You can also display tips even when the light bulb is not shown. Just right-click **Clippit** and select **See Tips**.

Turning Clippit On and Off

Although Clippit does a fine job of staying out of your way while you work, you may not like having an animated character ogling you. You can turn Clippit off at any time by clicking the **Close** button in the upper-right corner of Clippit's window or by right-clicking **Clippit** and selecting **Hide Assistant**.

When you turn Clippit off, he hides on the right end of the standard toolbar behind the Office Assistant button (the question mark button). To ask for Clippit's help, click this button or press the **F1** key. Clippit will also leap into action on his own accord and ask if you want help when you choose to use a wizard (a tool that helps you perform common tasks, such as composing a letter or inserting a formula).

Check This Out...

Drag Clippit
Clippit is set up to automatically move out of the way of dialog boxes and other objects. If Clippit doesn't move, drag it by its title bar. If you don't use Clippit for five minutes, he automatically shrinks to give you more room to work.

Customizing Clippit

Although Clippit is nearly perfect, there are some options you might want to play with to make him even better. To enter your preferences, right-click anywhere inside Clippit's window, and select **Options** or **Choose Assistant**. Both options bring up the Office Assistant dialog box; Options displays the Options tab in front, whereas Choose Assistant displays the Gallery tab.

To replace Clippit with some other animated character (who does the same thing), click the **Gallery** tab. Use the **Next>** and **<Back** buttons to scroll through the available characters until you find a character you like. If all you wanted to do was change characters, click **OK**.

To change other options for your Office Assistant (who may not be Clippit at this point), click the **Options** tab. This tab contains all sorts of options for controlling the behavior of your Office Assistant. I would give you a complete list of these options and tell you what each one does, but this is a chapter on how to get online help. To determine what an option does, right-click its name and select **What's This?**

When you are done setting your options, click **OK**.

You can replace Clippit with another animated character.

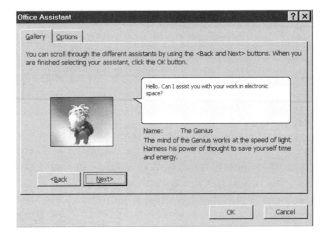

Finding Help Topics in the Table of Contents

If you can't stand the thought of having a cartoon character show you how to use your applications, you can opt for a more traditional approach and look for help in the table of contents. All of the Office 97 applications have online documentation that explains options and provides instructions.

To look up a topic, open the **Help** menu and select **Contents and Index**. If the Contents tab is hiding in the back, click it to bring it up front. To choose a topic, double-click its name or icon. In many instances, this reveals a sublist of more topics. Keep double-clicking to find the exact topic you want to view information about. You'll note several different Help icons among the lists.

➤ A closed book icon means there's a more detailed list to view. To see a list of topics in the book, double-click it, or click the book and click the **Open** button.

➤ An open book icon next to a topic means the topic is selected. You can close the book by double-clicking it.

➤ A question mark icon means there's detailed text about the topic. Double-click the topic to open a window that explains it and tells you how to use the feature.

Techno Talk

Web Work!

If you can't find the help you need, maybe you can get help from Microsoft's Web site. If you are connected to the Internet and you have a Web browser installed, open the **Help** menu and point to **Microsoft on the Web**. The submenu offers links that will take you and your Web browser to any of several Microsoft Web pages where you can find help, technical assistance, free files, and other goodies.

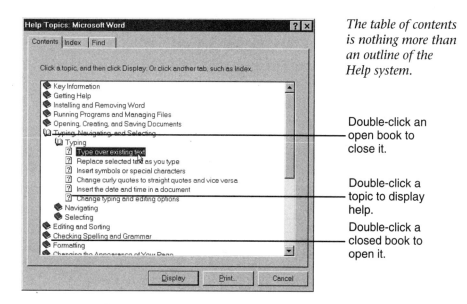

The table of contents is nothing more than an outline of the Help system.

Double-click an open book to close it.

Double-click a topic to display help.

Double-click a closed book to open it.

Navigating the Help Window

Whenever you choose a specific Help topic, your Office application closes the Contents and Index window and opens another window that displays information and instructions. These Help windows always contain some explanatory text, but they also might contain the following:

➤ Clickable buttons that can display help for a related topic.

➤ Green, solid-underlined text that can display help for a related topic.

➤ Green, dotted-underlined text that displays the definition of a term.

➤ Icons that represent a button or other screen item. You can click the icon to view a description of it.

To navigate the Help system, simply click on highlighted text, buttons, and icons, until you find what you need. If you go too far, step back through the various Help windows by using the **Back** button at the top of the window. To start from the beginning, click the **Help Topics** button. This returns you to the Help Topics window, where you can use the table of contents, the Index, or the Find feature to look up another topic.

By default, the Help window stays on top of all other windows so that you can see the instructions as you perform a task. Sometimes, however, the window can get in your way, preventing you from clicking a button or seeing what you're typing. You can close the window, or you can drag its title bar to move it. Or, possibly the best solution is to set an option that prevents the Help window from staying on top. Click the **Options** button, point to **Keep Help on Top**, and click **Not On Top**.

The Options menu contains these additional choices that you might find useful:

➤ **Annotate** lets you add your own notes to a Help topic. The next time you look up the topic, a paper clip icon appears in the corner of the Help window. Click it to view your note.

➤ **Copy** copies the topic to the Windows Clipboard. You can then paste the information into another document. (To copy a portion of the information, drag over it first.)

➤ **Print Topic** prints the information.

➤ **Font** lets you change the type style and size of the text in the Help window.

➤ **Use System Colors** tells the Help system to use standard Windows colors instead of its default colors.

Check This Out...

What's This?

In Chapter 2, you learned how to get help in a dialog box by right-clicking an option and clicking What's This? You can obtain similar help for any toolbar button or other control in your application's window. Open the **Help** menu and select **What's This?** (or press **Shift+F1**), and a question mark attaches itself to the mouse pointer (and the little sucker stays attached until you click on something). Now click on the button or other control for which you want help. A box pops up describing the control.

Searching the Index for Specific Help

Did you know that most users of technical documentation rank a thorough and well-organized index as the most important part of the documentation? That makes sense; after all, if you can't find the information you need, it doesn't matter how good that information is.

With that in mind, you will find the online Help system index a most valuable tool. To use it, open the **Help** menu, click **Contents and Index**, and click the **Index** tab. In the text box at the top of the Index tab, type a few letters of the topic you're looking for. As you type, the index scrolls down to show topics whose names match what you have typed so far. When you see the desired topic in the index, double-click it, or click it and click the **Display** button.

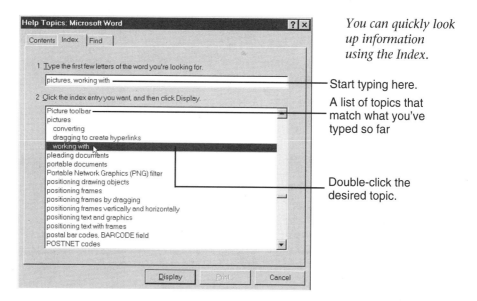

You can quickly look up information using the Index.

Start typing here.

A list of topics that match what you've typed so far

Double-click the desired topic.

Finding Help for Obscure Topics

The contents and index are great for people who know what they're looking for, but if you don't even know what a feature or button is called, you can't even start looking for it. In such cases, Clippit or one of his sidekicks is your best bet. However, if you can't stomach Clippit, you can search the Help database yourself.

To search through the Help database, open the **Help** menu, select **Contents and Index**, and click the **Find** tab. The first time you click on the Find tab, the Find Setup Wizard appears. The Wizard will create a list of words in the Help system, providing a more thorough list of topics than is available in the index. You can choose to Minimize the list (make a shorter but very thorough list), Maximize it (for an insanely thorough list), or Customize it (which is more trouble than it's worth). Pick the **Minimize** option, click **Next**, and then click **Finish**.

After the Wizard creates the Help database, it returns you to the Find tab. In the topmost text box, type the word or words you want to find. As you type, the list boxes change to display matching words. In the list marked 2, click the word that most closely matches what you are looking for (you can select several entries by dragging over them, or by Ctrl+clicking on additional entries). The bottom list (marked 3) displays all the topics that match the selected entries. Double-click the desired topic.

Check This Out...

Help Is Just a Right-Click Away Most of the time you need help, you just can't figure out which menu to open or which button to click. In many cases, you can solve your problem by selecting the text or object you want to work with and right-clicking on it. This displays a pop-up menu that lists the most common commands related to that item.

35

The Find option is thorough, but a little awkward.

Step 1: Type a word.

Step 2: Select one or more entries.

Step 3: Double-click the topic.

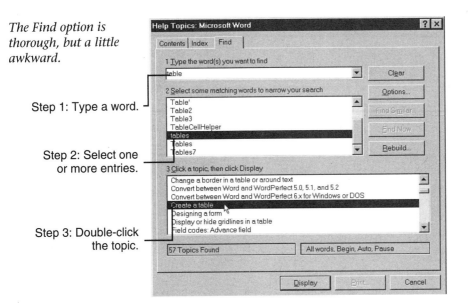

The Least You Need to Know

If you master an application's Help system, you can learn how to perform just about any task without having to flip through a book. (Did my publisher hear me say that?) The hard part is in trying to master the Help system.

➤ The Office Assistant (Clippit or one of his cronies) pops up whenever you start an Office application. Click the Office Assistant when you need help.

➤ To customize the Office Assistant, right-click it. This displays the menu you need.

➤ You can turn off the Office Assistant by clicking its **Close** button.

➤ If you can't see the Office Assistant, click the question mark button at the right end of the Standard toolbar.

➤ All other help options are available on the Help menu.

Part 2
Whipping Up Word Documents

Every office needs a good word machine, and Microsoft Word is one of the best. Its standard text layout tools allow you to easily set margins, indent text, and drop pictures and graphs anywhere on a page. The table feature gives you the power to easily align chunks of text in columns and rows. And the spelling and grammar checkers provide you with a professional, online proofreader that can catch errors as you type.

In this part, you will learn how to use these tools and others to crank out some high-quality documents with a minimal amount of effort.

Chapter 4

Making and Editing Word Documents

In This Chapter

➤ Using prefab documents with wizards and templates

➤ Typing, copying, and moving chunks of text

➤ Becoming a 500-word-per-minute typist with Auto Text

➤ Finding and replacing bits of text

Microsoft Word has been the superhero of word processing programs for several years now, kicking sand in the face of the former giant, WordPerfect, and pummeling ambitious newcomers such as WordPro. Its powerful features have won over several generations of computer users.

Even with this power, Word has not forgotten the simple tasks we need to perform, such as typing a letter, printing addresses on envelopes, and arranging text in columns. While beefing up Word with advanced features, Microsoft has continued to make it easier to perform these routine tasks.

In this chapter, you will see several of these improvements in action as you learn the basics of creating and editing your documents.

The Boilerplate Special

If you're in a hurry to create a document, and you don't have time to design and format your own, use one of Word's templates or wizards. A *template* is a ready-made document; all you have to do is add the text. A *wizard* is a series of fill-in-the-blank dialog boxes that lead you through the process of creating a custom document, allowing you to select design preferences and enter chunks of text.

Word's templates and wizards hang out in the New dialog box, shown in the following figure. To get there, open the **File** menu and select **New**. (Clicking the New button on the Standard toolbar won't open the New dialog box. You'll need to use the File menu to open it up.) The New dialog box contains several tabs full of wizards and templates. Click the tab for the type of document you want to create, and then double-click the desired template or wizard.

The New dialog box.

Click a tab.

Preview a template here by clicking it.

Double-click a template or wizard.

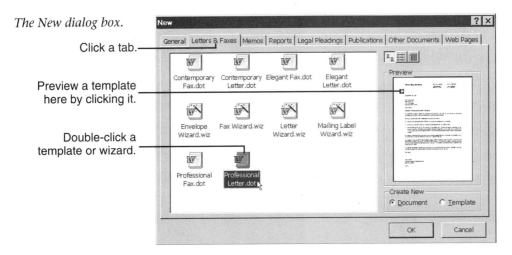

Template Tips

The Office 97 suite comes with lots of templates, but not all of them are installed with the Typical installation option. Run the setup program again, but this time use the Custom installation option to install additional templates.

What happens next depends on whether you selected a template or a wizard. If you selected a wizard (the wizard name has a .wiz extension at the end of it), a wizard dialog box appears, prompting you to make a selection. Simply follow the wizard's instructions and click the **Next>** button until you've reached the last dialog box; then click **Finish**. The wizard creates the document and returns you to the Word window, where you can further customize the document or print it as is.

If you picked a template (template names have .dot at the end), Word opens the template in its own document window, where you can start editing it. Many templates have placeholders that indicate the type of information you must enter. For example, if you use a letter template, [**Click here and type the recipient's name**] appears next to the greeting. Do whatever the placeholder instructs.

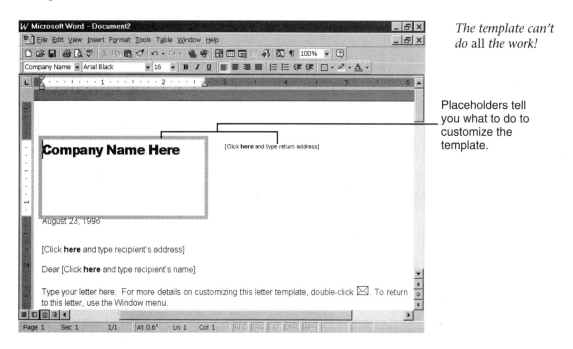

The template can't do all *the work!*

Placeholders tell you what to do to customize the template.

A hard-to-please Word customer, eh? If you don't see any templates or wizards that you like, you can create your own from scratch, or you can modify an existing template and save it under another name. In the New dialog box, click the **Template** option below the Preview area, and then double-click the template you want to modify (to create a template from scratch, select the **Normal** template). This allows you to create a template (with the .DOT extension) instead of a document (with the .DOC extension).

After entering your changes to the template, open the **File** menu, select **Save As**, and type a new name for the template. You don't have to type an extension; Word will automatically tack the .DOT extension to the end of the name. Be sure you save the template to one of the folders in the Templates folder so it will appear in the New dialog box. (Each folder in the Templates folder represents a tab in the New dialog box.)

Web Work! To create your own Web page in Word, check out the new Web Pages tab. This tab offers a Web page wizard and a blank Web page. See Chapter 31, "Creating Your Own Web Pages," for details.

Inserting, Typing Over, and Deleting Text

If you don't know your home keys from your house keys, you should probably take a typing course. Once you know how to type, typing in Word is easy—just do it. Here are a few tips that will help if you're making the transition from a typewriter to a computer keyboard:

➤ Don't press Enter at the end of a line. Word wraps the lines for you as you type. If the text disappears off the left or right side of the window, zoom out as explained in "Changing Views," later in this chapter.

➤ A blinking vertical bar, called the *insertion point*, indicates where text will be inserted as you type.

➤ At the end of the document, a horizontal line marks the end of the document. You can't type or insert anything below this line.

➤ Place the mouse pointer (shaped like an I-beam) where you want to start typing, and then click. The text you type is inserted, and any existing text moves to the right to make room for the new text.

➤ Double-click the **OVR** indicator in the status bar to change to Overtype mode. **OVR** (darkened) appears in the status bar at the bottom of the screen, and whatever you type replaces existing text to the right of it. To change back to Insert mode, double-click on **OVR** again.

➤ To replace text, drag over it and start typing.

➤ To delete text to the right of the insertion point, press the **Delete** (Del) key. To delete to the left, press the **Backspace** key.

➤ Don't use a whole bunch of tabs to align text in columns. Chapter 6, "Aligning Text in Tables and Columns," explains a much easier way.

➤ In Chapter 5, "Giving Your Text a Makeover," you will learn various techniques for making your text look pretty. For now, just type.

What's with the Red Pen?

As you type, you may get a strange feeling that your sixth-grade English teacher is inside your screen, underlining your spelling mistakes. Whenever you type a string of characters that does not match a word in Word's online spelling dictionary, Word draws a squiggly red line under the word to flag it for you so you can immediately correct it. (If you don't like this feature, you can turn it off; see Chapter 9, "Checking Your Spelling and Grammar," for details.)

The insertion point shows where the text you type will appear.

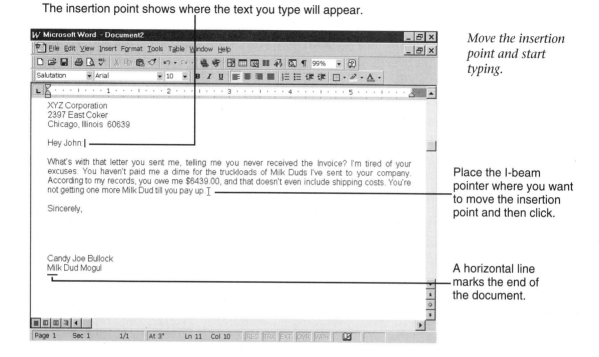

Move the insertion point and start typing.

Place the I-beam pointer where you want to move the insertion point and then click.

A horizontal line marks the end of the document.

You can backspace over the misspelling and type the word correctly, but Word offers a better option. Right-click the misspelled word, and Word displays a pop-up menu offering several possible correct spellings; you simply select the word you want. If you commonly mistype this word, right-click it, point to **AutoCorrect**, and click on the correct spelling. If you add a term to the AutoCorrect list, whenever you mistype the word and press the spacebar or type a period, AutoCorrect replaces the word with the correct spelling. You will learn more about AutoCorrect in Chapter 9, "Checking Your Spelling and Grammar."

Typing Text Has Never Been Easier!

I promised early on to teach you how to type 500 words per minute. The trick is to use AutoText. With AutoText, you can assign a term, quote, paragraph, or any other block of text to a couple of unique characters. To insert the block of text, all you have to do is type the unique characters and press **F3**. For example, you might create an AutoText entry that inserts "Democratic National Convention" whenever you type DNC and press F3.

To create an AutoText entry, type the block of text for which you want to create an AutoText entry, and then drag over the text to select it. Open the **Insert** menu, point to **AutoText**, and click **New** (or just press **Alt+F3**). The Create AutoText dialog box prompts you to type a name for the entry. Type the shortest possible name for the entry that you can think of, and click **OK**.

You can delete AutoText entries via the AutoCorrect dialog box. To display this box, open the **Insert** menu, point to **AutoText**, and click **AutoText**. To delete an entry, select its name and click the **Delete** button.

New AutoText Toolbar

Word now offers an AutoText toolbar that makes it easier to create and insert AutoText entries. To turn the toolbar on, right-click on any toolbar and select **AutoText**. This toolbar offers three buttons: click **AutoText** to display the AutoCorrect dialog box; click **All Entries** to display a list of AutoText entries you've created; click **New** to transform selected text into a new AutoText entry.

Scroll, Scroll, Scroll Your Document

As you type, the screen fills up, and your text starts scrolling off the top as Word "feeds you more paper." Eventually, you'll need to move back up to that text to edit it or at least read it. The easiest way to move is to point and click with your mouse. To move farther, use one of the following scroll bar methods:

➤ Drag the scroll box up or down. As you drag, a box shows you the number of the page you are about to visit.

➤ Click an arrow at the end of the scroll bar to scroll one line in the direction of the arrow. Hold down the mouse button to scroll continuously.

➤ Click inside the scroll bar above or below the scroll box to scroll up or down one screenful of text.

➤ Click the **Previous Page** or **Next Page** button (bottom of the scroll bar) to flip one page at a time. The dot between the two page buttons gives you additional options to scroll through a document's notes, graphics, or edits.

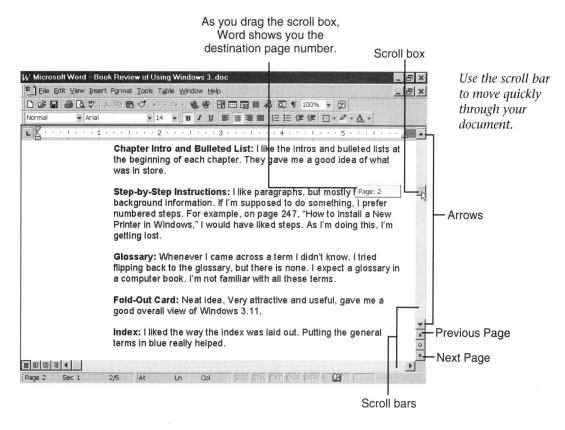

As you drag the scroll box,
Word shows you the
destination page number.

Scroll box

*Use the scroll bar
to move quickly
through your
document.*

Arrows

Previous Page

Next Page

Scroll bars

If you don't like taking your fingers off the keyboard, you can use the cursor keys to navigate your document. The following table lists the keys you can use to move in a hurry.

Navigating the Word Screen with the Keyboard

Press	To Move
⇐	Left one character
⇒	Right one character
⇑	Up one line
⇓	Down one line

continues

Navigating the Word Screen with the Keyboard   Continued

Press	To Move
Ctrl+⇐	Left one word
Ctrl+⇒	Right one word
Crtl+⇑	Up one paragraph
Ctrl+⇓	Down one paragraph
Home	To the beginning of a line
End	To the end of a line
PgDn	Down one screen
PgUp	Up one screen
Ctrl+PgDn	To the top of the next page
Ctrl+PgUp	To the bottom of the previous page
Ctrl+Home	To the start of the document
Ctrl+End	To the end of the document

Changing Views

When you start out in Word, it usually displays huge pages that look more like blocky billboard signs than typewritten pages. You might want to see more of your text (to give your thoughts some context), or you might want to zoom in when you're styling text. Word offers several ways to change views.

The first thing you'll probably want to do is zoom out so you can see entire lines of text. There's nothing more annoying than trying to read sentences that are chopped off on the right or left side of the window. Open the **Zoom** drop-down list in the Standard toolbar and click **Page Width**. Word automatically zooms in or out in order to make the text as large as possible and still fit it in the window. Note that the Zoom drop-down list has several other settings; in addition, you can click inside the text box and type your own setting (zoom percentage).

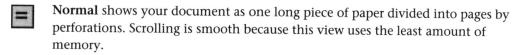

With the Zoom drop-down list, you can zoom in or out on a page.

Word also offers various views of a page, each of which is designed to help you perform a specific task. To change to a view, open the **View** menu and click one of the following view options (buttons for the first four views listed are also available in the lower-left corner of the document window).

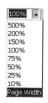 **Normal** shows your document as one long piece of paper divided into pages by perforations. Scrolling is smooth because this view uses the least amount of memory.

Online Layout is a new view that's supposed to make it easy to read your document. In reality, it divides the window into two panes, which always makes it more difficult to read the document. (Hey, Microsoft, view this!)

Page Layout displays the "edges" of your pages, giving you a more realistic look at your pages. However, this uses a lot of memory and makes scrolling a little jerky.

Outline view is covered in great detail in the next chapter, so I'm not going to say anything about it here.

Master Document allows you to create and organize a large document consisting of several smaller documents. Chapter 11, "Working with Long Documents," devotes some coverage to master documents.

Document Map is similar to Online Layout, providing you with a two-pane window. The left pane contains an outline, which makes it easy to see the overall organization of the document; the right pane displays the contents.

If you're new to word processing, stick with three views: Normal (which you'll use most of the time), Page Layout, and Outline.

Before you print the document, click the **Print Preview** button in the Standard toolbar. This gives you a bird's-eye view of the page, allows you to quickly flip pages, and provides rulers that you can use to drag the margin settings around. The following figure shows a document in Print Preview.

Click to start printing.

Click to zoom in or out.

Print Preview lets you make minor adjustments before you commit the document to paper.

Display or hide rulers for changing margins.

Click here to close Print Preview.

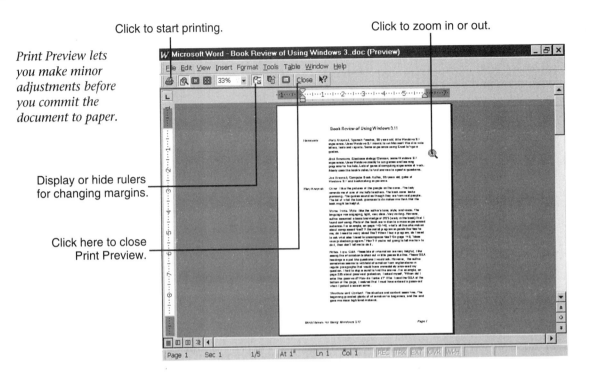

10 Ways to Select Text

Before you can do anything with the text you just typed, you must select it. You can always just drag over text to select it, but Word offers a multitude of quicker ways you can click to select text. The following table outlines those methods.

Selecting Text with Your Mouse

To Select This...	Do This...
Single word	Double-click inside the word.
Sentence	Ctrl+click inside the sentence.
Paragraph	Triple-click inside the paragraph. Or, position the pointer to the left of the paragraph until it changes to a right-pointing arrow, and then double-click.
Graphic	Click the graphic.
One line of text	Position the pointer to the left of the line until it changes to a right-pointing arrow, and then click.

To Select This...	Do This...
Several lines of text	Position the pointer to the left of the first line until it changes to a right-pointing arrow, and then drag up or down.
Several paragraphs	Position the pointer to the left of the paragraphs until it changes to a right-pointing arrow. Then double-click and drag up or down.
Large block of text	Click at the beginning of the text, scroll down to the end of the text, and Shift+click.
Entire document	Position the pointer to the left of any text until it changes to a right-pointing arrow. Then triple-click.
Vertical block of text	Hold down the Alt key and drag over the text.

In the selection area, the mouse pointer points right.

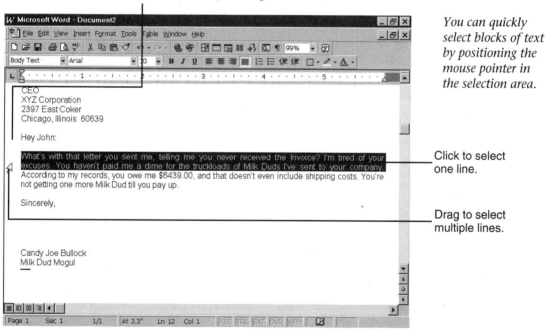

You can quickly select blocks of text by positioning the mouse pointer in the selection area.

Click to select one line.

Drag to select multiple lines.

Although selecting text with your keyboard is a little less intuitive, it can be done. The technique involves holding down the Shift key while moving the insertion point. So, for example, you can move the insertion point where you want to begin the selection, and then hold down the **Shift** key while using the arrow keys to stretch the selection over additional text. You can press **Shift+Page Down** to select screenfuls of text.

Select the Whole Document

To select an entire document, press **Ctrl+A**. This is especially useful if you want to format all of the text in a document. For instance, you might want to change the type style you used for all the text.

Dragging, Cutting, and Copying

You don't select text for the sheer joy of seeing it selected. You usually want to do something with it, such as copy or move it. In Word, the easiest way to copy or move text is to drag it. To move text, position the mouse pointer over any part of the selected text, hold down the left mouse button, and drag the text to where you want it inserted. To copy the text, hold down the **Ctrl** key while you're dragging it. Here are a couple of variations on this theme:

➤ If you drag text with the right mouse button, when you release the mouse button, a menu pops up asking if you want to move or copy the text.

➤ To quickly copy text, select it, hold down the **Ctrl** and **Shift** keys, and right-click where you want a copy of the selected text inserted.

Although the drag-and-drop method is the fastest way to copy and move small chunks of text a short distance, you may find it awkward for working with larger blocks of text or for moving text from one document to another. Therefore, Word offers the Cut, Copy, and Paste commands, which are better able to handle these tasks.

  To cut or copy text, select it, and then click either the **Cut** or the **Copy** button in the toolbar. (You can also access these commands by opening the **Edit** menu or by right-clicking the selected text.) When you select the Cut or Copy command, the selected text is placed on the Windows Clipboard. You can then use the Paste command (or button) to paste the text into a different place in the current document, into another Word document, or into a document in just about any other Windows application.

Splitting Your Document Window

Just above the vertical scroll bar is a tool that lets you split the document window in two. Move the mouse pointer just above the scroll bar until it turns into a two-headed arrow. Drag the tool down to split the window. Then you can scroll separately in each pane to show different parts of the document at the same time. This view makes it easy to copy and move text long distances within one document.

Juggling Two or More Documents

Word lets you work with more than one document at a time. Whenever you open a document or create a new one, Word opens it in its own window. All the other windows are hidden under the current window, just like a deck of cards. To switch from one window to another, open the **Window** menu and select the desired document. The selected document then pops up in front of the others.

If you have two documents open, you might want to display them both at the same time, so you can easily drag and drop between them. To arrange the windows, open the **Window** menu and select **Arrange All**. You can also do this with more than two windows, but then your screen will start looking like some twisted mosaic.

When two or more windows are displayed, don't forget that you can move the document windows and resize them, just as you can any windows. Drag the title bar to move the window, or drag a border to change its size. Your best bet is to arrange the windows so you can see the title bar of each window no matter which window is in front; then you can quickly switch to a window by clicking inside its title bar.

Spike it!

When most people think of the Windows Clipboard, they remember that it can hold only one stored item at a time. However, Word's *Spike* feature lets you do more than that. You know those metal spike desk accessories, the pointy stick-things that let you spear pieces of paper (like notes and bills)? Well, that's sort of what the Spike feature is like.

To Spike your text, select the text you want to move and press **Ctrl+F3**. Repeat this step for as many items as you're moving. When you're ready to paste them into a new location, position your cursor where you want them to appear and press **Ctrl+Shift+F3**. All the items in the Spike are pasted into the document in the order they were cut. Add that one to your repertoire of Word tricks!

The Ol' Find and Replace Trick

One of the things you'll encounter when editing is the old find-and-replace scenario. Let's say you've typed a long letter to the president of the Doohickey company, but then you find out that the name is supposed to be Doohackey not Doohickey. Because you used the name incorrectly in about 30 places in your letter, you need a way to change them all real fast. That's where the Find and Replace commands come in handy.

The Find command looks through the document for the text you specify. The Replace command replaces a word or words you designate with new text. You'll find both commands located on your Edit menu. In fact, they often work together. Here are steps for using both commands.

To search for text, follow these steps:

1. Pull down the **Edit** menu and select the **Find** command. The Find and Replace dialog box appears, displaying the Find tab in front.

2. Type the word you want to find and click **Find Next**. Word finds the specified text and highlights it.

The Find and Replace dialog box remains on-screen until you click the Cancel button. You can edit the found text as you normally would, or you can delete it. To find the next occurrence of the text, click **Find Next**.

The steps for replacing text are similar:

1. Open the **Edit** menu and choose **Replace**. The Find and Replace dialog box opens again, but this time, it displays the Replace tab up front.

2. Enter the word or phrase you want to replace in the **Find What** text box; enter the replacement word or phrase in the **Replace With** box.

3. (Optional) To take more control over the replace operation, you can click the **More** button and change any of the following settings:

   Match Case tells Word to find only those occurrences that use the same capitalization. For example, you might want to replace "College" with "University," but at the same time leave the lowercase "college" as "college."

   Find Whole Words Only replaces the search string only when it is a word by itself, not when it is part of another word or text string. For example, you might want to replace "book" but not replace "bookkeeper."

52

Use Wildcards tells Word to treat a question mark as a wildcard for an individual character, and to treat an asterisk as a wildcard that stands in for multiple unknown characters. If this option is off, Word treats question marks and asterisks as question marks and asterisks.

Sounds Like tells Word to find all occurrences of the word you typed plus any words that sound like the search word.

Find All Word Forms replaces both nouns and verbs with their appropriate forms. For example, if you replace "make" with "create," Word replaces "made" with "created" and "making" with "creating."

Format button displays a menu of character and paragraph formatting you can replace, such as bold or italic. (See Chapter 5, "Giving Your Text a Makeover," for details.)

> *Check This Out...*
>
> **I Just Want to Delete It** If you want to delete the specified text instead of replacing it with something else, leave the Replace With box empty in the Find and Replace dialog box.

Special button displays a menu of special items, such as tabs, paragraph marks, and spaces. This is useful for deleting tabs and spaces when you have used too many of them; for example, you can replace two spaces with one.

Word highlights the text it is about to replace.

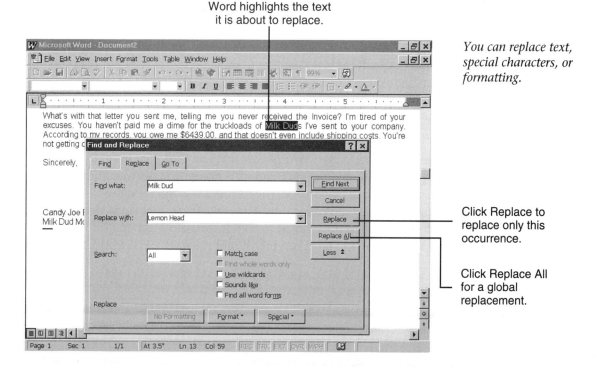

You can replace text, special characters, or formatting.

Click Replace to replace only this occurrence.

Click Replace All for a global replacement.

4. To start the search and replace, click the **Find Next** button.

5. Word highlights the first occurrence of the text it finds and gives you the opportunity to replace the word or skip to the next occurrence. Click one of the following buttons to tell Word what you want to do:

> **Find Next** skips this text and moves to the next occurrence.
>
> **Replace** replaces this text and moves to the next occurrence.
>
> **Replace All** replaces all occurrences of the specified text with the replacement text—and does not ask for your okay.
>
> **Cancel** aborts the operation.

On Second Thought: Undoing Changes

If you enjoy the slash-and-burn, never-look-back approach to editing your documents, you may just decide to live with whatever changes you enter. If you're a little more hesitant, and you get that sinking feeling whenever you delete a sentence, you will feel safe knowing that Word has an Undo feature that allows you to take back any of the most recent edits you've made.

To undo the most recent action, open the **Edit** menu and select **Undo**, or click the **Undo** button in the Standard toolbar. You can continue to click the **Undo** button to undo additional actions.

The Undo button doubles as a drop-down list that allows you to undo an entire group of actions or a specific action you performed some time ago. To view the list, click the drop-down arrow to the right of the Undo button. Then click the action you want to undo, or drag over two or more actions you want to undo. When you release the mouse button, Word undoes what you did.

The programmers who developed Word knew that the Undo feature could get you into as much trouble as it could get you out of. Suppose you get in a huff because you made a mistake, and you start undoing all the changes you made before you realize that some of those changes really improved the document. To recover from an accidental undo, use the Redo button (just to the right of Undo). It works just like the Undo button: Click the **Redo** button to restore the most recently undone action, or click the drop-down arrow to the right of the Redo button and select one or more actions from the list.

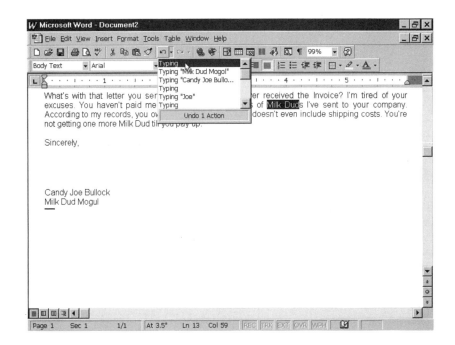

Open the Undo list and select the action you want to undo.

The Least You Need to Know

If you know how to type, you know about all you need to know to create documents in Word. However, there are a few tips that will make your life easier by giving you more control over that on-screen paper:

➤ The easiest way to create a document is to start with a template or wizard. To select from a list of templates and wizards, open the **File** menu and select **New**.

➤ If text disappears as you type, you're in Overtype mode. To turn it off, double-click the **OVR** indicator in the status bar.

➤ Press the **Delete** key to delete characters to the right of the insertion point or to remove selected text. Press **Backspace** to delete characters to the left of the insertion point.

➤ At the bottom of the Word window (just to the left of the horizontal scroll bar) is a set of buttons that let you specify how you want a document displayed. Try to stick with the Normal and Page Layout views.

➤ To select text, drag over it with the mouse pointer.

➤ To copy text, select it, press and hold the **Ctrl** button, and drag it. To move text, drag it without holding down the Ctrl button.

Chapter 5

Giving Your Text a Makeover

In This Chapter

➤ Making your text big and bold like in the magazines

➤ Aligning text left, right, and center

➤ Making bulleted and numbered lists

➤ Automated formatting with styles

➤ Knowing when to use tabs and when to avoid them

After working through Chapter 4, you can do gymnastics with your text—cutting, pasting, spiking, and so on. But those fancy moves don't make your text look any better. That 10-point Times New Roman makes your document look like some chalky ruins in ancient Rome.

You need to breathe some life into your document, spice it up with some big bold headings, drop in a few bulleted lists, maybe even add some color (you do have a color printer, don't you?). In this chapter, you'll learn how to use Word's formatting tools to give your document that much-needed facelift.

Fast and Easy Formatting with the Toolbar

The easiest way to format text is to use Word's Formatting toolbar. In case you haven't noticed this toolbar, it's the one with the B I U buttons in the middle of it. The following table lists the buttons and drop-down lists that appear in this toolbar, and provides a brief description of each.

Get to Know Your Formatting Toolbar

Control	Name	Description
Heading 1	Style list	Lets you select a style that contains several format settings. For example, in the Normal template, the Heading1 style uses Arial 14-point bold text. Skip ahead to "Baby, You've Got Style(s)," later in this chapter to learn more.
Arial	Font list	Provides typestyles from which you can choose. The typestyle is the design of the text.
14	Font Size list	Lets you select the size of the text.
B	Bold	Makes text bold.
I	Italic	Italicizes text.
<u>U</u>	Underline	Underlines text.
Align Left icon	Align Left	Pushes the left side of the paragraph against the left margin.
Center icon	Center	Centers the paragraph between the left and right margins.
Align Right icon	Align Right	Pushes the right side of the paragraph against the right margin.
Justify icon	Justify	Spreads the text evenly between the left and right margins, like in newspaper columns.
Numbering icon	Numbering	Creates a numbered list.
Bullets icon	Bullets	Creates a bulleted list.

Control	Name	Description
	Decrease Indent	Decreases the distance that the text is indented from the left margin.
	Increase Indent	Increases the distance that the text is indented from the left margin.
	Outside Border	Draws a box around the paragraph.
	Highlight	Highlights the text (you can select a different color from the drop-down list).
	Font Color	Changes the color of the text.

You can use any of the buttons in the Formatting toolbar to format your text before or after you type it. To format on the fly, use the Formatting toolbar to set your preferences, and then start typing. If you have already typed the text, select it as explained in Chapter 4, "Making and Editing Word Documents," and then use the tools to apply formatting to the text.

Two More Formatting Tricks

Yeah, the Formatting toolbar is pretty cool, but there are a couple other formatting shortcuts that you can use to dazzle your friends and impress your boss. The first is to right-click on selected text and choose one of the formatting options (Font, Paragraph, or Bullets and Numbering) in the pop-up menu. This displays the dialog box you need to use to apply the desired format.

The second trick is much cooler. You use the Format Painter to copy the format of the text without harming the text itself. This is sort of like copying the soul of the text. First, you drag over the text whose soul you want to steal. Then you click the **Format Painter** button. Now for the grand finale. Drag over the text to which you want to apply the format you copied. Voilà!

Boooo! Bad Form

When you first start using a word processor, you might be tempted to hit the Enter key a couple extra times to insert blank lines, to use the Tab key or spacebar to indent the first line of a paragraph, or to insert several tabs to line up columns of text. These techniques are considered bad form because they insert a bunch of unnecessary codes into your document. Try the following techniques, instead:

➤ To insert extra space before or after a paragraph, right-click the paragraph, select **Paragraph**, and increase the **Spacing Before** and **After** settings.

➤ To indent the first line of a paragraph, right-click the paragraph and select **Paragraph**. Under Indentation Special, select **First Line**. Then use the **Left** spin box to set the indentation distance.

➤ Instead of using several tabs to align text in columns, set the tab stops where you want them, and then use one tab between columns. Or better yet, create a table as explained in Chapter 6, "Aligning Text in Tables and Columns."

Visiting the Font Smorgasbord

The Font and Type Size lists are great for some light text formatting, but you're not going to start your own magazine with those limited choices. You need more power! You need the Font dialog box—a box overflowing with fonts, type sizes, and enhancements such as strikethrough, superscript, and double-underlining.

Before I set you loose in the Font dialog box, I feel obligated to caution you to avoid using too many different fonts in the same document. Feel free to vary the font size, but use only one or two different fonts. Otherwise, your document will look like some teenager's first experience with makeup.

Using the Font dialog box is simple. You drag over the text you want to format, right-click on the selection, and choose **Font**. The Font dialog box spreads out like a table full of choice grub. Just point and click to pick the font, size, and attributes you want. When selecting fonts and type sizes, keep the following font facts in mind:

➤ Font sizes are measured in points (72 points in an inch).

➤ Fonts with **TT** next to them are TrueType fonts, which offer unlimited variations in size. You can even specify a fraction of a point.

➤ Fonts with a printer icon next to them are fonts that are built into your printer. These typically print more quickly than do TrueType fonts.

➤ Fonts that have neither TT nor the printer icon are Windows fonts. The sizes listed are the only available sizes.

In addition, the Font dialog box contains a Character Spacing tab that lists options for controlling the space between characters. Use those options to scrunch the characters together or spread them out.

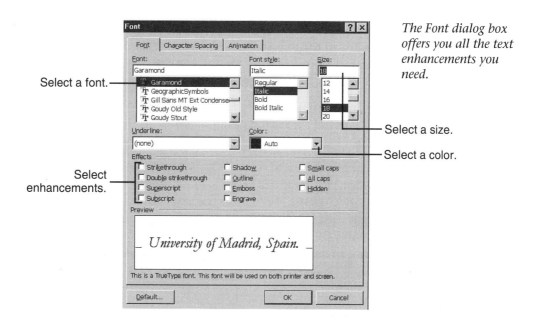

Select a font.

Select enhancements.

Select a size.

Select a color.

The Font dialog box offers you all the text enhancements you need.

Animated Text

If you're creating a document you're going to share with friends or colleagues, consider using Word's new Animated text feature. In the Font dialog box, click the **Animation** tab and select the desired effect. When someone opens the document, the text will do a little jig.

Paragraph Formatting: Line Spacing and Indents

After playing with fonts, paragraph formatting is going to seem a little on the boring side. However, you need to know how to shove paragraphs around on a page. First, if you want to format more than one paragraph, select the paragraphs. Then right-click on any portion of the selected paragraph(s) and click **Paragraph** (or choose **Format**, **Paragraph**). The Paragraph dialog box appears, giving you (basically) five options:

➤ **Alignment** sets the paragraph left, right, or center, or justifies it. You can also do this with the alignment buttons in the Formatting toolbar.

➤ **Line Spacing** sets the space between lines of text within the paragraph. Just like on a typewriter, you can choose single-space, double-space, or other settings.

61

➤ **Spacing Before and After** lets you set the amount of space you want between the current paragraph and the one above it (Before) or between the current paragraph and the one below it (After). Setting the spacing this way is more accurate than trying to set the spacing by pressing the Enter key repeatedly.

➤ **Left and Right Indents** allow you to indent the left and/or right sides of the paragraph. This is useful for setting off long quotes and other chunks of text from surrounding text.

➤ **First Line Indent** allows you to control the distance that the first line is indented from the rest of the paragraph. To set this, under Indentation, open the **Special** drop-down list. Select **First Line** to push the first line in from the left margin, or select **Hanging** to leave the first line flush against the left margin and indent the remaining lines of text (great for bulleted and numbered lists). Use the **By** spin box to set the distance of the indent. (See "Ruling Your Indented Servants," later in this chapter for an easier way to create hanging indents.)

In case you're wondering, the Line and Page Breaks tab in the Paragraph dialog box allows you to enter additional settings that are used mostly for preventing the lines of a paragraph from being split up by page breaks. In most cases, the default settings will prevent undesirable page breaks (for example, a page break that strands one line of a paragraph at the top or bottom of a page, creating a *widow* or *orphan).*

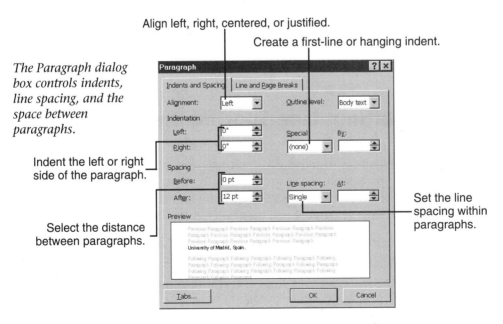

The Paragraph dialog box controls indents, line spacing, and the space between paragraphs.

Align left, right, centered, or justified.

Create a first-line or hanging indent.

Indent the left or right side of the paragraph.

Select the distance between paragraphs.

Set the line spacing within paragraphs.

Lists: You Gotta Love 'Em

From flipping through this book, you probably realize that I like lists. What's not to like? Nobody likes sifting through an entire paragraph to pick out bits of useful information. Lists allow you to quickly find the information you need and skip information that you don't need. So use lists.

You have already seen one way to create a simple bulleted or numbered list. In the Formatting toolbar, click the **Numbering** or **Bullets** button and type your list. Each time you press Enter, Word inserts another bullet or number so you can add an item to the list. To turn off the list and return to typing normal text, click the **Numbering** or **Bullets** button again.

To create fancier lists or sublists, or to control the look of the bullets or numbers, open the **Format** menu and select **Bullets and Numbering**. The Bullets and Numbering dialog box appears, offering several styles from which to choose. If you don't like the offerings, pick a style that's close to what you want, click the **Customize** button, and use the Customize dialog box to enter changes.

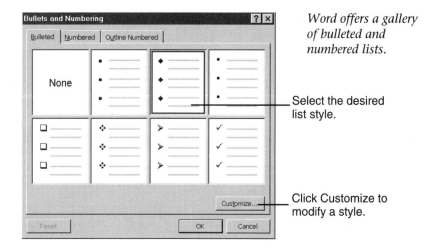

Word offers a gallery of bulleted and numbered lists.

Select the desired list style.

Click Customize to modify a style.

![Check This Out...] **Smart Formatting**

Word is pretty smart for a word processor; it can even tell when you want to create a bulleted or numbered list. Whenever you start a paragraph with a number, Word starts a numbered list for you. Whenever you start with an asterisk, Word assumes you want to create a bulleted list. To view or change these Auto Format options, open the **Tools** menu, select **Auto Correct,** and click the **Format As You Type** tab.

Ruling Your Indented Servants

Some people are good at judging measurements for the indents they want to create. Other people are men. We men need to see our indents in context in order to know whether they are right. For us, Word offers the horizontal ruler (just above the document viewing area). If the ruler isn't on your screen, some joker turned it off; open the **View** menu and select **Ruler**. The ruler contains three markers (the upward and downward pointing triangles), which you can drag:

➤ Drag the top left marker to indent the first line of the paragraph.

➤ Drag the bottom left marker to indent the rest of the lines in the paragraph.

➤ Drag the rectangle marker below the bottom left marker to move both of the left markers at the same time.

➤ Drag the rightmost marker to push text in from the right margin.

Inches, Centimeters, Points, or Picas?

By default, Word displays the rulers and all measurements for indents and margin settings in inches. If you would rather use centimeters, points, or picas (one pica is 12 points, or about 1/6 of an inch), open the **Tools** menu, select **Options**, click the **General** tab, open the **Measurement Units** drop-down list, and select the desired measurement.

When you adjust the indents, you indent only the selected paragraph(s) or the paragraph in which the insertion point is hanging out. These markers do not change the page margins. To change page margins, you need to play with the page setup, as explained in Chapter 8, "Taking Control of Your Pages."

 You can quickly indent paragraphs (including bulleted or numbered lists) by dragging over all the paragraphs you want to indent and clicking the **Increase Indent** button. This indents the paragraphs one tab stop (usually a half inch) to the right. The **Decrease Indent** button moves the paragraphs back one tab stop.

Drag to indent all but the first line. Drag to indent the right side of the paragraph.

*Use this picture as
your guide to indents.*

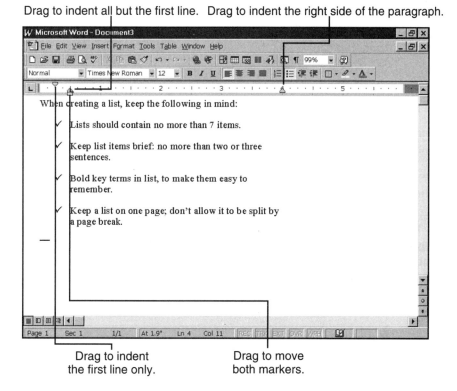

Drag to indent
the first line only.

Drag to move
both markers.

Are Tabs Even Necessary?

Tabs cause trouble. They're usually okay when you first insert them, but then when you go back and change a font size, nine out of ten times, they get all messed up and you have to redo them. But, I'm avoiding the question. The answer is yes, tabs are necessary—but you should avoid them whenever possible.

➤ To indent the first line of a paragraph, use the first line indent feature.

➤ To shove a date over to the upper right-corner of a page, click the **Align Right** button in the Formatting toolbar.

➤ Never use tabs to separate columns in a table. That's what the table feature is for. Check out Chapter 6, "Aligning Text in Tables and Columns," for details.

Now that you know when not to use tabs, when should you use them? Here are a few instances in which a tab can come in handy:

➤ *To shove a bit of text to the right when it is not in a paragraph of its own.* For example, if you want to type your name in the upper-left corner of the page and insert the date in the upper-right corner, you can use a tab between your name and the date.

➤ *To create a bulleted or numbered list.* To create a hanging indent, insert one tab before the bullet or number to indent it, and insert one tab after the bullet or number to create distance between it and the text that follows.

➤ *In a table of contents.* You use tabs to move page numbers to the right, across from their corresponding headings.

➤ *In a memo.* Press **Tab** between the memo headings (From, To, Re) and the text that follows those headings.

By default, regular paragraphs have tab stops at every half inch. That is, whenever you press the Tab key, the insertion point moves a half inch to the right. It's tempting to just keep pressing the Tab key until you've nudged the insertion point to where you want it. Don't. Instead, set the tab stops yourself, and press the Tab key only once to get there. The easiest way to set tab stops is to use the horizontal ruler. Take the following steps to set tabs on the ruler:

1. At the far left end of the ruler is a tab type symbol (which should be shaped like the letter L). Rest the mouse pointer on it to see which type of tab it is set to insert. Click it to pick the type of tab you want to set:

   Left (the default) left-aligns the text with the tab stop.

   Right aligns the text with its right side against the tab stop.

   Center centers the text on the tab stop.

   Decimal aligns the period (.) character on the tab stop. This is useful for aligning a column of numbers on the decimal point.

2. Click on the inside the lower half of the horizontal ruler where you want the tab stop inserted. An icon representing the tab stop appears in the ruler.

3. To move a tab stop, drag it to a new position.

4. To delete a tab stop, drag it off the ruler.

When you set tab stops, they apply to any paragraphs you've selected; if you don't select any paragraphs, they apply from the position of the insertion point forward to the end of the document.

Click this button to
select the tab stop type.

Click inside the bottom of
the ruler to set the tab stop.

*The easiest way to
set tab stops is to use
the horizontal ruler.*

Rest the mouse pointer
on this button to see
the selected type.

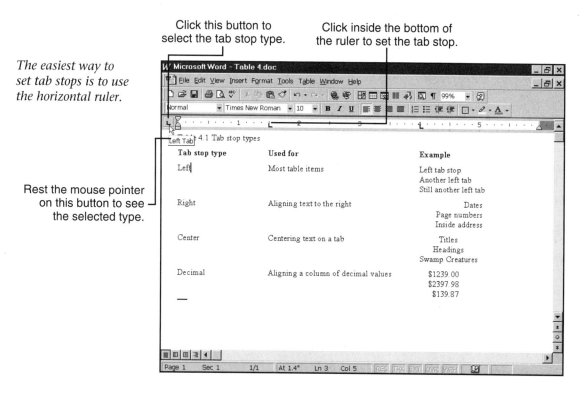

Tab stop type	Used for	Example
Left	Most table items	Left tab stop Another left tab Still another left tab
Right	Aligning text to the right	Dates Page numbers Inside address
Center	Centering text on a tab	Titles Headings Swamp Creatures
Decimal	Aligning a column of decimal values	$1239.00 $2397.98 $139.87

4.1 Tab stop types

Check This Out...

I Need More Control

For more control over the look and behavior of your tab stops, open the **Format** menu and select **Tabs**. The Tabs dialog box lets you set tab stops in inches, clear tab stops, and add *leaders* to tab stops. A leader is a string of characters that lead up to the text at the tab stop like this:

Chapter 14 155

The Painted Word: Using Text As Art

Fancy fonts are great for headings and running text, but sometimes you need something a little different. Maybe you want to add a curving banner to the top of a page, or maybe you want to set off a block of text in its own box. Word offers a couple of tools that you can use to create these special effects: WordArt and text boxes.

Inserting WordArt Objects

With WordArt, you can create three-dimensional text objects that curve, angle up or down, and even lean back. If you've used WordArt before, you'll notice that it has undergone some major reconstructive surgery that has made it a much more powerful tool and yet is simpler to use. To insert a WordArt object on a page, move the insertion point where you want the object inserted. Open the **Insert** menu, point to **Picture**, and click on **WordArt**. The WordArt Gallery appears, displaying a bunch of styles from which you can choose. Click the desired style and click **OK**. In the Edit WordArt Text dialog box, type your text and select the desired font, font size, and attributes (bold or italic). Click **OK**. Word creates the object and places it on the page along with the WordArt toolbar.

The WordArt object is essentially a graphic object. When it first appears (and whenever you click it), small squares called handles appear around it, and the WordArt toolbar appears. You can drag a handle to change the size of the object. If you move the mouse pointer over the object, the pointer appears as a four-headed arrow. You can drag the object to move it.

In addition to changing the object's size and position, you can use buttons in the WordArt toolbar to modify the object, as shown in the following table.

WordArt Toolbar Buttons

Button	Name	Description
![Insert WordArt icon]	Insert WordArt	Inserts another WordArt object on the page.
Edit Te_xt...	Edit Text	Lets you edit the text used in the WordArt object.
![WordArt Gallery icon]	WordArt Gallery	Lets you select a different style for this WordArt object from the WordArt Gallery.
![Format WordArt icon]	Format WordArt	Displays a dialog box that lets you change the WordArt object's size and position, control how surrounding text wraps around the object, change the object's color, and much more.
![WordArt Shape icon]	WordArt Shape	Lets you pick a different shape for the object.

Button	Name	Description
![Free Rotate button]	Free Rotate	Displays round handles around the object, which you can drag to spin the object on the page.
![Aa button]	WordArt Same Letter Heights	Displays all the characters in the object (uppercase or lowercase) the same height.
![Vertical Text button]	WordArt Vertical Text	Displays characters running from the top to the bottom instead of from left to right.
![Alignment button]	WordArt Alignment	Doesn't do anything if you have only one line of text. With two or more lines of text, this allows you to align the text left, right, or center, or to justify it (so it spreads out to touch both sides of the imaginary WordArt box).
![Character Spacing button]	WordArt Character Spacing	Lets you change the space between characters in the WordArt object.

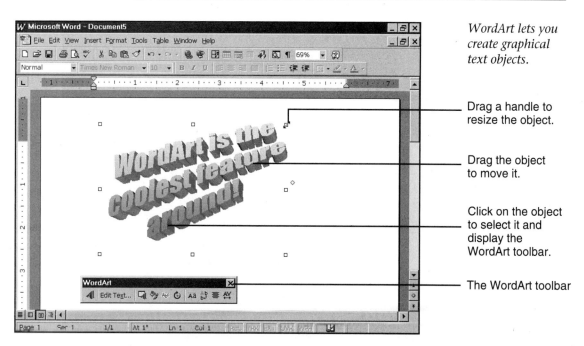

WordArt lets you create graphical text objects.

Drag a handle to resize the object.

Drag the object to move it.

Click on the object to select it and display the WordArt toolbar.

The WordArt toolbar

Setting Off Text in Text Boxes

Word is becoming more and more like a desktop publishing program with every new release. Now Word even offers text boxes, which you can use to set off a block of text from surrounding text. You've probably seen text boxes used in your favorite magazines to set off quotes or add a brief summary of the article. Because the text is in a box of its own, the reader can easily read it or skip it.

 To create a text box in Word, position the insertion point where you want the text box placed, open the **Insert** menu, and click **Text Box**. The mouse pointer turns into a crosshair pointer; drag it on your page to create the text box. Word inserts the box and displays the Text Box toolbar. Type your text in the box, and use the Formatting toolbar to style the text. As with WordArt, the text box is surrounded by handles that you can drag to change the size or dimensions of the box. You can use the Change Text Direction button (on the right side of the Text Box toolbar) to make the text run vertical instead of horizontal inside the box.

On the left end of the Text Box toolbar are two Link buttons: Create Text Box Link and Break Forward Link. These buttons allow you to continue the contents of one text box inside another text box on the same page or on another page. To create a link, make two text boxes and insert or type the desired text in the first text box. Then click the **Create Text Box Link** button and click inside the second text box. If the "story" doesn't fit in that text box, you can create a third text box and link to it. The Break Forward Link button allows you to break the link between text boxes.

Check This Out...

Why Use Columns? In Chapter 6, you'll learn how to create columns on a page for your newsletters or brochures. However, text boxes are much more flexible than columns, and they allow you to link to other pages in a newsletter. With the superior advantages offered by text boxes, who needs columns?

Two more buttons in the Text Box toolbar allow you to follow the link from one text box to the next. This is especially helpful if you have linked text boxes separated by several pages in a long document. You can use the **Previous Text Box** and **Next Text Box** buttons to quickly jump forward and back between text boxes.

One last text box trick, and I'll let you move on. Turn on the Drawing toolbar (right-click on any toolbar and select **Drawing**). All the way on the right are two buttons called Shadow and 3-D. To add a drop shadow to the text box, click the **Shadow** button and select the desired shadow. To give your text box a three-dimensional look like the one in the following figure, click the **3-D** button and select a 3-D effect.

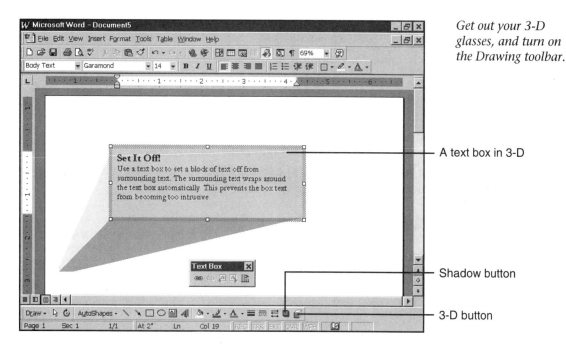

Get out your 3-D glasses, and turn on the Drawing toolbar.

A text box in 3-D

Shadow button

3-D button

More Text Box Options

If you drop a text box on top of existing text, you'll notice that it hides the text under it. If you prefer, you can have existing text wrap around the text box instead so that you can see all of the text. To enter text wrap and other format settings for your text box, open the **Format** menu and select **Text Box**.

Baby, You've Got Style(s)

You go through a lot of trouble creating a wardrobe for your documents. Maybe you've designed the perfect title, created some great-looking bulleted lists, and spent way too much time playing with the various levels of headings. You don't want to do all that work over again, and you don't have to. Instead, you can save your format settings as styles and apply the styles to the text in any other documents you create.

A *style* is a group of format settings. For example, if you create a heading using 18-point Arial bold italic type that's centered on the page, the first time you format the heading, you have to apply all those formats separately. However, if you then create a style for that heading (and name it, say, Heading1), you can apply all those format settings to some other text by selecting the Heading1 style from the style list.

Even better than that is that you can modify a style and have your changes affect all the text that you have formatted using that style. For instance, if you decided that you

71

wanted to bump the Heading1 type size down from 18-point to 16-point, all you have to do is change the Heading1 style. All the headings you've formatted using that style are then automatically changed from 18-point to 16-point.

There are two types of styles: paragraph and character. A *paragraph style* applies paragraph and character formatting to all the characters in the paragraph. Paragraph formatting includes alignment, indents, line spacing, space before and after the paragraph, and so on. Character formatting controls the font, size, and character attributes, such as bold and italic. A *character style* applies format settings only to selected text; it does not apply formatting to all the text in a paragraph. The style list (on the Formatting toolbar) marks paragraph styles with a ¶ and character styles with an a̲.

Applying Character and Paragraph Styles

Word's templates all come with a set of styles you can apply to your paragraphs and text. To apply a paragraph style, click anywhere inside the paragraph to which you want to apply the style, open the **Style** drop-down list, and click the desired style. To apply a character style, drag over the text to which you want to apply the style, open the **Style** drop-down list, and click the desired style.

Pick a style from the Style list.

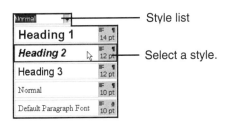

Style list

Select a style.

If the drop-down list doesn't have enough to choose from, you can open the **Format** menu and select the **Style** command. Open the **List** drop-down list and click **All Styles**. This displays a list of even more ready-made Word styles and styles you have created (which you will do in the next section).

Creating Your Own Styles

An easy way to create your own paragraph style is to use the **Style** box on the toolbar (you can't use this box to create a character style). First set up the paragraph on which you want to base your style; include any special formatting you want to use. Make sure your insertion point is somewhere in that paragraph, and then click inside the **Style** box in the Formatting toolbar. Enter a new style name, being careful not to duplicate an existing name. Click anywhere outside of the box or press **Enter**, and you have created a new style. You can now apply it by name to new paragraphs that you add to your document.

To create a character style, you can't use the Style box on the Formatting toolbar. You must use the Style dialog box, as covered in these steps:

1. Open the **Format** menu and select **Style** to display the Style dialog box.

2. Click the **New** button.

3. In the **Name** text box, type the desired name for the style.

4. Open the **Style Type** dialog box and select **Character**.

5. Open the **Format** menu at the bottom of the dialog box and select **Font**. This displays the Font dialog box.

6. Use the Font dialog box to select the desired character formatting and click **OK**. This returns you to the Style dialog box.

7. You can use the **Shortcut Key** button to assign a keystroke to this style. You can then quickly apply the style by selecting your text and pressing the keystroke.

8. Click **OK** to save your new style.

Type a name for the style.

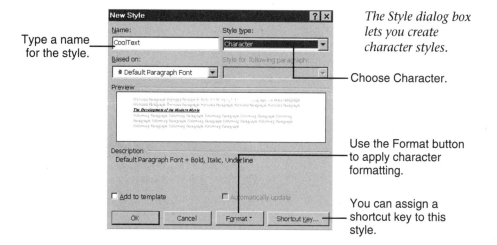

The Style dialog box lets you create character styles.

Choose Character.

Use the Format button to apply character formatting.

You can assign a shortcut key to this style.

The Least You Need to Know

About fifty percent of the time you spend creating a document is devoted to formatting it. If you have a severe case of writer's block, that percentage is even higher. So know the basics:

➤ The formatting toolbar places most of the common formatting options one click away.

➤ If you need more formatting options, right click on the text you want to format.

➤ To change line spacing within and between paragraphs, open the **Format** menu and select **Paragraph**.

➤ You can use the horizontal ruler to quickly indent paragraphs.

➤ Use the horizontal ruler to quickly set tabs.

➤ To insert a WordArt object, open the **Insert** menu, point to **Picture**, and click **WordArt**.

➤ The Style list in the formatting toolbar lets you quickly apply several format settings to text by applying a single style.

Chapter 6

Aligning Text in Tables and Columns

In This Chapter

➤ Avoiding tabs, for the most part

➤ Aligning text in columns and rows

➤ Drawing a table with your mouse—cool!

➤ Using columns to create your own newsletters

➤ Understanding section breaks

Creating a document with headings and paragraphs is relatively easy. You type some text, press the Enter key, and maybe assign a few styles and apply some character formatting to keep things interesting. However, if you need to create a more complex publication, such as a newsletter, a résumé, or instructional material, you need more powerful tools for aligning text in columns and rows.

Microsoft Word offers two such tools: the columns feature and tables. The columns feature allows you to place two or more columns of running text on a page, as in a newspaper or magazine. The tables feature provides the tools you need to align text in columns and rows. In this chapter, you will learn how to use these two powerful tools to take more control over your page layout.

Four Ways to Set Your Table

The most useful page layout tool you will find in any word processing program is the table feature. This tool allows you to align blocks of text side by side not only to create tables packed with small bits of information, but also to create professional-looking résumés, exams, study guides, and documentation. If you ever have trouble placing two items side by side in a document, the solution is usually a table. The following figure shows a table used to create a résumé.

A table disguised as a résumé.

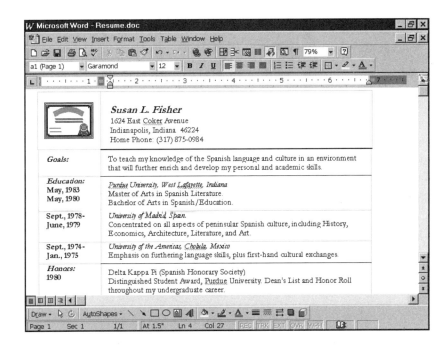

The key to Word tables is that the information is organized in a systematic fashion. Like a well-designed city, a table is a grid consisting of rows and columns that intersect to form cells. In the following sections, you will learn four techniques for creating your own tables. In later sections in this chapter, you will learn how to insert text and pictures in the cells that make up the table, and how to change the look and layout of the cells.

Using the Insert Table Button

The easiest way to create a table is to use the Insert Table button in the Standard toolbar. When you click that button, Word opens a menu showing a graphic representation of the columns and rows that make up a table. Drag down and to the right to highlight the number of rows and columns you want your table to have (you will learn how to insert and delete columns and rows later). When you release the mouse button, Word inserts the table.

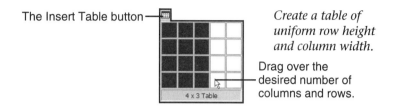

The Insert Table button

Create a table of uniform row height and column width.

Drag over the desired number of columns and rows.

4 x 3 Table

Setting Your Table with a Dialog Box

Another way to create a table is to use the Insert Table dialog box. Although it's not as fast as creating a table with the Insert Table button, this technique gives you additional control over your table, allowing you to set the column width and choose a design for your table.

To display the Insert Table dialog box, open the **Table** menu and select **Insert Table**. Set the desired number of rows and columns, and specify the column width if necessary. The default column width setting is Auto, which tells Word to make the table as wide as the margins allow and to divide it into columns of equal width.

If you want to give your table a professional look, you can choose a design for it. To do so, click the **AutoFormat** button and select a predesigned format from the **Formats** list. Enter any other formatting preferences and click **OK**. This returns you to the Insert Table dialog box. Click **OK** to create the table.

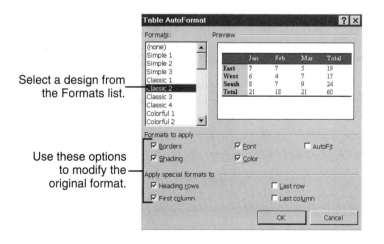

Select a design from the Formats list.

Use these options to modify the original format.

The AutoFormat options let you quickly format your table.

Drawing a Table with Your Mouse

If you're looking for a more intuitive way to create a table, why don't you just draw it? Word now offers a table drawing tool that allows you to create the overall table outline and then chop the table into little pieces by adding row and column lines.

To draw a table, open the **Table** menu and select **Draw Table**. The mouse pointer turns into a pencil, the Tables and Borders toolbar appears, and Word switches to Page Layout view. Drag a rectangle of the desired length and width where you want the table to appear. When you release the mouse button, Word inserts a one-cell table. You can then drag vertical horizontal lines across the table to create columns and rows (see below).

The Tables and Borders Toolbar

Whenever you choose to draw a table, the Tables and Borders toolbar appears. You can start drawing a table with simple lines, or you can select options from the toolbar (such as line color and thickness) before you start drawing. For more information on how to use this toolbar, see "Using the Tables and Borders Toolbar," later in this chapter.

You can now draw tables.

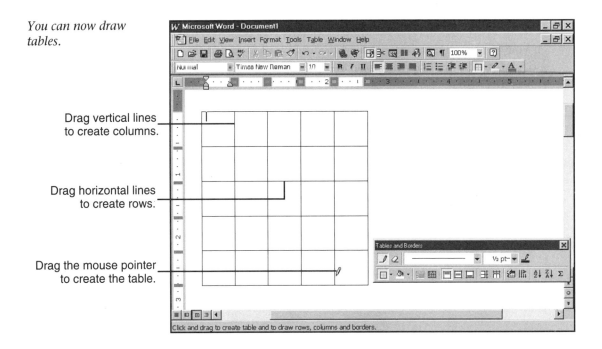

Drag vertical lines to create columns.

Drag horizontal lines to create rows.

Drag the mouse pointer to create the table.

Transforming Existing Text into a Table

Creating a table using tabs is like performing brain surgery with a meat cleaver; tabs just don't give you enough control over your columns and rows. However, if you're reading this after having set up a table with tabs, don't despair. You can recover from your ill-conceived mistake by converting your tabular table into a bona fide table.

¶   First, delete any extraneous tabs inside the existing table. You should press the Tab key only once between columns. To check for extra tabs, click the **Show/Hide ¶** button in the Standard toolbar (it's to the left of the Zoom list). This displays non-printing codes, such as paragraph symbols, spaces, and tabs (which are shown as arrows). Delete any extra tabs (arrows) that exist. The text may appear all jumbled, but the table will bring it back in line.

Aligning Graphics and Text   Although tables are traditionally used to align blocks of text, they're excellent for aligning pictures with text as well. Just place the insertion point in the cell where you want the picture to appear, and then select the **Insert, Picture** command.

When you have only one tab between columns, drag over all the text that you want to include in the table. Open the **Table** menu and select **Convert Text to Table**. The Convert Text to Table dialog box appears, prompting you to specify the number of columns and rows and to enter other preferences. Make the desired selections and click **OK**. Word converts the text to a table, and you can start modifying it if necessary.

Moving Around Inside Your Table

Navigating a table with the mouse is fairly straightforward. You click inside a cell to move the insertion point to that cell. You can also use the keyboard to quickly move from cell to cell. The following table lists the keystrokes to use for moving around in a table.

Moving Around in a Table

Press	To
Tab	Move to the next cell in the row.
Shift+Tab	Move to the previous cell in the row.
Alt+Home	Move to the first cell in the row you're in.
Alt+PgUp	Move to the top cell in the column you're in.
Alt+End	Move to the last cell in the row you're in.
Alt+PgDn	Move to the last cell in the column you're in.

You select text inside a table the same way you select text in a paragraph—by dragging over it. To select an entire row, move the mouse pointer to the left of the row (outside the table) until the mouse pointer points to the right, and then click. To select a column, move the mouse pointer over the topmost line of the column until the pointer points down, and then click. You can drag selected columns and rows to move them in the table.

Performing Reconstructive Surgery on Your Table

A table never turns out perfect the first time. Maybe you want more space between the topmost row and the rest of the table, or maybe you want to shade some of the cells or add lines to divide the columns and rows. In the following sections, you will learn all the tricks for restructuring and enhancing your table.

Adjusting the Row Height and Column Width

The contents of a table are rarely uniform in length. Tables typically display shorter entries in the leftmost column because the reader uses this column to scan for the needed information. Because of this, you will usually have to adjust the column widths to give a little more elbowroom to those entries that need it. In addition, you might have to adjust the row height if you use a larger font for some entries.

The easiest way to adjust the row height and column width is to drag the lines that divide the columns and rows. When you move the mouse pointer over a line, the pointer changes into a double-headed arrow; that's when you can start dragging. If you hold down the **Alt** key and drag, the horizontal or vertical ruler shows the exact row height or column width measurement. (You can also drag the column or row markers inside the rulers to change the row height and column width.)

Precise Control

For more precise control over the row height and column width, select the row(s) or column(s) you want to change, and then open the **Table** menu and select one of the following commands: **Distribute Rows Evenly** (to make all of the rows a uniform height), **Distribute Columns Evenly** (to make all columns equally wide), or **Cell Height and Width** (to enter exact measurements for the row height and column width).

Inserting and Deleting Columns and Rows

When you start typing entries in a table, you will find that you have either too many rows or columns or too few. Both problems are easy to correct:

➤ To insert a row, click inside the row above which you want the new row to appear, open the **Table** menu, and select **Insert Rows**.

➤ To insert multiple rows, select two or more rows in the existing table (for example, if you want to insert three rows, drag over three existing rows). Then open the **Table** menu and select **Insert Rows**. Word inserts the new rows above the rows you selected.

➤ To insert one or more columns, first select an existing column (for example, to insert two columns, select two columns). Then open the **Table** menu and select **Insert Columns**. Word inserts the new columns to the left of the selected columns.

➤ To delete rows or columns, drag over the rows or columns you want to delete, open the **Table** menu, and select **Delete Rows** or **Delete Columns**. (If you press the Delete key instead, Word removes only the contents of the rows or columns.)

In most cases, you'll want to insert a row at the end of the table or insert a column at the far right. However, the Insert command places the new rows up from the end of the table and to the left of any existing columns. To remedy the situation, select the bottom row or rightmost column, and drag it up or to the left. You can't drag the new blank rows or columns to the end of the table.

You can also insert and delete individual cells by selecting cells and using the **Insert Cells** or **Delete Cells** command on the **Table** menu. However, these operations require you to specify how you want surrounding cells shifted to accommodate the change. For example, if you delete two cells that have cells below them, Word will ask if you want surrounding cells shifted up or down.

Splitting and Joining Cells

Although not quite as exciting as splitting atoms, splitting cells and joining them (fusion, I guess) can keep you entertained for hours—and give you a great deal of control over your tables. The following figure shows some instances where you might want to join cells to create a single cell that spans several rows or columns.

To join cells, first drag over the cells that you want to transform into a single cell. Then open the **Table** menu and select **Merge Cells**. Word transforms the multiple cells into a single cell organism.

Column headings can span two or more columns.

You can join cells to form a single cell, or split one cell into many.

A row heading might span several rows.

Snack Type		Quantity	Calories	Total Fat	Cholesterol	Sodium
		Snack Table				
		Chips Ahoy (4 Cookies)	200	10g	0mg	27g
		Fritos (1 ¼ oz. Bag)	200	13g	0mg	200mg
		Pringles (1 can)	160	11g	0mg	340mg
		Cheese Crackers (1 pkg.)	130	8g	15mg	340mg

To split a cell into two or more cells, select the cell you want to split, and then open the **Table** menu and select **Split Cells**. The Split Cells dialog box appears, asking you to specify the number of rows and columns you want to split the cell into. Enter your preferences and click **OK**. Once the cells are split, you may have to drag the borders to adjust the width and height of the cells.

Giving Your Table a Face Lift with Borders and Shading

Tables are bland at first sight. However, Word offers several seasonings (such as borders and shading) that can add spice to your tables. By far, the easiest way to embellish your table is to use the AutoFormat feature. Click anywhere inside the table, open the **Table** menu, and select **Table AutoFormat**. Select the desired design for your table and click **OK**.

If you don't like the prefab table designs that Word has to offer, you can design the table yourself using the Borders and Shading dialog box. To change the borders or add shading to the entire table, make sure the insertion point is somewhere inside the table; you don't have to select the entire table. If you want to add borders or shading to cells, select the cells. Then open the **Format** menu and select **Borders and Shading**.

The Borders and Shading dialog box has three tabs, two of which you can use to format your table: the Borders tab and the Shading tab. On the Borders tab, you can select any of the listed border arrangements on the left, or you can create a custom border by inserting lines of a specific thickness, design, and color.

First, select a line style, thickness, and color from the options in the center of the dialog box. Next, open the Apply to drop-down list, and select Table (to apply the lines to the entire table) or Cell (to apply lines only to selected cells). In the Preview area (just above the Apply to list), click on the buttons or on locations in the preview to insert lines.

Select a predesigned border arrangement.

Shading tab

Select a line style, thickness, and color.

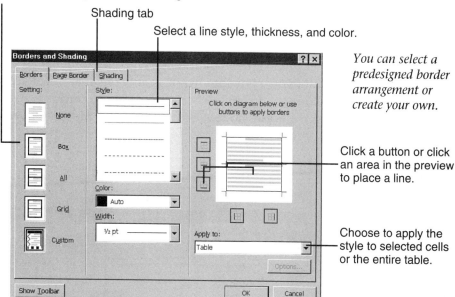

You can select a predesigned border arrangement or create your own.

Click a button or click an area in the preview to place a line.

Choose to apply the style to selected cells or the entire table.

To shade cells with color or gray shading, click the **Shading** tab. In the Fill grid, click the color you want to use to shade the table or selected cells. Under Patterns, click on a color and percentage to add a pattern of a different color to the shading. For example, you might choose green as the fill and then use a 50% yellow pattern to brighten the green.

When you finish entering all your border and shading preferences, click **OK** to apply your changes to your table.

Using the Tables and Borders Toolbar

The Table and Format menus provide you with all the tools you need to restructure and enhance your table, but there's an easier way: using the Tables and Borders toolbar. To display the toolbar, right-click on any toolbar and click on **Tables and Borders**.

Web Work!

If you've wandered the Web, you know that tables are a useful addition to many Web pages. When creating your own Web pages, feel free to use tables to control the layout of your page.

If you're not sure of what one of the buttons does, rest the mouse pointer on it to view its name. Most of the buttons are fairly intuitive. The only one that might give you trouble is the eraser, which allows you to remove lines from a table to merge two or more cells. To use the eraser, click the **Eraser** button, and then drag the mouse pointer over the line you want to remove.

The Eraser button

The Tables and Borders toolbar

The Tables and Borders toolbar allows you to quickly restructure and design your tables.

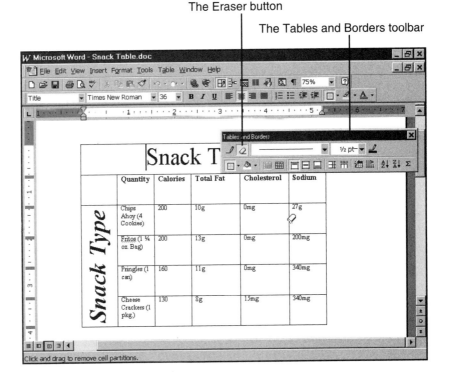

Sorting and Summing Table Entries

Tables commonly contain entries that you need to sort alphabetically or numerically. For example, if you create a table of phone numbers for people and places you frequently call, you may want to sort the list alphabetically to make it easy to find people when you need to. You might also create a table with numerical entries that you need to total. Word offers a couple of tools that can help.

To sort entries in a table, first select the entire table (or the portion that contains the entries you want to sort by). Open the **Table** menu and select **Sort**. Then open the **Sort By** drop-down list and select the column that contains the entries to sort by (for example, if you want to sort by last name and the last names are in the second column, select Column 2). Open the **Type** drop-down list and select the type of items you want to sort (**Number**, **Text**, or **Date**). Select the desired sort order: **Ascending** (1,2,3 or A,B,C) or **Descending** (Z,Y,X or 10,9,8). Click **OK** to sort the entries.

Although a Word table is not designed to perform the complicated mathematical operations that an Excel spreadsheet can handle, tables can add a column of numbers. Click inside the cell directly below the column of numbers you want to add, open the **Table** menu, and click **Formula**. By default, the Formula dialog box is set up to total the values directly above the current cell. Click **OK** to total the numbers.

Creating Your Own Newspaper Columns

Picture this. Due to your outstanding performance at work, your boss has put you in charge of writing and printing the company newsletter. Nobody wants to contribute to it, and very few of your coworkers really want to read it—but your boss thinks it'll be good for morale. The trouble is, you have never created a newsletter.

Never fear, with Word's Columns feature, you can at least make your second-rate publication look like a professional newsletter.

Creating Columns

Before you create columns, figure out where you want the columns to start and end. Maybe you want the entire document divided into columns, or maybe you want to apply columns to only a portion of the document. Perhaps you want a title at the top of the page that spans all the columns.

If you want to format the entire document with columns, it doesn't matter where the insertion point is within the document. If you want to divide the document and format only a portion of it in columns, place the insertion point where you want the columns to start, or drag over the text that you want to lay out in columns.

Open the **Format** menu and select **Columns**. The Columns dialog box appears, prompting you to specify the number of columns to use. Select one of the Preset column styles at the top, and specify additional preferences as desired to modify the style. You can click the **Line Between** option to insert a vertical line between the columns.

If you moved the insertion point to a place in the document where you want the columns to begin (instead of formatting the entire document with columns), open the **Apply To** drop-down list, and select **This Point Forward**. If you selected a block of text to transform into columns, **Selected Text** appears in the **Apply To** drop-down list. Click **OK**.

If you decide later to return the columns to normal text (turn columns off), position the insertion point where the columns start, and repeat the steps for setting columns. This time, pick the **One** column option from the Presets list. You can change the column layout anywhere inside the document; for example, you might want to shift from two columns on one page to three columns on the next. Again, move the insertion point to where you want the columns to change, and then repeat the steps for creating columns.

Adjusting the Column Width

Whenever you create columns, the horizontal ruler displays markers that you can use to control the column boundaries. To quickly change the width of a column, drag its marker. To display the column width measurements in the ruler, hold down the **Alt** key while dragging.

You can also adjust the column widths by resetting the columns. To do so, move the insertion point to where the columns begin, open the **Format** menu, and select **Columns**. Enter the desired measurements for the width of each column.

The easiest way to resize a column is to drag its marker.

Drag a column marker to change the column width.

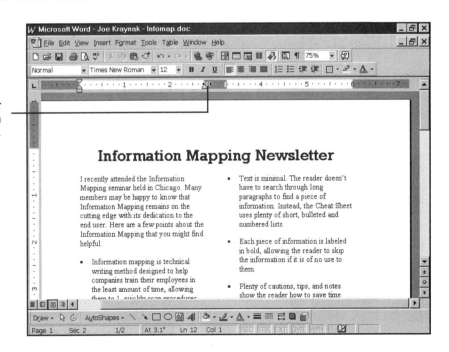

The Least You Need to Know

Once you learn how to use tables and columns, you can pry the Tab key off your keyboard. Until then, keep the following information in mind:

➤ The quickest way to create a table is to click the **Insert Table** button, and then drag to select the number of columns and rows you want your table to have.

➤ To create newspaper columns, place the insertion point where you want columns to start, open the **Format** menu, and select **Columns**.

➤ You can drag the markers in the horizontal and vertical rulers to adjust column widths and row heights.

➤ Use the Tables and Borders toolbar (View, Toolbars, Tables and Borders) to draw, restructure, and format tables.

Chapter 7

Spicing It Up with Graphics, Sound, and Video

In This Chapter

➤ Decorating your text-heavy pages with pictures

➤ Inserting audio and video clips

➤ Moving and sizing your pictures

➤ Adding graphs to reports and other documents

➤ Drawing your own masterpieces

With each generation, the world becomes a little more visual. Since the 1950s, people have flipped more channels than pages in search of news and entertainment. And since the early '70s when the Pinball Wizard was king, kids have spent more time playing video games and working on the computer than they have spent reading or playing board games. With the development of three-dimensional interactive educational programs, people will surely become even more visually oriented.

In order to catch the attention of such a media-savvy audience and convey your ideas and insights, you must now know how to communicate visually as well as verbally. You must use graphics both to attract the reader and to convey information. And if you really want to captivate the audience of the future, you will have to dazzle them with multimedia elements, as well.

In this chapter, you will learn how to use several tools in Word to add graphics, sound, and video to your documents.

Microsoft Photo Editor

Office 97 includes Microsoft Photo Editor, a high-tech tool for modifying electronic images. To run the Photo Editor, open the Windows Start menu, point to Programs, and click Microsoft Photo Editor. Photo Editor contains tools for adjusting the color, contrast, and sharpness of your images, and for modifying the images in other ways.

Inserting Pictures, Sounds, and Video Clips from the Gallery

Maybe you can hold your own in a doodling contest, or you can sketch Gumby and Pokey in your sleep, but chances are that you probably don't have the talent, ambition, or determination to become a professional artist. Fortunately, Word has gathered a collection of clip art, audio recordings, and video clips that you can use to transform your bland text into a dazzling multimedia document.

To insert an item from the gallery, first insert the Microsoft Office 97 CD in the CD-ROM drive. The CD contains additional clips that were not installed when you installed Office.

Techno Talk

Web Work! In the lower-right corner of the Microsoft Clip Gallery is a button that looks like a world with a magnifying glass over it. If you're connected to the Internet and you have Internet Explorer installed, you can click this button to connect to a special Web page that offers additional clip art.

Open the **Insert** menu, point to **Picture**, and click **Clip Art**. The Microsoft Clip Gallery appears, displaying several tabs full of images, sound clips, and video clips. Click on the desired tab. In the list on the left, click the category from which you want to select a clip, or leave (All Categories) selected so you can choose a clip from any category. The pane on the right displays the clips in the selected category. Use the scroll bar to view additional clips.

When you find the clip you want, click on it and click the **Insert** button. To replace a clip you've added with a different clip from the gallery, double-click the clip that's inside your document. This opens the Microsoft Clip Gallery dialog box, from which you can select a different clip.

Each tab lists a
different media type.   Click a clip.

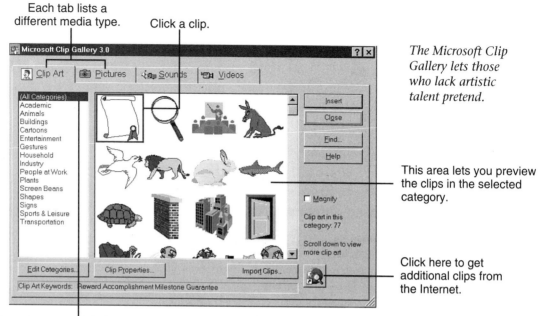

*The Microsoft Clip
Gallery lets those
who lack artistic
talent pretend.*

This area lets you preview
the clips in the selected
category.

Click here to get
additional clips from
the Internet.

Select a category to limit the number of clips.

Importing Graphics Files

Okay, maybe you're some professional artist who's trying to learn a little about word processing, and I underestimated your talent. I suppose you've been using CorelDRAW! since it first came out to do cover designs and to whip out technical illustrations and drawings. (Or maybe you've just downloaded a bunch of graphics files from the Internet and you want to paste them into your documents.) Whatever the case, Word can handle most types of graphics files.

To insert a graphic image that's stored on your disk, open the **Insert** menu, point to **Picture**, and click **From File**. The Insert Picture dialog box appears, prompting you to select the graphic file you want to insert. By default, this dialog box is set up to display all the graphic file types that Word supports. You can narrow the list by selecting a specific graphic file type from the **Files of Type** drop-down list.

Use this dialog box just as you would use the Open dialog box to open a document file. Select the drive, folder, and name of the graphics file you want to insert. Before you click the Insert button, check out the following options:

➤ **Link to File** links this graphic with the document so that whenever you edit the original graphic, the changes will appear in the document. If you do not want the graphic in the document to change, make sure this option is turned off.

➤ **Save with Document** saves the graphic image inside the document so that if you send the document to someone, the graphic image is included. By default, this option is on.

➤ **Float over Text** places the graphic image on the drawing layer, an imaginary layer that floats above the text. If you want to place the image on your page and have text wrap around it, turn this option off.

When you have entered your preferences, click the **Insert** button to insert the picture into your document.

Inserting a Scanned Image

If you have a scanner, you can insert a scanned image directly into your document using Microsoft Photo Editor (which comes with Office 97). Select **Insert, Picture, From Scanner**, and then use your scanner to scan in the desired image. The image appears in Microsoft Photo Editor, which you can use to crop the image, resize it, or change its color or contrast. When you're done modifying the image, open the Photo Editor's **File** menu and select **Exit and Return To**.

Moving Pictures Around on a Page

The Float over Text option explained in the previous section is an addition to Office 97 that is long overdue. This option (on by default for all images you insert) places the graphic on an imaginary drawing layer above the text. You can then drag the picture around on that layer even if you have no text on a page (something that was impossible in previous versions). This is a great improvement, bringing Word more in line with desktop publishing programs.

Now, to move a picture around on a page, click the picture, move the mouse pointer over it (the pointer turns into a four-headed arrow), and drag the picture to the desired location. When you release the mouse button, Word plops the picture on the page.

What happens to the surrounding text depends on the text wrapping setting for this picture. By default, the picture is set to have text appear above it and below it, but not on either side. To change the way text wraps, right-click the picture and select **Format Picture** or **Format Object**. Click the **Wrapping** tab, select the desired wrapping style, and select the distance you want between the text and the picture.

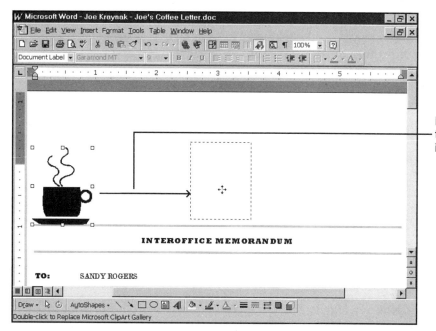

You move pictures by dragging them.

Drag the picture to the desired location in the document.

You can also control whether the picture moves with its surrounding text, so you can keep the picture on the same page as the text that refers to it. In the Format Picture (or Format Object) dialog box, click the **Position** tab and change any of the following options:

➤ **Horizontal** and **Vertical** settings you can ignore for now. It's easier to position the picture by dragging it. However, if you need precise figure placement on a page, you can enter the positions here. You can set the vertical position from the column, the top of the page, or the top margin. You can set the horizontal distance from the paragraph, the left margin, or the left edge of the page.

➤ **Move Object with Text** tells Word to keep this picture near the surrounding text, if this text moves due to edits. It changes the horizontal and vertical position settings to set the position of the picture relative to the column and paragraph it is in.

➤ **Lock Anchor** tells Word to keep this picture on the same page as the text to which it is anchored. The picture can move to the next page or previous page only if the anchor text moves.

Check This Out...

Copying and Cutting Pictures The Cut, Copy, and Paste commands on the Edit menu work for pictures as well as text. You can also copy a picture by holding down the **Ctrl** key and dragging it, or you can right-click a picture and select the desired command from the pop-up menu.

➤ **Float over Text** places the picture on a drawing layer above the page. If you turn this off, the picture is placed on the text page just as if it were a large character, which makes it difficult to move the picture.

After entering the desired preferences, click **OK**.

Resizing and Reshaping Your Pictures

Pictures rarely fit in. Either they're so large that they take over the entire page, or they're too dinky to make any impression at all. Changing the size of a picture is a fairly standard operation. When you click on the picture, squares (called *handles*) surround it. You can drag the squares to change the picture's size and dimensions:

➤ Drag a top or bottom handle to make the picture taller or shorter.

➤ Drag a side handle to make the picture skinny or fat.

➤ Drag a corner handle to change both the height and width.

➤ Hold down the **Ctrl** key while dragging to increase or decrease the size from the center out. For example, if you hold down the Ctrl key while dragging a handle on the right side out, the picture gets fatter on both the left and right sides.

If you need more control over the size and dimensions of an image, right-click the image, click **Format Picture** (or **Format Object**), and click the **Size** tab. This page of options lets you enter specific measurements for your picture.

You can use the handles around an object to resize it.

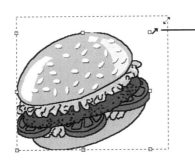

Drag a handle to resize or reshape a picture.

Touching Up a Picture with the Picture Toolbar

Microsoft never had this graphics thing under control. Previous versions of the Office products treated graphics as a nuisance, thinking that because pictures were trying to become integrated with text, the pictures should at least try to behave like text. However, all that has changed in Office 97 with the arrival of the Picture toolbar.

This toolbar is like a graphics program built right into your desktop. With about ten buttons, this toolbar allows you to adjust the picture's brightness and contrast, crop the image (to use only a portion of it), transform a color picture into grayscale or black-and-white, add a border around the picture, and even change the way text wraps around it:

Insert Picture lets you insert a graphics file from disk.

Image Control displays a menu that lets you transform a color image into grayscale, black-and-white, or a watermark (a ghost image that can lie on top of text without hiding it).

More Contrast is like a TV control that increases the contrast of the image.

Less Contrast decreases the contrast in an image.

More Brightness makes the image brighter.

Less Brightness makes the image darker.

Crop turns the mouse pointer into a cropping tool. Move the pointer over one of the handles and drag it to chop off a portion of the picture.

Line Style lets you add a border around the picture.

Text Wrapping does the same thing as the Wrapping tab in the Format Object dialog box you saw earlier, but this control is a lot easier to use.

Format Picture (or **Format Object**) displays the Format Picture or Format Object dialog box, which offers plenty of options but is nearly impossible to use.

Set Transparent Color makes the selected color in a picture transparent so that the background of the page (paper) or screen shows through. Click this button, and then click the color you want to make transparent. (This button is unavailable for most clip art images.)

Reset Picture changes the options back to their original settings in case you mess up while entering changes.

The Picture toolbar appears automatically whenever you insert a picture. If you turn it off, you can always turn it back on: just right-click on any toolbar and select **Picture**.

So You Think You're the Next Picasso

After you've spent a little time with the Picture toolbar, you might start to overestimate your artistic ability and think that you can actually create your own drawings or modify pictures that you've obtained from some outside source (such as the Internet). Maybe you're thinking of a career change right now.

Word offers a Drawing toolbar that offers several tools you can use to create your own drawings, logos, flow charts, illustrations, and other simple graphics. You can also use these tools to modify and enhance existing drawings. To turn on the Drawing toolbar, right-click on any toolbar and select **Drawing**.

Creating Drawings with Simple Lines and Shapes

Technical illustrators typically have a collection of rulers and templates that they use to draw lines, ovals, rectangles, curves, triangles, and other shapes. They assemble these very basic geometric shapes to create complex illustrations. This is the same technique you will use to create drawings in Word.

The Drawing toolbar allows you to place five different geometrical objects on a page: a line, an arrow, an oval, a rectangle, and an AutoShape (a predrawn object, such as a diamond, heart, or starburst). In addition, you can use the Shadow and 3-D tools to transform two-dimensional objects, such as a square, into three-dimensional objects, such as a cube.

You follow the same procedure for drawing any of these objects. Click on the button for the object you want to draw, and then drag the mouse on the page to create the object. For more control over the drawing tool, use the following techniques:

➤ Hold down the **Ctrl** key while dragging to draw the object out from an imaginary center point. Without the Ctrl key, you drag the object out from its corner or starting point.

➤ Hold down the **Shift** key while dragging to create a uniform shape (a perfect square or circle).

➤ Hold down **Ctrl+Shift** while dragging to draw the object out from its center point and create a uniform shape.

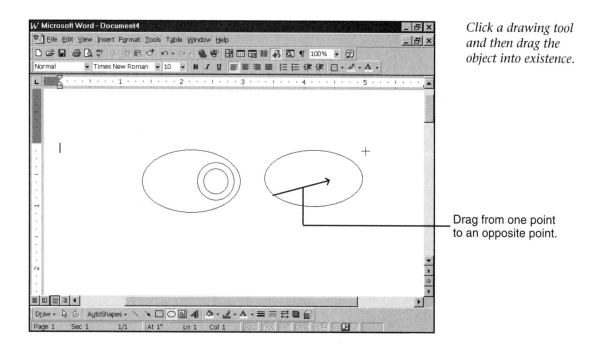

Click a drawing tool and then drag the object into existence.

Drag from one point to an opposite point.

Once you have an object on the page, you can use some of the other buttons in the Drawing toolbar to change qualities of the object (such as its fill color, and the color and width of the line that defines it). First select the shape whose qualities you want to change. Then use any of the following buttons to change the object's qualities.

Free Rotate lets you spin the object. When you click this button, little green circles surround the selected object. Drag a circle clockwise or counterclockwise to spin the object.

Fill Color colors inside the lines (like you would in a coloring book). Click the button to fill the object with the color that's shown. To change the fill color, click the arrow next to this button and select the color from the menu.

Line Color changes the color of the line that defines the shape. Click on the button to use the color that's shown. To change the color, click the arrow next to this button and select the color from the menu.

Font Color is for text boxes only. Drag over the text inside the box, and then open this menu and select the desired color.

Line Style displays a menu from which you can choose the line thickness and style you want to use for the line that defines the shape.

Dash Style lets you use dashed lines instead of solid lines.

 Arrow Style works only for arrows you have drawn. Select the arrow, and then use this menu to pick the type of arrow you want to use or to change the direction it points.

 Shadow works only for ovals, rectangles, AutoShapes, and other two-dimensional objects (including text boxes). This menu contains various drop-shadow styles you can apply to objects.

 3-D works for ovals, rectangles, AutoShapes, and text boxes. It turns rectangles into blocks and ovals into cylinders. What it does to AutoShapes, you have to see for yourself.

Graphics and Text

You can add some interesting special effects to a document by combining text with AutoShapes. For example, for sales brochures or announcements, you might consider placing small bits of text inside a starburst. Just lay a text box on top of the starburst. You can also use AutoShapes with text and arrows to create flow charts and organizational charts.

Working with Layers of Objects

Working with two or more drawing objects on a page is like playing with a Colorforms toy; you know, those storyboards with the vinyl characters you stick on and peel off to create various scenes? The trouble with these objects is that when you place one on top of another, the top object blocks the bottom one and prevents you from selecting it. You have to flip through the deck to find the object you want.

Word offers a couple of drawing tools that can help you flip through the stack and create groups of objects, which makes it easier to maneuver them.

The first thing you'll need to do is reorder the objects. You can send an object that's up front back one layer or all the way to the bottom of the stack, or you can bring an object from the back to the front. First, click on the object you want to move (if possible). Some objects are buried so deep that you can't get to them; in such a case, you will have to move objects from the front to the back.

After selecting the object you want to move, right-click it, point to **Order**, and select the desired movement: **Bring to Front**, **Send to Back**, **Bring Forward**, **Send Backward**, **Bring in Front of Text**, or **Send Behind Text**.

Working with Two or More Objects as a Group

Once you've created a drawing or a portion of a drawing consisting of several shapes, it becomes difficult to move this loose collection of shapes or resize it. If you drag one object, you ruin its relative position with the other objects. Similarly, if you need to shrink or enlarge the drawing, you shouldn't have to resize each object separately. And, you don't have to. Word lets you group two or more objects so that you can move and resize them as if they were a single object.

 To create a group, click the **Select Objects** button in the Drawing toolbar and drag a selection box around all the objects that you want to include in the group (or just **Shift**+click on each object). Handles appear around all the selected objects.

Then open the **Draw** menu in the Drawing toolbar and select **Group**. The handles around the individual objects disappear, and a single set of handles appears around the group. You can now drag a handle to resize all the objects in the group, or you can drag any object in the group to move the group.

To turn off grouping so you can work with an individual object, open the **Draw** menu again and click **Ungroup**. After you're done working with the individual object, you can regroup the objects by opening the **Draw** menu and selecting **Regroup**.

A single set of handles appears around the group.

Drag any object in the group to move all objects.

You can group two or more objects and treat them as a single object.

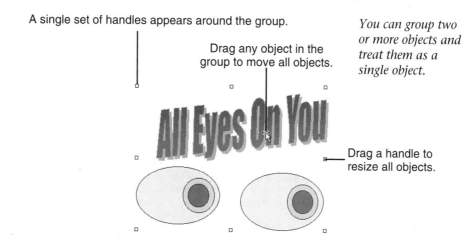

Drag a handle to resize all objects.

Editing Existing Pictures

Suppose one of your friends or colleagues sent you a graphic, or you copied one off the Internet. You like the overall design, but it needs a few minor adjustments. You definitely don't want to redraw it from scratch. The solution? Insert the graphic into a Word document (as explained earlier in this chapter) and then double-click on it. This opens the picture in a drawing window.

You'll notice that the picture is surrounded by gray lines. These define the object's boundaries; whatever is inside the gray lines will be inserted as a picture into your document. Anything outside the lines will be chopped off. To change the position of these lines, drag the markers in the vertical and horizontal toolbars.

Once you've set up the markers, use the buttons in the Drawing toolbar to add shapes to the existing drawing. Keep in mind that you can use the Picture toolbar to modify the existing picture. When you're done, click the **Close Picture** button.

Adding Captions

You can insert captions below pictures, tables, drawings, charts, and other items. To do so, select the object below which you want the caption to appear. Then open the **Insert** menu, select **Caption**, and type the desired caption. If you want Word to insert the captions for you and automatically number them, select **AutoCaption** and enter your preferences. Click **OK**.

Accenting Your Reports with Graphs

You can insert Excel graphs and parts of Excel spreadsheets into your Word documents, as you'll see in Chapter 28, "Sharing Data Dynamically." However, if all you need is a simple graph showing your boss how your overtime hours have grown exponentially over the last year, you can insert a basic graph right in Word.

To insert a graph, open the **Insert** menu, point to **Picture**, and click **Chart**. A datasheet appears, showing sample data for a graph. You can change this data to meet your needs. To edit an entry, click inside a cell and type the desired entry.

After you've entered the data you want to graph, you can use the graph tools at the top of the screen to select a different graph type, add X and Y axis labels, change the color of the graph, and so on. When you're done, click anywhere outside the graph to return to your document. Word pastes the graph in the document, and you can move it and resize it like any graphic object. If you want to edit the graph later, double-click on it.

You can select a different graph style.

You can insert a graph into your document.

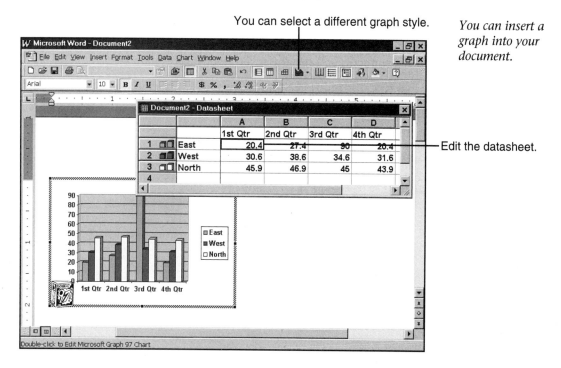

Edit the datasheet.

Grouping Pictures and Text with Text Boxes

Previous versions of Word used Frames to group text, pictures, tables, captions, and other objects, so they would move as a single object when you edited your document. In this version of Word, Microsoft has replaced the Frames feature with text boxes, which were described in Chapter 5, "Giving Your Text a Makeover."

What Chapter 5 did not mention, however, is that you can insert all sorts of objects into a text box, including pictures, tables, captions, and even charts. If you set the text box to move with the surrounding text, all of the objects in the text box will move together. If you drag the text box to move it, all of the objects move.

The Least You Need to Know

Microsoft has revamped the way Word and other Office products deal with graphics. With Office 97, placing graphics on a page is very similar to working with graphics in a desktop publishing program:

➤ To insert clip art, pictures from disk, video clips, graphs, WordArt, or your own drawings into a Word document, use the Insert, Picture command.

➤ The Picture toolbar lets you adjust the brightness and contrast of a picture and crop a picture, just as if you were using a separate graphics program.

➤ To move a picture, drag it.

➤ To resize a picture, drag one of its handles.

➤ The Drawing toolbar contains several buttons you can use to create basic shapes and arrange them to create a drawing.

Chapter 8

Taking Control of Your Pages

In This Chapter

➤ Making a two-page paper run three pages with a few clever margin adjustments

➤ Forcing Word to number your pages for you

➤ Printing a footer on the bottom of every page

➤ Adding a fancy border around a page

Up to this point, you have been micro-managing the document—formatting blocks of text, adding tables and columns, and inserting pictures and other clips. Before you print your document, however, there are a few macro-management tasks you need to perform, such as setting the page margins, correcting for any funky page breaks, adding page numbers (if desired), and perhaps decorating your page with an attractive border.

This chapter shows you how to perform these tasks. While you are working through the chapter, you may want to flip back and forth to Print Preview to see how your changes will affect the printed document. See Chapter 4, "Making and Editing Word Documents," for details.

Setting Up Your Pages for Printing

We have progressively moved from printing at central locations (such as printing presses) to printing at less centralized locations (such as copy shops) to printing with a completely decentralized system in which every individual has a desktop printer.

This has caused a major problem. Instead of relying on the print shop to lay out our pages and create our documents, we now have to do it ourselves. And to do it right in Word, you have to master the Page Setup options.

To display the Page Setup options, open the **File** menu and select **Page Setup**. The Page Setup dialog box appears, presenting four tabs for changing various page and print settings. In the following sections, you will learn how to use this dialog box to set margins and control the way Word prints text on the pages.

Setting the Page Margins

When the Page Setup dialog box first appears, the Margins tab is up front. This tab lets you change the top, bottom, left, and right margins. Click the up or down arrow to the right of each margin setting to change the setting in increments of .1 inch. Or, you can click inside a margin setting text box and type a more precise measurement.

The Margins tab offers several additional options for special printing needs:

➤ **Gutter** allows you to add margin space to the inside margin of the pages, in case you plan to insert the pages into a book or binder.

➤ **From Edge** specifies the distance from the top of the page to the top of the header and from the bottom of the page to the bottom of the footer. (For details about headers and footers, see "Head-Banging Headers and Foot-Stomping Footers," later in this chapter.)

➤ **Mirror Margins** is useful if you plan to print on both sides of a page. When this option is on, Word makes the inside margins of facing pages equal.

➤ **Apply To** lets you apply the margin settings to the entire document or to selected text only. (In Chapter 5, "Giving Your Text a Makeover," you learned how to set the margins for selected text using the ruler and the Paragraph dialog box.)

Keep in mind that you can also change page margins in Print Preview by dragging the margin markers on the horizontal and vertical rulers. To quickly switch to Print Preview, click the **Print Preview** button in the Standard toolbar.

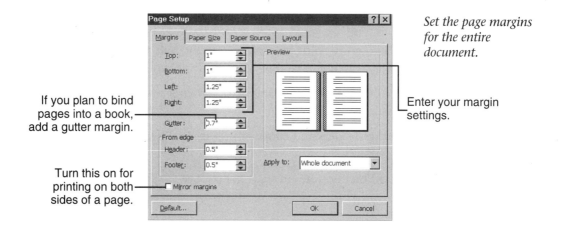

If you plan to bind pages into a book, add a gutter margin.

Turn this on for printing on both sides of a page.

Set the page margins for the entire document.

Enter your margin settings.

Picking a Paper Size and Print Direction

Most people print right-side-up on 8 1/2-by-11 inch paper. But maybe you're special. Maybe you need to print on legal size paper, or maybe you're creating a sign for your garage sale and you want to print it sideways on the page. If that's the case, check out the Paper Size tab.

There you can pick from a list of standard paper sizes, or you can specify a custom size. You can also select a print orientation: Portrait (to print normal, like in this book) or Landscape (to print sideways on the page).

Again, you can use the **Apply To** drop-down list to specify these settings for the entire document or from this point in the document forward. In most cases, you will want to apply the paper size and orientation to the entire document. However, if you have a wide table or graphic that you want to print sideways on a page, you might want to pick Landscape orientation before the table or graphic, and then change back to Portrait orientation after it.

Where's Your Paper Coming From?

When you went shopping for your printer, you probably bought the least expensive printer that offered color and near laser quality output. That is, you probably purchased an inkjet printer. If so, you and your applications know where the paper is coming from: it's coming from that little tray in which you stick the paper. However, if you have a fancy printer with trays for different paper sizes and types (lucky you), you'll need to check the Paper Source tab before you start printing just to make sure Word is set up to use the right tray for this document.

Laying Out Your Pages

The last tab in the Page Setup dialog box is the Layout tab. It contains several unrelated options, most of which I discuss in later sections in this chapter:

➤ For information about the Section Start drop-down list, see "Controlling Page Breaks and Section Breaks."

➤ To learn about the Headers and Footers options, see "Head-Banging Headers and Foot-Stomping Footers."

➤ I don't even mention endnotes in this chapter. See Chapter 11, "Working with Long Documents."

We've just whittled the options on the Layout tab to two: Vertical Alignment and Line Numbers. The Vertical Alignment drop-down list is very useful for making one-page documents (such as a short letter) look good on the page. Open the drop-down list and select **Center** to center the document on the page. To make the document fill the page, select **Justified**.

The Line Numbers button is useful for legal and literary pieces. These types of documents often contain line numbers so people can refer to the line numbers when discussing the documents (instead of quoting entire lines). To insert line numbers, click the button and enter your preferences.

Adding Page Numbers

If you plan to share your document with others, it's a good idea to number the pages. That way, if the person tosses the pages up in the air in disgust (or just by mistake), it's easy to get the pages back in order. Page numbers also allow your audience to peek ahead to see how much they still have to read.

There's really no excuse for not numbering the pages in a multipage document because Word can do it for you. You can insert a page number code in a header or footer (see "Head-Banging Headers and Foot-Stomping Footers" later in this chapter), or you can use the Insert, Page Numbers command. Follow these steps to use the latter method:

1. Open the **Insert** menu and select **Page Numbers**. The Page Numbers dialog box appears.

2. Open the **Position** drop-down list and specify whether you want the page numbers printed at the top or bottom of the page.

3. Open the **Alignment** drop-down list and select where you want the page number placed in relation to the left and right margins. (The Inside and Outside options are for positioning page numbers on pages that will be bound in a book.)

4. If the first page is a cover page or you just don't want a page number on the first page, make sure there is no check in the **Show Number on First Page** box.

5. Click the **Format** button to enter additional settings (see the figure below):

   Number Format lets you pick a numbering scheme other than the standard 1, 2, 3.

   Include Chapter Number lets you precede the page number with the chapter number, assuming you used a Heading style for the paragraph that includes the chapter number. To include chapter numbers, turn this option on, and then select the heading style you applied to the paragraph that contains the chapter number.

   Page Numbering lets you start with a number other than 1. For example, if you left the page number off the first page, you may want to start numbering the second page with the number 2.

6. Click **OK** to return to the Page Numbering dialog box, and then click **OK** to save your changes. The page number is inserted inside a header or footer.

Select a numbering scheme.

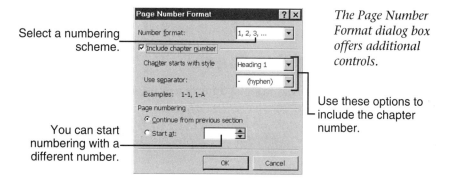

The Page Number Format dialog box offers additional controls.

Use these options to include the chapter number.

You can start numbering with a different number.

Viewing Page Numbers

Page numbers do not appear in Normal view. To view page numbers, switch to Page Layout view or Print Preview. Or, view them in the header or footer; open the **View** menu and select **Header and Footer**.

Controlling Page Breaks and Section Breaks

Typing in Word is like working in a sausage factory. As you type, Word stuffs your text and divides it into neat little pages. The trouble is that you might not like where Word divides your text. Word might divide an important list over two pages or perform other similar atrocities. You need some way to control these breaks.

Dividing Pages and Columns

The first, and easiest, type of break to deal with is a page break. In Page Layout view, you can easily identify a page break by the top or bottom edges of the on-screen pages. In Normal view, a page break appears as a dotted horizontal line. If you don't like where Word inserted the page break, insert your own break. Move the insertion point to the beginning of the paragraph before which you want the break inserted. Open the **Insert** menu, select **Break**, make sure **Page Break** is selected, and click **OK**. Word inserts a dotted line with the words **Page Break** in the center to indicate the position of the break.

Check This Out...

Quick Page Breaks To quickly insert a page break, move the insertion point where you want to insert the break and press **Ctrl+Enter**.

If you used the Columns feature (see Chapter 6, "Aligning Text in Tables and Columns"), you can insert a column break to move text after the column break over to the next column. Open the **Insert** menu, select **Break**, select **Column Break**, and click **OK**.

Working with Section Breaks

Page and column breaks are easy to understand; inserting them is like snipping the page with a pair of scissors. However, section breaks are a little more difficult to master. With a section break, you tell Word that you're going to use a different layout for the text from this point on, or up to the next section break. (Initially, Word treats the document as a single section.)

For instance, say you are creating a newsletter and you want it to have two columns on the first page and three columns on the next. To do this, you must insert a section break between the section in which you want two columns and the section in which you want three columns. Otherwise, when you select the number of columns you want, Word assumes you want to use that number for the entire document. Section breaks also allow you to change the formatting within a document for the following elements:

➤ **Headers and footers:** You can use different headers and footers for different sections in a document.

➤ **Footnotes and endnotes:** You can number footnotes and endnotes separately in each section. See Chapter 11, "Working with Long Documents," for details.

➤ **Page numbers:** You can number pages separately for each section.

➤ **Margins:** You might want to change the margins for a section (for instance, to indent a long quotation).

➤ **Paper size and source:** If you have parts of a document that must print in a different orientation (landscape or portrait) or on different paper, you can create a section break before and after that section.

➤ **Line numbers:** If you choose to number the lines in a document, you can number the lines separately for each section.

To insert a section break, position the insertion point where you want the new section formatting to begin, open the **Insert** menu, and select **Break**. Under Section Breaks, choose where you want the section to begin:

➤ **Next Page** inserts a section break and page break; the next section starts at the top of the next page.

➤ **Even Page** starts the section on the next even page.

➤ **Odd Page** starts the section on the next odd page.

➤ **Continuous** starts the section immediately; the new section starts on the same page as the previous section ends.

Check This Out...

Inserting Section Breaks Automatically

To have Word handle section breaks for you, drag over the text you want to include in a section, and then enter your section formatting. If given the option, choose to apply formatting to only the current section. For example, you can drag over text and select columns. Word inserts a section break before and after the selected text, and then applies the new section formatting only to the text that's sandwiched between the two section breaks.

Deleting and Moving Breaks

If you insert a break and later decide that it's not working out, you can delete the break or move it. First, change to Normal view (**View, Normal**). To select a break, click on it. To delete a selected break, press the **Del** key. To move a break, drag it. If you delete a section break, the section formatting for the previous section takes control of the text.

Head-Banging Headers and Foot-Stomping Footers

Headers and footers are great tools for stitching together a document and helping your audience find specific pages and information. Headers and footers can include all sorts of useful information, such as the title of the document or of a section inside the document, the date on which the document was created, chapter numbers, page numbers, and the total number of pages in the document.

To insert a header or footer, open the **View** menu and select **Header and Footer**. This displays the Header and Footer toolbar and the header of the first page (which should be empty, unless you have gremlins or you inserted page numbers earlier). Before you start typing, familiarize yourself with the Header and Footer toolbar buttons:

Insert Page Number automatically inserts the correct page number on each page.

Insert Number of Pages is a new button that inserts the total number of pages in the document.

Format Page Number displays the Page Number Format dialog box, which allows you to include the chapter number and enter other preferences.

Insert Date inserts the date from your computer's internal clock.

Insert Time inserts the current time from your computer's clock.

Page Setup lets you create a different header or footer for odd pages and even pages. If you choose to do this, use the Show Previous and Show Next buttons to move between the boxes for entering the odd and even page headers or footers.

Show/Hide Document Text turns the document text display on or off. If you click this button to hide the document text, all you see on the screen is the header or footer text box.

Same as Previous allows you to use the same header or footer for this section that you used for the previous section, or to create a new section with a different header or footer than the one you used in the previous section.

Switch Between Header and Footer tells Word to display the footer box if you are currently using the header box, and vice versa.

Show Previous moves to the previous header or footer so you can edit it.

Show Next moves to the next header or footer.

Once you are familiar with the buttons, click the **Switch Between Header and Footer** button to display the Header box or the Footer box. Type your text, using the Insert buttons as desired to insert the page number, date, time, or total page count. You can use any of the text formatting options to enhance the look of your header or footer. When you're done playing around, click the **Close** button.

Inserting Pictures in a Header or Footer

In addition to enhancing text in the header or footer, consider adding a logo or other graphic, a WordArt object, or a simple line to accent it.

Framing Your Page with a Border

In Chapter 5, "Giving Your Text a Makeover," you learned that you could add a border around a paragraph by using the Outside Border button in the Formatting toolbar. You also learned that you could use a text box border. As if you don't have enough borders to defend, Word allows you to insert a border around entire pages.

To add a border to one, all, or some pages in your document, open the **Format** menu and select **Borders and Shading**. Click the **Page Border** tab, and then enter your preferences:

➤ **Setting** lets you pick a predesigned page border.

➤ **Style** displays a list of line styles from which you can select.

➤ **Color** lets you specify a line color.

➤ **Width** controls the thickness of the border.

➤ **Art** lets you use a graphical border, such as Christmas trees or stars (definitely a desktop publishing feature carried over from Microsoft Publisher).

➤ **Preview** allows you to turn the lines that make up the border on or off individually. Click on a button or a line in the Preview area to remove or add a side of the border.

➤ **Apply To** lets you print the border on all pages of your document or on selected pages only.

You can add a border that surrounds all the text and other items on the page.

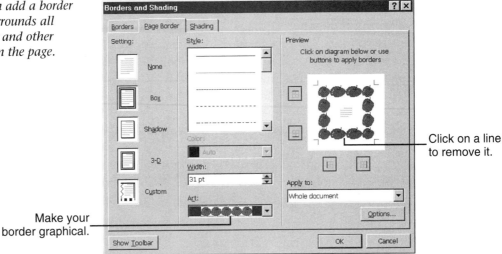

Click on a line to remove it.

Make your border graphical.

The Least You Need to Know

Sometime before you print your document, you should stop fiddling with the font controls and take an aerial view of your document so you can modify any page settings to suit your tastes:

➤ To change most page settings, open the **File** menu and select **Page Setup**.

➤ When you change margins with the ruler, you affect only selected paragraphs. When you change margins with the Page Setup dialog box, you affect the entire document or a section of it.

➤ To insert a page break, press **Ctrl+Enter**.

➤ Columns are controlled by section formatting. To return columns to normal text, click on the section code (in Normal view) and press **Delete**.

➤ To insert, delete, or edit a header or footer, open the **View** menu and select **Header and Footer**.

➤ You can add a border to a page by opening the **Format** menu and selecting **Borders and Shading**.

Chapter 9

Checking Your Spelling and Grammar

In This Chapter

➤ Proofreading for lazy people

➤ Checking your spelling as you go

➤ Grammar checkers—blah!

➤ Using AutoCorrect to automatically correct common typos

➤ How to use a thesaurus to make people think you are well educated

In this era of electronic communications, where people are sharing documents, rifling off e-mail messages, and having virtual meetings with chat programs, written communication skill are becoming much more important. No matter how well you speak, if your writing is unclear and packed with typos and grammatical errors, your colleagues (and perhaps even your boss) are going to think you're a dolt. Of course, if you are a dolt, you aren't giving anyone a false impression.

Word offers a couple of tools that can help you clean up your writing. The spell checker can catch most of your spelling errors and typos; the grammar checker can help you avoid passive voice and other grammatical no-nos; and the thesaurus can help you think of just the word you need. In this chapter, you will learn how to use these tools and a few others to improve at least the mechanics of your writing.

Looking for Ms. Spellings

You won the sixth grade spelling bee, you know that "potatoes" is spelled with an "e," and for any words that you're unsure of, you can use a dictionary. I'm sure your mother's proud of you, but you still need to use the spell checker to catch any errant typos that you might overlook in your hurry to meet deadlines.

Word provides more than one way for you to check your spelling. Word can check your spelling on the fly as you type, or after you're done typing. You can also customize the spell checker to have it skip over things like acronyms (NAACP for instance) and Internet addresses (such as www.mcp.com). The following sections explain your options.

Spell Checking on the Go

By default, Word is set up to check for possible spelling errors as you type. If you type a word that does not have a matching entry in Word's spelling dictionary, Word displays a squiggly red line below the word. You have several options at that point:

➤ Ignore the line.

➤ Backspace over the misspelled word and type the correct spelling.

➤ Right-click the word in question to see a pop-up menu that may contain suggested correct spellings for the word. If you see the correct spelling, click it.

➤ Right-click the word and select **Ignore All** to have Word remove its annoying red squiggly line and tell it not to question the spelling of this word in this document again.

➤ Right-click the word and select **Add** to add the word to Word's spelling dictionary. Once the word is in the dictionary, Word will not question its spelling in any document ever again.

➤ Right-click the word, point to **AutoCorrect**, and select the correct spelling of the word. (See "Making Word Automatically Correct Your Typos," later in this chapter for details.)

➤ Right-click the word and click **Spelling** to see more options.

Personally, I find it offensive to see squiggly red lines popping up as I type (even though these lines don't print). They give me flashbacks to grade school, where good writing meant every word was spelled correctly and you followed the grammar rules. To turn off automatic spell checking, open the **Tools** menu, select **Options**, and click the **Spelling & Grammar** tab. Click **Check Spelling As You Type** to remove the check from the box, and then click **OK**.

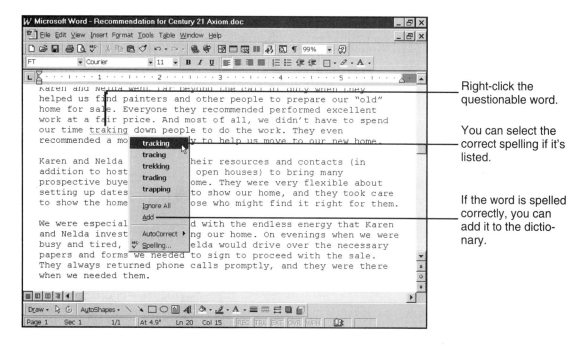

Right-click the questionable word.

You can select the correct spelling if it's listed.

If the word is spelled correctly, you can add it to the dictionary.

Spell Checking Just Before You Hand It In

As you write, you rarely have time to deal with spelling errors. When you're pulling an all-nighter just to get the term paper in on time or to meet your project deadline, a spell check is a mere afterthought—something you do only if you have five minutes to spare and you already had your first cup of coffee. That's the way it is with me anyway.

If you took my advice and turned off the check-as-you-type option, you can use Word to perform one of these last minute spell checks for you—a lot faster and more accurately than your droopy eyes could ever do it. To do so, open the **Tools** menu and select **Spelling and Grammar**. Word starts checking your document and stops on the first questionable word. The Spelling and Grammar dialog box displays the word in red, and it usually displays a list of suggested corrections. You have several options:

➤ Backspace over the word (assuming it is misspelled) and type the correction.

➤ Click **Ignore** if the word is spelled correctly and you want to skip it just this once. Word will stop on the next occurrence of the word.

➤ Click **Ignore All** if the word is spelled correctly and you want Word to skip any other occurrences of this word in this document.

➤ Click **Add** to add the word to the dictionary so the spell checker will never question it again in any of your documents.

➤ If the word is spelled incorrectly and the Suggestions list displays the correct spelling, click the correct spelling and click **Change** to replace only this occurrence of the word.

➤ To replace this misspelled word and all other occurrences of the word in this document, click the correct spelling in the Suggestions list and click **Change All**.

➤ Create an AutoCorrect entry for the misspelling so Word will correct it whenever you type the misspelling. See "Making Word Automatically Correct Your Typos," later in this chapter for details.

If Word finds a misspelling and displays the correct spelling, your options are easy.

Click the correct spelling if it's listed.

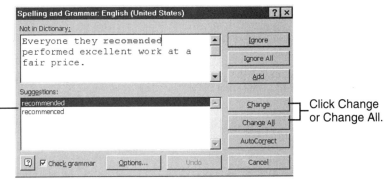

Click Change or Change All.

The Spelling and Grammar Button You can start spell-checking your document by clicking the **Spelling and Grammar** button in the Standard toolbar. If the Check Grammar with Spelling option is off in the Options dialog box (on the Spelling and Grammar tab), this starts only the spell checker. If Check Grammar with Spelling is on, Word checks both at the same time.

When Word completes the spell check, it displays a dialog box telling you so. Click **OK**.

Oh yeah, one more thing. If you want to check the spelling of a single word, double-click the word to select it before you start the spell checker. To check the spelling in one or more sentences or paragraphs, select them first. When Word is done checking the selection, it displays a dialog box asking if you want to check the rest of the document.

Customizing the Spell Checker

The spell checker is your flunkie. You tell it what to do and how to do it, and the spell checker carries out your instructions. But how do you give the spell checker its job description? Through the Options dialog box. To display the spell checker options, either click the **Options** button during a spell check, or open the **Tools** menu, click **Options**, and select the **Spelling & Grammar** tab.

Most of the options on this tab are self-explanatory, but a couple might give you trouble, such as Hide Spelling Errors in This Document. This option tells Word to hide the squiggly red lines under questionable words as you type. Always Suggest Corrections tells Word to display a list of possible corrections for any questionable words. You should probably keep this option on. If any other options confuse you, right-click the option and select **What's This?**.

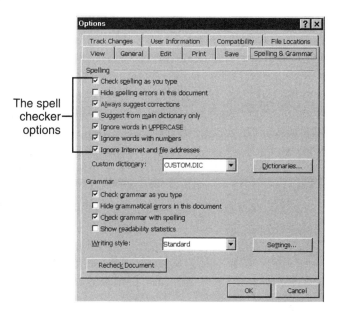

The spell checker options

You can tell the spell checker how to do its job.

You might also wonder about the dictionary options. Word uses two spelling dictionaries to perform a spell check—the standard dictionary and a custom dictionary, which you create. Whenever the spell checker stops and questions the spelling of a word, it gives you the option of adding the word to the dictionary. If you click the **Add** button, the spell checker adds the word to the custom dictionary. As long as a word is in either the standard or the custom dictionary, the spell checker will never question its spelling.

Multiple Custom Dictionaries

Do you need more than one custom dictionary? Probably not. But say you're a technical writer and you have one project dealing with electrical engineering and another dealing with destructive testing. Each project may have a unique vocabulary. By creating separate custom dictionaries, you can create a unique list of correct spellings for each project.

The dictionary options (Custom Dictionaries and the Dictionary button) allow you to create additional custom dictionaries and delete them, pick the custom dictionary you want to use, and edit the list of words in the custom dictionary.

Making Word Automatically Correct Your Typos

One of my favorite features in Word has always been AutoCorrect. I type **teh**, and Word inserts **the**. I start a sentence with a lowercase character, and AutoCorrect capitalizes it. Now *that's* a feature! When I'm up at 2 a.m. gulping coffee, and my fingers are hitting two or three keys at a time, that AutoCorrect feature sure comes in handy.

You have probably used this feature already, adding AutoCorrect entries by right-clicking on misspelled words and then selecting AutoCorrect. Or maybe you used the AutoCorrect button in the Spelling dialog box. In either case, when you create an AutoCorrect entry, you pair a misspelled word with its correct spelling.

You can edit the list of paired words to create additional AutoCorrect entries or to delete entries. Open the **Tools** menu and select **AutoCorrect**. The AutoCorrect dialog box appears, displaying a list of options for controlling the behavior of AutoCorrect, and displaying a list of AutoCorrect pairs. Set your preferences using the check box options at the top of the dialog box.

To create a new AutoCorrect pair, click inside the **Replace** text box and type the text that you want Word to automatically replace. Tab to the **With** text box, and type the text that you want Word to replace it with. You can type more than one word in either or both text boxes, and you can choose to have the replacement text formatted. Click the **Add** button. To remove a pair from the list, click on the pair, and click the **Delete** button.

Create AutoCorrect entries for all of your most common typos.

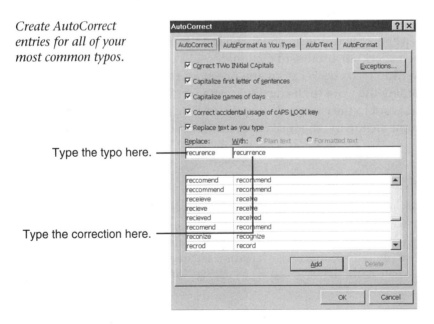

Type the typo here. ⎯⎯

Type the correction here. ⎯⎯

Create Your Own Shorthand

You can create your own shorthand by using AutoText entries, as explained in Chapter 4, "Making and Editing Word Documents," but then you have to type and press the F3 key to insert a word or phrase. Instead of creating AutoText entries for single words, create an Auto-Correct entry. That way, you don't have to press F3 to insert the word.

The Useless Grammar Checker Just Got Better

Grammar checkers are easy to fool. If you write short subject-verb sentences without contractions, the grammar checker will rank your writing skills right up there with Dr. Seuss and Forrest Gump. The grammar checker doesn't care if your writing is entertaining, if it expresses a brilliant insight, or even if it's well organized. As long as you don't break any rules, you're a genius.

With that in mind, I'm going to keep this section brief. The grammar checker options are similar to those of the spell checker. To change them, open the **Tools** menu, select **Options**, and click the **Spelling & Grammar** tab. Enter your preferences:

➤ **Check Grammar As You Type** draws a green squiggly line under questionable phrases and sentences.

➤ **Hide Grammatical Errors in This Document** hides the green squiggly lines.

➤ **Check Grammar with Spelling** tells Word to check both grammar and spelling at the same time whenever you choose to spell check a document.

➤ **Show Readability Statistics** displays a message at the end of the grammar check showing the reading level required to understand your writing. If you're writing a children's book and the readability statistics show that you're writing for college kids, you might need to simplify your vocabulary and sentence structure.

➤ **Writing Style** lets you pick a set of grammatical rules for various types of writing, such as technical or business writing.

➤ **Settings** lets you turn individual grammar rules on or off.

➤ **Recheck Document** rechecks the document using the preferences you just entered.

Word's Helpful, Useful, Beneficial Thesaurus

Suppose you're writing your letter of resignation to your supervisor, and you can't think of a less offensive word than "moron." The dictionary's no help, and you can't really ask around the office. What do you do? Take the following steps:

1. Click on the word to place the insertion point somewhere inside it.

2. Open the **Tools** menu, point to **Language**, and click **Thesaurus** (or just press **Shift+F7**). Word displays the Thesaurus dialog box, providing a list of alternative words or phrases. (Wouldn't it be nice if you could right-click the word and pick Thesaurus? Write Microsoft a letter.)

3. If the Meanings list has more than one word, click the word that most closely matches your intended meaning. For example, if you look up "moron," the Meanings list displays "simpleton," and "fool." The Replace with Synonym list displays suggested replacement words.

4. If the Replace with Synonym list contains a word that's pretty close to the one you want but just not quite it, click it and click the **Look Up** button. (If the list of synonyms you get next is worse than the previous list, click the **Previous** button.)

5. When you find the word you want or a word that's as close as the thesaurus can find, click it and click the **Replace** button.

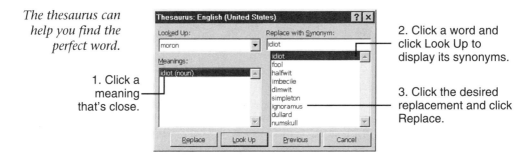

The thesaurus can help you find the perfect word.

1. Click a meaning that's close.

2. Click a word and click Look Up to display its synonyms.

3. Click the desired replacement and click Replace.

The Least You Need to Know

In this chapter, you learned how to use several of Word's writing tools to clean up and perfect your documents:

➤ If Spell As You Go is on, Word draws a squiggly red line below any words of questionable spelling.

➤ To view suggested corrections for a word that's underlined, right-click it.

➤ AutoCorrect automatically corrects misspellings and typos as you type.

➤ To view and edit the AutoCorrect list, open the **Tools** menu and select **AutoCorrect**.

➤ The grammar checker is a useless piece of computer code.

➤ To view a list of synonyms for a word you typed, click inside the word, open the **Tools** menu, point to **Language**, and click **Thesaurus**.

Chapter 10

Creating Mailing Labels and Form Letters

In This Chapter

➤ Addressing an envelope with your printer

➤ Making your own address book

➤ Laying out and printing address labels

➤ Creating your very own personalized form letters

➤ Doing mass mailings with mail merge

Face it, you're a mail junkie. Your motivation to wake up in the morning comes only from the possibility that you might receive a piece of mail addressed specifically to you. You stare out the window to catch the familiar gait of your mail carrier. You're on a first name basis with the mail room clerk at your company. You just can't get enough. And you know that the only way to get mail is to send mail, lots of mail, to anyone who will listen.

In this chapter, you will learn how to use a couple of features that can help you create and address your paper mail correspondence. You'll learn how to easily print on an envelope or mailing labels, how to create a letter with the Letter Wizard, and how to merge a form letter with a list of names and addresses to create a stack of personalized letters for mass mailings.

Creating the Perfect Letter with the Letter Wizard

In Chapter 4, "Making and Editing Word Documents," you learned how to use the File, New command to display a collection of templates and wizards for quickly creating new documents. Perhaps you used one of the templates on the Letters & Faxes tab to create a letter. That's one way to do it.

Another way to create a letter is to create a new document and then use the Letter Wizard from within Word. You can run the Letter Wizard before you start typing your letter or after you've typed it. Just open the **Tools** menu and select **Letter Wizard**. The Letter Wizard dialog box appears (see the next figure), displaying a fill-in-the-blank form that you can use to specify your preferences and enter information such as the inside address, the salutation, and the closing. Mark your selections and type the requested entries on the following four tabs:

➤ **Letter Format**   To insert a date, click **Date Line** and select the desired date format. Pick a page design and style from the drop-down lists in the middle of the tab. The preview areas show how the letter will look. If you plan to print on letterhead, click **Pre-printed Letterhead** and use the options below it to specify the amount of room to allow for the letterhead.

➤ **Recipient Info**   Type the name and address of the person to whom you are writing. Under Salutation, pick the salutation you want to use (Informal, Formal, Business), or type your own salutation in the text box.

➤ **Other Elements**   This tab contains additional items you might want to include in the letter, such as cc (courtesy copy) if you plan to send a copy of the letter to other people.

➤ **Sender Info**   Enter information about yourself, including your name and address, a closing (such as "Yours Truly"), your job title, and, if you really want to impress the recipient, your secretary's initials.

Click **OK**. The Letter Wizard creates the letter and plops it on the page. A placeholder appears where you will type the body of your letter, indicating that you should type something. Start typing.

Addressing an Envelope or Mailing Label

Most of the letters I receive from friends and family members have obviously been typed and printed using a computer, but for some strange reason, they arrive in handwritten envelopes. I guess it just takes too much time and effort to position the two addresses on the front of that skinny little envelope.

Fortunately, Word can print addresses for you, either on envelopes or on mailing labels.

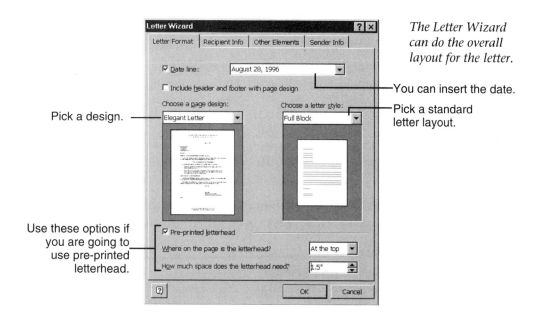

The Letter Wizard can do the overall layout for the letter.

You can insert the date.

Pick a standard letter layout.

Pick a design.

Use these options if you are going to use pre-printed letterhead.

Addressing an Envelope

To print an address on an envelope, open the **Tools** menu, click **Envelopes and Labels**, and make sure the Envelopes tab is up front. Type the recipient's name and address in the **Delivery Address** text box. Tab to the **Return Address** text box, and type your address.

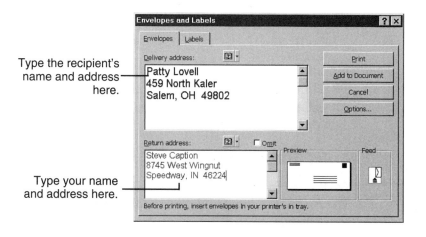

Enter the information you want Word to print on the envelope.

Type the recipient's name and address here.

Type your name and address here.

Before you print, you should preview the envelope and check the printer settings. Click the **Options** button, make sure the **Envelope Options** tab is in front, and check the following:

123

➤ **Envelope Size** Check the box that your envelopes came in, and make sure the Envelope Size setting matches it.

➤ **Delivery Point Barcode** If you are mailing this letter in the United States, you can have Word print a barcode on the envelope to help the postal service sort the mail. You can also choose to have an FIM (Facing Identification Mark) printed near the location of the stamp to mark the front of a courtesy reply envelope.

➤ **Delivery Address** You can choose a font and adjust the position of the delivery address on the envelope. Check the Preview area to see how your changes will affect printing.

➤ **Return Address** You can choose a font and adjust the position of the return address. Again, check the Preview area to determine the effects of your change.

Default Return Address

When you attempt to print an envelope for the first time, Word asks if you want to use the return address you entered as the default. If you select Yes, Word automatically inserts the return address for you whenever you choose to print an envelope.

While you're in the Envelope Options dialog box, click the **Printing Options** tab and enter the settings to specify how you will feed the envelope into your printer. Click **OK** to save your options and return to the Envelopes and Labels dialog box.

Having Trouble? If you have trouble with your inkjet printer, don't feel bad—envelopes aren't the easiest pieces of paper to print on. My inkjet likes to kick out the envelope the first time I load it, forcing me to reload it and press the Online key.

If you need to manually load the envelope into your printer, load away. All printers are different; check your printer's documentation to determine the proper loading technique. When the envelope is in position, click the **Print** button to print it.

Addressing a Mailing Label

The trouble with mailing labels is that there's no easy way to print just one. If you need to print a whole page of them or a long strip, no problem. But a single mailing label will give you all sorts of trouble. My advice is to avoid printing one label. See "Using Mail Merge to Do Mailing Labels," later in this chapter, to learn how to print a whole page of labels containing different addresses.

However, if you really need to print a single label or a whole page of labels with the same address, go ahead and give it a shot. Open the **Tools** menu, select **Envelopes and Mailing Labels**, and make sure the **Labels** tab is up front. In the Address text box, type the name and address you want printed on the mailing label. (You can print your return address by clicking the **Use Return Address** option, instead.) Under Print, specify whether you want to print a single label (and specify the location of the label on the label sheet) or a full page of labels.

Click the **Options** button and use the Label Options dialog box to specify the type of label on which you are printing. Click **OK**. Load the sheet of labels into your printer and click the **Print** button.

Your Very Own Address Book

You may have noticed that just above the text boxes in which you type the delivery and return addresses is the Insert Address button. This button lets you create and use a personal address book to store the names, addresses, and phone numbers of the people you frequently write to. Instead of typing a person's name and address each time you want to send a letter, you can click the Insert Address button and select the person's name from a list.

To create your address book and add names to it, click the **Insert Address** button (not the arrow to the right of it). The Select Name dialog box appears, but there are no names to select. Click **New** to add a name to the book. In the New Entry dialog box, select **Other Address** and click **OK**. The New Other Address Properties dialog box appears.

Click the Business tab to enter the address.

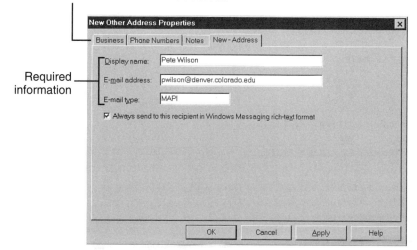

You can add names and addresses to a personal address book for easy access.

The New Other Address Properties dialog box prompts you to type the recipient's name, e-mail address, and e-mail type. Unfortunately, these three entries are all required, so if the person does not have an e-mail address, type anything in the e-mail text boxes. Use the other tabs to enter the person's address, phone number, and other information. When you are done entering information, click **OK**. This adds the person's name and address to the phone book.

Now, whenever you want to insert a person's name and address, click the **Insert Address** drop-down arrow and select the person's name.

Merging Your Address Book with a Form Letter

You've been getting them for years from Publisher's Clearing House, Ed McMahon, Reader's Digest, Mastercard, Visa, window installers, and even AOL, all addressed to you (or some guy by the name of Current Resident), selling you magazines and money and dreams of someday being someone you're not.

Now it's your turn.

In the following sections, you'll learn how to do your own mass mailings right from your desktop. Word's Mail Merge feature can't lick your stamps, but it can do just about everything else.

First You Need Some Data

It takes two to merge merengue. You need a form letter that has codes for pulling pieces of data into the letter, and you need the pieces of data themselves. You can use any of several data sources for the mail merge. If you created a personal address book as explained earlier in this chapter, it will work just fine. You can also use any of the following files as your data source:

➤ An Outlook address book. See Chapter 26, "Keeping Track of Dates, Mates, and Things to Do."

➤ An Access database.

➤ An Excel spreadsheet with column headings.

➤ A Word table. The first row must contain headings describing the contents of the cells in that column. Each row contains information about an individual. See the figure below. (You can create a Word table data source on the fly as you are performing the merge.)

The topmost row must contain labels
(field names) that will match the
codes you insert in the form letter.

A field name can be up to 40
characters, no spaces, and
must begin with a letter.

Each cell contains a
piece of information.

Title	FirstName	LastName	Address	City	State	ZIP
Mr.	William	Kennedy	5567 Bluehill Circle	Indianapolis	IN	46224
Ms.	Marion	Kraft	1313 Mockingbird Lane	Los Angeles	CA	77856
Ms.	Mary	Abolt	8517 Grandview Avenue	San Diego	CA	77987
Mr.	Joseph	Fugal	2764 W. 56th Place	Chicago	IL	60678
Mr.	Gregg	Lawrence	5689 N. Bringshire Blvd.	Boston	MA	56784
Ms.	Lisa	Kasdan	8976 Westhaven Drive	Orlando	FL	88329
Mr.	Nicholas	Capetti	1345 W. Bilford Ave.	New Orleans	LA	12936
Ms.	Allison	Milton	32718 S. Visionary Drive	Phoenix	AZ	97612
Mr.	Barry	Strong	908 N. 9th Street	Chicago	IL	60643
Mr.	Chuck	Burger	6754 W. Lakeview Drive	Boston	MA	56784
Ms.	Carey	Bistro	987 N. Cumbersome Lane	Detroit	MI	88687
Ms.	Marie	Gabel	8764 N. Demetrius Blvd.	Miami	FL	88330
Ms.	Adrienne	Bullow	5643 N. Gaylord Ave.	Philadelphia	PA	27639
Mr.	John	Kramden	5401 N. Bandy	Pittsburgh	PA	27546
Mr.	Mitch	Kroll	674 E. Cooperton Drive	Seattle	WA	14238
Mr.	Gary	Davell	76490 E. Billview	New York	NY	76453
Ms.	Kathy	Estrich	8763 W. Cloverdale Ave.	Paradise	TX	54812

*You can use a Word
table or an Excel
spreadsheet as your
data source.*

Each row, called a
record, contains
information for one
person.

Then You Need a Form Letter

How you compose your form letter is your business. You can type it from scratch, use a
template, or seek help from the Letter Wizard. Omit any information that you will obtain
from the data source during the merge, such as the person's name and address. You will
insert codes into the letter during the merge operation. These codes will pull information
from the database and insert it in each letter.

Now You Can Merge

Once you have your form letter and data source, let the fun begin! This is a long process,
but as long as you follow me step-by-step, you can pull off this merge thing without a
hitch:

1. Open the form letter.

2. Crank down the **Tools** menu and select **Mail Merge**. The Mail Merge Helper dialog
   box appears; it will lead you through the merge operation.

3. Click **Create** (under Main Document), select **Form Letters**, and click **Active Window**. This tells Word to use your letter as the main document in the merge.

The Mail Merge Helper dialog box leads you through the three-step process.

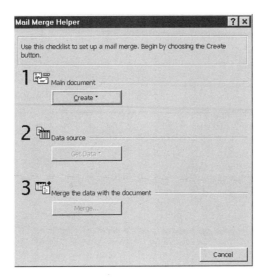

4. Under Data Source, click **Get Data**. Then select one of the following options and perform the necessary steps to select the source of data you want to use for the merge:

   Create Data Source leads you through the process of creating a Word table containing the data you want to merge with your form letter.

   Open Data Source lets you select an Excel spreadsheet file, another Word file (which contains a properly formatted table), a text file, or a database file (created in Access, Paradox, dBase, or FoxPro) as your data source.

   Use Address Book displays a dialog box asking if you want to use your personal address book or an address book created in Schedule+ or Outlook.

   Header Options lets you use one file that contains the names of the data fields and another file that contains the data entries themselves. You can live a full life without ever selecting this option.

5. The Microsoft Word dialog box appears, telling you that your form letter has no merge fields (as if you didn't know). Click **Edit Main Document**. Word returns you to your form letter and displays the Mail Merge toolbar.

6. Position the insertion point where you want to insert a piece of data from the database. For example, you might move the insertion point just below the date to insert the person's name and address.

7. Open the **Insert Merge Field** drop-down list in the Mail Merge toolbar and click the name of the field you want to insert. This inserts a code (such as **<<FirstName>>**) that will pull specified data (a person's first name) from the data source and insert it into your letter.

8. Repeat step 7 to insert additional merge field codes. Add punctuation between the codes as necessary. For example, if you are assembling codes to create an inside address, you need to add spaces and commas like this:

   <<Title>> <<FirstName>> <<LastName>>
   <<Address>>
   <<City>>, <<State>> <<ZIP>>

9. If your database contains information that you want to insert in the salutation or body of the letter, insert a field merge code wherever you want that information to appear. For example, you might use the following salutation:

   Dear <<Title>> <<LastName>>,

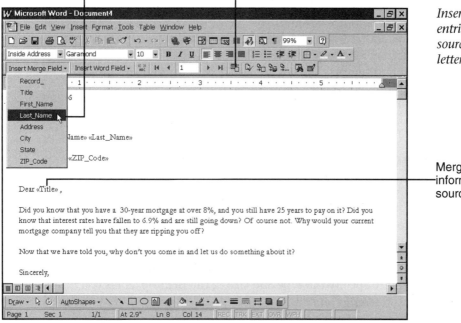

Select a field name to insert a code in your letter.

Click the Mail Merge Helper button to display the Mail Merge Helper dialog box at any time.

Insert codes to pull entries from the data source into your letter.

Merge field codes pull information from the data source into the letter.

10. Click the **Mail Merge** button. The Merge dialog box appears, offering the following options for controlling how Word merges the form letter and data source:

> **Merge To** lets you merge to the printer, to a new document, or to your e-mail program.

> **Records to Be Merged** allows you to select a range of records (so you can create letters only for selected records in the data source).

> **When Merging Records** tells Word whether or not to insert blank lines when a particular field in a record is blank.

> **Query Options** displays a dialog box that lets you sort the merged letters or create letters for a specific collection of records.

11. Enter your merge preferences, and then click the **Merge** button. If you chose to merge to the printer, Word starts printing the letters. If you chose to merge to a new file, Word opens a new document window and places the merged letters in this window. You can then print them.

Other Data You Can Merge

If your data source contains specific information about each person, you can insert that information into the body of your letter. For instance, a financial advisor might keep a list of clients along with the dates of their last appointments. The advisor could then insert something like, "The last time we discussed your finances was on <<LastDate>>. We should meet soon to reevaluate your financial situation."

Using Mail Merge to Do Mailing Labels

Now that you have a stack of letters, you need to address them. You can do this by using a mailing label as your main document and merging it with the database. Perform the same steps you performed in the previous section, but in step 3, open the **Create** menu and select **Mailing Labels**.

After you select the data source to use, the Mail Merge Helper displays the Label Options dialog box, asking you to specify the type and size of the mailing labels you intend to print on. Enter your preference and click **OK**.

The Mail Merge Helper then displays the Create Labels dialog box, which allows you to insert the merge field codes for creating the label. Click the **Insert Merge Field** button to insert the codes. Type any required punctuation between codes. To change the font used for the label, drag over the codes, right-click on the selection, and click **Font**.

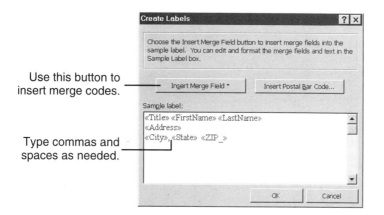

Use this button to insert merge codes.

Type commas and spaces as needed.

You can use mail merge to create pages of address labels.

The Least You Need to Know

Microsoft's letter templates and Letter Wizard make writing and sending letters a no-brainer. The only challenge is what you're going to put in the body of the letter. However, you do need to know the basics:

➤ You can now find the Letter Wizard on the Tools menu as well as in the New dialog box.

➤ To print an envelope or mailing label, open the **Tools** menu and select **Envelopes and Labels**.

➤ The Envelopes and Labels dialog box has an Insert Address button. Click it to create your own address book.

➤ You can merge data from an address book you created in Word, Outlook, or Schedule+; from a Word table; from an Excel spreadsheet; or from a database created in Access, dBase, Paradox, or FoxPro.

➤ To use mail merge with a form letter, first create the letter, and then open the **Tools** menu and select **Mail Merge** to run the Mail Merge Helper.

Chapter 11

Working with Long Documents

In This Chapter

➤ Using Outline view to shuffle your document

➤ Assembling short documents to create a long document

➤ Do-it-yourself table of contents

➤ Tacking on an index

When you're writing a letter, slapping together a brochure, or typing a memo, you have very few concerns. These one- or two-page documents are self-contained and easy to handle. You might need to adjust the margins, change the character formatting, and perhaps fiddle with the paragraphs—but those are all relatively easy tasks.

However, if you're writing something lengthy, such as a procedures manual, a chapter for a book, or your dissertation on the life cycle of the corporate slacker, you need some additional tools to organize and manage your tome. This chapter teaches you where to find these tools in Word, and how to use them.

Reorganizing Your Document in Outline View

Writing is a lot like life itself. You can start with a plan and try to follow it, or you can wing it and deal with the consequences. Personally, I prefer winging it (just ask my editor) but planning does have its advantages. By planning and outlining your work before you start, you give yourself a big fill-in-the-blank form. Once you have the headings in place, all you have to do is add some text to fill up the white space.

In addition, the outline makes it easy for you to reorganize your document. You just move the headings around, and Word takes care of moving the body text (the text that's under the headings). You'll see all this and more in the following sections.

Marking Headings in an Outline

Most Word templates contain styles for various heading levels: Heading 1, Heading 2, Heading 3, and so on. Before you can work with an outline, you need to use these styles to format your headings. Click inside the paragraph that you want to use as a heading, and then open the **Style** drop-down list and select the desired heading level.

Another way to mark a paragraph as a heading is to use the Paragraph Formatting dialog box. Click anywhere inside the paragraph you want to use as a heading, and then open the **Format** menu and select **Paragraph**. Open the **Outline Level** drop-down list, and select the desired heading level.

You can also create your own heading styles. When creating your own styles, make sure you include a setting for the Outline Level in the Paragraph formatting dialog box. If you don't specify an outline level, Word will think the paragraph is normal body text.

Turning on Outline View

Outlining doesn't require major surgery. You simply open the **View** menu and select **Outline**, and you're in Outline view. The Outlining toolbar appears at the top of the screen. If the document viewing area was blank before, it's blank now. If you start typing, each paragraph you type is marked as a top level heading. If you've already typed some or all of the document, you'll see some weird symbols off to the left of your text, marking headings and normal text.

The Incredible Expanding (and Shrinking) Outline

If you have a bare-bones outline, you don't have to worry much about the text below the headings. However, as you start filling in your outline (adding paragraphs, pictures, tables, and other neat stuff), you may want to hide some of the text so you can see the big picture and work on the overall structure of the document. You do this by expanding and collapsing the outline.

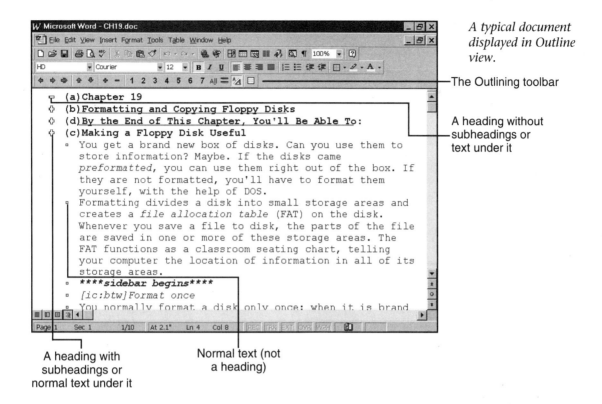

A typical document displayed in Outline view.

The Outlining toolbar

A heading without subheadings or text under it

A heading with subheadings or normal text under it

Normal text (not a heading)

The easiest way to expand and collapse the outline is to click the topmost heading in the document and then click the **Show All Headings** button in the Outlining toolbar. Click **All** once to collapse all the body text under the current heading and show just the subheadings. Click it again to expand all the body text.

You may not need any of the other collapse/expand buttons, but if you do, here's how you use them:

Click a collapsed heading and click the **Expand** button to expand the subheadings and body text one level at a time.

Click an expanded heading and click the **Collapse** button to hide subheadings and body text one level at a time.

The 1, 2, 3, 4, 5, 6, and 7 buttons indicate the number of heading levels you want Word to display in Outline view. Click **1** to display only the main heading; click **2** to display the main heading and the next level of headings; and so on.

Click the **Show First Line Only** button to display the first line of the body text (instead of entire paragraphs) below each heading. This gives you a general idea of what each section contains.

Collapse All displays only the headings and subheadings.

Click the Show All Headings button to collapse or expand all body text below the currently selected heading.

A collapsed outline makes it easy to copy and move entire sections.

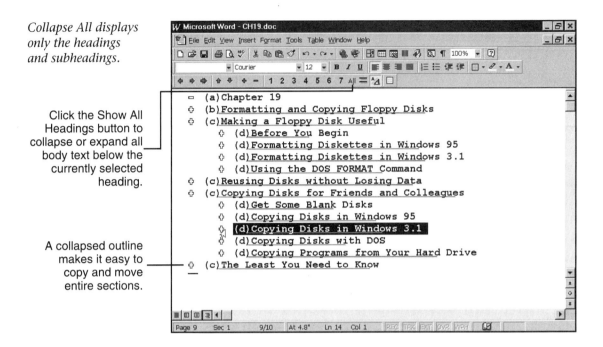

Move It!

You're done. The 100-page thesis you've been working on for the better part of your adult life is complete. But now that you've collapsed the outline, you realize that your sections don't flow logically. You need to shuffle them around a bit. You could, of course, do this in Normal or Page Layout view by cutting and pasting, but it's a whole lot easier in Outline view. Just move a heading, and all the subheadings and body text below it move along with it.

To rearrange sections, first click anywhere inside the heading you want to move. Then take one of the following steps:

➤ Click the **Move Up** or **Move Down** button in the Outlining toolbar until the heading is where you want it.

➤ Press **Alt+Shift+Up Arrow** or **Alt+Shift+Down Arrow**.

➤ Drag the symbol to the left of the heading up or down.

Promoting and Demoting Headings

As you probably know, an outline consists of headings, subheadings, and sub-subheadings. In the process of creating an outline, you decide who gets to be head

honcho, who qualifies as middle management, and who has to settle for the bottom
rung. To do this, you use the Promote and Demote buttons in the Outlining toolbar, as
described in the following steps:

1. Place the insertion point in the heading you want to promote or demote.

2. Click one of the following Promote or Demote buttons:

   Promotes a heading to a higher level. On the keyboard, you can press
   Shift+Tab to promote a heading.

   Demotes a heading to a lower level. On the keyboard, you can press **Tab** to
   demote a heading.

   Transforms a heading into body text.

Giving Your Headings a Makeover

If you used one of Word's templates to format the headings in your document using
styles (Heading1, Heading2, and so on), you can quickly give your headings a new look.
Open the **Format** menu and select **Style**. Click the Heading style you want to change,
click the **Modify** button, and use the Modify Style dialog box to enter your formatting
preferences. After you've changed the format settings for a style, Word applies those
settings to all the headings formatted with that style.

Treating Many Documents As One with a Master Document

Suppose you're doing a book that contains 20 chapters about 10 pages each. Say you want
the pages numbered consecutively throughout the book, you want the book's title at the
top of all even-numbered pages, and you want to generate an index and table of contents
for the entire book. Pretty tall order.

If you tried to manage the book as one file, you would probably go bonkers, and your
computer would run about as fast as Bill Clinton after a trip to McDonalds. But if you try
to manage each chapter as a separate file, you'll be cutting and pasting table of contents
and index entries until your fingers bleed.

The solution: create a *master document*. A master document acts as a big book cover in
which you can bind several small files called *subdocuments*. If you need to edit a
subdocument, you simply open it and edit it as a separate file. If you need to replace text
throughout the book, create a table of contents or index, or perform any other global
task, you can work with the master document as one big document.

The Making of a Master

Word offers three ways to make a master document: from an existing collection of subdocuments (Word files), from an outline, or from a long document you want to transform into a collection of shorter documents. To create a master document, you first need to be in Master Document view. If you are transforming a long document into two or more subdocuments, open the long document. If you are transforming an outline into a master document, open the outline. To create a new master document, click the **New** button. Then open the **View** menu and select **Master Document**. Word displays the Outlining toolbar and the Master Document toolbar. Do one of the following to create your master document:

 ➤ If you have subdocuments that you want to insert in the master, click the **Insert Subdocument** button in the Master Document toolbar. Use the Insert Subdocument dialog box to select the file you want to insert.

 ➤ If you have created an outline of your book, you can transform sections (chapters) of the outline into subdocuments. Drag over the headings that you want to transform into a subdocument and click the **Create Subdocument** button. Word inserts a horizontal line above and below the selected section and displays a document icon in the upper-left corner. Word places the selected section of the outline in a new document window, but does not automatically display that window.

➤ If you have a massive document, you can divide it into subdocuments. Collapse the document so that only the headings are shown. Drag over the headings that you want to include in the new subdocument and click the **Create Subdocument** button. Word inserts a horizontal line above and below the selected section and displays a document icon in the upper-left corner. Word places the selected section headings and associated body text in a new document window, but does not automatically display that window.

Check This Out...

Saving the Subdocuments Once you have created a master document, you should save it. Word saves the master document and all its subdocuments, and assigns names to each of the subdocuments based on its headings.

If you have an outline or a massive document that you want to divide into subdocuments, you can divide the entire document or outline into subdocuments with a single Create Subdocument command. The trick is in how you mark your chapter headings and how you select them. For example, if you mark the title of your book as a Heading 1, and mark each chapter title as a Heading 2, you must select all headings that use the Heading 2 style (and any headings below it), but be careful *not* to select the book title marked Heading 1. When you click the **Create Subdocument** button, Word creates a subdocument for each heading that uses the Heading 2 style.

138

Create Subdocument   Insert Subdocument

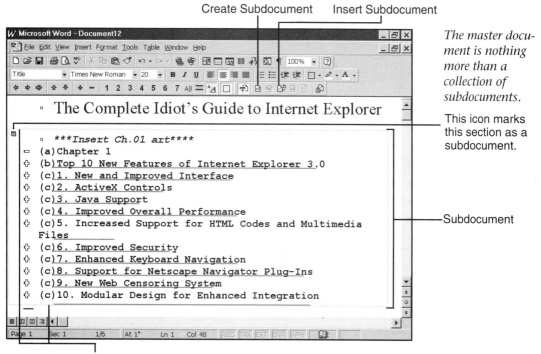

The master document is nothing more than a collection of subdocuments.

This icon marks this section as a subdocument.

Subdocument

Horizontal lines indicate where the subdocument starts and ends.

Working with the Master and the Loyal Subdocuments

In Master Document view, the master document is more like an outline than a document. You can collapse or expand it, and you can drag subdocument icons up or down to restructure the master. If you switch to Normal view, Word opens all the subdocuments on a single screen, and the master document appears to be a normal file—big, but normal. In Normal view, you can cut and paste text from one subdocument to another, find and replace text, and perform other editing as if the master document were a single file.

To work with a subdocument in the Master document, double-click the subdocument's icon (to the upper-left of the subdocument). This opens the subdocument in its own document window, where you can edit the subdocument and save your changes.

Here are a couple of things you *shouldn't* do while working with a master document:

➤ Don't delete a subdocument file until you've removed it from the master document. (To remove a subdocument, click its icon in the Master document and press **Del**.)

➤ Don't rename or move subdocument files unless you let the master know. To rename or move a document, double-click its icon in the Master document and use the **File**, **Save As** command to save the file under another name or to another folder.

Oh, the Things You Can Do with Your Master

You didn't make a master document just so you could open it and drag the subdocuments from one spot to another inside the master document. You created a master document so you could format and edit your gargantuan work without having to open 40 different files. So here's a list of cool, timesaving things that a master document allows you to do (along with some very sketchy instructions on how to do them):

➤ **Apply section formatting.** You can set any section formatting for the entire book by setting it in the master document. This includes adding a header or footer, changing the margins, and specifying page numbering options. Here's the catch: any section formatting you apply to a subdocument overrides the section formatting in the master document. In other words, if you want to set up a header for the entire book, set the header in the master document, not in the subdocuments. Likewise, if you want section formatting (say columns) to apply to only one subdocument, apply the formatting only in that subdocument.

➤ **Search and replace.** You can search for and replace text in a master document to ensure consistency throughout your book.

➤ **Apply a template.** You can create a template for your master document, complete with all the styles you want applied to all the subdocuments. The formatting of styles in the master document will override the formatting of any styles that have the same name in the subdocuments.

➤ **Create a table of contents.** You can create a table of contents as another subdocument or as part of the master document. By creating the table of contents from the master document, you ensure that the table includes all headings from the subdocuments. See "Setting Your Very Own Table of Contents" later in this chapter for details.

➤ **Index your book.** Create an index from the master document instead of from the subdocuments. Because the master document numbers pages throughout the book instead of numbering them separately for each section, your index will include the correct page numbers. See "Indexing Key Terms and Concepts," later in this chapter.

Setting Your Very Own Table of Contents

In most technical and business documents, a table of contents is essential. Why? Because people need some way of skipping all the boring drivel to find what they need. So if you have a document that contains a lot of boring drivel—a training manual, policies handbook, the Republican platform—you should include a table of contents (henceforth nicknamed TOC). Fortunately, creating a TOC is easy. You tell Word which headings you want included in the TOC, and Word does the rest, pulling the headings into a table, formatting the table, and inserting page numbers.

Branding Your Headings

Have you ever hired a moving company to move your stuff? Before they start moving, they come in and put a sticker on everything that's going. The sticker tells the mover two things: that this thing needs to be moved, and where this thing needs to be moved to. That's sort of what you have to do before you create a TOC.

The easiest way to mark your headings is to use Word's built-in Heading styles: Heading 1, Heading 2, Heading 3, and so on. You can edit these styles as explained in Chapter 5, "Giving Your Text a Makeover," to change the look of the headings, or you can create your own paragraph styles for your headings (be sure to specify an outline level for the paragraph). To transform a paragraph into a heading, click the paragraph, open the **Style** drop-down list, and click the style for the desired heading level.

Tabling Your Contents

The hard part is over. Now you get to sit back and watch Word do its thing. However, you do need to spur Word into action:

1. Place the insertion point where you want the TOC. You might want to type a title for your TOC first (maybe something clever like "Table of Contents"). If you are creating a TOC in a master document, make sure the insertion point is not inside of any subdocuments.

> **Check This Out...**
>
> **Displaying the Style Bar**
> You can display paragraph styles on the left side of the document window. Open the **Tools** menu, select **Options**, and click the **View** tab. Under Window, use the **Style Area Width** spin box to set the style area to .5" or more. When this area is minimized, you can determine a paragraph's style setting by clicking the paragraph and looking in the Style box.

2. Open the **Insert** menu, select **Index and Tables**, and click the **Table of Contents** tab. Word displays the table of contents options (shown in the following figure).

3. In the **Formats** list, click the desired TOC design. Look in the Preview area to check the appearance.

The Table of Contents tab asks you to make a few simple choices.

Pick a design for your TOC.

Enter your preferences here.

Click OK to create the TOC.

Use the Options button if you marked your headings with funky new styles.

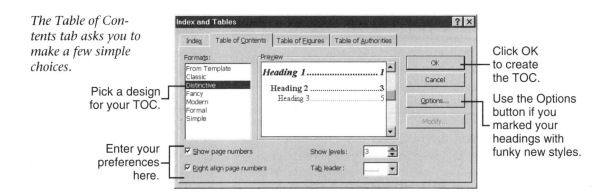

4. Select any of the following TOC preferences:

> **Show Page Numbers:** Turn this on to have page numbers included in the TOC.

> **Right Align Page Numbers:** This shoves the page number to the right, the way the pros do it.

> **Show Levels:** Use this spin box to tell Word how many levels you want included in the table.

> **Tab Leader:** A tab leader is a line or series of dots that stands between the heading and the page number if you right-align the page numbers. Select the type of tab leader you want.

5. If you used Word's Heading styles to mark your headings, skip to the next step. If you used your own heading styles, click the **Options** button and use the Table of Contents Options dialog box to specify which styles should appear at which levels in the TOC. Click **OK**.

6. Click **OK**. Word creates the TOC and plops it into your document.

Dealing with Change

What happens when you change a heading or edit your text so that a heading gets pushed to the next page? Does Word update your TOC? Heck no. You have to do it yourself. To do so, click anywhere inside the TOC and press the **F9** key. Then take your pick between these options:

➤ **Update Page Numbers Only** changes only the page numbers, not the headings. If you applied any formatting to the TOC, that formatting remains intact.

➤ **Update Entire Table** updates the entire table, wiping out any formatting you may have applied to the table.

Indexing Key Terms and Concepts

I've had a lot of bad jobs in my life—everything from cleaning kennels at the neighborhood animal hospital to driving a taxi in a city I had just moved to. But the worst job I've ever had was as a grocery store "facer." I was the guy who had to make sure that each can of Campbell's Chicken Noodle Soup was on the right shelf and that the labels were all facing forward. Well, indexing ranks right up there with facing.

To create an index, you first have to figure out which words or terms you want to index. Then you have to comb through your document and mark each significant occurrence of those words or terms. Luckily, Word can pull marked items into the index, alphabetize them, insert page numbers, remove duplicate entries from the same page, and insert the completed index. In the following sections, you will learn how to mark terms you want to index, and how to generate the index.

The Easy (But Overly Thorough) Way to Mark Terms for Indexing

If you have a 300-page book to index, you don't want to search through the entire book and manually flag each occurrence of each term you want to index. That would drive you mad. An easier way is to create a *concordance file*. A concordance file is a Word document consisting of a two-column table. In the left column, you type the word or phrase you want to index, and in the right column, you type how you want the word or phrase to appear in the index.

In some cases, you might need to list a term in the index as a subentry below a broader topic. For example, you might list "tonsillectomy" under "surgical procedures." To do this, you would type **tonsillectomy** in the left column, and then you would type **surgical procedures:tonsillectomy** in the right column. (A quick way to create another row in a table is to move to the end of the entry in the right column and press the **Tab** key.)

passing	soccer:passing
goalkeeper	soccer:goalie
passing	soccer:receiving pass
throw-in	soccer:throw-in
kick-off	football:kick off
holding	football:penalties
holding	penalties:football:holding
home run	baseball
home run	scoring:baseball
field goal	scoring:football
quarterback	football:positions
center	hockey:positions
center	soccer:positions

A concordance file is nothing more than a two-column table.

Type the term as you want it to appear in the index here.

Type the term you want to index here.

After you have created the concordance file, save it. Then perform the following steps to use your concordance file to mark terms in your document:

1. Open the document you want to index.

2. Open the **Insert** menu, select **Index and Tables**, and click the **Index** tab.

3. Click the **AutoMark** button. The Open Index AutoMark File dialog box appears.

4. Select the drive, folder, and name of your concordance file and click **Open**. Word does its thing and then turns on hidden text so you can see the field codes used to flag the index entries (see the next figure).

If the field codes are not displayed, click this button.

Word slaps a field code after each indexible entry.

Index field code

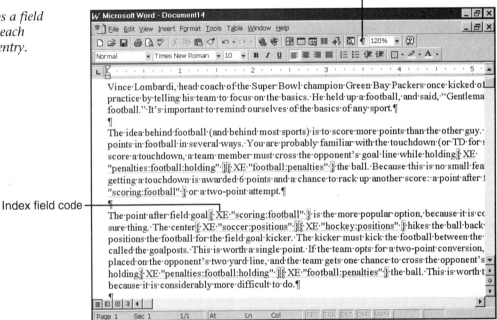

Valuable Indexing Tip

Most indexers do not mark every occurrence of each term. For example, if this book included a reference for each occurrence of the word "button," it would have about 25 pages of index entries for "button." To avoid that fate, go back through your document and delete the field codes surrounding each passing reference to a particular term.

Flag 'Em and Tag 'Em Index Entries

If you want to have more control over the terms you include in your index, you can mark each occurrence of a term manually. Here's what you do:

1. Open the document you want to index. (To index a master document, switch to Normal view.)

2. Select the term you want to index, or click next to it to position the insertion point near it.

3. Press **Alt+Shift+X**. The Mark Index Entry dialog box appears.

4. Edit the contents of the Main entry and Subentry text boxes as desired:

   ➤ If you want the item to appear in the index as it is displayed in the Main Entry text box, leave it as is.

   ➤ You can edit the entry in the Main Entry text box.

   ➤ To have the item listed as a subentry below another index entry, press **Ctrl+X** to cut the entry from the Main Entry text box, click in the **Subentry** text box, and press **Ctrl+V** to insert the text. Then type the main index entry in the Main Entry text box.

   ➤ You can format the index entry by highlighting it and pressing **Ctrl+B** (for bold), **Ctrl+I** (for italics), or **Ctrl+U** (for underlining).

5. Select one of the following options:

   Cross Reference: You can reference another index entry by selecting this option and typing the entry's name in the Cross-Reference text box.

   Current Page: This is the default setting. It places the current page number after the index entry you are marking.

   Page Range: To mark a range of pages (for example, 7–13), you first have to mark the range with a bookmark. Then choose **Page Range** and select the name of the bookmark from the Bookmark list. (To mark pages, you select the text and use the **Insert, Bookmark** command.)

6. Select **Bold** or **Italic** if you want to enhance the look of the page numbers in the index.

7. Select one of the following Mark options:

   Mark: Marks only this occurrence of the term.

   Mark All: Marks the first occurrence of the term in every paragraph in which the term appears.

8. Repeat steps 2–7 for each item you want to index.

9. Select **Close**.

Now for the Easy Part

You've done your job. Now it's Word's turn to take your magnificently coded text and make an index out of it.

1. Place the insertion point where you want the index inserted.

2. Open the **Insert** menu, select **Index and Tables**, and click the **Index** tab.

3. Select **Indented** or **Run-In** to specify the type of index you want to use. (Indented tells Word to indent subentries under the main entries. Run-In places subentries on the same line as their corresponding main entries.)

4. Select the overall format you want to use for the index.

5. Select any of the following preferences for your index:

   Headings for Accented Letters tells Word to list terms that start with an accented letter, such as À separately from terms that start with an unaccented letter, such as A.

   Right Align Page Numbers pushes the page numbers to the right.

   Columns tells Word how many columns of entries it should place across a page.

   Tab Leader inserts a line or series of dots between the index entry and its page number.

6. Click **OK**. Word creates the index and inserts it in your document. This may take awhile, depending on the speed of your computer, the length of the document, and the number of terms you marked.

Check This Out...

Updating Your Index Suppose you've created your index, and now you have to insert a page at the beginning of your document—which will throw off the entire page count (NUTS!). Don't worry, Word can fix it. Click inside the index and press **Shift+F9**.

When you index a document, Word assigns a style to each paragraph in the index: Index 1, Index 2, Index 3, and so on, all the way up to Index 9. If you want to change the look of your index, modify these styles as explained in Chapter 5, "Giving Your Text a Makeover." If you simply apply formatting to the index, Word will remove that formatting if you update the index later.

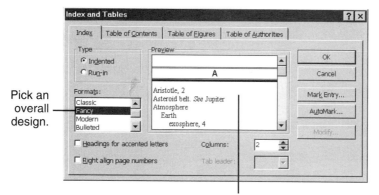

Specify how you want your index to look.

Pick an overall design.

The Preview area shows you how the index will look.

The Least You Need to Know

This chapter contains way too much information for any one person to know. If you're having trouble remembering all this, just keep a few points in mind:

➤ To change to Outline view, open the **View** menu and select **Outline**.

➤ The Show All Headings button in the Outline toolbar is probably the only expand/collapse button you'll really need.

➤ A master document lets you treat a collection of smaller documents as one document. This is great for numbering pages, creating a table of contents or an index, or applying margin settings.

➤ To create a master document, open a new document, open the **View** menu, and select **Master Document**. Use the **Insert Subdocument** button to insert shorter documents into the master document.

➤ Before you create a table of contents, make sure you mark the headings with the Heading styles.

➤ Use **Alt+Shift+X** to mark terms you want to include in your index.

Part 3
Crunching Numbers with Excel Spreadsheets

You know your multiplication tables. You've mastered long division. Now you would like to spend a little less time with your calculator and a little more time with your golf clubs.

Well, blow the dust off your clubs. Excel is ready and willing to do your math homework for you. You type some text and values, insert a few formulas, and Excel takes care of the rest—adding, subtracting, multiplying, dividing, and even graphing the results!

Whether you're refinancing your home, analyzing sales figures, or creating a business plan, the chapters in this part will show you that Excel is a tool you can't live without.

Chapter 12

Becoming a Data Entry Clerk

In This Chapter

- ➤ A nickel tour of the Excel screen
- ➤ The types of data you can put in a spreadsheet
- ➤ Typing entries in tiny boxes
- ➤ Automated data entry
- ➤ Home on the range(s) with Excel

Contrary to popular belief, you don't have to be a mathematical wizard or a CPA in order to crunch a few numbers. All you need is a good spreadsheet program such as Excel (and a little instruction), and soon you *too* will be juggling numbers, entering complex formulas and calculations, balancing budgets, and doing other high-profile tasks to impress your friends and coworkers.

But before you start juggling numbers, you have to enter them. In this chapter, you'll learn how to move around in Excel and enter the raw data Excel needs in order to perform its magic. Along the way, I'll even show you some quick ways to pour data into your spreadsheets.

Terminology Check

The term "spreadsheet" comes from the green paper ledgers that some accountants still use to keep track of information. The paper forms have tidy little rows and columns in which one can neatly record all manner of data. Basically, it's one big table with data spread out all over the page, hence the name *spreadsheet*. To further confuse you, Microsoft insists on calling its spreadsheets *worksheets*. When you first run Excel, it displays a *workbook* consisting of three worksheets.

Taking Excel on the Open Road

How do you start Excel? First, you have to know where to find the Excelerator. Get it? Excel-erator! Okay, enough of that. Although I told you how to start the Office programs back in the first part of this book, I'll tell you again. To run Excel, use one of these methods:

➤ Open the **Start** menu, point to **Programs**, and click **Microsoft Excel**. Excel opens, displaying a blank spreadsheet window. You can create a new spreadsheet using one of Excel's many templates by opening the **File** menu and selecting **New**.

➤ Click the **New Office Document** button on your Microsoft Office Shortcut bar. Click the **Spreadsheet Solutions** tab to bring it to the front of the New dialog box, choose one of the Excel spreadsheet templates, and then click **OK** to open Excel.

➤ If you set up your Office Shortcut bar to show an Excel icon (see Chapter 6), you can click the **Excel** icon to open the program.

After Excel starts, you're left staring at a big blank workbook (shown in the next figure) containing three worksheets. The area surrounding the workbook shows you all the typical program elements you learned about previously, including toolbars, menu bars, scroll bars, and so on. You'll also see several items that you might not be as familiar with:

➤ **Worksheet tabs** let you flip sheets in your workbook. Click a tab to select it; right-click a tab for additional options.

➤ **Formula bar** lets you enter data into cells (the little boxes in the worksheet) and edit entries. You'll learn all about this bar when you start typing entries.

➤ **Column headings** are the gray boxes at the top of the columns. Each column is labeled with a letter of the alphabet. To select a column, click its column heading.

➤ **Row headings** are the gray boxes at the left of the rows that indicate the number of the rows. To select a row, click its row heading.

Row headings   Column headings

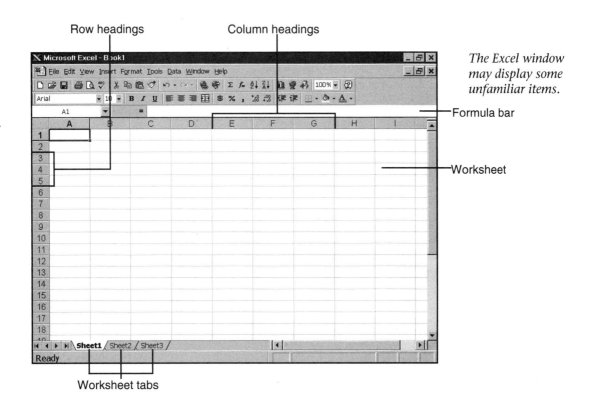

The Excel window may display some unfamiliar items.

Formula bar

Worksheet

Worksheet tabs

What's with the Letters and Numbers?

In a worksheet, rows and columns intersect to form the tiny boxes we fondly refer to as *cells*. Each cell has an *address* made up of its column letter and row number. For example, the address of the cell in the upper-left corner of the worksheet is A1. Addresses are used in formulas to refer to values in particular cells. For instance, the formula =A1+A2+A3 would determine the total of the values in cells A1 through A3.

All Data Entries Are Not Created Equal

As with most high-end applications, Excel can accept just about any kind of data that can be digitized. You can insert pictures, sounds, video clips, Web page addresses, e-mail addresses… you name it. But that type of data is merely a decoration for a worksheet. What a worksheet really needs are numbers and formulas, and some labels to indicate what the numbers and formulas stand for.

153

➤ **Labels** are the text entries that you usually type at the top of a column or the left end of a row to indicate what is in that column or row.

➤ **Numbers** (values) are the raw data that Excel needs. You enter this data in rows or columns to keep it all neat and tidy.

➤ **Formulas** are entries that tell Excel to perform calculations. For example, if you type the formula =A6*C3 into cell D5, Excel multiplies the value in cell A6 by the value in C3 and inserts the answer in cell D5.

➤ **Functions** are predesigned formulas that perform relatively complex calculations with a single operator. For example, the AVG function determines the average of a set of values, and FV determines the future value of an investment given the rate of return, the number of periods, the amount invested per period, and the present value of the investment.

You can enter labels, values, formulas, and functions into your worksheet.

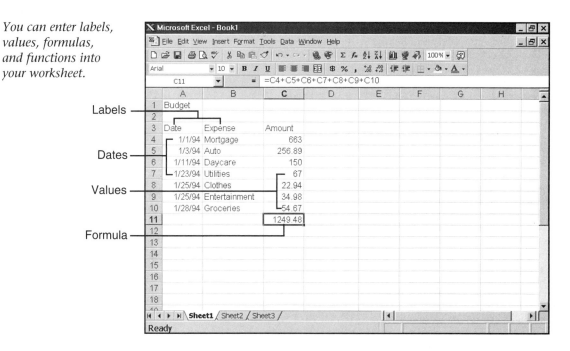

Excel usually knows which data category you're using and guesses what you're going to do with it. For that reason, you'll notice that Excel displays different data types in different positions in your worksheet cells. For example, plain old text always lines up against the left side of the cell it's in, and numbers always line up against the right side of the cell.

Entering Data

To enter data, you first have to select a cell; click on it or use the arrow keys. A bold box (the *selection box*) appears around the selected cell. When you start typing data into a selected cell, the data immediately appears in that cell and in the Formula bar above the worksheet window. Two buttons also appear in the Formula bar—a red X and a green check mark. Click on the green check mark (or press **Enter**) to accept your entry and insert it into the cell. Click on the red X (or press **Esc**) to cancel the entry.

To edit an entry as you type it, use the backspace and Delete keys as you normally would to delete characters, and then type your correction. If you accept your entry and then decide to change it, you have two options. You can double-click the cell that contains the entry and edit it right in the cell, or you can select the cell and edit its entry in the Formula bar.

If you type a relatively long entry in a cell, the entry remains in its own cell, but it may appear to spill over into the cells on the right. If the cell on the right is occupied by another entry, your long entry may appear to be chopped off (if it is a label) or it may appear as a series of pound signs (########) if it is a value. In any case, don't panic. Although you can't see your entry, it's still there. You just need to widen your column. Open the **Format** menu, choose **Column**, and choose **AutoFit Selection**. This command automatically widens the column so that your text will fit. As an alternative, you can place your mouse pointer between the column headings until it becomes a double-headed arrow and then double-click.

> **Check This Out...**
>
> **My Text Corrected Itself!**
> AutoCorrect automatically corrects common misspellings immediately after you type them when you press the **Spacebar** or **Enter** key. To add your own common misspellings to the list, open the **Tools** menu, select **AutoCorrect**, and use the AutoCorrect dialog box to add words.

The address of the selected cell   Click here to accept.

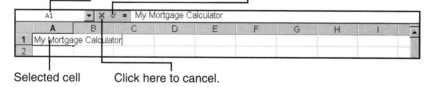

Selected cell   Click here to cancel.

As you type, your entry appears in the selected cell and in the Formula bar.

Are Your Values Valid?

Entering text data is pretty straightforward, but entering numeric data is a little more complicated. When you enter numbers as data (remember, they're called *values*), you need to know the difference between valid numbers and invalid numbers. (Here come the rules.)

Valid numbers include the numeric characters 0–9 and any of these special characters: . + – ( ) , $ %

Invalid numbers would be any other characters not mentioned as valid numbers. (So the letter Z, for example, would not be considered a valid number because it's a letter.)

Perhaps you're wondering why special characters, such as a percent sign, are recognized as numeric data. It's because you use special characters to write mathematical problems, equations, formulas, and so on. When you enter numeric values, you can include commas, decimal points, dollar signs, percent signs, and parentheses.

Although you can include punctuation when you enter numeric values, you may not want to. Why? Because you can apply formatting that adds punctuation for you. For example, instead of typing a column of hundred dollar amounts including the dollar signs and decimal points, you can type numbers such as 700 and 19.99, and change the column to Currency format. Excel will change your entries to $700.00 and $19.99, adding your beloved dollar signs where needed. (You'll learn how to do this in Chapter 14, "Giving Your Spreadsheet a Professional Look.")

Numbers As Text

What if you want your numbers to be treated like text? You know, say you want to use numbers for a ZIP code instead of a value. To do this, you have to precede your entry with a single quotation mark (') as in '90210. The single quotation mark is an alignment prefix that tells Excel to treat the following characters as text and left-align them in the cell.

Numbers As Dates and Times

Check This Out...

We're in the Army Now?
Unless you type AM or PM, Excel assumes that you are using a 24-hour military clock. Therefore, Excel interprets 8:20 as AM (not PM) unless you type 8:20 PM. In military time, you would have to type 20:20 for 8:20 PM.

What about dates and times? Dates and times are data, too, and there are a variety of ways to enter them. They're values because you can perform calculations on them (for example, you can have Excel calculate how many days until your birthday).

To use any date or time values in your spreadsheet, type them in the format you want them to appear (see the table that follows). When you enter a date using one of the formats shown in the table, Excel converts the date into a

156

number that represents how many days it falls after January 1, 1900. (Don't ask me why. I didn't invent this stuff!) But you'll never see that mysterious number. Excel always displays a normal date on-screen. I thought you ought to know that.

Valid Formats for Dates and Times

Format	Example
MM/DD	9/9 or 09/09
MM/DD/YY	9/9/97 or 09/09/97
MMM-YY	Aug-97 or August-97
DD-MMM-YY	16-Sep-97
DD-MMM	29-Mar
Month, D, YYYY	March 29, 1997
HH:MM	16:50
HH:MM:SS	9:22:55
HH:MM AM/PM	6:45 PM
HH:MM:SS AM/PM	10:15:25 AM
MM/DD/YY HH:MM	11/24/97 12:15

The Trouble with Long Worksheets

As you are entering data, selecting cells, creating ranges, and performing all the other worksheet mumbo jumbo covered in this chapter, you may notice that your worksheet is becoming quite lengthy. This isn't all that bad until you scroll down or to the right and find that the column and row headings you typed are no longer on the screen. You *need* these headings to see what each row and column are supposed to contain.

If you run into this problem, never fear. You can split the window into panes that contain separate scroll bars. You can then display the row headings in one pane, the column headings in another, and the main body of your spreadsheet in the third. Here's what you do to create a pane or remove one.

➤ Drag a split box to the position on the screen where you want the window divided. The split boxes are located above the vertical scroll bar and to the right of the horizontal scroll bar.

➤ To remove a pane divider, drag it to the top or right side of the screen.

Drag this split box to divide the window horizontally.

You can divide a window into panes to view two sections of the worksheet at the same time.

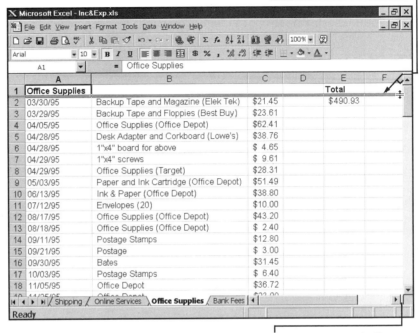

Drag this split box to divide the window vertically.

Secrets of the Data Entry Masters

Microsoft realized a long time ago that people don't like to type. In Word, Microsoft built in the AutoCorrect and AutoText features so people wouldn't have to waste time correcting common typos and typing every character of commonly used words and phrases. In Excel, Microsoft offers these same features and more. The following sections explain how you can use these timesaving features to turbocharge your data entry.

Fill 'Er Up

Let's say you need to insert the same label, date, or value in 20 cells. The mere thought of retyping a date 20 times makes your hands cramp. You could use the Copy and Paste commands to do it, but that's only slightly less tedious. The solution? Use the Fill feature.

To fill neighboring cells with the same entry, drag over the cell that contains the entry and the cells into which you want to copy the entry (up, down, left, right—doesn't matter). Open the **Edit** menu, point to **Fill**, and click the direction you want to fill: **Up**, **Down**, **Left**, or **Right**. Excel "pours" the entry into the selected cells.

Filling to Different Worksheets

You can copy the contents and formatting of cells from a worksheet to one or more worksheets in your workbook. First, click the tab for the worksheet you want to copy from, and then **Ctrl+click** the worksheets you want to copy to. Then select the cells you want to copy. Open the **Edit** menu, select **Fill**, and select **Across Worksheets**. The Fill Across Worksheets dialog box appears. Select **All** (to copy the cells' contents and formatting), or select **Contents** or **Formats** (to copy only the contents or only the formatting). Then click **OK**.

A Faster Fill Up

That submenu thing was fun, but there must be an easier way. There is. First click the cell that contains the entry you want to insert into neighboring cells. You'll notice that in the lower-right corner of the cell is a tiny square: that square is called the *fill handle*. Move the mouse pointer over fill handle, and it turns into a crosshair. Drag the fill handle over the cells you want to fill, and then release the mouse button.

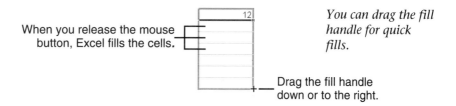

When you release the mouse button, Excel fills the cells.

Drag the fill handle down or to the right.

You can drag the fill handle for quick fills.

In some cases, this inserts the same entry into all the cells. In other cases, it inserts entries that complete a series. For example, if you use the fill handle to fill January into six neighboring cells, Excel inserts February, March, April, May, June, and July. Why? Because Excel has some built-in *fill series*, which it uses to make AutoFill a more intelligent tool. You will learn how to create your own fill series in later sections.

Excel now offers a way for you to see the last entry in a fill series. As you drag the fill handle, a tiny yellow text box pops up next to the mouse pointer, showing the name of the last item in the series. In previous versions of Excel, you had to guess how far to drag the fill handle.

159

Before you get too carried away with the fill handle, you should know a little more about it. Here are a few background pointers and tricks you can try:

➤ If you click a row heading to select a row, a fill handle appears in the lower-left corner of the row. Drag it to fill rows with any entries from the selected row.

➤ If you click a column heading, a fill handle appears in the upper-right corner of the column. Drag it to fill columns with entries from the selected column.

➤ Hold down the **Shift** key and drag the fill handle to insert blank cells, rows, or columns.

➤ To display a pop-up menu that contains fill options, drag the fill handle with the right mouse button. When you release the mouse button, the menu appears, offering you all the fill options you'll ever need.

Create Your Own AutoFill Series Data

You like this AutoFill feature. It's nice that Excel can insert a series of days, weeks, and months and intelligently fill in a series of regularly escalating numbers. However, you would like to use AutoFill to insert a list of employees or products or some other series that Excel is not set up to handle. You need to know how to create your own fill series.

The easiest way to create a series is to first type the series in a column or row (or open a workbook that already has the series in it). Drag over the entries in the series. Open the **Tools** menu, select **Options**, and click the **Custom Lists** tab. Click **Import**. You can add items to the AutoFill list by typing them in the **List Entries** text box. Click **OK** when you're done.

You can now use the AutoFill list you created. Simply type any of the entries from your AutoFill list into a worksheet cell. Then drag that cell's fill handle over the cells into which you want to insert the remaining entries from the list. When you release the mouse button, AutoFill inserts the entries for you.

Fill In the Blanks with AutoComplete

Many spreadsheet users spend a lot of time entering repetitive data or the same labels over and over again in their columns. Excel can help you speed up such entries with AutoComplete. It works like this: Excel keeps track of your column entries for each cell. Instead of retyping an entry, you right-click an empty cell and select **Pick from List**. A list of entries you already typed appears below the selected cell. You can then choose from the list, which is a lot faster than typing the word again.

Right-click inside a cell
and select Pick from List...

...and then select the
AutoComplete entry.

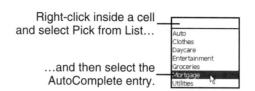

*You can quickly
insert entries you
have already typed.*

You may notice the AutoComplete feature kicking in while you enter text. If you repeat the first few letters of a previous entry, AutoComplete guesses that you're typing in repeat information and finishes your word for you. If the word it inserts is not the correct word, keep typing and ignore AutoComplete.

AutoComplete will also try to enter values for you, which can become annoying if all the values you're typing are different. To turn off AutoComplete for values, open the **Tools** menu, select **Options**, click the **Edit** tab, and click **Enable AutoComplete for Cell Values** to remove the check from the box.

Annotating Your Cells with Comments

For those of you who like to include notes in your worksheets that explain what's going on with your data, Excel has a Comments feature for you (formerly known as Cell Notes or Cell Tips). You insert comments into any cell you like. The comments don't need to have anything to do with the data inside the cell; they won't affect the data, and they do not appear in print (unless you want them to). Anytime you pass your mouse pointer over the cell, however, its comment pops up next to the cell.

Comments are great for reminding you of the significance of specific data in your worksheet and for helping you communicate with coworkers. For example, if you create a worksheet into which another employee (or a temp) is going to enter data, you can add comments that tell the employee specifically how to enter the data.

To insert a comment, take the following steps:

1. Click in the cell you want to add a comment to.

2. Open the **Insert** menu and choose **Comment**. A small text box pops up with your name in it.

3. Type your clever message explaining what this data represents or providing in-structions on how to type the entry. Or, just type some wisecrack to keep things interesting.

4. Click anywhere outside the text box. A red triangle now appears in the upper-right corner of the cell with the comment attached. Whenever you move your mouse over the cell, a tiny box appears with your text.

To delete or edit a comment later, right-click the cell that contains the comment and click **Edit Comment** or **Delete Comment**.

Life in the Cell Block: Selecting Cells

So far, we've talked about typing entries into cells. Once you have some entries, however, you might need to select the entries to copy, move, delete, or format them to perform other operations. To select cells, use the following techniques:

➤ To select a group of cells, drag over them.

➤ To select a column, click the letter at the top of the column. Drag over column letters to select more than one column.

➤ To select a row, click the number to the left of the row. Drag over row numbers to select more than one row.

➤ To select an entire worksheet, click the **Select All** button. (It's above the row numbers and to the left of the column letters.)

➤ To select multiple neighboring cells, columns, or rows, select the first cell, column, or row in the range. Then press and hold down the **Shift** key and select the last cell, column, or row in the range.

➤ To select multiple non-neighboring cells, columns, or rows, select the first cell or group of cells, columns, and rows. Then press and hold down the **Ctrl** key and click other cells, columns, or rows.

Roaming the Range

Once you become accustomed to selecting cells, you may notice that you often need to select the same group of cells to format, copy, print, or refer to them in other cells. Instead of dragging over this group of cells every time you want to perform some operation with it, consider creating a range. A *range* is a rectangular group of connected cells. You can name the range to make it even easier to select and refer to. (In Chapter 13, "Doing Math with Formulas," I'll show you how to use ranges in formulas.)

We refer to ranges by specific anchor points: the upper-left corner and the lower-right corner. For instance, if you were to drag over the cells from C3 to E5, you would create a range that Excel would fondly refer to as C3:E5. (Doesn't this sort of remind you of that game Battleship? You know, A5:D10—Hey! You sunk my battleship!) A range with more than one cell uses a colon to separate the anchor points.

Once you've selected a range, you should name it to make it easier to recognize and go to. To name the range, click in the **Name** box (at the left end of the Formula bar), type the desired name according to the following rules, and press **Enter**.

➤ Start the range name with an underscore or a letter. You can type numbers in a range name, but not at the beginning.

➤ Do not use spaces. You can use an underscore character, a period, or some other weird character to separate words.

➤ You can type up to 255 characters—but if you type any more than 15, you should be committed.

➤ The name can't be the same as a cell address. (As if you'd want a range name to be the same as a cell address.)

To quickly select a range, open the **Edit** menu and select **Go To** (or press **Ctrl+G**). Excel displays a list of named ranges. Click the desired range and click **OK**.

> *Techno Talk*
>
> **Web Work!** If you plan to place your worksheet on the Internet or on your company's intranet, you can link the worksheet to other documents by inserting a hyperlink. Open the **Insert** menu, select **Hyperlink**, and type the address of the file or Web page you want to link to. For more information about preparing your documents to publish them electronically, see Chapter 31, "Creating Your Own Web Pages."

The Least You Need to Know

Without data, a worksheet is just an overpriced piece of graph paper. To start transforming your worksheet into a useful tool, you need to first enter some data:

➤ Data consists of text labels, values, and formulas.

➤ Don't worry about formulas. You'll get your fill of those in the next chapter.

➤ Entering data is a snap: click in a cell, type your entry, and press **Enter**.

➤ You can have Excel fill selected cells with the entry in one cell or with a series of entries. Drag the little black box in the lower-right corner of a selected cell (the fill handle) over additional cells to fill them.

➤ Right-drag the fill handle to display a pop-up menu that offers additional fill options.

➤ To name a range of cells, select them, and enter a name in the **Name** box (at the left end of the Formula bar).

Chapter 13

Doing Math with Formulas

In This Chapter

➤ Transforming your spreadsheet into a high-speed calculator

➤ Determining quick totals with AutoSum

➤ Using functions for those incredibly complex calculations

➤ Special concerns when you move formulas

➤ Playing "What If?" with sets of values

Although an Excel worksheet is ideal for arranging entries in columns and rows, that's not its sole purpose. You can do that with Word's Table feature. What makes a worksheet so powerful is that it can perform calculations using various values from the worksheet and values you supply. In addition, you can set up unlimited scenarios for your worksheet that supply different numbers in the calculations, allowing you to play "What if...?" with different sets of numbers!

In this chapter, you'll learn how to unleash the power of Excel's formulas, functions, and other calculation tools.

Understanding and Concocting Your Own Formulas

The term "formula" might conjure up images of Grecian Formula or Formula 44 cough syrup. Excel formulas are nothing like that. Instead, formulas perform mathematical operations (addition, subtraction, multiplication, and division) on the entries in your worksheet. To get you started, here are some helpful facts about formulas:

➤ You type a formula into the cell in which you want the answer to appear.

➤ All formulas start with an equal sign. If you start with a letter, Excel thinks you're typing a label.

➤ Formulas use cell addresses to pull values from other cells into the formula. For example, the formula =A1+D3 calculates the sum of the values in cells A1 and D3.

➤ Formulas use the following symbols: + (addition), – (subtraction), * (multiplication), / (division), and ^ (raise to the ___ power).

➤ You can include numbers in formulas. For example, to determine your annual income, you would multiply your monthly income by 12. If your monthly income were in cell C5, the formula would be =C5*12.

A simple formula might look something like =A1+B1+C1+D1, which determines the grand total of the values in cells A1 through D1. However, formulas can be much more complex, using values from two or more worksheets in the workbook.

Get Your Operators in Order

You're probably dying to start entering formulas to see what happens. Whoa, little filly. First you need a refresher course on a little rule in math that determines the *order of operations*. In any formula, Excel performs the series of operations from left to right in the following order, which gives some operators precedence over others:

1st (All operations in parentheses)

2nd Exponential equations or operations

3rd Multiplication and division

4th Addition and subtraction

This is important to keep in mind when you are creating equations, because the order of operations determines the result.

For example, if you want to determine the average of the values in cells A1, B1, and C1, and you enter =A1+B1+C1/3, you'll probably get the wrong answer. Excel will divide the value in C1 by 3 and then add that result to A1+B1. Why? Because division takes precedence over addition. So how do you correctly determine this average? You have to group your values in parentheses. In our little equation, we want to total A1 through C1 first. To do that, you enclose that group of values in parentheses: =(A1+B1+C1)/3. That way, Excel knows to total the values before dividing them.

Memory Jogger Another way to remember the order of operations is to use this mnemonic device: "Please Excuse My Dear Aunt Sally," in which P stands for parentheses, E for exponential equations, M for multiplication, D for division, A for addition, and S for subtraction.

Tell Me How to Put Them in Already!

You can enter formulas in either of two ways: by *typing* the formula or by *selecting* cell references. To type a formula, use these steps:

1. Select the cell in which you want the formula's calculation to appear.

2. Type the equal sign (=) because it won't be a formula without an equal sign. Then type the formula. You'll notice that as you type the formula into the cell, it also appears in the Formula bar.

3. When you finish, press **Enter**. Excel calculates the result and enters it into your selected cell (assuming you have entered some values to calculate).

Error!

If an error message appears in the cell in which you typed your formula, make sure that you did not enter a formula that told Excel to do one of these things: divide by zero or a blank cell, use a value in a blank cell, delete a cell being used in a formula, or use a range name when a single cell address is expected.

To enter a formula by selecting cell references, here's what you do:

1. Select the cell in which you want the formula's result to appear.

2. Type the equal sign (=).

3. Click the cell whose address you want to appear first in the formula. The cell address appears in the Formula bar.

4. Type a mathematical operator after the value to indicate the next operation you want to perform.

5. Continue clicking cells and typing operators until you finish entering the formula.

6. When you finish, press **Enter** to accept the formula, or press **Esc** to cancel the operation.

Start with an equal sign. Type mathematical operators between cell addresses.

The easiest way to compose formulas is to point and click.

	A	B	C	D	E	F	G	H	I
1	Hokey Manufacturing								
2									
3	Income	1st Qtr	2nd Qtr	3rd Qtr	4th Qtr				
4	Wholesale	55000	46000	52000	90900				
5	Retail	45700	56500	42800	57900				
6	Special	23000	54800	67000	45800				
7	Total	123700	157300	161800	+E5+E6				
8									
9	Expenses								
10	Materials	19000	17500	18200	20500				
11	Labor	15000	15050	15500	15400				
12	Rent	1600	1600	1600	1600				
13	Misc.	2500	2500	3000	1500				
14	Total	38100	36650	38300	39000				
15						Total Profit			
16	Profit	85600	120650	123500	155600	485350			
17									
18									

Formula bar: =E4+E5+E6

Click a cell to insert its address.

If you make a mistake while entering a formula, simply backspace over it and enter your correction as you would with any other cell entry. If you already accepted the entry (by pressing Enter or clicking the check mark button), double-click the cell (or click it and then click in the Formula bar).

As you enter formulas, you may notice that Excel automatically performs the calculation. If you change a value in a cell that the formula uses, Excel recalculates the entire worksheet again. If your worksheet is fairly small and contains few calculations, this automatic recalculating is great. However, if you have a long worksheet with lots of formulas, this can slow down Excel significantly, so you may want to change the recalculation settings. To turn off the Auto Calculation option, open the **Tools** menu, choose **Options**, and click the **Calculation** tab. Select **Manual** and click **OK**. From now on when you want to recalculate the worksheet, press **F9**.

Going Turbo with Functions

Functions are ready-made formulas that you can use to perform a series of operations using two or more values or a range of *values*. For example, to determine the sum of a series of values in cells A5 through G5, you can enter the function =SUM(A5:G5) instead of entering +A5+B5+C5+ and so on. Other functions may perform more complex operations, such as determining the monthly payment on a loan for which it's given the principle, interest rate, and number of payment periods.

Every function must have the following three elements:

➤ The *equals sign (=)* indicates that what follows is a formula, not a label.

➤ The *function name* (for example, SUM) indicates the type of operation you want Excel to perform.

➤ The *argument*, such as (A3:F11), indicates the cell addresses of the values the function will act on. The argument is often a range of cells, but it can be much more complex.

A function can also be part of another formula. For example =SUM(A3:A15)/7 uses two functions along with the division operator to determine the average of the values in cells A3 to A15. (Of course, it would be easier to simply use the AVERAGE function.)

Demystifying Functions with the Paste Function Feature

Although you can type functions and arguments yourself, the Paste Function feature can make the process a lot less painful. To paste a function into a cell, take the following steps:

1. Select the cell in which you want to insert the function.

 2. Open the **Insert** menu and choose **Function**, or better yet, click the **Paste Function** button in the Standard toolbar. The Paste Function dialog box appears, displaying a list of available functions.

169

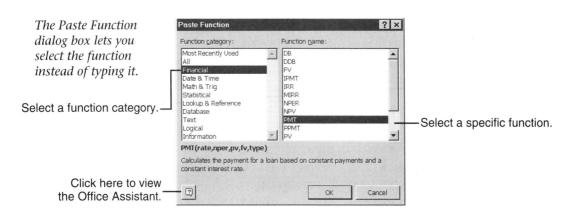

The Paste Function dialog box lets you select the function instead of typing it.

Select a function category.

Select a specific function.

Click here to view the Office Assistant.

Function Rookie Tip

When you select a function in the Function Name list, Excel displays a description of the function. Read this description to find out the purpose of the function (or the function of the purpose). If you need more help, you can use the Office Assistant to get help on using the Paste Function feature or on the selected function.

3. From the **Function Category** list, select the type of function you want to insert. If you're not sure, select **All**, and the Function Name list displays the names of all the functions in the selected category.

4. Select the function you want to insert from the **Function Name** list and click **OK**. Another dialog box appears, prompting you to type the argument. The second box's appearance varies depending on the function you selected. (The figure below shows the dialog box you would see if you chose the AVERAGE function.)

5. Enter the values or cell ranges for the argument. You can type a value or argument, or you can drag the dialog box (by its title bar) out of the way and click the desired cells.

The second step is to enter the values and cell references that make up the argument.

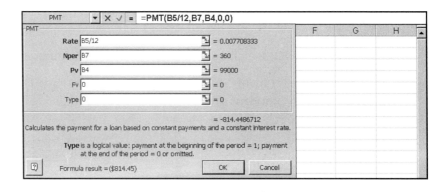

6. Click **OK** or press **Enter**. Excel inserts the function and argument in the selected cell and displays the result.

When you need to edit a function using the Function Wizard, select the cell that contains the function you want to edit. (Make sure you're not in Edit mode; that is, the insertion point should not appear in the cell.) Open the **Insert** menu and choose **Function**, or click the **Paste Function** button. This displays a dialog box that lets you edit your argument.

The Awesome AutoSum Tool

One of the tasks you'll perform most often is summing up values you've entered in your worksheet cells. Because summing is so popular (voted most popular function in its graduating class), Excel provides a tool devoted to summing: AutoSum.

To quickly determine the total of a row or column of values, first click in an empty cell to the right of the row or just below the column of values. Then click the **AutoSum** button in the Standard toolbar. AutoSum assumes that you want to add the values in the cells to the left of or above the currently selected cell, so it displays a "marching ants" box around those cells. If AutoSum selects an incorrect range of cells, you can edit the selection by dragging across the cells whose values you want to add. Press **Enter** or click the green check mark button in the Formula bar.

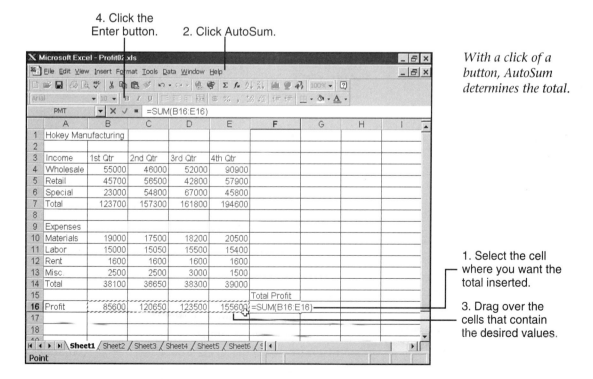

4. Click the Enter button. 2. Click AutoSum.

With a click of a button, AutoSum determines the total.

1. Select the cell where you want the total inserted.

3. Drag over the cells that contain the desired values.

171

AutoCalculate

Drag over a range of values and look in the status bar. You'll see **Sum=**, followed by the total of the values in the selected cells. This feature, called *AutoCalculate*, can help you determine totals without inserting the total in a cell. Right-click the status bar to display a pop-up menu that lets you see the average of the selected cells or the count (the number of values in the cells).

Controlling Cell Addresses When You Copy or Move Formulas

Moving a value or label is as easy as moving a dining room chair. You pick it up, and then you set it down somewhere else. With formulas and functions, moving and copying become a little more difficult. Instead of moving a fixed, absolute entry (such as 4), when you move a function or formula, you're moving cell references (such as B52).

When you copy a formula from one place in the worksheet to another, Excel adjusts the cell references in the formulas relative to their new positions in the worksheet. Let me give you an example. In the following figure, cell B9 contains the formula =B4+B5+B6+B7, which determines the total sales revenue for Fred. If you copy that formula to cell C9 (to determine the total sales revenue for Wilma), Excel automatically changes the formula to =C4+C5+C6+C7.

My References Are Mixed Up

Once in a blue moon, you may need to mark the column letter or the row number (but not both) as absolute. This allows the column letter or row number to change when you copy or move the formula. A reference that is partially absolute, such as A$2 or $A2, is called a *mixed reference*. To create a mixed reference, keep pressing the F4 key until you have the proper combination of dollar signs.

The preceding example shows a formula in which the cell references are *relative:* Excel changes the cell addresses relative to the position of the formula.

Sometimes, however, you may not want Excel to adjust the cell references. For example, say you have a formula in cell E2 that shows the sales revenue goal for each individual salesperson, and you want to find out whether any salesperson surpassed that goal and if so, by what percentage. To determine the percentage for each salesperson, you type =B9/E2 in cell B10 (see the previous figure). If you copy that formula into C10 to determine Wilma's percentage, the formula changes to =C9/F2, and you get an error because F2 contains no value.

In order to keep a cell reference (E2) from changing when you copy or move the formula, you must mark the cell reference in the formula as an *absolute reference*. To mark a

172

reference as an absolute, press the **F4** key immediately after typing the reference. This places a dollar sign before the column letter and the row number (as in E2). You can type the dollar signs yourself, but it's usually easier to let Excel do it.

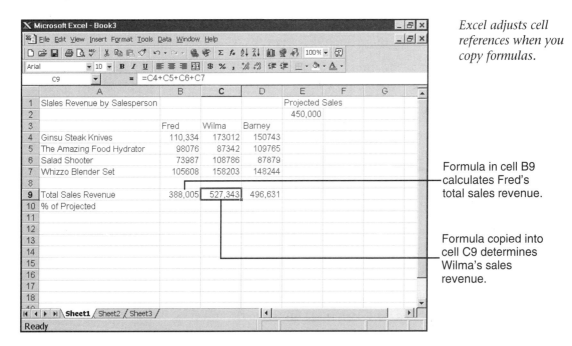

Excel adjusts cell references when you copy formulas.

Formula in cell B9 calculates Fred's total sales revenue.

Formula copied into cell C9 determines Wilma's sales revenue.

Playing "What If?" with Scenarios

Once you have some values and formulas in place, let the fun begin! Excel offers a tool that allows you to plug different sets of values into your formulas to determine the effects of different values on the outcome.

For example, say you're purchasing a home and you need some idea of how much your monthly mortgage payment is going to be for various loan amounts. You have successfully created a worksheet that determines the monthly payment for a $120,000 house at 8.5%, but you want to know what the payment would be for a $110,000, a $130,000, and a $140,000 home. And you want to see the effects of other loan rates.

You could create a bunch of separate worksheets. But a better solution would be to create several scenarios for the same worksheet. A *scenario* is simply a set of values that you plug into variables in the worksheet.

The Making of a Scenario

Making a scenario is fairly simple. You name the scenario, tell Excel which cells have the values you want to play with, and then type the values you want to use for the scenario. The following step-by-step instructions walk you through creating a scenario:

1. Display the worksheet for which you want to create a scenario.

2. Open the **Tools** menu and click **Scenarios**. The Scenario Manager appears, indicating that this worksheet has no current scenarios.

3. Click the **Add** button. The Add Scenario dialog box appears.

4. Type a name for the scenario that describes the specific changes you're going to make. For example, if you were creating this scenario to determine payments for a $110,000 house at 9.25%, you might type **110K @ 9.25%**.

5. Tab to the **Changing Cells** text box and click the cell that contains the value you want to change in your scenario. To change values in other cells, hold down the **Ctrl** key and click them. (This inserts the addresses of the changing cells, separating them with commas.)

6. Click **OK**. The Scenario Values dialog box displays the current values in the cells you want to change.

7. Type the values you want to use for this scenario and click **OK**. The Scenario Manager displays the name of the new Scenario.

8. To view a scenario, click its name and click the **Show** button. Excel replaces the values in the changing cells with the values you entered for the scenario.

To make a scenario, enter different values for the variables.

This entry will replace the loan rate in cell B5.

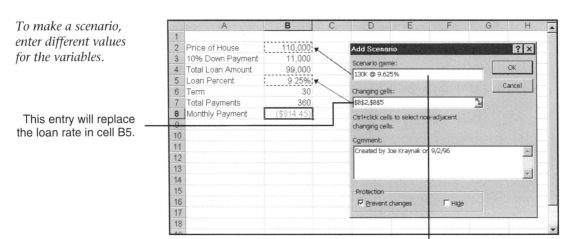

This entry will replace the price of the house in cell B2.

Managing Your Scenarios

Whenever you want to play with the various scenarios you've created, open the **Tools** menu and select **Scenarios**. This displays the Scenario Manager, which you met in the previous section. The Scenario Manager offers the following buttons for managing and displaying your scenarios:

➤ **Show** displays the results of the selected scenario right inside the worksheet.

➤ **Add** lets you add another scenario.

➤ **Delete** removes the selected scenario.

➤ **Edit** lets you pick changing cells and insert different values for the variables.

➤ **Merge** takes scenarios from various worksheets and places them on a single worksheet.

➤ **Summary** displays the results of the various worksheets on a single worksheet. As you can see in the following figure, this is great for comparing the different scenarios you've created.

Scenario Summary				
	Current Values:	120K @ 8.25%	110K @ 9.25%	130K @ 9.625%
Changing Cells:				
B2	110,000	120,000	110,000	130,000
B5	9.25%	8.50%	9.25%	9.63%
Result Cells:				
B8	($814.45)	($830.43)	($814.45)	($994.49)

Notes: Current Values column represents values of changing cells at time Scenario Summary Report was created. Changing cells for each scenario are highlighted in gray.

Scenario Manager can create a summary of the results from different scenarios.

The Conditional Sum Wizard, and Other Wizardry

Excel comes with several wizards that can help you perform complex operations, such as creating a lookup table. (A *lookup table* typically specifies an entry to insert for a specific range of values. For example, if you have a grade sheet, the lookup table might match percentage grade ranges to their letter grade equivalent; for instance 92–100=A.) Following are a list of the wizards that Excel offers, complete with brief descriptions. You will find these wizards on the **Tools, Wizard** submenu.

Web Work! The Tools, Wizard submenu also contains the Web Form Wizard. It leads you through the process of transforming your worksheet into a form for entering data into an Access database. You can then place this form on the Web or on your company's intranet for collecting data or processing orders.

➤ **Lookup** helps you create a formula that can find specific information in a workbook and insert it into a cell. Before running the Lookup Wizard, make sure your workbook has a table with the entries you need to pull and insert.

➤ **File Conversion** helps you convert spreadsheets created in other spreadsheet applications, such as Lotus or Quattro Pro, into a Excel workbooks.

➤ **Conditional Sum** totals values that meet the criteria you specify. For example, if you have a worksheet that totals sales figures in various cities (Chicago, New York, San Francisco), you can use the Conditional Sum Wizard to add only the sales figures for a specific city (for instance, New York).

The Least You Need to Know

This chapter is merely an appetizer, showing you some of the basics of entering formulas and functions in your worksheets. You must now rely on your own mathematical creativity and the help of the Paste Function feature to write the formulas you need. While you're doing that, keep the following information at your fingertips:

➤ Formulas are mathematical statements that perform calculations (such as addition or subtraction) on your data.

➤ Excel performs a calculation from left to right, performing multiplication and division before addition and subtraction.

➤ You can group various values and cell references by enclosing them in parentheses. This tells Excel to perform those calculations first.

➤ Use built-in functions to sum or average a range of numbers or to perform more complex calculations, such as determining monthly payments on a loan.

➤ An absolute reference is a cell reference in a formula that does not change when you copy the formula to a new location.

➤ To mark a cell reference in a formula as absolute, select it inside the formula and press **F4**.

➤ A relative reference is a cell reference in a formula that is adjusted when you copy the formula.

Chapter 14

Giving Your Worksheet a Professional Look

In This Chapter

➤ Inserting blank rows, columns, and cells

➤ Adding dollar signs, decimals, percent signs, and other valuable ornaments

➤ Spiffing up a worksheet with clip art

➤ Adding borders, shading, and other fancy stuff

➤ Formatting tricks and shortcuts

If you win the lottery or you go to see a numerologist to have your future told, numbers might grab your attention. In most cases, however, numbers have that sort of ashen Al Gore look to them.

To make your numbers a little more appealing, and to make the rows and columns easier to follow, you need to format your worksheet. You can format by inserting blank rows and columns to give your values a little elbow room, laying down a few lines around your cells, or even shading individual cells, rows, or columns to make them stand out.

In this chapter, you will learn several ways to adorn your worksheets and make your numbers a little more exciting.

Add a Few Rows, Toss in Some Columns

As you are building your worksheet, you may have some need to add a few columns or rows to insert data you hadn't thought of when you were laying out your worksheet. Or maybe you need to delete a row or column if you were a little too ambitious in your design. Whatever the case, adding and deleting cells, rows, and columns is fairly simple.

To insert cells, rows, or columns, first select the number of cells, rows, or columns you want to insert (drag over the row or column headings to select entire rows or columns).

➤ If you select rows, Excel will insert the new rows *above* the selected rows.

➤ If you select columns, Excel will insert the new columns to the *left* of the selected columns.

➤ If you select a block of cells, Excel will insert the new cells where the selected cells are located, and it will shift the data from the selected cells *down* or to the *right* (your choice).

Look to the Insert Menu
If your right mouse button is broken, you can always use the Insert menu to insert cells, rows, or columns.

After selecting columns, rows, or cells, right-click anywhere inside the selection and click **Insert**. If you selected columns or rows, Excel inserts them immediately. If you selected a block of cells, the Insert dialog box appears, asking which way you want the data in the currently selected cells to be shifted. Select **Shift Cells Right** or **Shift Cells Down** and click **OK**. Be careful! If you have formulas in your worksheet that rely on the contents of the cells that Excel moves, it could throw off your calculations.

Specify the direction in which you want data from the currently selected cells to be shifted.

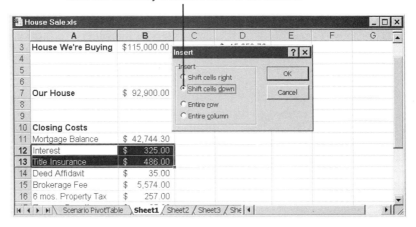

When you insert a block of cells, Excel shifts data down or to the right to make room.

Nuking Rows, Columns, and Cells

When you delete data in a worksheet, all sorts of things can happen. For example, you might destroy only the data in the cells, or you might wipe out the cells or columns entirely, forcing adjacent cells to shift. Therefore, when you set out on any mission of mass destruction, keep the following things in mind:

➤ If you select columns, rows, or cells, and press the **Delete** key, Excel leaves the cells intact, deleting only the contents of the selected cells. This is the same as entering the Edit, Clear, Contents command.

➤ The Edit, Clear command opens a submenu that allows you to clear All (contents, formatting, and comments), Contents (just cell entries, not the formatting), Format (cell formatting, not the contents), or Comments (only the cell comments).

➤ To completely remove cells, columns, or rows, select them, open the **Edit** menu, and select **Delete**. (Or right-click inside the selection and select **Delete**.)

➤ When you remove a row, rows below it are pulled up to fill the space. When you delete a column, columns to the right are pulled left to fill the void.

➤ If you choose to remove a block of cells (otherwise known as a cell block), Excel displays a dialog box asking you how to shift the surrounding cells.

Now that you know what is going to happen when you choose to delete cells, go ahead and do it. Select the cells, columns, or rows you want to delete, open the **Edit** menu, and select **Delete**.

Making It All Look Nice in 10 Minutes or Less

Personally, I don't subscribe to the moronic wisdom of corporate America that says things like "The clothes make the man," and "Dress for success." In business (and in worksheets), performance far outweighs appearance. However, if your worksheet is creative, well-designed, error-free, *and* attractive, you'll find that it will not only catch the attention of your audience, but perhaps also convince them to use it. The following sections show you how to use the various formatting tools available in Excel to give your worksheets a more professional look.

Drive-Through Formatting with AutoFormat

Excel offers a formatting feature called AutoFormat that makes formatting your worksheet as easy as picking up a bag of burgers at the local drive-through. With AutoFormat, you apply a predesigned format to selected cells. The format controls everything from fonts and alignment to shading and borders.

To use AutoFormat, drag over the cells you want to format, open the **Format** menu, and select **AutoFormat**. In the AutoFormat dialog box, click the desired format in the **Table Format** list. The preview area shows a sample of the selected format. To turn off any format settings, such as shading or borders, click the **Options** button and select your preferences, as shown in the following figure.

You can pick a predesigned table format for your worksheet.

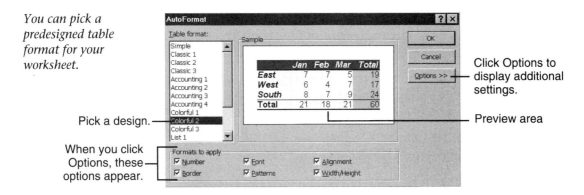

Click Options to display additional settings.

Pick a design.

Preview area

When you click Options, these options appear.

Conditional Formatting

Worksheets don't really care if your expenses exceed income or your bottom line drops off the page. They display the numbers just as if everything were going okay. Now, however, Excel allows you to apply *conditional formatting* to a cell; this tells Excel to display a value in a unique way if the value falls in a certain range. For example, you can apply a conditional format telling Excel that if this value falls below zero, it should shade the cell red and place a big, thick border around it to alert you. To apply a conditional format, take the following steps:

1. Select the cell that contains the formula or value you want to format.

2. Open the **Format** menu and select **Conditional Formatting**. The Conditional Formatting dialog box appears.

3. In the drop-down list at the left, you usually want the option set to **Cell Value Is**. Select Formula Is only if the cell contains a formula whose result is either True or False. If the formula produces a value as a result, leave this set to Cell Value Is.

4. Use the next drop-down list and the text box(es) to the right of the list to specify the range in which the value must fall in order to apply the conditional format. For example, you might select **Less Than** from the list and type **0** in the text box to tell Excel to apply the format if the value in the cell drops below zero. See the following figure for another example.

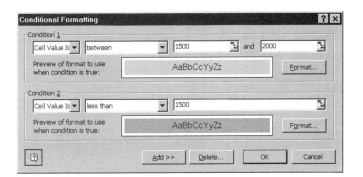

Tell Excel when to apply the special formatting.

5. Click the **Format** button. The Format Cells dialog box appears.

6. Use the Format Cells dialog box to specify a font, border, or cell shading to use as the conditional format. Click **OK**.

7. To add another conditional format to the cell, click the **Add** button and repeat steps 3–6. For example, you might want to shade the cell red if its value falls below 0 and green if it's above 0.

8. To delete a conditional format, click the **Delete** button, select the conditions you want to delete, and click **OK**.

9. When you finish setting conditions, click **OK**.

Don't Forget Your Formatting Toolbar

Overlooking the Formatting toolbar in any of the Microsoft Office applications is like forgetting your laptop when you're going on a business trip. Without it, you have to resort to a system of awkward pull-down menus, dialog boxes, and pop-up menus to get anything done.

The Formatting toolbar offers the fastest way for you to change fonts, increase or decrease the type size, align text in cells, change the text color, add borders, and more. You should already know how to use the Formatting toolbar from working in Word. If you don't, here are a few pointers:

➤ To figure out what a button does, rest the mouse pointer on it. (Or press **Shift+F1** and click the button.)

➤ You can format text before or after typing it.

➤ The Font and Font Size boxes are both pull-down menus. Click the arrow to the right of the box to open the menu.

181

➤ The Borders, Fill Color, and Font Color buttons are each actually two buttons. To select a border or color, click the arrow button to the right of the main button. Select a border or color, and then apply it by clicking the main button.

Font   Font Size   These are your alignment buttons. Use the last one to center data across cells.   Indents   Fill Color (cell shading)

Excel's Formatting toolbar.

Use these to make your data bold, italic, or underlined.   These buttons let you format your numbers as currency style or with decimal points.   Borders   Font Color

Web Work! If you are formatting your worksheet to place it on the Web or on your company's intranet, try to keep the worksheet narrow. If the worksheet is wider than the Web browser window, the people viewing your worksheet will have to use the horizontal scroll button to bring columns into view. This may make the worksheet difficult to navigate.

Okay, You Can Use the Menu, Too

You can also control formatting through the Format Cells dialog box. Open the **Format** menu and select **Cells** to open the dialog box. You can change many of the formatting features for your data by clicking the appropriate tabs in this dialog box; the next section shows you how.

Step-by-Step Formatting Basics

General instructions such as "Use the toolbar" are fine until you need to apply a specific formatting to cells. You might want to give your values dollar signs and a couple of decimal places to remind yourself that these numbers represent real values. Or, maybe you need to add borders and shading to help you follow a row of numbers across a worksheet. Whatever the case, the following sections give you instructions for applying specific format settings.

How to Make Your Numbers Attractive

Numeric values represent dollar values, dates, percentages, and other real values. So instead of showing plain old digits on your worksheet, you can indicate what particular values they stand for. If you're working with dollars, let's see some dollar signs! If you're calculating percentages, let's see some percent signs! And how do you do this, you may ask? Well, you can use the buttons on your Formatting toolbar, or you can make additional selections in the Numbers tab of the Format Cells dialog box. Here's what you do:

1. Select the cell or range that contains the values you want to format.

2. Open the **Format** menu and choose **Cells**. The Format Cells dialog box appears.

3. Click the **Number** tab to make sure it's at the front of the dialog box.

4. In the **Category** list, select the numeric format category you want to use. Excel shows you a sample of what the format looks like.

5. If you select a format that prompts you to specify additional preferences, make the desired selections. For example, if you pick the Currency format, you can specify the number of decimal places to display, the dollar sign symbol to use, and how you want negative values displayed.

6. Click **OK** or press **Enter**.

Get in Line!

By default, Excel automatically aligns data according to what type of data it is: text aligns bottom left; numbers align bottom right. You can change all that by entering the desired alignment settings.

Drag over the cells whose entries you want to align differently, open the **Format** menu, select **Cells**, and click the **Alignment** tab. Select the desired alignment and click **OK**. Here's a rundown of the alignment options.

Horizontal options enable you to specify a left/right alignment in the cell(s). With the Center Across Selection option, you can center a title or other text inside a range of cells.

Vertical options enable you to specify how you want the data aligned in relation to the top and bottom of the cell(s).

Orientation options let you flip the text sideways, print it from top to bottom, or place it on an angle inside the cell. (I'll bet you're dying to try this trick.)

Text Control check boxes allow you to wrap long lines of text within a cell, shrink text to fit inside a cell, and merge cells. (Normally, Excel displays all text in a cell on one line.)

Changing the Font Design and Size

You can use the Font tab in the Format Cells dialog box to change fonts, but it's much easier to use the Formatting toolbar. Just drag over the cells whose font settings you want to change, and then select the desired font, size, attributes (bold, italic, underline), and color from the Formatting toolbar.

Changing the Default Font

To use any font as the normal font for all your worksheets, you can change the default font. Open the **Tools** menu, select **Options**, and click the **General** tab. Open the **Standard Font** drop-down list and click the desired font. Open the **Size** drop-down list and click the font size you want. Then click **OK**.

Adding Borders and Shading

If you've printed a worksheet, you know that those lines separating the cells don't print. They are there merely to help you see where the various cells are located. If you want similar lines (or different ones) on your printout, or if you want to add shading to your cells, you can add formatting via the Format Cells dialog box.

First, select the cells you want to format. Then open the **Format** menu and select **Cells**. The familiar Format Cells dialog box appears. You have two tabs you need to look at: Border and Patterns.

To add a border, click the **Border** tab. Before you select a border, select a line style from the **Style** list and select a color from the **Color** drop-down list. The Presets buttons allow you to add an outline (a line around the outside of the entire selection) and inside lines (between all the cells in the selected area). Click a button to turn the lines on or off. The Border buttons (below the Presets) allow you to add or remove individual lines.

The Border tab lets you place lines between and around cells.

2. Select one or more presets.

3. Click a border button to turn an individual line on or off.

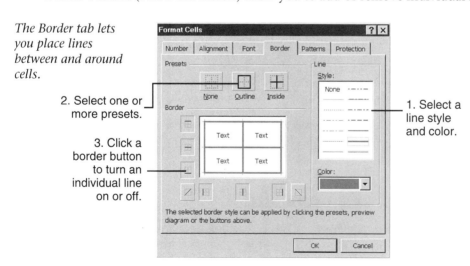

1. Select a line style and color.

To shade the selected cells, click the **Patterns** tab. Under Color, click the main color you want to use for the cell shading. If you want to use a solid color, you're done; click **OK**. To overlay a pattern of a different color, open the **Pattern** drop-down list and click a pattern (from the top of the list); then open the **Pattern** drop-down list again and click a color (from the bottom of the list). Click **OK**.

Applying Formats with a Few Brush Strokes

You can quickly copy the formatting from one cell or a block of cells to other cells by using the Format Painter. Select the cell that contains the formatting you want to copy and click the **Format Painter** button. Drag your pointer (which now has a paintbrush icon next to it) over the cells to which you want to copy the formatting. Format Painter applies the formatting!

Page Break Preview
Before you print your worksheet, change to Page Break Preview to see how Excel plans to divide the worksheet into pages. Open the **View** menu and select **Page Break Preview**.

Formatting Tricks to Help with Printing

The toughest challenge in creating a worksheet is how to print it. Worksheets are usually too wide for an 8.5-by-11-inch page. How do you get it to fit? Following are a few tricks you might try:

➤ Print sideways on a page. Choose **File**, **Page Setup** and click the **Page** tab. Pick **Landscape** and click **OK**.

➤ Scale the fonts to fit on a page. Choose **File**, **Page Setup** and click the **Page** tab. Under **Scaling**, click the **Fit To** option and select **1 Page Wide** by **1 Page Tall**. Excel shrinks the text to make it fit—but it might be too small to read.

➤ Decrease the margins. In the Page Setup dialog box, click the **Margins** tab and shrink the margins.

➤ Print only a portion of the worksheet. Drag over the cells you want to print. Open the **File** menu, point to **Print Area**, and select **Set Print Area**. If you decide later to print the entire worksheet, use the **File**, **Print Area**, **Clear Print Area** command to cancel this option.

➤ Hide some columns. In many cases, all you need are two columns: the first column with the row labels, and the last column that displays the totals. Drag over the columns in-between, right-click the selection, and click **Hide**. To display hidden columns, select the entire worksheet, open the **Format** menu, point to **Columns**, and select **Unhide**.

Hanging a Few (Graphical) Ornaments

In the next chapter, "Graphing Your Data for Fun and Profit," you will learn how to add graphs to your worksheets to give your data meaning and to make your worksheets more graphical. However, Excel offers a few additional tools for adding graphics to your worksheets. For instance, you can insert maps of various countries by opening the **Insert** menu and selecting **Map**.

Web Work! If you're planning to place your Excel worksheet on the Web, give it a background design. Open the **Format** menu, point to **Sheet**, and select **Background**. In the Sheet Background dialog box, select a background design. Look in the Microsoft Office/ Clipart/Backgrounds folder for backgrounds you can use.

The Insert, Picture submenu contains additional options for inserting clip art images, graphics stored on your disk, organizational charts, WordArt, AutoShapes, and even scanned images (assuming you have a TWAIN-compatible scanner).

These graphic tools are similar (some are even identical) to the tools that Word offers. To learn how to use these tools (Clip Art, WordArt, AutoShapes, drawing, and so on), refer to Chapter 7, "Spicing It Up with Graphics, Sound, and Video."

The Least You Need to Know

Before this chapter, your Excel worksheets probably looked pretty dreary. But now, with all the formatting tricks you learned, your worksheets should inspire some "wows" from friends and colleagues alike. As you're sprucing up your other worksheets, don't forget the following basics:

➤ To let Excel make the formatting decisions for you, drag over the cells you want to format, open the **Format** menu, and click **AutoFormat**.

➤ Conditional formatting applies special formatting to a cell if the value in that cell falls in a certain range that you specify.

➤ To insert cells, rows, or columns, drag over the number of columns, rows, or cells you want to insert, and then right-click the selection and choose **Insert**.

➤ Added rows are inserted above the currently selected rows; added columns are inserted to the left of currently selected columns.

➤ You can apply most formatting quickly by selecting the cells you want to format and using the Formatting toolbar.

➤ To apply a bunch of formatting settings to a cell or group of cells, select them, and then open the **Format** menu and select **Cells**.

Chapter 15

Graphing Data for Fun and Profit

In This Chapter

➤ Graphing without graph paper

➤ In your face with pie charts

➤ Making a chart more understandable with legends

➤ Labeling your chart axes just for fun

During the 1992 presidential race, Ross Perot made charts famous. With his prime time voodoo pointer and his stack of charts, he managed to upset an election and change the political strategies of both parties. At the same time, he proved that a well-designed graph could convey data much more clearly and effectively than could any page full of numbers.

In this chapter, you'll learn how to use Excel's charting tools to make your data more graphical and give your numbers context.

Graphs or Charts?

Completely ignoring the fact that most of us grew up calling graphs *graphs*, Excel and most other spreadsheet programs insist on calling them *charts*. They're still graphs, but to make Excel happy and to prevent confusion, I'll try to call graphs charts from now on.

Charting Your Data

If you've ever graphed any data in chemistry or math class, you know how tedious it can be. You have to draw your axes and label them, figure out which data to place on each axis, plot your points, and connect the dots. Assuming you didn't draw any points in the wrong spots, your graph eventually revealed some hidden truth that you probably already knew before you started.

To make charting less painful, Excel offers a tool called the Chart Wizard. You select the data you want charted, and then start the Chart Wizard, which leads you step-by-step through the process of creating a chart. All you have to do is enter your preferences. To use the Chart Wizard, take the following steps:

1. Select the data you want to chart. If you typed names or other labels (for example, Qtr 1, Qtr 2, etc.) and you want them included in the chart, make sure you select them.

2. Click the **Chart Wizard** button in the Standard toolbar. The Chart Wizard Step 1 of 4 dialog box appears, asking you to pick the desired chart type. (Ignore the Custom Types tab for now.)

3. Make sure the **Standard Types** tab is up front, and then click the chart type you want in the **Chart Type** list. The Chart sub-type list displays various renditions of the selected type.

4. In the **Chart sub-type** list, click the chart design you want to use. (To see how this chart type will appear when it charts your data, point to **Press and Hold to View Sample** and hold down the mouse button.)

5. Click the **Next>** button. The Chart Wizard Step 2 of 4 dialog box appears, asking you to specify the worksheet data you want to chart. (I know, I already told you to select the data, but the Chart Wizard is just making sure you selected the right data.)

6. If the data you want to graph is already selected, go to step 7. If Chart Wizard is highlighting the wrong data, drag over the correct data in your worksheet. (You can move the Chart Wizard dialog box out of the way by clicking the **Collapse Dialog Box** button that's just to the right of the Data Range text box.)

188

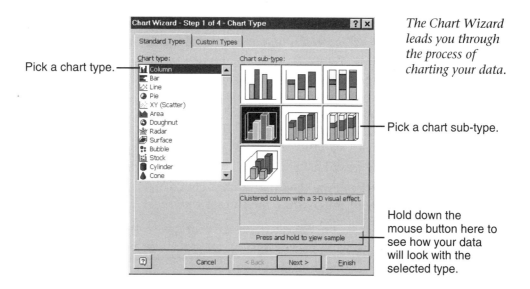

Pick a chart type.

The Chart Wizard leads you through the process of charting your data.

Pick a chart sub-type.

Hold down the mouse button here to see how your data will look with the selected type.

Drag over the data you want to graph.

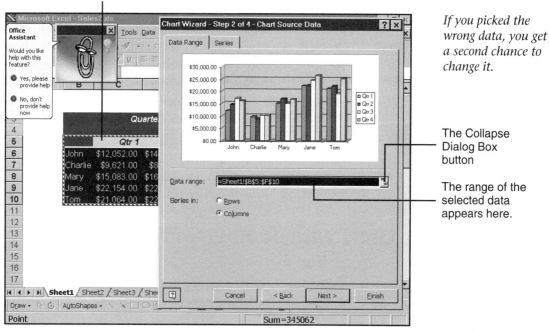

If you picked the wrong data, you get a second chance to change it.

The Collapse Dialog Box button

The range of the selected data appears here.

7. Under Series In, click **Rows** or **Columns** to specify how you want the data graphed. This is a tough choice that is best done by trial and error.

8. Click the **Next>** button. The Chart Wizard Step 3 of 4 dialog box appears, prompting you to enter additional preferences for your chart.

9. Enter your preferences on the various tabs to give your chart a title, name the x- and y-axes, turn on additional gridlines, add a legend, enter data labels, and more. (Most of these options are described in "Adding Text, Arrows, and Other Objects," later in this chapter.)

10. Click the **Next>** button. The Chart Wizard Step 4 of 4 dialog box appears, asking if you want to insert the chart on the current worksheet or on a new worksheet.

11. If you want the chart to appear alongside your data, select **As Object In**. To have the chart appear on a worksheet of its own, select **As New Sheet** and type a name for the sheet.

12. Click **Finish**. Excel makes the chart and slaps it on a worksheet.

Controlled Dragging
When resizing a chart, you can hold down the **Ctrl** key and drag to expand or shrink the chart from the center. You can hold down the **Shift** key and drag to ensure that the chart retains its relative dimensions.

If your chart has only two or three data types to graph, it probably looks okay. If you chose to graph several columns or rows, chances are that all your data labels are scrunched up, your legend is chopped in half, and several other eyesores have popped up. Fortunately, you can fix most of these problems by resizing the chart.

To resize or move a chart, first click on it to select it. Excel displays tiny squares around the chart, called *handles*. To resize the chart, drag one of its handles. To move the chart, position the mouse pointer over the chart (not on a handle), and drag the chart where you want it.

Changing Your Chart with Toolbars, Menus, and Right-Clicks

Before you get your hands dirty tinkering with the many preferences that control the look and behavior of your chart, you need to know where you can find these options.

The first place to look for options is the Chart menu. If you don't see the Chart menu, you haven't selected a chart yet. Click on a chart, and the Chart menu appears. This menu contains options for changing the chart type, selecting different data to chart, adding data, and even moving the chart to its own page.

A quicker way to bring up these same options is to right-click on a blank area of the chart to display a pop-up menu. Why a blank area? Because if you right-click on a legend, axis, title, or other element in the chart, the pop-up menu displays options that pertain to that element, not to the entire chart.

The third way to format your chart is to use the Chart toolbar. To display it, right-click any toolbar and click **Chart**. The Chart toolbar offers the following formatting tools:

> **Chart Objects** displays a list of the elements inside the chart. Select the item you want to format from this list, and then click the **Format Selected Object** button.

 Format Selected Object displays a dialog box that contains formatting objects for only the specified chart object, so you don't have to view a bunch of formatting options you can't apply to it.

 Chart Type lets you change the chart type (bar, line, pie, and so on).

 Legend turns the legend on or off.

 Data Table turns the data table on or off. A data table displays the charted data in a table right next to (or on top of) the chart, so you can see the data and chart next to each other.

 By Row charts selected data by row.

 By Column charts selected data by column.

 Angle Text Downward lets you angle text entries so they slant down from left to right.

 Angle Text Upward lets you angle data labels so they slant up from left to right.

Now that you know the various paths to the chart options, you're ready to tackle some hands-on formatting.

Bar Charts, Pie Charts, and Other Chart Types

Choosing the right chart type for your data is almost as important as choosing the right data. If you want to see how your salespeople are doing relative to each other, a bar chart would clearly illustrate the comparisons. However, if you wanted to show the percentage of the total sales revenue that each salesperson was contributing, a pie chart would be better. Excel offers a wide selection of charts, allowing you to find the perfect chart for your data.

To change the chart type, right-click your chart and click **Chart Type**. The Chart Type dialog box appears, providing a list of chart types from which you can choose. Click the **Standard Types** or **Custom Types** tab (the Custom Types tab offers special chart types most of which are combinations of two chart types, such as a bar chart and a line chart). Select the desired chart type from the **Chart Type** list. On the Standard Types tab, pick the desired chart design from the **Chart Sub-type** list.

Formatting the Elements That Make Up a Chart

The Chart Wizard is pretty good about prompting you to specify preferences when you first create a chart. But if you were in a hurry, you may have skipped some of the options. Maybe you left off the legend or you decided later that you would like to give your chart a title. Whatever the case, you can always add and format chart objects later.

The easiest way to add objects to a chart is to use the Chart Options dialog box. To display this dialog box, right-click on your chart and click **Chart Options**. You can then add or remove the following items:

➤ **Chart Title**   Click the **Titles** tab and type a title in the **Chart Title** text box. The title appears above the chart, providing a general description of it.

➤ **Axis Titles**   Click the **Titles** tab and you can type a title for the vertical (Y) axis or horizontal (X) axis. (Axis titles describe the data that's charted along each axis.)

➤ **X and Y Axes**   Bar, column, line, area, and stock charts all have two axes (X and Y). You can hide either (or both) of these axes by clicking on the Axes tab and removing the check next to the axis you want to hide. This tab is not available for charts that do not use axes (such as pie charts).

➤ **Gridlines**   Every chart that has x- and y-axes displays hash marks along the axes to show major divisions. You can extend these hash marks to run across the chart (sort of like graph paper). Click the Gridlines tab and turn on any gridlines you want to use.

➤ **Legend**   This tab allows you to add a legend to your chart. Legends display a color chart matching each color in the chart to the data that the color represents.

➤ **Data Labels**   The Data Labels tab allows you to add text entries from your worksheet above the various bars or lines that graph specific data. These labels usually make the chart more cluttered than it already is.

➤ **Data Table**   This tab lets you turn on a data table to display specific values alongside the graph. This is another option that will make your chart overly cramped.

Run the Chart Wizard Again

If you love the Chart Wizard, you can use it to add items to your chart. Click on your chart to select it, and then click the **Chart Wizard** button. This displays the Step 1 through Step 4 dialog boxes that you used to create the chart in the first place.

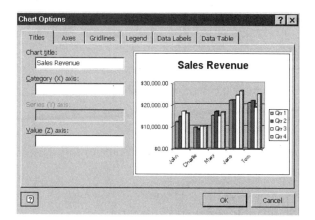

The Chart Options dialog box lets you add items to your chart.

Adding Text, Arrows, and Other Objects

You have a chart decorated with all sorts of embellishments, but it's still missing something. Maybe you want to stick a starburst on it that says "Another Record Year!" or point out to your business partner that the new product he developed five years ago is still losing money.

You can add items to your chart by using the Drawing toolbar. Click the **Drawing** button in the Standard toolbar to turn on the Drawing toolbar. For details on using the Drawing toolbar's tools, see "So You Think You're the Next Picasso," in Chapter 7, "Spicing It Up with Graphics, Sound, and Video."

If you're too lazy to flip back to that chapter (I don't blame you), just rest the mouse pointer on a button to figure out what it does. In most cases, you can draw an object by clicking a button and then dragging the object into existence on your chart. When you release the mouse button, the shape or object appears. You can then drag the object to move it, or drag a handle to resize it. The following figure shows some of the ways you can add to your chart.

193

You can doodle on top of your chart.

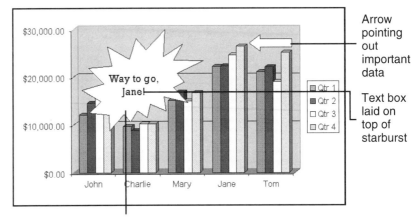

Arrow pointing out important data

Text box laid on top of starburst

Starburst created with AutoShapes

The Least You Need to Know

The Chart Wizard makes it easy to create charts. You can forget almost everything in this chapter, as long as you remember three things:

➤ To create a chart, drag over the data you want to chart, click the **Chart Wizard** button (in the Standard toolbar) and follow the instructions.

➤ To change a chart later, click it, and then click the **Chart Wizard** button again.

➤ You can drag a chart to move it; you can drag a handle to resize the chart.

Chapter 16

Working with Worksheets

In This Chapter

➤ Working with more than one worksheet

➤ Tucking additional worksheets between existing sheets

➤ Naming your worksheets

➤ Grouping and ungrouping worksheets

To this point, we have been working on individual worksheets—typing entries, entering formulas and functions, formatting values and text, and even creating graphs. You may not have even noticed that at the bottom of the worksheet window are tabs for two additional worksheet pages.

In most cases, you won't need these tabs. They just sort of sit there like benign growths. Sometimes, however, the additional worksheets come in handy. For example, if you need to keep track of income and expenses for a small business, you might want to keep each category of expenses on a separate worksheet. In such a case, you will need to learn how to use the tools that Excel provides for working with worksheets.

Scrolling Through and Selecting Worksheets

Chapter 12, "Becoming a Data Entry Clerk," told you almost all you need to know to work with worksheets: You click on a worksheet's tab to select the worksheet, and you right-click for additional options. Here are a couple of additional worksheet tips that might make your life easier:

➤ To the left of the worksheet tabs is a set of four tab scrolling buttons. The two buttons in the middle scroll one tab at a time back or forward. The button on the left displays the first tab, and the button on the right displays the last tab in the workbook.

➤ Hold down the **Shift** key and click one of the middle tab scrolling buttons to scroll several tabs at a time.

➤ To display a menu of worksheets in the workbook, right-click a tab scrolling button. You can then select the desired worksheet from the menu.

➤ To select more than one worksheet, **Ctrl**+click on the tab of each worksheet you want to select. Or, click the first tab you want to select, and then **Shift**+click on the last tab in the range.

Tab scrolling buttons.

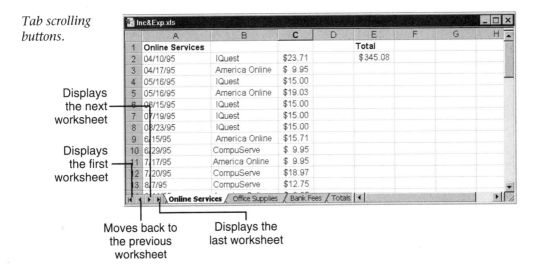

Displays the next worksheet

Displays the first worksheet

Moves back to the previous worksheet

Displays the last worksheet

Adding and Deleting Worksheets

The previous version of Excel got a little carried away with the workbook concept. Whenever you opened a new workbook, Excel presented you with a volume consisting of 16 worksheets, 15 of which you probably would never touch.

In Office 97, Excel has smartened up. Now, new workbooks have three pages. If you need more pages, you can easily insert them as described here:

1. Click the worksheet tab before which you want the new worksheet inserted. The worksheet will be inserted to the left of the selected worksheet.

2. Open the **Insert** menu.

3. To insert a plain, blank worksheet, select **Worksheet**. Excel inserts the new worksheet, naming it Sheet#, where # represents the number of worksheets in your workbook.

The trouble with inserting worksheets, is that you can never insert a worksheet after the last worksheet, which is usually where you want the new sheet placed. To get around that dilemma, insert a worksheet anywhere in the workbook. Then drag the worksheet's tab to the right to move it. For more information about moving worksheets, see "Moving and Copying Worksheets," later in this chapter.

Deleting worksheets is even easier than inserting them. However, you have to be careful. If you delete a worksheet that contains data, you delete the data, too. So before you delete a sheet, make sure it does not contain any data you will need. Then right-click the worksheet's tab and click **Delete**. A warning appears, asking you to confirm the deletion. Click **OK**.

Check This Out...

Right-Click Insert Another way to insert a worksheet is to right-click a worksheet tab and click **Insert**. This displays the Insert dialog box, prompting you to specify the type of object you want to insert. Click **Worksheet** (or click the **Spreadsheet Solutions** tab and pick the desired worksheet template) and click **OK**.

Naming Your Worksheets

Excel learned how to name worksheets from George Foreman, the world champion heavyweight boxer who named all of his sons George. Whenever you create a worksheet, Excel slaps the name "Sheet" on it and adds a number. Of course, that often leaves you wondering what's on a particular sheet. And who knows?

To make it easier for you to tell what's on a worksheet, you should give all your worksheets concise but descriptive names. To name a worksheet, right-click its tab and select **Rename**. The sheet's current name is highlighted on the tab. Type a name for the sheet (up to 31 characters) and press **Enter**. (Keep names short, so the tab doesn't take up the entire tab area.)

As with range names (discussed in Chapter 12, "Becoming a Data Entry Clerk"), tab names are useful when you are entering formulas. If your formula needs to refer to a cell on another worksheet, you'll need to enter the worksheet's name in the cell reference. The easiest way to do this is to use the point-and-click method of creating formulas. However, you can also type cell addresses. For example, if your formula needs a value from cell E5 on a worksheet page called Income, the cell reference would be as follows:

'Income'!E5

Moving and Copying Worksheets

As you work with your workbook, you will start to notice that you use some worksheets more often than others. You get tired of having to scroll to use the worksheet you use most often. The solution: Move that worksheet to the beginning. Moving a worksheet is easy. Click the tab for the worksheet you want to move, and then drag the tab to the left or right. Excel displays a tiny arrow, showing where the sheet will be placed. When the arrow is in the right place, release the mouse button.

To copy a worksheet (and its contents), hold down the **Ctrl** key and drag it to the location where you want to place the copy.

To copy or move a worksheet to another workbook, first make sure both workbooks are open. Then right-click the tab for the workbook you want to copy or move and click **Move** or **Copy**. The Move or Copy dialog box appears. Open the **To Book** drop-down list and select the workbook to which you want to copy or move the selected worksheet. In the **Before Sheet** list, click the worksheet before which you want the selected tabs inserted. If you want to copy the worksheet, select **Create a Copy**. Click **OK**.

You can copy or move selected worksheets to another open workbook.

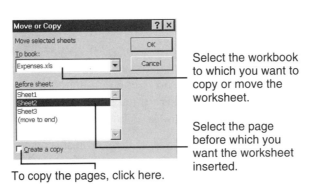

Select the workbook to which you want to copy or move the worksheet.

Select the page before which you want the worksheet inserted.

To copy the pages, click here.

198

Grouping and Ungrouping Worksheets

If you have several worksheets that are similar in design and/or content, you can group the worksheets to work with them as a single unit. For example, you might want to apply the same cell formatting to all the worksheets or type the same entry into the same cell on a several worksheets. You can do this by grouping the worksheets.

To group two or more worksheets, simply select them. Click the tab for the first worksheet you want to include in the group, and then **Ctrl**+click on the tabs for additional worksheets. Or, to group neighboring worksheets, click the tab for the first worksheet and then **Shift**+click the tab for the last worksheet.

When you've grouped worksheets, whatever you enter in a cell on one of the worksheets is inserted into the same cell on all the other worksheets in the group. If you format a cell or cells on one of the worksheets, the same formatting is applied to the same cells on all the other worksheets.

To ungroup the worksheets, click the tab for a worksheet that is not in the group, or right-click a tab for one of the worksheets that is in the group and select **Ungroup**.

The Least You Need to Know

You can keep life simple by creating only one-page workbooks. However, if you ever need to create a workbook with more than one worksheet in it, you should know the basics of working with worksheet tabs:

➤ To work with two or more worksheets, click the tab for the first sheet and **Ctrl**+click on additional tabs.

➤ The tab scroll bar is to the left of the worksheet tabs.

➤ To insert a tab, right-click the tab before which you want the new worksheet inserted and click **Insert**.

➤ To rename a tab, right-click it and click **Rename**.

➤ To move a tab, drag it.

➤ To copy a tab, hold down the **Ctrl** key and drag the tab.

Part 4
Snapping Slide Shows in PowerPoint

You've seen business presentation programs on TV—probably on your favorite sitcom or during the commercial break. Some suit stands in front of a group of other suits, usually in a cramped board room with a big oak table, and flips through a series of slides, pitching a new product or showing how profitable the company is. Each slide is packed with graphs, illustrations, and bulleted lists, carefully designed to drive home the speaker's point.

Now, with PowerPoint and the chapters in this part, you'll get your chance to play slide show presenter. You'll learn how to create a professional-looking slide show; add graphs, pictures, and lists; and display your slide show on your computer screen, or output it on paper, 35mm slides, or even overhead transparencies. You'll even learn how to make a slide show that runs on any PC, even if it's not running PowerPoint!

Chapter 17

Slapping Together a Basic Slide Show

In This Chapter

➤ Using PowerPoint's ready-made slide shows

➤ Changing the overall design of your slides

➤ The five faces of PowerPoint

➤ Controlling all of your slides by changing one master slide

Creating a slide show sounds like a complicated operation. You might wonder if you should have joined the photography club in high school. You know nothing about 35mm cameras, shutter speeds, or f-stops, and you think *exposure* is simply what political candidates want more of.

The fact is that PowerPoint makes it fairly easy to create slide shows. With PowerPoint, you start with a predesigned show, change the background color and design for all your slides, and plop objects (pictures, bulleted lists, graphs, sounds, and video clips) on each slide.

In this chapter, you'll learn how to create a basic slide show in PowerPoint. In later chapters in this part, you will learn how to take control of your slide show and transform it into a real live presentation.

Start from Scratch? Nah!

Most applications greet you with a blank screen, as if daring you to do something. PowerPoint is different. Whenever you start PowerPoint (**Start, Programs, Microsoft PowerPoint**), a dialog box appears, asking you what you want to do. You have four choices: you can use the AutoContent Wizard to help you design a slide show based on what you want to present, you can use a PowerPoint template, you can open a blank presentation (start from scratch? No way!), or you can open a presentation you or someone else has already created.

Assuming you don't have a presentation and you don't want to start from scratch, you'll create a presentation using the AutoContent Wizard or a template. The following sections provide instructions for each method.

Using the AutoContent Wizard

What kind of presentation do you want to create? Are you pitching a marketing strategy, selling a product, training new employees, or advertising your company on the World Wide Web? Whatever you need to do, just tell the AutoContent Wizard and let the wizard lead you through the process of creating a starter slide show. The wizard picks the template you need, lets you specify how you will want to output the presentation, and allows you to give your presentation a title. To use the AutoContent Wizard take the following steps:

1. Start PowerPoint, make sure **AutoContent Wizard** is selected, and click **OK**. The first wizard dialog box appears on your screen—the introduction to AutoContent Wizard. (If this is the first time you have run PowerPoint, the Office Assistant also appears, welcoming you to PowerPoint and offering help.)

   If the startup dialog box is no longer on the screen, there's another way to run the wizard. Open the **File** menu, select **New**, click the **Presentations** tab, and double-click the **AutoContent Wizard** icon.

2. Click the **Next>** button or press **Enter** to continue. The next AutoContent Wizard dialog box displays a long list of presentation types from which you can choose. (You can display the previous dialog box at any time during this process by clicking the <**Back** button.)

3. To narrow the list, click a category button for the type of presentation you want to create. The list on the right changes to display various presentations in the selected category.

4. Click the desired presentation and click the **Next>** button. The next dialog box asks how you intend to use your slide show. Select **Presentations**, **Informal Meetings**, **Handouts**, or **Internet Kiosk**.

Click AutoContent and click OK.

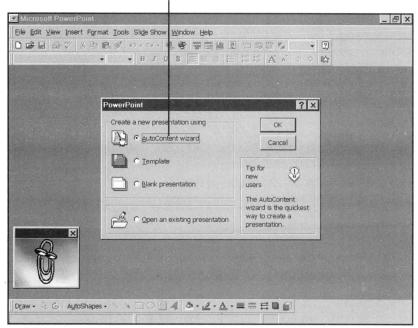

When you start PowerPoint, it asks how you want to proceed.

Select a presentation category.

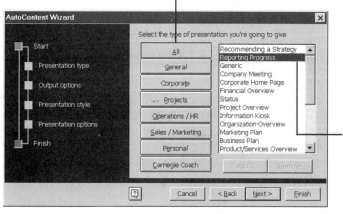

The AutoContent Wizard lets you select from a long list of presentations.

Select the specific presentation you want to create.

5. Select the option that best describes how you intend to use the slide show and click **Next>**. The wizard displays another dialog box asking the type of media you will use to output the presentation.

6. Select the desired output type (**On-Screen presentation**, **Black and White Overheads**, **Color Overheads**, or **35mm Slides**) and specify whether you will want to use handouts. Click **Next>**. The next dialog box asks you to type a title for your presentation.

205

35mm Slides?

If you have the right equipment, you can transfer your presentation to 35mm slides to create a slide show like those used in the old days. If you don't have the proper equipment, you can send your slide show on disk or via modem to a company that does have the required equipment. See Chapter 20, "Shuffling and Presenting Your Slide Show," for details.

7. Type a title for your presentation, and then type your name and any additional text that you want to appear on the first slide in the presentation. Click **Next>**. The last dialog box appears, indicating that you are almost done.

8. Click the **Finish** button. The AutoContent Wizard creates the slide show and displays the first slide on your screen.

When you're done jumping through wizard dialog box hoops, your presentation appears on-screen in Outline view. You'll learn how to work in different views later in this chapter, in "Changing Views to Edit and Sort Your Slides."

When you have a presentation on your screen, PowerPoint should display the new Common Tasks toolbar. This smart toolbar changes its options according to the task you are currently performing to give you quick access to the options you probably need. If the toolbar is not displayed, right-click on any toolbar and select **Common Tasks**.

Dale Carnegie on Your Computer?!

PowerPoint 95 offered a presentation that taught you about the seven habits of highly effective people. In PowerPoint 97, you can pick up some presentation tips from the Dale Carnegie Training seminars. When the AutoContent Wizard displays its list of available templates, click the **Carnegie Coach** button. PowerPoint provides a list of templates for introducing a speaker, motivating a team, selling your ideas, and much more.

Starting with a Template

Like all the other Office 97 applications, PowerPoint comes with many predesigned templates. These templates provide the basic color scheme and design for all the slides in the presentation.

There's no wizardry involved in creating a presentation from a template. After you start PowerPoint, click the **Template** option and click **OK**. Or, open PowerPoint's **File** menu and select **New**. Either way you do it, PowerPoint displays the New Presentation dialog box, offering you a collection of templates for creating various types of presentations.

Click the template you want to use (a sample is displayed in the Preview area) and click **OK**. The New Slide dialog box appears, prompting you to pick a layout for the first slide. Click the desired structure and click **OK**. PowerPoint creates the first slide for you and displays it in Slide view, where you can start editing it.

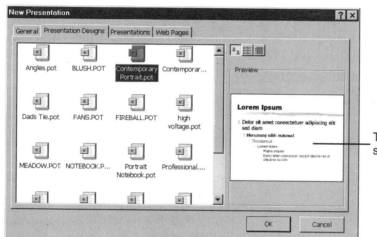

The template supplies the look; you supply the content.

The design of the selected template.

Changing Views to Edit and Sort Your Slides

Assuming that all has gone as planned, you now have a slide show (or at least one slide) on your screen. If you used the AutoContent Wizard, you have a slide show displayed in Outline view. If you used a template, you have a single slide displayed in Slide view. PowerPoint allows you to display your slide show in the five different views, enabling you to work more easily on different aspects of your presentation. Before you start modifying your slide show, familiarize yourself with these different views:

➤ **Slide** is the best view for adding objects (such as titles, lists, graphs, and pictures) to individual slides. See the following section, "Working in Slide View," for details.

➤ **Outline** is best for working on the content of your presentation. Outline view allows you to organize your slides so they flow logically. See "Organizing Your Content in Outline View," later in this chapter, for details.

➤ **Slide Sorter** is great for rearranging the slides in your presentation. Slide Sorter view displays thumbnail versions of each slide, which you can drag to move slides. Slide

Sorter view is explained in greater detail in Chapter 20, "Shuffling and Presenting Your Slide Show."

➤ **Notes Page** displays speaker notes pages (should you choose to create them). A copy of the slide appears at the top of the page, and your notes appear at the bottom. Chapter 20 discusses speaker notes in greater (not much greater) detail.

➤ **Slide Show** is the best view for previewing your slide show. It allows you to check the transitions from one slide to another and test any animation effects you may have added. Again, you'll have to see Chapter 20 for more information.

The easiest way to change from one view to another is to click the button for the desired view in the lower-left corner of the window (see the following picture). If you have something against buttons, you can select the desired view from the View menu. A quick way to change from Outline view to Slide view is to double-click the icon next to the slide's title in Outline view.

Use the View buttons to quickly change from one view to another.

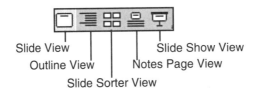

Slide View   Slide Show View

Outline View   Notes Page View

Slide Sorter View

Black and White View

If you're doing a presentation about the films of Woody Allen and Spike Lee (or if you're planning to print your slide show using a black-and-white printer), it's a good idea to change to Black and White view. Open the **View** menu and select **Black and White**, or click the **Black and White View** button in the Standard toolbar.

Working in Slide View

When creating a presentation, you will spend most of your time in Slide view. If you created a slide show using the AutoContent Wizard, you can switch to this view to change slide titles, edit bulleted lists, and insert graphs and other graphics where they are called for.

To work in Slide view, you need to know very little. The most important element in Slide view is the scroll bar. At the bottom of the scroll bar are the Next Slide and Previous Slide buttons (the double-headed arrow buttons). These buttons enable you to quickly move from one slide to the next. You can also drag the scroll box or click the regular scroll bar arrows to move from slide to slide.

While you are in Slide view, click any of the text objects. When you select an object, a box appears around it with several selection handles (small white squares). To work with these text boxes, use any of the following techniques:

➤ To move a box, position the mouse pointer over an edge of the box until it turns into a four-headed arrow, and then drag the box.

➤ To resize a box, position the mouse pointer over one of the handles (the mouse pointer turns into a two-headed arrow). Drag the handle.

➤ To edit text inside a box, drag over the text and type new text.

Turning Toolbars On and Off As with all other Office 97 applications, PowerPoint contains toolbars that allow you to quickly enter commands without having to poke around in a poky menu system. To turn these toolbars on or off, open the **View** menu, point to **Toolbars**, and click a toolbar's name to turn it on or off. You can also display a list of toolbars by right-clicking any toolbar that is displayed.

If you created a slide using the AutoContent Wizard, you probably have at least one slide that has a box telling you to "Double click" to add something. Simply double-click where PowerPoint tells you to click and follow the on-screen instructions. Chapter 18, "Adding Lists, Graphics, and Sounds to a Slide," tells you how to place additional text boxes and other objects on your slides.

Organizing Your Content in Outline View

Most people prefer working in Slide view because they get to look at the pretty slide backgrounds while typing their boring presentation text. However, when you need to look at the big picture and focus on the *content* of your presentation, Outline view is best. In Outline view, you can quickly move slides, rearrange items in a list, move lists, and enter other changes that can make your presentation flow more logically.

To work in Outline view, familiarize yourself with the buttons in the Outlining toolbar:

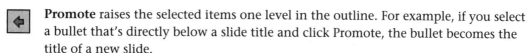 **Promote** raises the selected items one level in the outline. For example, if you select a bullet that's directly below a slide title and click Promote, the bullet becomes the title of a new slide.

Demote lowers the selected items one level in the outline. For example, if you click an item in a bulleted list and click Demote, the bullet becomes part of a bulleted sublist.

Move Up moves any items you select up in the outline. You can use this button to rearrange items on a slide or move items from one slide to another.

Move Down is the same as the Move Up button, but in the other direction. You can also move items up or down by selecting them and then dragging their icons or bullets up or down.

Collapse displays less detail on a slide. Select the slide's title before clicking this button to hide any bulleted items or other subtext.

Expand redisplays the detail on a slide that you hid using the Collapse button.

Collapse All hides all the bulleted text in your slide show, so that only slide titles are displayed.

Expand All redisplays bulleted text that you hid by clicking Collapse All.

Summary Slide inserts a slide that allows you to jump to different slide show sequences. This is an advanced option that requires you to first create two or more custom slide shows (sort of sub slide shows) in the current slide show.

Show Formatting turns the character formatting for the slide show text on or off. (Sometimes you can focus more effectively on the content if you don't have to look at the formatting.)

Controlling the Miniature Slide

In past versions of PowerPoint, Outline view gave no indication of what your slides would look like. In the 97 version, PowerPoint displays a miniature slide. You can change the miniature slide's options by right-clicking it and selecting **Color View**, **Black and White View**, or **Animation Preview**. To close the Miniature Slide window, right-click in its title bar and click **Close**.

Inserting and Deleting Slides

PowerPoint's prefab presentations are great, but they either stick you with a bunch of slides you don't need or they leave you short, providing you with a lone slide that's supposed to divide by some law of cellular biology. In other words, you're going to have to either delete slides or insert them. Deleting slides is pretty easy. In Outline or Slide

Sorter view, you click the slide you want to nuke and press **Delete**. In Slide view, display the slide, open the **Edit** menu, and select **Delete Slide**.

Inserting slides is a little more challenging, but it still doesn't require a college degree. Select the slide after which you want the new slide inserted. Open the **Insert** menu and select **New Slide**, or click the **New Slide** button in the Standard toolbar. The New Slide dialog box appears, asking you to pick an overall layout for the slide. Click the desired layout and click **OK**. PowerPoint inserts the slide, giving it the same background and color as all the other slides in the presentation.

Changing the Background, Color Scheme, and Layout

When you use a wizard or a template to sire your presentation, PowerPoint gives all the slides in the presentation the same overall look, which is usually what you want. However, the color scheme and background design are not carved in stone. You can easily change them for one slide or for all of the slides in the presentation.

To change the background, color scheme, or layout for a single slide, first select the slide. (You don't have to select a slide if you're changing the background or color scheme for the whole show.) Once you select a slide (or choose not to select a slide), read the following sections to learn how to change the background, color scheme, and layout for the slide(s).

Applying a Different Design to the Entire Presentation

When you first created your slide show, you picked an overall look for your presentation that appealed to you at the time. But now it might not look so good to you. No problem. You can change it by picking a different template.

Open the **Format** menu and select **Apply Design**, or click the **Apply Design** button in the Standard toolbar. The Apply Design dialog box appears, displaying a long list of templates. Click on the name of a template that looks promising, and you see a sample of it in the Preview area (you can use the Down Arrow key to step through the list). When you find a design you like, click the **Apply** button.

Check This Out...

Lifting a Design from a Presentation

If you or someone else has already created a custom design for a presentation, you can apply that design to the current presentation. In the Apply Design dialog box, change to the drive and folder where the presentation is stored. From the **Files of Type** drop-down list, select **Presentations and Shows (*.ppt;*.pps)**. You can then click on a presentation to preview its design. If you like it, click the **Apply** button to apply it to your current presentation.

Changing the Background

Behind every slide is a color background. You can change the background color and pattern and even use a picture as your background.

To change the background, open the **Format** menu and select **Background** to display the Background dialog box. If all you want to do is pick a different background color, your job is easy. Open the **Background Fill** drop-down list and select the desired color swatch. To use a custom color, click on **More Colors**, and then use the Colors dialog box to pick a color or create your own custom color.

Colors are swell, but if you want to jazz up a slide show, you need to give your slides a background pattern or texture. To do this, open the Background dialog box, open the **Background Fill** drop-down list, and select **Fill Effects**. The Fill Effects dialog box appears, offering four tabs packed with options for adding shading styles, textures, patterns, or a background picture to your presentation. The best way to get a feel for these options is to experiment, while keeping an eye on the Preview area.

Experiment with the background fill effects to give your background a unique look.

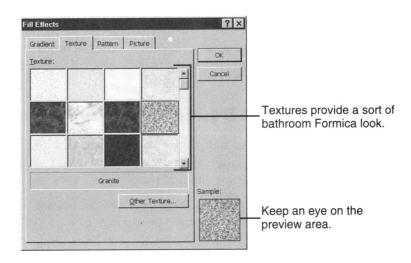

Textures provide a sort of bathroom Formica look.

Keep an eye on the preview area.

Web Work!

If you've spent much time on the World Wide Web, you know that some people have no common sense when it comes to backgrounds. Some backgrounds can make the text on a Web page (or a slide) impossible to read. Before you present your slide show or place it on the Web, preview it and maybe have an honest friend look at it. The background should be attractive, but it shouldn't interfere with your presentation's content.

Picking a Different Color Scheme

Every template is set up to display the various elements on a slide in a different color. Slide titles are one color, bulleted items are another color, and fills are another color. You can change the colors used for the various elements. Open the **Format** menu and select **Slide Color Scheme**.

The Color Scheme dialog box lets you choose a predesigned color scheme or create your own custom color scheme. To stay on the safe side, select one of the prefab color schemes to ensure that you won't have clashing colors or a weird text/background mix. If you're feeling a little adventuresome, click the **Custom** tab and select a color for each element on the slides. When you're done, select **Apply to All** (to apply the new color scheme to all the slides) or **Apply** (to apply the scheme to only the selected slide).

Restructuring a Slide

If you inserted new slides, you have already encountered the Slide Layout dialog box. It displays a bunch of sample slides that allow you to select a structure for a slide. For example, you can create a slide that has a title and a bulleted list; one with a title, a graph, and a bulleted list; one with a title, a picture, and a bulleted list; or ...well, you get the idea.

If you have a slide whose structure you want to change, you have two options: you can manually change the structure by adding or deleting objects from the slide (skip ahead to the next chapter), or you can use the Slide Layout dialog box. Select the slide and click the **Slide Layout** button, or open the **Format** menu and select **Slide Layout**. (To change the layout for more than one slide, **Shift**+click each slide in Slide Sorter view before clicking the Slide Layout button.)

Taking Control with the Master Slide

Behind every good slide show is a good Master slide, which acts as the puppeteer, pulling the strings that make the other slides behave the way they do. The Master slide controls the font and font size for the slide titles and bulleted lists, and it contains any graphics that appear on all the slides. In addition, it inserts the date, slide number, and any other information you want to display on *all* the slides in the presentation.

To display the Master slide, open the **View** menu, point to **Master**, and pick **Slide Master** (or hold down the **Shift** key and click the **Slide View** button in the lower-left corner of the window). Then make any of the following changes to the Master slide that you want to affect all the slides in the presentation:

➤ To change the look of the slide titles, drag over the slide title on the Master slide, and then use the **Font** and **Font Size** drop-down lists in the Formatting toolbar to change the font. For additional font options, open the **Format** menu and select **Font**.

➤ To change the look of the text in bulleted lists, drag over the bullet level, and then use the **Font** and **Font Size** drop-down lists to change the font.

➤ You can place additional text or graphics on the Master slide just as if you were placing them on any slide in the show. See Chapter 18, "Adding Lists, Graphics, and Sounds to a Slide."

➤ If the Master slide has a text box that inserts the date or slide number on every slide, you can edit the text in the box, or you can change its font and alignment.

Format the Master slide to control the look of all the slides in the presentation.

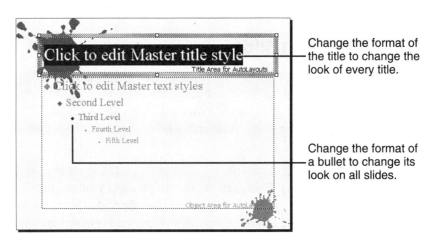

Change the format of the title to change the look of every title.

Change the format of a bullet to change its look on all slides.

Although the Master slide initially controls all aspects of every slide in your slide show, any changes you make to an individual slide override the formatting of the Master slide. For example, you can change the font used for the title on one slide. If you decide later that you want to use the formatting from the Master slide, select the slide that contains the special formatting, click the **Slide Layout** button, and click **Reapply** in the Slide Layout dialog box.

If you add a graphic such as a company logo to the Master slide, it appears on all the slides in the presentation. To prevent the graphic from appearing on a particular slide, select the slide, open the **Format** menu, select **Background**, click **Omit Background Graphics from Master**, and click **Apply**.

The Least You Need to Know

You're at least half done. You now have a collection of slides you can start tweaking in the next few chapters. Whenever you need to create another presentation, keep the following information handy.

➤ When you start PowerPoint, it displays a dialog box in which you can create a presentation using the AutoContent Wizard or a template. The AutoContent Wizard is probably the best way to go.

➤ You can change views to edit and sort your slides. Click the button for the desired view in the lower-left corner of the window.

➤ Slide view is best for editing individual slides. Use Outline view to reorganize the presentation content.

➤ To insert a new slide, click the slide after which you want the new slide inserted, and then click the **Insert New Slide** button in the Standard toolbar.

➤ The Format menu has all the options you need for changing the background, color scheme, and layout for one or all of the slides in your presentation.

➤ To change the look of all the slides in your presentation, make changes to the Master slide.

Chapter 18

Adding Lists, Graphics, and Sounds to a Slide

In This Chapter

➤ Adding titles and bulleted lists

➤ Making your presentation more serious with graphs

➤ Spicing up your presentation with clip art and line drawings

➤ Exploring the third dimension with sound and video

Starting with a template or even with the AutoContent Wizard doesn't give you much to work with. These tools provide you with a background design and color scheme, and they may give you some direction on what to include in your presentation. But most of the slides consist merely of titles, bulleted lists, and an occasional space for a graph. If you decide to go with this arrangement, your audience will be nodding off long before the grand finale.

To keep your presentation interesting and to hook your audience, you need to spice it up with graphics, sound, video and any other media that reduces the time you have to speak and cuts down on the amount of reading your audience has to do. In this chapter, you'll learn how to add various media objects to your slides.

One-Minute Refresher Course on Managing Existing Objects

Throughout this chapter, you're going to be placing new objects on your slides, which may obstruct existing objects. In Chapter 19, "Taking Control of Objects on a Slide," you will learn all about moving, deleting, resizing, and formatting objects. However, as you work through this chapter, you'll need to know the following basics:

Don't Forget the Master
As you insert text and other objects on your slides, don't forget about the Master slide. If you want the text or graphic to appear on all slides in the presentation, insert it on the Master slide. See the end of the previous chapter for details.

➤ Click an object to select it, and tiny white squares called *handles* surround the object. If you select a text box or chart, a gray box, called a *frame*, appears around the object.

➤ To move an object, drag its frame.

➤ To resize an object, drag one of its handles.

➤ To delete an object, press the **Delete** key.

➤ To cut or copy an object, right-click the gray box that defines it, and click **Cut** or **Copy**. You can then paste the object somewhere else, even on another slide.

As If You Didn't Have Enough Text

I know… I just said that your slides were probably *too* texty, and now I'm going to tell you how to add even more text. The problem is that the text boxes you have on your slides might not be the text boxes you want to use.

To insert a text box on a slide, display the slide in Slide view. Then open the **Insert** menu and select **Text Box**. Drag the mouse pointer over the slide where you want the text box to appear, and then release the mouse button. Type your text. For information about formatting the text, transforming it into a list, or changing the text alignment, see Chapter 19, "Taking Control of Objects on a Slide."

Jazzing Up Your Slides with Clip Art and Other Pictures

Office 97 comes with a Clip Gallery that works for all of the Office applications. You may have met the Gallery in Chapter 7, "Spicing It Up with Graphics, Sound, and Video." You can insert clip art pictures from the Clip Gallery into your slides. Take the following steps to do just that:

1. In Slide view, display the slide on which you want to insert the clip.

2. Open the **Insert** menu, point to **Picture**, and click **Clip Art**. The Microsoft Clip Gallery appears.

3. From the list on the left, click the category of clip art from which you want to choose. The list on the right shows small samples of the images in that category.

4. Click the image you want to insert and click the **Insert** button. The Clip Gallery pastes the image on the current slide and displays the Picture toolbar.

5. (Optional) Use the Picture toolbar to touch up the picture (crop it, change its brightness and contrast and so on). See "Touching Up a Picture with the Picture Toolbar," in Chapter 7 for details.

6. You can drag one of the handles that surround the image to resize it, and drag the box that surrounds the image to move it to the desired location.

Click the image you want to insert.

You can decorate your slides with predrawn art from the Clip Gallery.

Click the Insert button.

The Insert, Picture submenu also allows you to insert graphics files that you may have on your hard drive but that are not in the Clip Gallery. Open the **Insert** menu, point to **Picture**, and select **From File**. In the Insert Picture dialog box, pick the graphics file you want to insert.

PowerPoint can handle most common graphics file formats, including JPG, PCX, BMP, Kodak Photo CD, CorelDRAW!, WordPerfect Graphics, and many more. You can add graphic files created in other programs to the Clip Gallery. Display the Clip Gallery dialog box, and then click the **Import Clips** button. Use the Add Clip Art to Clip Gallery dialog box to select the graphic files you want to add, and then click the **Open** button.

219

Adding Shapes, Lines, and Arrows

If none of the predrawn images work for you, you can use the Drawing toolbar to create your own drawings, insert AutoShapes, add lines and arrows, and do much more. This is the same Drawing toolbar you saw in Word. To learn more about using it to draw, see Chapter 7, "Spicing It Up with Graphics, Sound, and Video."

Inserting WordArt Objects on Your Slides

Another tool that makes itself available to all the Office 97 applications is WordArt. With this tool, you can insert text that acts like a graphic object, and you can twist it, stretch it, flip it, and make it perform other gymnastic feats that most text can't even dream of.

To insert a WordArt object on a slide, display the slide in Slide view. Open the **Insert** menu, point to **Picture**, and click **WordArt**. The WordArt gallery appears, displaying a bunch of styles from which you can choose. Click the desired style and click **OK**. In the Edit WordArt Text dialog box, type your text and select the desired font, font size, and attributes (bold or italic). Click **OK**. WordArt inserts the new object on the current slide. You can drag it to move it, or you can drag a handle to resize or reshape the object.

Below the WordArt object is the WordArt toolbar, which you may have met in Chapter 5. This toolbar enables you to change the color, shape, and alignment of the WordArt object, rotate the object, and edit the text. For details, see "Inserting WordArt Objects," in Chapter 5.

A Slide Show Isn't a Presentation Without a Graph

The staple of most effective presentations is the graph (or *chart*, as Microsoft likes to call it). Charts provide a great way of conveying numerical information visually so that your audience doesn't have to think about the numbers in order to grasp their significance.

Inserting Excel Charts If you've already created a chart in Excel, there's no sense wasting your time re-creating it in PowerPoint. Simply copy the chart in Excel, and then paste it on a slide in PowerPoint.

If you created slides with the AutoContent Wizard or with the Slide Layout dialog box, the slide may already have a space for the chart. You should see something like **Double click to add chart**. Double-click the chart icon. If there is no designated space for the chart, click the **Insert Chart** button on the Standard toolbar.

Either way you do it, the Datasheet window appears, displaying some sample data. To enter the data you want to graph, click inside the cell (the box) where you want to insert the data, type your entry, and press **Enter** or use one of the arrow keys to move to the next box. Initially, data is graphed by rows, so the column headings appear below the horizontal (X) axis in the chart. To graph by column (so the row headings appear below the axis), click the **By Column** button in the Standard toolbar.

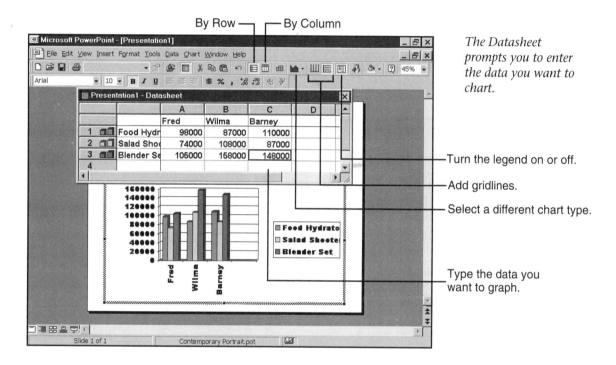

The Datasheet prompts you to enter the data you want to chart.

More Chart Options

When the Datasheet window is displayed, PowerPoint's menu bar changes to include the Chart menu. To pick a different chart type (bar, line, pie, stock, etc.) open the **Chart** menu and select **Chart Type**. The Chart Type dialog box provides a list of chart types a mile long. Pick the desired chart type and click **OK**.

The Chart menu also contains the Chart Options command, which displays the Chart Options dialog box. This dialog box allows you to give your chart a title, add or remove a legend, control the look of the axes, and much more.

To further control the look of the various objects that make up your chart (the legend, axes, colors of the bars or pie pieces), right-click the object whose look you want to change and click the option for formatting it.

Pick a chart type that works for you.

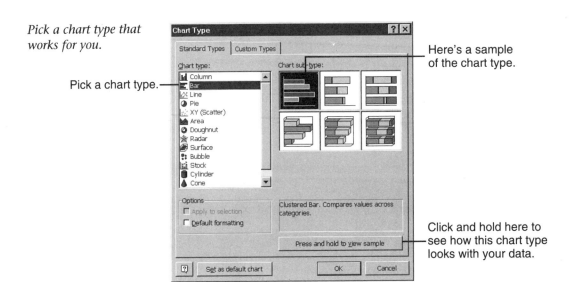

Pick a chart type.

Here's a sample of the chart type.

Click and hold here to see how this chart type looks with your data.

Accepting Your Chart for What It Is

When you're done playing around with your chart, click anywhere outside the Datasheet window and outside the chart area. PowerPoint inserts the chart on the slide. You can then move it and resize it to fit in with the other objects on the slide.

To edit the chart later, simply double-click it. PowerPoint displays the Datasheet window again, adds chart buttons to the Standard toolbar, and displays the Chart menu in the menu bar. When you're done entering changes, click outside the Datasheet window and the chart.

Do-It-Yourself Organizational Charts

Suppose you've landed a job in the personnel department of a major corporation, and it's your job to explain the company pecking order to new employees so they know whom they have to kiss up to in order to climb the corporate ladder. You could type up a list of the managers' names from the top down, but if you really want to etch the hierarchical scheme into the virgin mind of a newcomer, there's no better way to do it than by using an organizational chart.

Inserting a chart on a slide is easy. If you used the Slide Layout dialog box to pick a slide that included an organizational chart, there's a message on the slide telling you to **Double click to add org chart**. Just do it. Or if you prefer, you can open the **Insert** menu, point to **Picture**, and click **Organizational Chart**. The Organizational Chart window appears, prompting you for information.

In each box in the organizational chart, you can type the name, position, and up to two additional comments about a person. Press **Enter** after typing each piece of information. To move from box to box, click a box, or use the arrow keys (the up and down arrow keys move from one level to another; the left and right arrow keys move from box to box on the same level).

If you need more boxes, click on the type of box you need at the top of the screen (for example, Subordinate or Manager), and then click the box to which you want the new box attached.

Selecting One or More Levels

As you are editing, adding to, or enhancing an organizational chart, you will need to select the boxes you want to work with. The following list explains how to select one or more boxes or levels:

➤ To select a single box, click it.

➤ To select more than one box, **Shift**+click additional boxes.

➤ To select a specific group of boxes (for example, all Manager boxes), open the **Edit** menu, point to **Select**, and click the desired group.

➤ To select a specific level in the organization, open the **Edit** menu, choose **Select Levels**, and type the range of levels you would like to select (for example, 2 through 5).

Copying, Moving, and Pasting Boxes

Say the president of your organization has a major mid-life crisis, divorces his wife, and donates his shares of company stock to an ashram in New Delhi. The VP is beside himself. Upper management starts clawing for open positions. Just to keep up, you have to edit your organizational chart daily. How do you do it? Just use the ol' cut and paste commands.

To delete or move a box (and its contents), select the box (or boxes), open the **Edit** menu and select **Cut**. To copy one or more boxes, select them, open the **Edit** menu, and select **Copy**. You can then attach the cut or copied boxes to another box in the organizational chart by clicking the box to which you want to attach the boxes, opening the **Edit** menu, and selecting **Paste**.

Changing the Chart's Appearance

Organizational charts can become unwieldy. They usually end up too shallow and too wide or too long and too narrow. You can change the overall structure of the organizational chart by changing its style. Open the **Styles** menu and select the desired style.

If the overall structure of the organizational chart is sound but the text looks a little drab, you can spruce it up by changing the text font, size, or color. To change the look of all the text in one or more boxes, first select the boxes. To change the look of only a portion of text (for example the job title) in one text box, drag over the text. Open the **Text** menu, select **Font**, and use the Font dialog box to enter your formatting options.

You can also change the look of the lines that define the organizational chart. To do so, first click the boxes and lines whose look you want to change. Then open the **Boxes** menu and point to the item whose look you want to change. From the submenu that appears, select the desired color, style, or shading for the selected lines or boxes.

Once you've perfected your organizational chart, you can insert it on the slide. Click anywhere outside the Organizational Chart window. You can edit the organizational chart at any time by double-clicking it.

Adding Sounds to Your Slide Shows

Does your voice shake when you speak in front of a group? Does your mouth go dry? Do you have a bad case of Tourette's syndrome? Instead of dealing with the cause of the problem, just avoid public speaking altogether! You can do it in PowerPoint by attaching sounds and recordings to your slides. (Of course, there may be other reasons you want to attach sounds to your slides.)

Here's a list of the types of sounds PowerPoint lets you use:

➤ Sounds from the Microsoft Clip Gallery.

➤ Sounds recorded and saved in files on your disk. These files must be in one of the following formats: MID, RMI, or WAV.

➤ CD audio tracks. You can tell PowerPoint to play a specific track from an audio CD in the background while the slide show is playing. Just make sure you have the right CD in the drive when you're presenting your slide show.

➤ Microphone input. PowerPoint can record your voice or whatever else you want to input and display an icon for it on the slide. You can make PowerPoint play the sound automatically during the slide show or whenever you click the icon for the sound.

To insert a sound, first display the slide on which you want the sound to play. Open the **Insert** menu, point to **Movies and Sounds**, and click the desired sound option: **Sound from Gallery**, **Sound from File**, **Play CD Audio Track**, or **Record Sound**.

What you do next depends on the option you selected. The Sound from Gallery and Sound from File options are fairly straightforward: you select the audio clip or sound file you want to use and then confirm the action. If you chose Play CD Audio Track, use the Play Options dialog box to select the track on which you want PowerPoint to start playing and the track on which PowerPoint should stop playing. If you chose **Record Sound**, the process is a bit more complicated; see the following section for details.

Attaching a Recorded Sound to a Slide

If you chose the Insert, Movies and Sounds, Record Sound option, you now have the Record Sound dialog box on your screen. First, make sure your microphone is connected to your sound card and is turned on. Drag over the entry in the **Name** text box and type a name for the recording. When you are ready to speak, click the **Record** button and start speaking into the microphone (or making whatever sound you want to record). When you're done recording, click the **Stop** button and click **OK**. PowerPoint inserts a little speaker icon on the slide. Drag it to where you want it to appear. You can double-click the speaker icon to play the recorded sound.

Assuming you present your slide show on-screen (instead of with 35mm slides, overhead transparencies, or handouts), whenever you advance to a slide on which you have placed a sound, the speaker icon appears. To play the sound, double-click the icon.

You can make it so the sound plays automatically whenever you advance to the slide. You do this by adding animation effects, which are described in greater detail in Chapter 20, "Shuffling and Presenting Your Slide Show." Here's a quick rundown of what you need to do:

1. Open the **Slide Show** menu and click **Custom Animation**.
2. Click the **Effects** tab.
3. Under **Entry Animation and Sound**, open the first drop-down list and click **Appear**.
4. Open the second drop-down list and click the sound you recorded. Click **OK**.

You can make sounds play automatically when you advance to a slide.

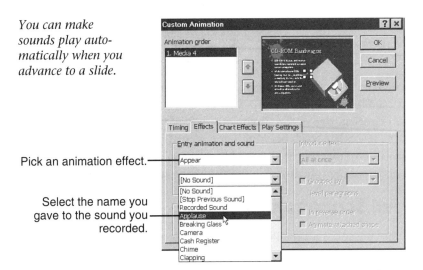

Pick an animation effect.

Select the name you gave to the sound you recorded.

Narrating an Entire Slide Show

You could use the Record Sound option as described in the previous section to narrate your slide show. Just add a separate recorded sound to each slide. An easier way to narrate an entire slide show is to use the Narration feature. With this feature, you simply advance through the slide show while speaking into your microphone. PowerPoint records your voice and attaches your narrative to the correct slide.

Before you start recording, you should know how to pause and resume your narration. To pause the narration, right-click anywhere on the slide and click **Pause Narration**. To resume, right-click and choose **Resume Narration**. Okay, turn on your microphone and follow these steps to get started:

1. Open the **Slide Show** menu and click **Record Narration**. The Record Narration dialog box appears, showing how many minutes of recording time you have (based on the free space on your hard drive).

2. Click **OK**. PowerPoint changes to Slide Show view.

3. Start narrating your slide show by speaking into your microphone. Click anywhere on the slide to advance to the next slide. Keep talking. Although it looks as though PowerPoint is doing nothing, it is actually recording your voice. At the end of the show, a message appears, asking if you want to save the timing of the slide show along with your narration.

4. To save the slide timing along with the narration, click **Yes**. To save the narration without the timing, click **No**. PowerPoint displays a speaker icon in the lower-right corner of each slide you added narration to.

When you run the slide show, the narration will automatically play with the show. To run the slide show without narration, open the **Slide Show** menu and click **Set Up Show**. Select **Show Without Narrations** and click **OK**.

The recording toolbar

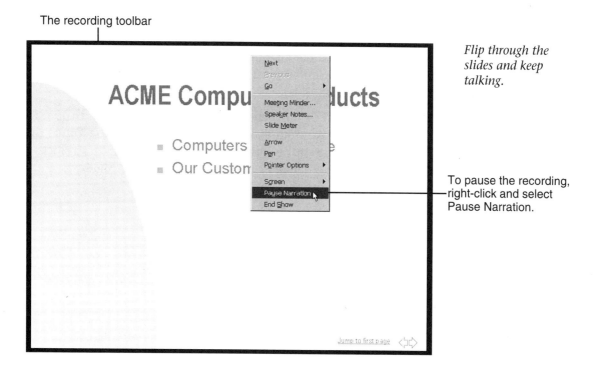

Flip through the slides and keep talking.

To pause the recording, right-click and select Pause Narration.

Going Multimedia with Video Clips

Even though the computer offers about the worst video quality imaginable, everyone seems to think that no presentation or Web page is complete without a video clip. PowerPoint has followed this lead by making it possible for you to insert video clips into your slide show.

To insert a video clip, display the slide into which you want to insert the clip. Then open the **Insert** menu, point to **Movies and Sound**, and click one of the following options: **Movie from Gallery** (you'll need to insert the Microsoft Office 97 CD) or **Movie from File**. If you selected the Gallery option, the Microsoft Clip Gallery dialog box appears, presenting you with a list of feature films from which to choose. If you selected the File option, use the Insert Movie dialog box to pick a flick from your disk. PowerPoint supports most movie clip formats, including MPG, MPE, and VDO, so anything you lift off the Web should work.

Adding Slide Numbers, Dates, and Other Novelties

If you created a slide show using a template or the AutoContent Wizard, your Master slide should have a footer that inserts the date, the slide number, and a tiny bit of text at the bottom of each slide.

You can turn off or change any of this footer information. Open the **View** menu and click **Header and Footer**. The Header and Footer dialog box appears, with the **Slide** tab up front. Change any of the following options and click **Apply to All** (or click **Apply** to enact your changes for only the current slide):

➤ **Date and Time** Make sure this box has a check in it if you want the date to appear in the footer area. Select **Update Automatically** and pick the desired date format to have PowerPoint automatically insert the current date from your computer's clock. Or, select **Fixed** and type the date that you want to display on all the slides.

➤ **Slide Number** To insert the slide number on each slide, make sure this box is checked.

➤ **Footer** To insert additional text in the footer area, select this option and type your text.

➤ **Don't Show on Title Slide** To prevent any footer information from appearing on the first slide in your show, select this option.

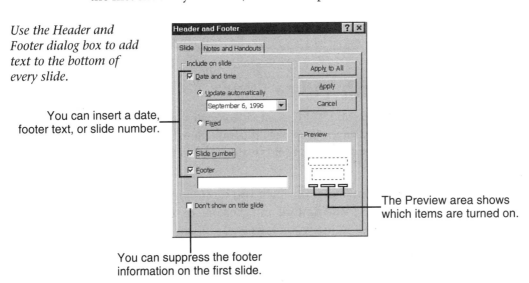

Use the Header and Footer dialog box to add text to the bottom of every slide.

You can insert a date, footer text, or slide number.

The Preview area shows which items are turned on.

You can suppress the footer information on the first slide.

228

To change the appearance or location of the date, footer text, or slide number, make your changes to the Master slide. To learn how to view the Master slide and work with it, check out the end of Chapter 17, "Slapping Together a Basic Slide Show."

The Least You Need to Know

When you break a slide show down into its component parts, as we have in this chapter, it becomes clear that a slide show isn't all that complicated:

➤ A slide show consists of a collection of slides.

➤ Each slide has one or more objects that you stick on a background layer.

➤ You can add a text box, WordArt object, picture, sound, video clip, or any other object by selecting it from the Insert menu.

➤ If you want to get an "A" on your first slide show, be sure to add a couple of charts.

➤ The best way to show the hierarchical structure of corporate America is to use an organizational chart.

➤ You can narrate your slide show so that you can golf while your colleagues are watching it on their big-screen home PC-TV units.

Taking Control of Objects on a Slide

In the previous chapter, you sprinkled text boxes, graphics, and other objects on your slides. Now your slides might look a little cramped and overdone. Maybe the chart you added is blocking the view of your bulleted list, or your slide titles are so large that you can't fit anything else on the slide.

In this chapter, you'll learn how to take control of the objects on your slide, to change their appearance, position, and size. You'll learn a lot of other things, too.

Giving Your Text a Unique Look

When you create slides using the AutoContent Wizard or the Insert, New Slide option, the Master slide dictates the formatting on the slide. If you type in the slide title text box, the text appears big and bold. In the other text boxes, whatever you type usually ends up as a bulleted list.

You need some way to control the look and layout of the text inside these boxes and the text inside any new text boxes you've created (in Chapter 18). The following sections show you how to take control.

Right-Click Formatting

If you're ever wondering what you can change about an object on a slide, right-click the object. This displays a pop-up menu showing you most of the formatting options available for the object.

Selecting and Formatting Text in Different Views

In Chapter 17, you learned the benefits of the various views that PowerPoint offers. Before you start reformatting your text, you must consider which view is best for what you want to do:

➤ Slide Master view enables you to change the appearance of the text on all the slides. To give your slide titles and bulleted lists a consistent look, enter your formatting changes on the Master slide. (If you added text boxes to individual slides, the Master slide does not control text in these boxes.)

➤ Slide view displays individual slides. To give the text on a slide a look that differs from text on the Master slide, enter your change in Slide view. This view also allows you to see how your text will appear on the slide.

➤ Outline view displays only text, showing you how the text on one slide looks next to the text on other slides. Outline view is excellent for changing the font or font size of all text on all slides in the show. For example, you can open the **Edit** menu, choose **Select All**, and then select a different font from the **Font** drop-down list in the Formatting toolbar. Or you might click the **Increase Font Size** button or the **Decrease Font Size** button to change the size of the text.

To select text in any view, simply drag over it with your mouse. Double-click a word to select it, or triple-click inside a paragraph to select the entire paragraph. In Outline view, you can select all the text on a slide by clicking the slide icon or the number next to the slide title. In Slide view, you can select all the text inside a text box by selecting the text box and pressing **Ctrl+A**.

Select a font here. Select all the text. Decrease Font Size

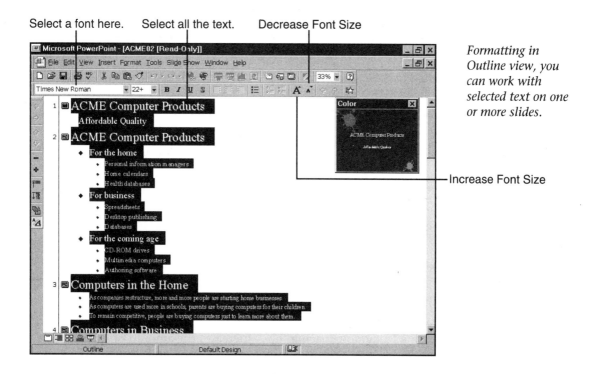

Formatting in Outline view, you can work with selected text on one or more slides.

Increase Font Size

Changing Fonts, Sizes, and Other Text Attributes

Once you have selected the text you want to format, the easiest way to format it is to use the drop-down lists and buttons in the Formatting toolbar. These controls work like the formatting controls you use in Word and Excel. For example, if you want to make the text in one of your slides bold, select the text and click the **Bold** button. (You can also open the **Format** menu and choose the **Font** command to change formatting.) If you want to change the point size of the text, click the **Increase Font Size** button or use the **Font Size** drop-down list. The following table provides an overview of the available formatting tools.

Formatting Toolbar: Buttons and Drop-Down Lists

Icon	Name	Description
Arial	Font	Displays type styles
24	Font Size	Displays font sizes in points
B	Bold	Bolds text or numbers

continues

233

Formatting Toolbar: Buttons and Drop-Down Lists   Continued

Icon	Name	Description
I	Italic	Italicizes selected text
U	Underline	Underlines text
S	Shadow	Creates a shadow effect
≡	Left Alignment	Pushes text to the left
≡	Center Alignment	Centers text
≡	Right Alignment	Pushes text to the right
≔	Bullets	Turns bulleted list on or off
≣	Increase Paragraph Spacing	Increases the amount of space between lines and paragraphs
≣	Decrease Paragraph Spacing	Decreases the amount of space between lines and paragraphs
A	Increase Font Size	Increases size with one click
A	Decrease Font Size	Decreases size with one click
⬅	Promote	Raises selected text to the next level in the outline
➡	Demote	Lowers selected text to the next level in the outline

You'll also find these same formatting controls on the Format menu. Use the Fonts command to change the type style, size, and color of the text. Select the **Format, Line Spacing** command to change the line spacing within and between paragraphs. And display the **Format, Alignment** submenu to specify how you want PowerPoint to align the selected text in the text box.

Taking Control of Bulleted Lists

Effective slide show presentations don't have huge blocks of text that the audience is supposed to read. The slide shows highlight key points by using bulleted lists. As you fine-tune your slide show, you may feel the need to take control of these lists. Because the Master slide controls most of the bulleted lists, you'll probably want to change to the Slide Master view to enter your changes. If you want to create your own bulleted list, work in Slide view.

You can change two aspects of a bulleted list: the bullet itself, and the distance that the list is indented. To change the look of the bullet, perform the following steps:

1. Select the text in the bulleted list. If you are working on the Master slide, click anywhere inside the bullet level you want to change. In Slide view, you must select all the items in the bulleted list.

2. Open the **Format** menu and select **Bullet**. The Bullet dialog box appears.

3. Open the **Bullets From** drop-down list and click a font to display the available symbols you can use for a bullet. A collection of symbols appears at the bottom of the dialog box.

4. Click the symbol you want to use as the bullet. (Hold down the mouse button to see a larger version of the bullet.)

5. Open the **Color** drop-down list and click the color you want to use for the bullet.

6. Use the **Size** spin box to set the size of the bullet as a percentage of the text size.

7. Click **OK**.

Making Numbered Lists You can use the indent markers to create numbered lists, too. Just set the indents as you normally would, and use numbers in place of bullet symbols.

Once you have the bullet you want to use, you might consider adjusting the indent. The best way to do this is to use the ruler. Open the **View** menu and select **Ruler** to turn on the layout rulers. Indent markers appear, showing the current indents. Drag the top marker to where you want the bullet placed. Drag the triangular part of the bottom marker to where you want the text placed. (You can drag the rectangular portion of the bottom marker to move both indent markers but retain their relative positions.) If you selected a bulleted list that contains a bulleted sublist, the ruler shows two sets of indent markers.

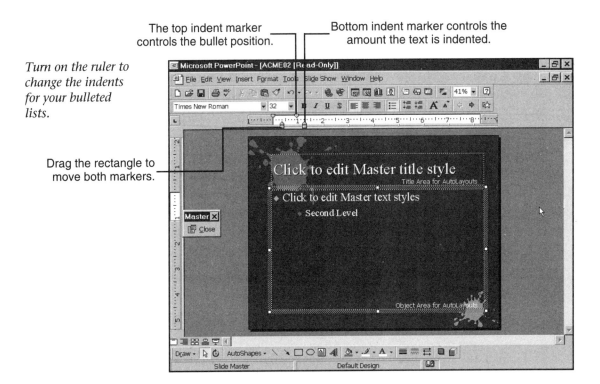

The top indent marker controls the bullet position.

Bottom indent marker controls the amount the text is indented.

Turn on the ruler to change the indents for your bulleted lists.

Drag the rectangle to move both markers.

Move It! Repositioning and Sizing Objects

Slides seem large until you start dropping in 40-point titles and 30-point bulleted lists. As the landscape shrinks, you may suddenly feel the need to resize, reposition, crop, and delete some objects to make the best use of space. The following sections provide the basic instructions you need to shuffle the objects on your slides. They also offer a few tips and tricks for more precise movement.

Selecting Objects Buried Under Other Objects

As you stack objects on a slide, some objects are bound to end up at the bottom of the stack. If you need to work with an object at the bottom, you must first bring it up front. If any portion of the object is visible, you can bring it to the front by clicking it.

However, if the object is completely buried, you need to use another technique. To rearrange the objects in a stack, you can use the Order options. To do so, right-click an object, click **Order**, and click the desired option:

➤ **Bring to Front** brings the selected object to the front of the stack.

➤ **Send to Back** sends the selected object all the way to the bottom of the stack.

➤ **Bring Forward** moves the selected object up one layer in the stack.

➤ **Send Backward** moves the selected object back one layer.

Resizing, Moving, Copying, and Deleting Objects

When you select an object (a text box, graphic, chart), tiny squares called *handles* surround it. If you select a text box or a chart, a gray box called a *frame* appears around the text box. You can then use these methods to move, resize, copy, and delete objects:

➤ To move a text box or chart, drag its frame. To move a graphic, drag any part of the image.

➤ To move an object from one slide to another, select the object, open the **Edit** menu, and select **Cut**. Change to the slide on which you want the object placed, open the **Edit** menu, and select **Paste**.

➤ To resize an object, drag one of its handles. Hold down the **Ctrl** key and drag to resize the object from the center out. Hold down the **Shift** key and drag to retain the relative dimensions of the object.

➤ To delete an object, press the **Delete** key. (With some objects, this may not work; you may have to open the **Edit** menu and select **Delete**.)

Drag the box around an object to move it.

Drag a handle to resize the object.

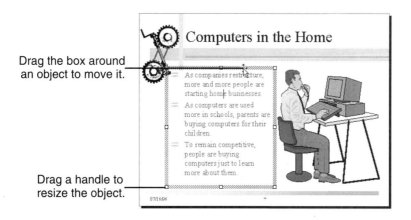

You can move or resize an object using the box that surrounds the object.

Precise Positioning with Rulers and Guides

If you have a good eye for graphics, you can probably drag items around on slides until the slide looks good. However, for the rest of us, PowerPoint offers a couple of alignment tools that help us position objects more precisely: rulers and guides.

You may have already encountered rulers if you changed the bulleted list indents earlier in this chapter. To turn rulers on or off, open the **View** menu and select **Ruler**. In addition to helping you set indents for paragraphs and lists, the rulers can help you align objects on a slide. Whenever you drag an object, a dotted line appears in the rulers, showing the position of the object's edges. These indicators can help you position an object at a specific location on the slide.

Guides are useful for setting the position of an object relative to another object. To turn on the guides, open the **View** menu and select **Guides**. The guides appear on your screen as a vertical and a horizontal dotted line that intersect near the middle of the slide. As you drag an object over a guide, the object's edge or center point "sticks" to the guide (as if the guide were magnetic). Using a guide is a simple two-step process:

1. Drag the guides so they align with another object on the slide. For example, if you want to align another object with the title, drag the guides so they align with some point on the title (maybe the bottom and left side of the title).

2. Drag the object toward the guides until it sticks to the guides.

More Control with the Drawing Toolbar

Although you can spice up your presentations by changing the look and color of your text, you can do more by changing the look of boxes that surround the various objects on your slides. The Drawing toolbar offers controls that enable you to add borders and shading to boxes, place boxes and their contents on an angle, give boxes a third dimension, and much more.

The Drawing toolbar should be displayed at the bottom of the PowerPoint window. If it's not there, turn it on (open the **View** menu, point to **Toolbars**, and click **Drawing**). Although the main purpose of the Drawing toolbar is to enable you to draw lines, shapes, and arrows on your slides, the following tools also enable you to control the look of existing objects, such as text boxes and graphics:

Free Rotate lets you spin the object. When you click this button, little green circles surround the selected object. Drag a circle clockwise or counterclockwise to spin the object. You can spin a text box to place the text at an angle on a slide.

Fill Color colors inside the lines like in a coloring book. Click the button to fill the object with the color that's shown. To change the fill color, click the arrow next to this button and select the color from the menu.

Line Color changes the color of the line that defines the shape. Click the button to use the color that's shown. To change the color, click the arrow next to this button and select the color from the menu. (This option does nothing until you select a Line Style from the toolbar.)

Font Color is for text boxes only. Drag over the text inside the box, and then open this menu and select the desired color.

Line Style displays a menu from which you can choose the line thickness and style you want to use for the line that defines the shape. This enables you to add a border around an object.

Dash Style lets you use dashed lines instead of solid lines.

Arrow Style lets you pick an arrow type to use. Arrows come in handy if you need to label a figure or point out trends on a chart.

Shadow works only for ovals, rectangles, AutoShapes, and other two-dimensional objects (including text boxes). This menu contains various drop-shadow styles you can apply to objects.

3-D works for ovals, rectangles, AutoShapes, and text boxes. It turns rectangles into blocks and ovals into cylinders. The options on this menu are great for making text boxes stand out on a slide.

Many of the Drawing toolbar buttons are not listed here because they don't control the look of existing objects. However, don't overlook these options. The AutoShapes menu, for example, is very useful for adding such predefined shapes as starbursts, banners, and callouts, to your slides. For details on how to draw with these tools, see Chapter 7, "Spicing It Up with Graphics, Sound, and Video."

Check This Out...

Treating Objects As a Group

If you have several objects on a slide that you want to resize and move as a single object, group them. Click the **Select Objects** arrow in the Drawing toolbar and drag a selection box around the objects you want to include in the group. Handles appear around all the objects. Right-click one of the selected objects, point to **Grouping**, and click **Group**. A single set of handles appears around the group. Drag the group to move it, or drag a handle to resize it.

239

Finding and Replacing Text or Fonts

As you're working with a presentation, certain terminology may be in transition. For instance, say your company is developing a new tool for unclogging drains, and so far the company has called it the SuperSucker. You put together a presentation for your sales department, boasting of the SuperSucker's performance. However, due to design issues, the engineering department changes the tool so that instead of sucking the clog out of the plumbing, the tool blows it out. The name changes from SuperSucker to ClogBlower. Now you have to consistently replace "SuperSucker" with "ClogBlower."

Changing Fonts on the Master Slide If the Master slide is controlling the fonts you want to replace, don't bother with the Replace Fonts command. Simply display the Master slide and enter your font changes on it. This replaces the fonts used for all the other slides in the show.

Instead of flipping through the slides one-by-one and facing the risk of missing an occurrence of SuperSucker, you can have PowerPoint make the replacement for you. Open the **Edit** menu and select **Replace**. In the **Find what** text box, type the word or phrase you want to replace. In the **Replace with** text box, type the replacement word or phrase. To replace all occurrences of the word or phrase, click **Replace All**. To have PowerPoint ask for your confirmation each time, click **Find Next** and proceed through the slide show, replacing only the desired occurrences of the word or phrase.

In addition to replacing text, PowerPoint can replace the fonts you've used in your presentation to give your slides a more consistent look. To replace a font, open the **Format** menu and select **Replace Fonts**. Open the **Replace** drop-down list and select the font you want to replace. Then open the **With** drop-down list and select the replacement font. Click the **Replace** button, and PowerPoint replaces one font with the other throughout the slide show, but does not change any of the font sizes. To change the font sizes, you must enter your changes on each slide or on the Master slide.

Checking Your Spelling

When you are working with small chunks of text, such as slide titles and bulleted lists, it is easy to overlook spelling errors. You figure that with such brief text entries, there's no way you could possibly overlook a spelling error or typo. However, a spelling error in a presentation is much more embarrassing than a spelling error in a printed report. The presentation is live, and you have to continue speaking while you hear people talking about your lousy spelling. To avoid embarrassment, check your spelling.

Spell Checking on the Fly

As in Word, the spell checker in PowerPoint checks your spelling as you type. If you type a misspelled word or a word that the spell checker has no match for, the spell checker displays a squiggly red underline below the word. You then have the following options:

➤ Ignore it. Maybe it's correct.

➤ Backspace over the misspelled word and type your correction.

➤ Right-click the misspelled word and select the correct spelling from the pop-up menu.

➤ Right-click the word and select **Ignore All** to have Word remove the red line and never question the spelling of this word in this document again.

➤ Right-click the word and select **Add** to add the word to Word's spelling dictionary.

Change the Spelling Options

You can turn off automatic spell checking and enter other options for the spell checker. Open the **Tools** menu, select **Options**, and click the **Spelling** tab. To turn off the automatic spell checking feature, click **Spelling** (under Check Spelling As You Type) to remove the check mark.

Checking the Spelling in Your Entire Slide Show

If you turn off the automatic spell checker, you can check for misspellings and typos throughout your slide show whenever you want to. To start checking your slide show, click the **Spelling** button. PowerPoint starts checking your slide show for typos and spelling errors, and it stops on the first questionable word. The Spelling dialog box displays the questionable word and usually displays a list of suggested corrections.

If the word is incorrect and you see the correct spelling in the list of suggested corrections, click the correct spelling and choose **Change** or **Change All**.

If the word is spelled correctly, you have several options. To add the word to the spelling dictionary so PowerPoint won't question it again, click **Add**. To skip only this occurrence of the misspelling, select **Ignore**. To skip all occurrences of this word, click **Ignore All**.

PowerPoint checks for spellings and typos, and offers suggestions.

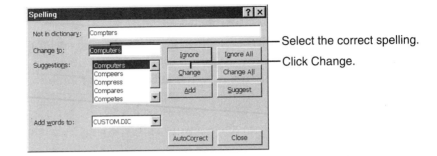

The Least You Need to Know

You could just drop objects on a slide and make them fight for slide space, but then your slide show probably wouldn't make it on the First Annual MTV PowerPoint Awards show. You need to know a few tricks to take more control over the objects on a slide.

➤ To select an object, click it.

➤ To move an object, drag the gray box that surrounds it.

➤ To resize an object, drag one of its handles.

➤ The Formatting toolbar has most of the tools you need to change the look of your text. Drag over the text and then select your preferences from the toolbar.

➤ In a bulleted list, you can change two things: the appearance of the bullet and the distance that the text is indented.

➤ The Drawing toolbar offers several tools that enable you to add borders, shading, and color to your text boxes.

Chapter 20

Shuffling and Presenting Your Slide Show

In This Chapter

➤ Shuffle your slides in Slide Sorter view

➤ Animate an on-screen slide show with special effects

➤ Rehearse and give on-screen presentations

➤ Create speaker notes and handouts

Before you lift the curtain for your slide show presentation, leave it for a day or two, and then come back and try to look at it from the perspective of your audience. Maybe you need to tweak one or two slides, move a bulleted list, fix a chart, or perform some other minor maintenance in Slide view.

You also may need to make some more substantial changes, such as rearranging your slides and animating your slides to make your presentation more active. Before you take the stage, you may want to draw up some speaker notes, prepare handouts for your audience, and even rehearse. This time spent in preparation will help you perfect your slide show and will help you become more comfortable presenting it. In this chapter, you'll learn how to use PowerPoint's power presentation tools to do all this and more.

Rearranging Your Slides

When creating a slide show, you usually focus on individual slides, making each slide the best it can be. When you step back, however, you notice less of what's on each slide, and more of how the slides are arranged in your presentation. From this bird's eye perspective, you may notice that you need to rearrange the slides in your presentation.

The following sections show you how to step back in Outline and Slide Sorter view, and how to drag your slides to different positions in the presentation.

Rearranging Slides in Slide Sorter View

The best view for arranging slides is Slide Sorter view. In this view, PowerPoint displays a small version of each slide. To change to Slide Sorter view, click the **Slide Sorter View** button. You can use the scroll bar to scroll down the list of slides.

Do you see a slide that would look better in another location? No problem. Position the mouse pointer over the slide you want to relocate, hold down your mouse button, and drag the slide to the desired location. As you drag, a vertical line appears, showing where PowerPoint will insert the slide. When you release the button, the slide moves to the new position. To copy a slide (instead of moving it), hold down the **Ctrl** key and drag.

In Slide Sorter View, you can move slides by dragging them.

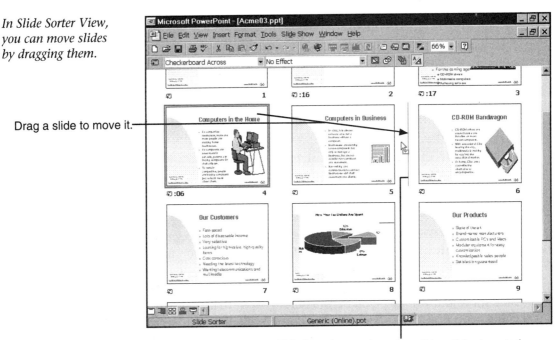

Drag a slide to move it.

This line shows where the slide will be inserted.

Although Slide Sorter view offers the most graphical way to shuffle your slides, Outline view also allows you to easily move slides. Before you move slides in Outline view, you may want to collapse your outline so that PowerPoint displays only the slide titles (no bulleted lists or other text). To collapse the outline, first change to Outline view (click the **Outline View** button) and then click the **Collapse All** button in the Outlining toolbar.

You can then move a slide by dragging the slide icon next to the slide title up or down in the outline. As you drag, a horizontal line appears, showing where PowerPoint will insert the slide. Release the mouse button when the line is where you want it. You can also move a slide by clicking the **Move Up** or **Move Down** arrow in the Outlining toolbar.

Adding Special FX

Now for the fun stuff. Adding effects to your presentation can really jazz up the message, and keep your audience awake. For example, if you plan to present your slide show using a computer, you can animate the transitions from one slide to the next. Perhaps you want one slide to fade out while the next fades in, or maybe you would like a vertical blind effect—when you draw the blinds, the next slide appears on the back of the blinds.

What's on the Slide Sorter Toolbar?

First up, let's finish looking at all the details found in Slide Sorter view. Switch to Slide Sorter view by clicking the **Slide Sorter View** button at the bottom of your screen. Each slide in your presentation appears on-screen, as shown in the next figure. You also see the Slide Sorter toolbar. As you begin working with slide effects in the paragraphs to come, you'll have occasion to use the Slide Sorter toolbar to assign effects or open dialog boxes. This table explains what each toolbar button does:

Slide Sorter Toolbar Buttons

Toolbar Button	Name	Description
	Slide Transition	Opens the Slide Transition dialog box, which offers options for animating the transition from one slide to the next.
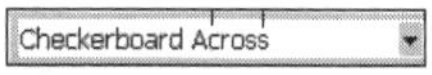 Checkerboard Across	Slide Transition Effects	Displays a list of animation effects for slide transitions.

continues

Slide Sorter Toolbar Buttons Continued

Toolbar Button	Name	Description
Fly From Left ▾	Text Preset Animation	Allows you to animate the movement of bulleted lists and other text on the screen. For example, you can make items on a list fall onto a slide from above.
▣	Hide Slide	Hides the currently selected slide, so it will not appear in the show.
▣	Rehearse Timings	Switches to Slide Show view and provides a dialog box that lets you set the amount of time each slide remains on the screen.
🗗	Summary Slide	Allows you to create a slide that links you to other slides in the presentation.
ᴬ₄	Show Formatting	Turns your presentation's formatting on or off.

I will soon explain how to use the elements described in this table, so be patient and keep reading.

The Slide Transition dialog box.

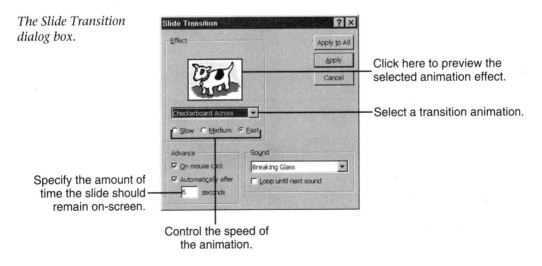

Click here to preview the selected animation effect.

Select a transition animation.

Specify the amount of time the slide should remain on-screen.

Control the speed of the animation.

Animating the Transition from Slide to Slide

Back when I was in school, slide show timing and narration was in its beginning stages. A slide show came with a phonograph record that contained the slide show narration and sounded a beep whenever it was time for the next slide. One student was always in charge of listening for the beep and then manually advancing the slide. The timing was always off, but it gave rise to some humorous moments.

If you are planning to present your slide show with 35mm slides or overhead transparencies, your transitions may retain some of this vintage humor. However, if you're using a computer to project your slide show, you can time the transitions and add interesting animation effects. Here's how:

1. To create an animated transition for only one slide, click the slide. (Usually, you will want to use the same animated effect for all slides in the show, in which case you do not need to select a slide.)

2. In Slide Sorter view, click the **Slide Transition** button. The Slide Transition dialog box appears.

3. Open the **Effect** drop-down list and pick a transition option. Look in the preview area (above the list) to see a demonstration of the transition.

4. Under the Effect drop-down list, click **Slow**, **Medium**, or **Fast** to set a speed for the transition.

5. Under Advance, select **On Mouse Click** to advance slides whenever you click the mouse, or select **Automatically, After ___ Seconds** to have PowerPoint automatically display the next slide for you.

6. To add a sound to the transition, open the **Sound** drop-down list and select the desired sound. (If you want to use a sound not found on the list, select **Other Sounds** and locate the sound file you want to use.) To have the sound continue to play until the next sound starts, click **Loop Until Next Sound**.

7. When you finish with the dialog box, click **Apply**.

Using Animated Builds

Slide transitions are cool, but you can use them only on entire slides. PowerPoint also offers animation effects for objects on the slide. For example, you can make your slide text appear on-screen as if it is being typed; you can even accompany the animation with the clicking sounds of a keyboard. Or how about making your slide title drop down from the top of the slide? Or maybe you'd like to add a flash of text or art?

Build It!

The effect of having your slide items appear at different times and in different ways on-screen is called a *build*. There are lots of different builds you can use with PowerPoint, such as bulleted items appearing one bullet at a time when you click the slide, or a graphic flying in from the side of the screen.

PowerPoint offers all these options via the Animation Effects toolbar. To display it, first change to Slide view, and then click the **Animation Effects** button (the one with a yellow star on it) in the Standard toolbar. The following table lists and describes the buttons you'll find on this toolbar.

The Animation Effects Toolbar

Button	Name	Description
	Animate Title	Turns on the animation effect for the slide title.
	Animate Slide Text	Turns on animation effects for other text on the slide.
	Drive-In Effect	Drives the object onto the slide and plays the sound of a speeding car.
	Flying Effect	Flies the selected object onto the slide.
	Camera Effect	Inserts object into slide with the sound of a camera click.
	Flash Once	Flashes object onto slide and then off again.
	Laser Text Effect	Writes text onto slide with a laser-like effect and sound.
	Typewriter Text Effect	Inserts slide text one character at a time, as if it is being typed on your screen.
	Reverse Order	Builds your text block from bottom up.
	Drop-In	Drops in each word one at a time, as if the words are falling from the top of the slide.

Button	Name	Description
	Animation Order	Lets you specify the order in which items should appear on the slide.
	Custom Animation	Displays the Custom Animation dialog box, which offers additional options for controlling build animations.

You can add these animation effects to any object on your slide—slide title, bulleted list, or graphic. If you apply the effect to a bulleted list, the effect applies to all items in the list.

To apply an animation effect, first click the object to which you want to apply the effect. Then click the desired effect. Open the **Animation Order** drop-down list and select the order in which this object should appear on the slide. (If this is the first item you are choosing to animate, you have only one Animation Order option, 1.) You can select the animation order at any time.

PowerPoint 97 offers another way to quickly animate objects. Click the object, open the **Slide Show** menu, and point to **Preset Animation**. This displays a list of animation effects available for this object. Click the desired effect.

When you're ready to run your slide show (which I'll tell you how to do shortly), the assigned slide effects will appear on your screen on command.

Previewing Your Animations

Instead of flipping from Slide view to Slide Show view every time you want to check out the effects of your animation settings, open the **Slide Show** menu and select **Animation Preview**. A small window appears, showing the current slide. Click inside the window to view the animation effects in action.

Animating Your Charts

PowerPoint 97 now offers animation effects for your charts. For example, if you have a bar chart showing company profits for 1996, 1997, and 1998, you can have the bar showing each year's net profit fly onto the chart separately. To add animation effects to a chart, take the following steps:

1. Right-click the chart you want to animate and click **Custom Animation**. The Custom Animation dialog box appears, with the Chart Effects tab up front.

2. Open the **Introduce Chart Elements** drop-down list and select the option that specifies how you want the chart elements introduced: **All at Once**, **By Series**, **By Category**, **By Element in Series**, or **By Element in Category**.

3. To animate the grid and legend, make sure there is a check in the **Animate Grid and Legend** check box.

4. From the **Entry Animation and Sound** drop-down lists, select the desired animation effect and any sound you want to accompany that effect.

5. To have the chart disappear after it is displayed, select an option from the **After Animation** drop-down list.

6. You can click the **Preview** button to see the animation effects in action. When you're satisfied, click **OK**.

Now you can animate your charts.

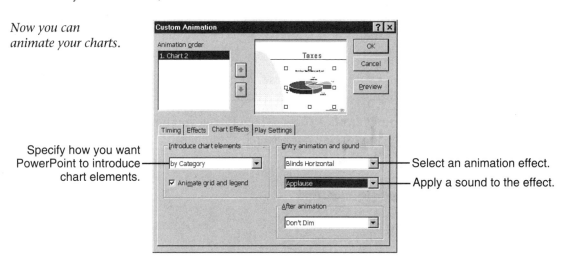

Specify how you want PowerPoint to introduce chart elements.

Select an animation effect.

Apply a sound to the effect.

More Animation Effects

If you're looking for more control over the timing and execution of your animation effects, use the Custom Animation dialog box. To display it, open the **Slide Show** menu and select **Custom Animation**. This dialog box offers four tabs full of animation options, including all the options available on the Animation Effects toolbar and on the Preset Animations submenu.

Making an Interactive Presentation with Action Buttons

Typical slide shows are designed to give the presenter total control. The presenter sets the pace, deciding which slide appears when, advancing slides, and introducing data. However, there are times when you want to give that control to your audience. For example, if you are creating a presentation to place on the Web, or you are developing a training presentation for individual workers, you want a presentation that is more self-directed and interactive. You want the person who is viewing the presentation to set the pace, pause when needed, and determine the next course of action.

You can give your audience control over the presentation by adding *action buttons* to your slides. For example, a simple action button may allow the user to click it to advance to the next slide. Another button may prompt the user to click it to play a video. To add an action button to a slide, take the following steps:

1. Display the slide on which you want the action button to appear. (Use the Master slide, if you want the button to appear on all slides in the presentation.)

2. Open the **Slide Show** menu and point to **Action Buttons**. A submenu appears, showing the available buttons. If you rest the mouse pointer on a button, its name appears.

3. Click the button you want to insert. The submenu closes, and the mouse pointer transforms into a crosshair.

4. Drag the mouse pointer to create a box where you want the button to appear. When you release the mouse button, the action button appears on the slide, and the Action Settings dialog box appears, prompting you to assign some action to the button. (A dialog box may appear, prompting you to save the presentation before you continue. Respond to the dialog box as desired, and then proceed to the next step.)

5. To have the button perform an action when the user clicks it, make sure the **Mouse Click** tab is selected. To have the button act when the mouse pointer passes over it, select the **Mouse Over** tab.

6. Under **Action on Click** (or Action on Mouse Over, if the Mouse Over tab is selected), click the type of action you want the button to perform. Then select the action:

   None assigns no action to the button. The button is there basically for decoration or to drive the user crazy.

Hyperlink To pulls up the specified slide, connects to another slide show, opens a page on the Web, links to a custom slide show, or opens some other file on the disk. If you select this option, you must indicate where the item you want to link to is located.

Run Program runs another application. If you choose this option, specify the drive and folder where the application's files are stored and specify the name of the file that runs the application.

Run Macro runs a series of recorded commands.

Object Action opens, edits, or plays the object that you specify in the drop-down list.

7. To have a sound play when the user clicks the button, click **Play Sound** and select an audio file from the drop-down list.

8. To make the button look as though it is pressed when the user clicks it, select **Highlight Click**.

9. Click **OK**. The button appears on the slide. You can drag the button to move it or drag one of the button's handles to resize it.

Web Work: Using the Control Toolbox

If you want to get fancy with your presentation, you can add *controls* to your slides, allowing your audience to input data or make selections. This is useful if you plan to place your slide show on the Internet or on your company's intranet. To insert controls on a slide, you use the Control Toolbox. To turn it on, right-click any toolbar and click **Control Toolbox**. You can then add controls by clicking the desired control in the Control Toolbox, and then dragging the mouse pointer onto the slide.

Creating Custom Slide Shows

The presentation you just created may not be suitable for all audiences. For example, you may have created a very thorough presentation of a new product to convince investors that you have clearly planned its design and that you intend to place marketing dollars behind it. You may also need to present the design to your suppliers, who need to know nothing about how much you're spending to market the product. And you may want to present the marketing portion of the presentation to your accountants, who probably wouldn't understand the design if you showed it to them.

Do you have to create a separate presentation for each audience? Heck no! PowerPoint enables you to create several custom presentations, each containing a separate set of slides from the main (complete) presentation.

To create a custom presentation, open the **Slide Show** menu, select **Custom Shows**, and click the **New** button. The Define Custom Show dialog box appears. You can type a name for the custom slide show in the **Slide Show Name** text box at the top of the dialog box. In the **Slides in Presentation List**, click the first slide you want to appear in the custom slide show. **Ctrl+click** additional slides to select them, and then click the **Add** button. This copies the names of the slides to the **Slides in Custom Show** list. To change the order of the slides in the custom show, click a slide's name and click the **Up** or **Down** arrow button. Click **OK** to save the show.

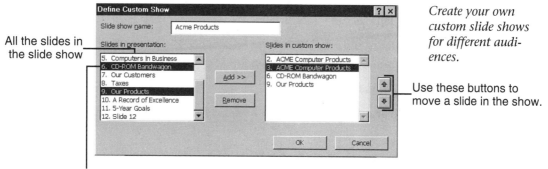

All the slides in the slide show

Create your own custom slide shows for different audiences.

Use these buttons to move a slide in the show.

Click a slide's name and click Add to place it in the custom show.

Another Way to Customize

There's another way to change the overall look and behavior of your slide show for specific situations. Open the **Slide Show** menu and click **Set Up Show**. The Set Up Show dialog box appears, offering options for turning off narration and animation, for giving control of the show to the user, for including a specific range of slides in the show, and for controlling how the slides advanced. Enter your preferences and click **OK**.

Jumping Around in a Slide Show with Summary Slides

If you're creating a self-directed slide show to run on a PC or on the Web, you might want to use one slide as a jumping off point for other series of slides in the show. You can do this with *summary* (or *agenda*) slides. The summary slide contains a bulleted list of other slides in the slide show. When the user runs the presentation, the summary slide pops up on-screen, allowing the user to choose the direction in which to proceed. To create a summary slide, follow these steps:

1. Make a custom show for each series of slides you want the summary slide to point to. (Skip back to the previous section for details about creating custom shows.)

2. In Slide Sorter or Outline view, click the first slide of the first custom show that you want the summary slide to point to.

3. **Shift**+click the first slide of each additional custom show you want to list on the summary slide.

4. On the Slide Sorter or Outlining toolbar, click the **Summary Slide** button. The summary slide appears as the first slide in the presentation. It contains a list of the first slides in each custom slide show.

5. Select the summary slide and change to Slide view so you can link the bullets to their corresponding custom slide shows.

6. Select one of the bulleted items.

7. Open the **Slide Show** menu and click **Action Settings**. The Action Settings dialog box appears.

8. Click **Hyperlink To**. Then open the drop-down list and select **Custom Show**. The Link to Custom Show dialog box appears.

9. Click the name of the custom show that you want this bulleted item to link to. To automatically return to the summary slide after viewing the custom show, click **Show and Return**. Click **OK**.

10. Click **OK** to create the link and return to the summary slide.

11. Repeat steps 6–10 to link additional bulleted items on the summary slide to their custom shows.

It's Show Time!

This is it—the moment you finally get to see how your presentation looks and runs. I'll tell you how to electronically show your presentation, give you tips for stopping and adding notes, and even show you how to write on your slides during the presentation. Places, everyone! Cue monitor …lights, camera, action!

You're On!

When you have your show in order, take it for a spin. Starting from the first slide in the presentation, click the **Slide Show** view button on the View button bar. (You can also start the presentation by opening the **View** menu and selecting **Slide Show**.) Your first slide fills the screen, obscuring all the toolbars and window features. You can now do the following:

➤ To progress to the next slide, click anywhere on the screen or press the right arrow or down arrow key on the keyboard.

➤ If you set up a specific transition time (as described earlier in this chapter), it will kick in automatically.

➤ To quit the show at any time, press **Esc**.

➤ To see a menu of slide show controls, click the inconspicuous button in the lower-left corner of the slide.

➤ If you selected a build effect for your slide or any slide elements, click your screen to "build" each effect (unless, of course, you have timed the builds).

➤ If you've inserted any sound clips, movie clips, or other special effects, you can double-click their icons to start them during the presentation.

Check This Out...

Rehearsing

You can rehearse your slide show while specifying the amount of time each slide is to appear on-screen. When you're ready to rehearse, open the **Slide Show** menu and select **Rehearse Timings**. PowerPoint displays the Rehearsal dialog box, showing the number of seconds that the slide has been on-screen. When you are ready to advance to the next slide, click the **Advance** button (the one with the right-pointing arrow on it). When you reach the end of the show, PowerPoint asks if you want to save your slide show timings. Click **Yes**.

Slide Show Controls

Take a gander at PowerPoint's slide show controls by clicking the control button in the lower-left corner of the slide screen. It opens a menu from which you can select controls for moving to the next slide, turning the arrow pointer into a pen that writes on-screen, and even ending the show.

A slide during the course of the slide show.

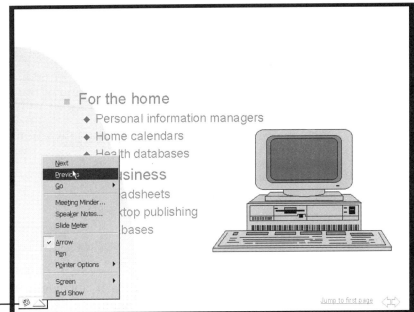

Click here to view a menu of slide show controls.

Here's what each menu item controls:

Next takes you to the next slide or the next build effect. (It's easier to use the arrow keys or just click a slide.)

Previous takes you back to the previous slide or build effect.

Go opens a submenu that allows you to select the name of a specific slide you want to view.

Meeting Minder lets you stop your slide show and compose notes, comments, and other observations made by your audience. Meeting Minder even lets you type the meeting minutes during the presentation, so you can quickly review the meeting at a later date.

Speaker Notes allows you to add notes about a specific slide or to view notes you've already typed. (See "Creating Speaker Notes for Yourself," later in this chapter.)

Slide Meter opens a dialog box for timing your slide show.

Arrow lets you use the mouse pointer arrow to navigate the screen.

Pen turns your mouse pointer into a pen that you can use to scribble on the slides you show. The scribbles are not saved as part of your presentation; however, the effect is kind of like using an electronic chalkboard. Just select **Pen** and start dragging the pen pointer around on your screen.

Pointer Options lets you hide the mouse pointer altogether or change your pen's color.

Screen opens a submenu for blacking out your current slide, pausing the show, or erasing your pen scribbles.

End Show puts a stop to your slide show.

Screen Show, 35mm Slides, Overhead Transparencies?

Throughout this chapter, you have probably noticed that the instructions lean toward on-screen slide shows, which allow you to incorporate dazzling animation effects. However, not all slide shows are high-tech. Small companies and individuals may not have the projection equipment available to make on-screen presentations feasible. Many users have to resort to transferring the slide show to 35mm slides, overhead transparencies, or even (gasp) paper!

If you are technically deprived, you'll need to enter page setup options to specify the medium on which you want to output your slides. Open the **File** menu and select **Page Setup**. Your slides are originally sized for an on-screen presentation. To adjust the size for another medium, open the **Slides Sized For** drop-down list, and select one of the following options:

➤ **Letter Paper** to print on 8.5-by-11-inch paper.

➤ **A4 Paper** to print on 210-by-290-millimeter paper.

➤ **35mm Slides** to transfer the presentation to 35mm photographic slides.

➤ **Overhead** to print the slides on overhead transparencies.

➤ **Banner** to print the presentation on continuous form paper (assuming your printer can print on continuous form paper).

➤ **Custom** to adjust the size of the slides to fit the print area for your printer. This makes the slides as big as your printer can make them.

The Page Setup dialog box also enables you to change the orientation for your slides. By default, slides are printed sideways so they are wider than they are long. You can print them in Portrait orientation to print them in a standard layout.

Professional Slide Service

Most people don't have the equipment needed to place their presentations on 35mm slides or transform them into overhead transparencies. If you are one of the many unfortunates, you can send your presentation to a service called Genigraphics that can output your presentation for you. To reach Genigraphics, open the **File** menu, point to **Send To**, and click **Genigraphics**. This starts the Genigraphics Wizard, which prompts you to pick the presentation, the type of output, and shipping and billing information. Assuming you have a modem or a network connection to the Internet, the wizard can establish a connection to Genigraphics and transmit your presentation.

Making Notes and Handouts

Before you give your presentation, you may need to do a little preparation. Will you need to refer to notes while you're speaking, or would you rather wing it? Are any slides so important that you would like your audience to take them home so they can study them at their leisure? PowerPoint can help you make speaker notes pages and audience handouts, as explained in the following sections.

Creating Speaker Notes for Yourself

We've all witnessed presentations in which the speaker merely read the information on the slides, never elaborating on anything or making the visual meaningful. Don't let yourself fall into giving that kind of presentation. Instead, create some speaker notes to help you organize your thoughts, cover all the crucial points, and make your presentation cohesive and effective.

Notes pages consist of two parts: the slide itself and your notes. Because you've already put together your presentation, you have to worry only about the notes:

1. Open your presentation and switch to **Notes Pages** view.

2. On the first slide that appears, click the notes text box in the lower half of the page. This selects the notes text box so you can start typing notes. If you're having trouble seeing what you're typing, click the **Zoom** drop-down list on the toolbar to display a list of zoom percentages (if you prefer, you can use the **Zoom** command on the **View** menu). Try 100%; it's up close and personal.

3. Go ahead and type in your note text. If you're at a complete loss about what to type, consider noting supporting information, explanations and tie-ins, jokes, and so on. You can format your text any way you want it on the page.

4. When you finish with one slide, click the **Next Slide** button to move to the next one in line.

You can readjust the sizes of the slide picture or the notes text box at any time. Click either one, and a frame with handles appears around it. Drag one of the handles to resize the frame. When you're ready to print your notes, open the **File** menu and select **Print**. In the Print dialog box, open the **Print What** drop-down list and select **Notes Pages**. Click **OK**.

Format the Notes Master
You have seen that every slide show has a Master slide that controls the formatting for all slides in a show. Your notes pages also have a Master slide. **Shift+click** the **Notes Page View** button in the View toolbar to display the Notes Pages master. Any formatting changes you enter here (including resizing the slide and notes areas) affect all your notes pages.

Making Handouts for Your Audience

Slide shows go by fairly quickly, and there's rarely time for the information to sink into the collective mind of your audience. So back up your presentation with handouts—they're easy to make:

1. Open the **File** menu and choose **Print**.

2. In the Print dialog box, pull down the **Print What** drop-down list and select the **Handouts** option you want to use.

3. When you have that squared away, click the **OK** button to print your handouts.

There's also a Handout Master you can use to make the appearance of all your handout pages uniform. Open the **View** menu, select **Master**, and select **Handout Master**. This switches your screen to Handout Master mode. Make any necessary changes to the handout page that appears. To exit, click any of the View buttons.

Pack and Go to Make a Slide Show That Plays on Any Computer

Are you ready to take your show on the road? Then you'll need PowerPoint's new Pack and Go feature. This little wizard assists you in loading your presentation onto a floppy disk, including all the relevant files that are linked to it. For example, if you're taking the presentation to an important sales meeting back at the home office in Timbuktu, you can use the Pack and Go Wizard to load the presentation files nicely onto a set of floppy disks to take with you. Here's how it works.

1. Open the **File** menu and select **Pack and Go**. The Pack and Go Wizard box appears.

2. Click the **Next>** button to proceed.

3. Choose the presentation you want to pack. By default, PowerPoint selects the current presentation that you have opened. You can choose another, however, by selecting **Other Presentations** and clicking the **Browse** button. Click **Next>** to continue.

4. The next box lets you pick which drive you're packing the presentation onto. (By default, PowerPoint selects drive A, but you can change to another.) Select a drive and click **Next>**.

5. The next box lets you choose to include linked files or to embed TrueType fonts along with your presentation (in case the computer you're going to use to show the presentation doesn't have the same fonts you used). Make the appropriate selection and click **Next>** to continue.

6. If the computer you're going to use to show your presentation doesn't have PowerPoint, the next Wizard box lets you load a PowerPoint Viewer. (The viewer will work with previous versions of Windows.) Click **Next>** to continue.

7. Now click the **Finish** button in the final box, and the Wizard starts packing your data onto a floppy disk. Make sure a disk is in the appropriate drive. (Chances are, you'll need more than one floppy disk.)

Check This Out...

Hold a Conference

PowerPoint comes with a Presentation Conferencing Wizard to help you manage or view presentations over a network, via modem, or on the Internet. The participants can even add their own notes on the slides. First, get on the phone and make sure everyone is connected. Then open the **Tools** menu and select **Presentation Conference**. This runs the Presentation Conference Wizard, which leads you through the steps necessary to hold a virtual presentation conference.

Keeping Up-to-Date with PowerPoint Central

PowerPoint 97 comes with a special presentation called PowerPoint Central that contains links to several helpful resources, including tutorials, additional templates and textures, sounds, and animation clips. These resources are stored both on the Microsoft Office CD (in the ValuPack) and on the Web (at Microsoft's PowerPoint Web site and at other vendor sites). PowerPoint Central can also check Microsoft's Web site for any updates to PowerPoint, ensuring that you have the latest version of the product.

To run PowerPoint Central, open the **Tools** menu and select **PowerPoint Central**. If you haven't checked for updates to PowerPoint, a dialog box appears, asking if you want to check for updates now. Click **Yes** and follow the on-screen instructions. After PowerPoint Central checks for and installs any updates, it displays a multi-tabbed window that allows you to check out free additions, PowerPoint news, tips and tricks, animation effects, and more.

The Least You Need to Know

You're a presentation pro now. Get out there and visually communicate:

➤ Practice running through your slide show several times, and use the Slide Sorter view to quickly move slides around.

➤ You can animate the slide transitions for all the slides in a show. To set transitions, open the **Slide Show** menu and select **Slide Transition**.

➤ The best way to animate individual objects on a slide is to change to Slide view and turn on the Animation Effects toolbar. Click the **Animation Effects** button in the formatting toolbar.

➤ To set the timing for your slide show, open the **Slide Show** menu and click **Rehearse Timings**.

➤ To preview your slide show before presenting it to the public, click the **Slide Show View** button.

➤ Action buttons enable you to add controls to your slides that allow the viewer to interact with the show. To add an action button, change to Slide view. Open the **Slide Show** menu, point to **Action Buttons**, and click the desired button.

➤ Use the Pack and Go Wizard to help you put your presentation on disk.

Part 5
Mastering the Information Age with Access

Information is power. But too much information, if not managed properly, can cripple the intelligence and derail any train of thought. Fortunately, we people of the late twentieth century have computerized databases that can manage the information for us. We type in the data (in the proper form), and the database does the rest: sorting it, summarizing it in reports, and helping us pull it into our other documents.

Although databases can be complicated beasts, Access provides a complete, yet simple set of tools designed to make it easy to work with databases. In this section, you will learn how to use these tools to create and manage your own databases.

Making Your First Database

Our society thrives on information. Magazines and TV news shows broadcast results of the latest polls. Telemarketers and junk mailers pay for lists of names, addresses, and phone numbers of prospective customers. People call and show up at our doors asking survey questions. Television networks use the Nielsen ratings to figure out which shows to create.

We collect this data and pour it into computers, but then what? Someone (or something) has to tally the results and arrange the data in some meaningful form so we can use it. This something is a *database*. In this chapter, you'll learn how to create your own database so you can start dumping data into it and organizing your data in some manageable format.

What Is a Database, Anyway?

A database is a collection of data. A phone book is a database. Your collection of cooking recipes is a database. Even your summer reading list is a database. How do you know if what you're creating is a database? I asked Jeff Foxworthy this question, and he said, "You might be a database, if..."

➤ Your head is packed with names and addresses of people you've never even met.

➤ You ask people to *type* entries, instead of asking them to *print clearly*.

➤ You have a full time job at the Department of Motor Vehicles—and you like it.

➤ You've never lost a game of Trivial Pursuit.

➤ You can alphabetize a list of 1,000 names in less time than it takes to tie your shoes.

Database Lingo You Can't Live Without

Before you dive in and start creating a database, there's some terminology you need to know. Of course, you can proceed in ignorance, but then you wouldn't know what I was talking about when I told you to "create a field" or "select a record." Here's a quick rundown of the terms you should know (and, of course, their definitions):

➤ **Form**   A fill-in-the-blanks document you use to type entries into your database. This is just like a form you would fill out at your doctor's office.

➤ **Field**   On a fill-in-the-blanks form, fields are the blanks. You type a unique piece of data (such as last name, first name, or middle initial) into each field.

➤ **Record**   A completed form. Each record contains data for a specific person, thing, or other being or non-being. For example, in a Rolodex, each card is a record.

➤ **Table**   Another way to display records in a database. Instead of displaying data on separate forms, you can have Access display the data in a table. Each row displays a record. Each column represents a separate field.

➤ **Query**   To pull data from one or more databases. For example, if you have one database that contains customer names and addresses, and another database that contains a record of bills you have sent out, you can use a query to pull information from both databases and create a list of customers who owe you money. You'll learn more about queries in Chapter 23, "Finding, Sorting, and Selecting Records."

➤ **Report**   A document that pulls data from one or more databases and arranges it in various ways to present the data in a meaningful context and help you analyze it.

Entering Data with Tables and Forms

When you create a database in Access, you are essentially designing a fill-in-the-blanks form. You provide field names that tell you what to type in each space, and you try to make your spaces wide enough to handle any lengthy entries you need to type.

Once you have a form, you can use it to start dumping data into your database. You type an entry into each field (blank) on the form to create a record. You then save the record to your database.

Another way to enter records into your database is to switch to Table view. In this view, records are listed as they might appear in an Excel worksheet. You type your entries into the various "cells" in a row to create a record. In Chapter 22, "Entering Data: For the Record," you will learn how to type entries in both Form and Table views.

Check This Out...

Word and Excel Databases

Word tables and Excel worksheets can double as databases. To create a database in Word, you must create a table with column headings that act as field names. In Excel, you do the same thing. These databases are useful for mail merges and for short lists of records, but neither Excel nor Word offers the powerful database management tools you will find in Access.

Planning Your Database

For most people, database planning is a lot like family planning—once they have two or three kids, they start planning how to avoid having more. Although the consequences of creating a database without planning are a lot less serious than the consequences of having children without planning, an unplanned database can cause problems later. For example, if you omit a blank on your form, you'll have to add the blank later and then go back to any records you've already entered to make sure it has that piece of data.

In planning a database, you have to focus on two things: forms and tables. The forms must have blanks for all the data that makes up a record. In addition, you should try to make each blank large enough for the longest entry you will ever need to enter in that blank, but not so large that it takes up unnecessary space. Before creating an electronic form, sit down with a pencil and paper and draw the form. If you already have a paper form that you use to collect data, you can use the paper form as your model.

Primary and Foreign Keys

Access uses primary and foreign keys to establish relationships between tables. In most cases, the two tables have fields of the same name. The primary key is the field that supplies information to the foreign key field in the other table. For example, you might have a Customer table that supplies the Customer ID to the Orders table.

In addition to planning your form, you should spend some time thinking about the tables that will make up your database. Tables enable you to break your database into smaller units, making each unit more manageable, and preventing you from having to type duplicate entries. When designing your tables, keep the following rules in mind:

➤ *Use a separate table for each related collection of data.* For example, create a table for customer information, such as the customer ID, name, address, and phone number. Another table might contain product information, such as the Product ID, name, and price. By keeping related data in separate tables, you can delete a record in one table without affecting an entry in another table.

➤ *Tables should not contain duplicate entries, and a column in one table should not be duplicated in another table.* For example, only one table should contain a column for customer IDs. By typing an entry in only one table, you can easily update it, and you eliminate the possibility of entering conflicting pieces of data in two or more tables.

➤ *Try to give the records in each table a unique identifier* (called a *primary key*), such as a product ID, customer ID, or order number. This makes it easy to access or extract data from a table and to sort the records.

Cranking Out a Database with the Database Wizard

Now that you can recognize a database when you see one, you should be ready to create your own database. If you need to create a standard database, such as an inventory list, address book, or a membership directory, this is going to be easy. The Access Database Wizard can lead you step-by-step through the process:

1. Start Access. (Click **Start**, point to **Programs**, and click **Microsoft Access**.) The Microsoft Access dialog box appears, asking if you want to create a new database or open an existing database.

2. Click **Database Wizard** and click **OK**. The New dialog box appears, prompting you to select a database template.

3. Click on the **Databases** tab, and click on one of the template icons. The preview area shows a sample of the selected template.

268

4. Click the database template you want to use and click **OK**. The File New Database dialog box appears, prompting you to name your database file.

5. Type a name for your new database file in the **File Name** text box, and then select the drive and folder in which you want to store the file. Click the **Create** button. As Access creates the database file, it displays a Database dialog box and then the first Database Wizard dialog box.

6. Read the information in the first Database Wizard dialog box, to find out what the wizard is going to do. Click the **Next>** button. The Database Wizard displays a list of tables it will create for your database, and a list of fields on each table.

Running the Database Wizard If the Microsoft Access dialog box that appears when you start Access is not displayed, you can create a new database by using a template. Open the **File** menu, select **New Database**, click the **Databases** tab, and double-click a template for the type of database you want to create. This runs the Database Wizard.

7. In the **Tables in the Database** list, click the table whose fields you want to change. The Fields in the Table box lists the available fields; optional fields appear in italics.

8. Click a field name to turn it on or off. A check mark next to a field name indicates that the field will be included in the table. Repeat steps 7 and 8 to specify which fields you want included in each table.

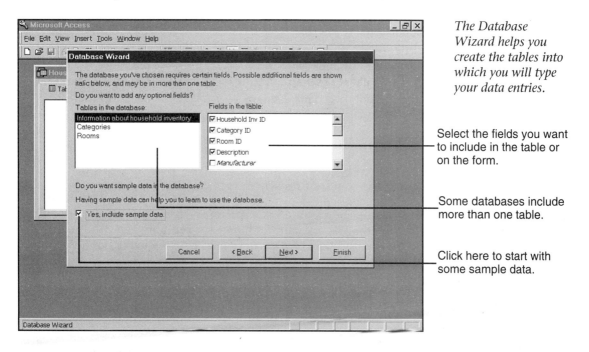

The Database Wizard helps you create the tables into which you will type your data entries.

Select the fields you want to include in the table or on the form.

Some databases include more than one table.

Click here to start with some sample data.

9. Click **Yes, Include Sample Data**. (Throughout this chapter and the next three Access chapters, I'm going to assume that your database contains data; so turn this option on.) Click **Next>**. The next dialog box asks you to pick the desired appearance of your database.

10. Use the down arrow key to move through the list of styles. The sample area lets you preview the currently selected design. Select the desired design and click **Next>**. The wizard now asks you how you want your printed reports to look.

11. Click a report style to preview it in the sample area. When you find a style you like, click it and click the **Next>** button. The wizard asks you to type a title for the database and insert a (optional) picture.

12. To replace the suggested database title with your own title, type the title you want to use. The title will appear on printed reports.

13. To include a picture (such as a logo) next to the database title on reports, click **Yes, I'd Like to Include a Picture**. Click the **Picture** button, select the graphic file you want to use, and click **OK**. Click the **Next>** button. At long last, the wizard informs you that you are nearly finished.

14. Make sure **Yes, Start the Database** is selected so the Database Wizard will run the database after creating it.

15. If you want Access to display on-screen help while you are creating your database, click **Display Help on Using a Database**.

16. Click the **Finish** button.

Access makes the database and then displays the *Main Switchboard*, a tool for working with various tables in the database. To start entering data, you can click the **Enter/View** button at the top of the switchboard. This displays a form you can use to start creating records. See Chapter 22, "Entering Data: For The Record," for details.

Household Inventory

The Database Wizard allows you to create a household inventory database for insurance purposes. I guess Microsoft thinks that burglars will be courteous enough to leave your computer behind when they steal the rest of your stuff, and that no house fire could possibly harm your computer. If you use Access to keep track of inventory for insurance records, be sure to print your inventory later and store the printout in a lock box at the bank.

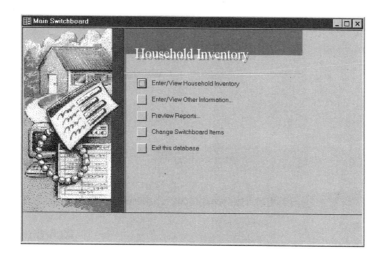

The Main Switch-board gives you access to your database tables and tools.

Working with That Other Database Window

The Main Switchboard is sort of like that white mask that the Phantom of the Opera wears. It covers a less-attractive database window that actually gives you greater access to your database tables, forms, and reports. To see this database window, click the **Close** or **Minimize** button in the Main Switchboard window. You should see a minimized version of the Database window. Click its **Maximize** or **Restore** button to bring it into view, as shown in the following figure.

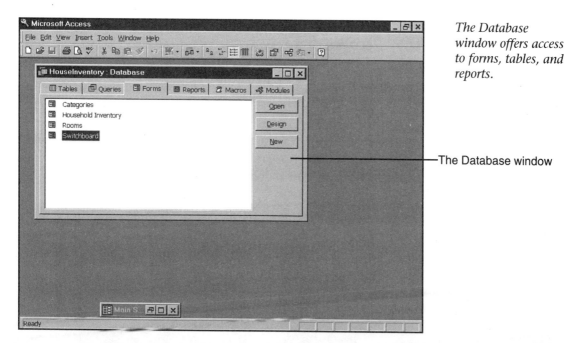

The Database window offers access to forms, tables, and reports.

The Database window

Are You Happy? If you're happy with the database you created, skip to Chapter 22 right now. The rest of the sections in this chapter deal with customizing your database. These sections are fairly complicated, so avoid them if possible. However, if you need to tweak your database before using it (or if you're just curious about how to do that), read on.

The Database window has tabs for the various elements that make up your database: tables, queries, forms, reports, macros, and modules. Many of these tabs (including Queries and Macros) are blank because neither you nor the wizard has created any of these objects. However, the Tables, Forms, and Reports tabs should contain a list of the objects in your database.

The buttons on the right side of the window enable you to enter commands for the items on the tab. For example, to open a form so you can start entering data, click the **Forms** tab, click the form you want to use, and click the **Open** button. You can click the **Design** button to customize the form, table, report, or other object. The **New** button lets you create a new object on the tab.

Creating and Customizing Tables

The central element in any database is the *table*. This is the structure that stores all the data you enter and supplies that data when you create a query or report, or choose to flip through your records using a form. Before you start entering data into your tables, make sure you have all the tables you need, and that each table contains fields for the required data entries. The following sections show you how to take control of existing tables and create new tables from scratch.

Understanding How Tables Interact

Tables allow you to divide a database into several parts to make it easier to enter and manage your data. For example, a company might have a database that has one table for products (ProductInfo), another for suppliers (Suppliers), and a third for purchase orders (PO). A product ID number in each table can link the tables together, allowing you to pull information out of all three tables. For example, if you needed to order a part, you could use the product ID number to pull the part's name, description, and price from the ProductInfo table, the supplier's name and address from the Suppliers table, and the preferred shipping method from the PO table.

If you were to place all this data in one table, you would have multiple entries for the same supplier and product. For example, say you use three different parts (product ID number X04, X20, and X54). You would have to include the supplier's name, address, and contact information in the record for *each* part. Not only would this require a lot more typing from you, but it would also increase the chance that you would mistype an entry.

By using separate tables and linking them with a common field, you reduce the number of entries you must type, streamline your database, and avoid errors.

Configuring Tables: Pick a View

You can display tables in either of two views to configure them: Datasheet view or Design view. Datasheet view displays the table as if it were an Excel worksheet. Design view displays a list of all the fields in the table, and specifies the data type of each field. To switch views, open the **View** menu and select **Design View** or **Datasheet View**.

In either view, you can move or delete fields or insert new fields. To select a field in Datasheet view, you click the field name at the top of the column. You can then perform the following tasks:

➤ To move a field, drag it to the left or right.

➤ To delete a field, select it and press the **Delete** key.

➤ To insert a field, select the column to the left of which you want the new column (field) inserted, open the **Insert** menu, and click **Column**.

➤ To rename a field, right-click on the column name and select **Rename Column**. Type a new field name.

Click the field name to select the column.

Household Inv	Category ID	Room ID	Description	Model	Model Numb
1	Sports Equip	Bedroom	Exercise Bike	Deluxe	KK200
2	Furniture	Living Room	Gray three-cush	70" sleeper	
3	Sports Equip	Garage	Mountain Bike		
4	Electronic	Den	Computer	375	1089
5	Tool	Garage	Cordless drill	Deluxe	PK200
6	Furniture	Dining Room	Ebony inlaid tab		
7	Tool	Garage	Table saw		BKV100
8	Collectible	Den	Baseball card c		
9	Jewelry	Bedroom	Pearl necklace		
10	Electronic	Living Room	Audio-Visual Re		AV-520
(AutoNumber)					

Record: 1 of 10

In Datasheet view, a table looks and acts like an Excel worksheet.

You can perform the same actions in Design view, but the layout is a little different. Design view does not show the data in the table. Instead, it shows the field names and the settings that control each field. The following figure shows you how to move, delete, and insert fields in Design view.

273

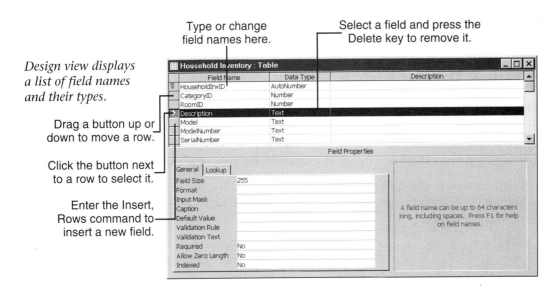

Design view displays a list of field names and their types.

Type or change field names here.

Select a field and press the Delete key to remove it.

Drag a button up or down to move a row.

Click the button next to a row to select it.

Enter the Insert, Rows command to insert a new field.

Inserting Fields That Take Data from Other Tables

To insert a field that can copy data from another table in your database, you should create a *lookup field*. Instead of selecting **Insert, Rows**, select **Insert, Lookup Field**. This runs the Lookup Wizard, which leads you through the process of connecting this field to the corresponding field in the other table.

Changing the Field Properties

Whenever you create a new field, you must type two entries for the field: the *field name* and the *data type*. The field name appears at the top of the column in the table, and tells you what is stored in that field. The *data type* controls the type of entry you can type into the field. For example, if you set a field's data type as Number, you can't type a regular text entry in that field.

To change the data type for a field, change to Design view. Click in the **Data Type** box next to the field whose data type you want to change. A button appears inside the box; click the button to open the **Data Type** drop-down list. Select the desired data type from those described in the following table.

Access Data Types and What They're Good For

Data Type	What It's Good For
Text	Text entries or combinations of text and numbers: names, addresses, phone numbers, ZIP codes, and any other text or number that doesn't have to be sorted numerically or included in a calculation. (Text fields hold up to 255 characters.)
Number	Any number except a dollar amount. Use the Number data type for numbers you might include in calculations or for numbers you may want to sort, such as record numbers or part numbers. Don't use this data type for numbers you want to treat as text, such as addresses and phone numbers.
Date/Time	A calendar date or a time.
Currency	Dollar amounts.
Memo	Lengthy descriptions up to 64,000 characters.
AutoNumber	A field that automatically inserts a number for you. Excellent for numbering records sequentially.
Yes/No	True/False or Yes/No entries.
Lookup Wizard	Entries from other tables in the database. Choosing this data type runs the Lookup Wizard, which prompts you to pick the table from which you want to insert data. If you create a Combo box, you can then select entries from a drop-down list instead of typing them into the table.
OLE Object	A picture, sound, spreadsheet, document, or other file created using some other application. (You can insert an object as large as 1 gigabyte!)
Hyperlink	A link to another file on your hard drive or on the network, or to a Web page.

At the bottom of the Design view window are additional options for changing the properties of fields. For example, for the Currency data type, you can specify that you want no decimal places used so that amounts are shown only in dollars, or you can specify that this field is required (so Access won't accept the record unless you type an entry in the required field). When you click a field name in the upper half of the window, the options in the lower half show the settings for that field. You can then change the settings.

In Design view, you can change the data types and enter additional field properties.

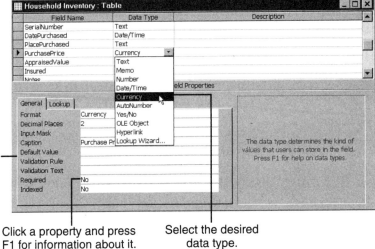

The Field Properties area offers additional options for controlling the appearance and behavior of data in a field.

Click a property and press F1 for information about it.

Select the desired data type.

Creating New Tables

So far we have talked about rearranging the fields and changing field data types in existing tables. But what if your database needs another table? How do you create one? First, return to the main Database window, the one with all the tabs in it, and click the **Tables** tab.

On the right side of the Tables tab are three buttons: Open, Design, and New. Click **New**. The New Table dialog box appears, offering three options for creating a new table; you can create the table in Design View or in Datasheet View, or you can use the Table Wizard. Click **Table Wizard**, click **OK**, and follow the on-screen instructions to create the table.

Making a Table from Scratch

If the Table Wizard does not offer options for the type of table you want to create, you can create the table from scratch in Design view or Datasheet view. In such a case, you must insert fields manually and set the data type for each field. For a long table, this can be a fairly complicated and drawn out process.

Creating and Customizing Data-Entry Forms

Forms are powerful tools in Access. You can use them to enter data in a table, to display a collection of commands (like the Main Switchboard), or even to accept input (like a dialog box). The main purpose of a form, however, is to allow you to enter data into a table.

If you created a database using the wizard, you already have some forms you can start using. However, if you changed your table in the previous section or created a new table, you may need to customize your data entry forms or create a new form. The following sections provide the instructions you need to get started.

Restructuring a Form

What do you get when you cross a row and a dialog box? A data-entry form. A form looks and acts like an electronic version of the paper form you might fill out at the doctor's office. It consists of a bunch of blanks into which you type your entries. In most cases, the data entry form contains all the fields in a corresponding table; for example, if the Product Information table has a Product ID field, the Product Information form should have a Product ID field, too.

If you open a form and find that it does not contain the fields you want, or that the fields are not in the correct order, you can restructure the form in Design view. In the Database window, click the **Forms** tab and click on the name of the form you want to restructure. Click the **Design** button. The form appears in Design view, displaying the various controls that make up the form. When you click a control, handles appear around it, indicating that it is selected. You can then perform the following tasks:

➤ To move a control, drag it.

➤ To resize a control, drag one of the control's handles.

➤ To change the look of the text inside the control, select a font, font size, or attribute (bold, italic, underline) from the toolbar.

➤ To delete a control, press the **Delete** key. (Be careful about deleting controls. Controls link the form to your table. If you delete a control, you won't be able to use the form to enter that piece of data into the table.)

➤ To change a label, drag over the existing text in the label box, and type new text. (This label should match the field name in the table or at least resemble it.)

➤ To change the control source (the field into which you type your entries), see the next section cleverly entitled "Changing the Control Source and Other Control Properties."

➤ To add a field or control, see "Adding Controls to a Form," later in this chapter. (You can also change the control type.)

➤ You can change the overall look of the form by using AutoFormat. Open the **Format** menu and select **AutoFormat**, or click the **AutoFormat** button in the Form Design toolbar.

You can change
the text of a label.

When you click a control,
handles appear around it.

*In Form Design view,
you can change the
look and arrange-
ment of the controls.*

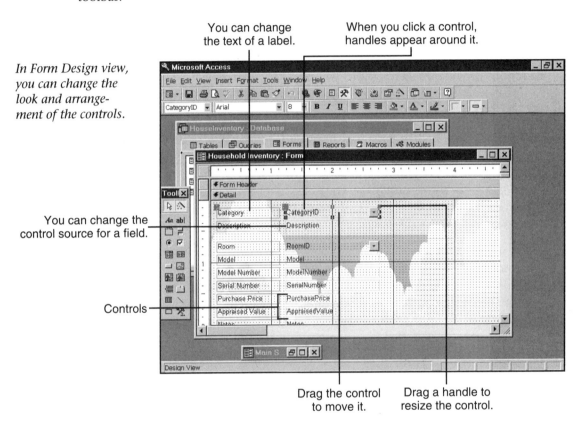

You can change the
control source for a field.

Controls

Drag the control
to move it.

Drag a handle to
resize the control.

Changing the Control Source and Other Control Properties

The *control source* links the field into which you type your entries to the table in which the entries are inserted. For example, say your form has text boxes into which you type a contact's last name and first name. The control sources for these text boxes are the LastName and FirstName fields in the table. If you created your database using the Database Wizard, you probably don't want to mess with the control source settings. However, if you're creating a new form, you may need to specify the control source for a field.

To change a control source, first right-click the field whose control source you want to change and click **Properties**. Click the **Data** tab, open the **Control Source** drop-down list, and click the name of the field into which you want the data from this control inserted.

Adding Controls to a Form

If you added any fields to a table earlier in this chapter, you'll have to add controls to the corresponding form. You do this by using the Toolbox toolbar and by drawing the controls on the form in Design view. You can add controls such as text boxes, check boxes, option buttons, drop-down lists, and image boxes to your form.

To draw a control, select the button for the type of control you want to draw from the Toolbox toolbar. Then position the mouse pointer over the form and drag the mouse pointer to draw a box where you want the control to appear. When you release the mouse button, the control appears, and you can change its properties as explained in the previous section. With some controls, a dialog box appears after you create the control, asking you for more information.

In most cases, the control is accompanied by a box that allows you to type a label describing the control. If a label box does not appear next to the control, you can use the **Label** button to add a Label control to the form.

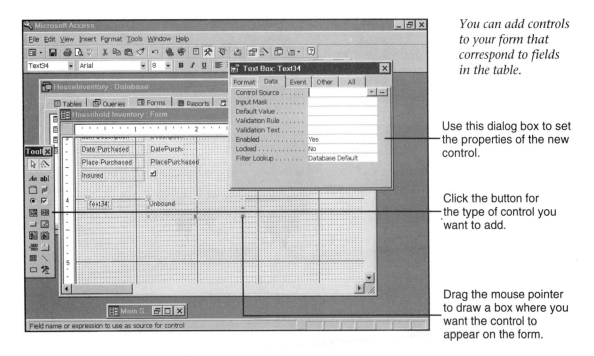

You can add controls to your form that correspond to fields in the table.

Use this dialog box to set the properties of the new control.

Click the button for the type of control you want to add.

Drag the mouse pointer to draw a box where you want the control to appear on the form.

Weaving Your Way Through Control Properties

When you click Properties for a control source, you get a dialog box that's packed with options. Most of the options allow you to change the position or appearance of the control. For example, the Format tab lets you change the font, border color, background, and font style and size. The Data tab contains options that are a bit more cryptic, allowing you to pick a different control source, add an input mask (which forces you to type an entry in a certain way), and enter other data input control settings. For some properties, you simply type an entry (for example, a measurement) in the property's text box. Other boxes act as drop-down lists, which you can open to display a list of options. When you click on some property text boxes, a button with three dots appears to the right of the box; click the button to display a dialog box. If you have trouble understanding a property, click it and press the **F1** key for additional help.

Creating a New Form

Once you have all the tables you need for your database, creating forms for entering data into those tables is pretty easy. The Form Wizard can lead you step-by-step through the process. All you have to do is tell the wizard which table fields you want included on your form and the order in which you want the fields placed.

Select the fields from one or more tables.

Select the table that has the fields you want to insert on your form.

Select the field you want to insert.

Click this button to copy the selected field to your form.

These fields will be included on the form in this order.

This button copies all the fields from the table to your form.

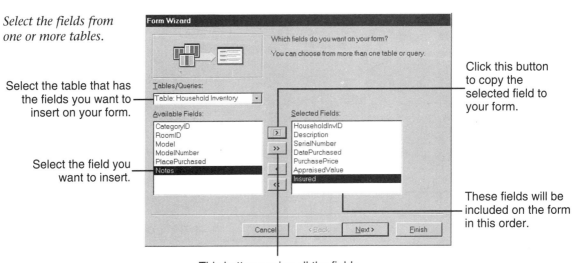

To run the Form Wizard, click the **Forms** tab in the Database window and click the **New** button. The New Form dialog box appears. Click **Form Wizard** and click **OK**. The first Form Wizard dialog box asks you to pick all the fields you want included on the form from the various tables in your database. You can select fields from more than one table. Try to insert the fields in the order in which you want them to appear on the form; you can change the order later, but it's easier to do it right the first time.

After you select the fields, click the **Next>** button and follow the wizard's instructions to select the layout and design for the form and to give the form a title. Click the **Finish** button when you reach the last dialog box. Congratulations, you're the proud parent of a new form!

The Least You Need to Know

This chapter introduced you to a lot of customization options you may not even need. What you do need to know, however, is how to use the Database Wizard, the Database window, and the Main Switchboard:

➤ You can run the Database Wizard when you first start Access. Click **Database Wizard**, click **OK**, and follow the wizard's instructions.

➤ You can run the Database Wizard by creating a database from a template. Open the **File** menu, select **New**, and click on the **Databases** tab. Double-click the template for the type of database you want to create, and then follow the wizard's instructions.

➤ After the wizard creates the database, and whenever you open the database for the first time, the Main Switchboard opens, displaying buttons for performing most of the tasks you need to perform with your database.

➤ The Database window is minimized when you first open a database, and it hides behind the Main Switchboard. To bring it into view, minimize the Main Switchboard, and then restore or maximize the Database window.

➤ The Database window has tabs for working with forms, tables, and reports. Click a tab to display a list of forms, tables, or reports.

➤ Use the Form Wizard to create new forms, and use the Table Wizard to create new tables.

Entering Data: For the Record

Now that you have all your tables and forms in place, you're ready to start typing data and entering the records that make up your database. This is the drudge work behind database creation, the kind of job that can give you a bad case of carpal tunnel syndrome and make you wish you had stayed in school.

You can enter data in three ways: by filling out pages full of forms, by typing entries in a table, or by entering the data in a Query. This chapter shows you how to enter data using a form and a table. In Chapter 23, "Finding, Sorting, and Selecting Records," you'll learn more about queries.

How Forms, Tables, and Datasheets Differ

Before you start entering data into your database, you should understand the differences between Datasheet view, forms, and tables so you can make an educated decision on how to enter data. The following list will help you decide.

➤ If you create a form that matches one table blank for blank, you can use either the form or the table to enter data. You are filling in the same blanks, so it really doesn't matter.

➤ A form can have blanks that correspond to fields in more than one table. In such a case, it makes a big difference whether you type the data on a form or use a table.

➤ Datasheet is a *view* that is available for both tables and forms. A table in Datasheet view is very similar to a form displayed in Datasheet view, but the function of a form differs from that of a table. Even though a form in Datasheet view *looks* like a table, remember that you're still working with a form.

Filling Out Forms

We are all accustomed to filling out forms. You do it in your checkbook, at the dentist's office, when you apply for a job, and even when you fill out an application for a credit card. Because you know how to fill out forms, the most intuitive way to enter data in your database is to use a fill-in-the-blanks form.

To complete a form, first display the form you want to fill out. If the Main Switchboard is displayed, click the **Enter/View** button. You can also display a form by selecting it from the Database window; click the **Forms** tab and double-click the name of the form you want to use. Either way you do it, the form pops up on your screen.

Check This Out...

Editing Records You perform the same steps to edit your records. However, when you press the Tab, Enter, or arrow keys to move from one blank to the next, Access highlights the entire entry in that blank. If you want to replace the entry, go ahead and start typing. However, if you just want to edit the entry, click on the entry to move the insertion point to the position where you want to type your change.

If you have any records in the database, the form displays the data that makes up the first record. You can click the arrow buttons at the bottom of the Form window to flip from one record to another. To display a blank form for entering a new record, click the button that has the asterisk (*) on it.

If you choose to create a new record, a blank form appears, prompting you to fill in the blanks. How you fill in the blanks depends on the blanks you're filling. Some blanks are drop-down lists that contain entries from other tables. To enter data, you open the drop-down list and select the desired entry. Other blanks are text boxes; type an entry in the text box. Still other blanks may require that you insert a picture. In such a case, right-click the blank, select **Insert Object**, and use the Insert Object dialog box to select the picture (or other object) you want to insert.

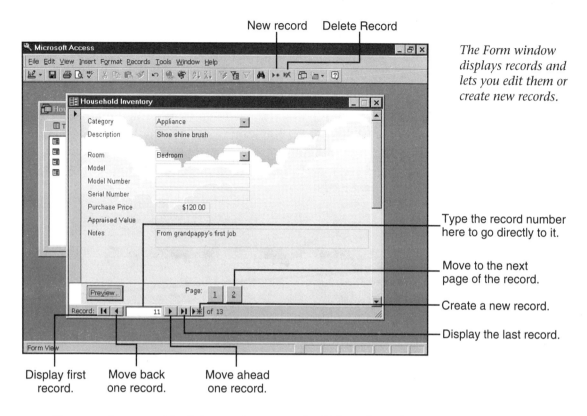

New record   Delete Record

The Form window displays records and lets you edit them or create new records.

Type the record number here to go directly to it.

Move to the next page of the record.

Create a new record.

Display the last record.

Display first record.   Move back one record.   Move ahead one record.

To move from one blank to another, press the **Tab** or **Enter** key, or point and click with the mouse. (If a blank is too short for the entry you're typing, you can expand the blank by pressing **Shift+F2**.) If the form has another page, you can view the page by scrolling down or by clicking the desired page button at the bottom of the form.

Once you have entered all the data for a record, click the **New Record** button (the one with the asterisk). This transfers all the data you entered into the corresponding table(s) and displays a new record for you to fill out.

Keep in mind that you can change from Form view to Datasheet view to enter records into rows instead of using a separate form for each record. Depending on how you like to work, this may help you enter data more quickly. To change to Datasheet view, open the **View** drop-down list in the Form View toolbar and select **Datasheet view**. To enter data in Datasheet view, follow the same process you would to enter data in a table. See the following section, "Entering Data in a Table," for details.

Entering Data in a Table

Although forms provide a more intuitive way to enter records into your database, a table may be more efficient. A table also allows you to focus on a single set of data, whereas a form might contain data fields for several tables.

To enter records in a table, click the **Tables** tab in the Database window, and then double-click the name of the table to which you want to add records. In a table, you can create a new record by typing data into the last row of the table. After you type an entry in the last field in the row and press the **Tab** key, Access creates a new row into which you can type entries for the next record.

Datasheet View lets you type records in a table.

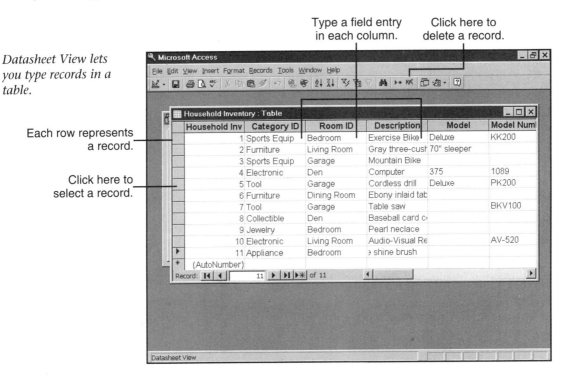

Type a field entry in each column.

Click here to delete a record.

Each row represents a record.

Click here to select a record.

If a column is too narrow to display the entries, you can widen the column. Move the mouse pointer over the field name at the top of the column, and then slide it over one of the lines separating the columns until the mouse pointer turns into a double-headed arrow. Hold down the mouse button and drag the line to make the column the desired width.

What Are These Drop-Down Lists For?

As you enter data in tables and forms, you'll start to notice that some of the blanks are actually drop-down lists from which you can choose an entry. You might also notice that you can't type any entries into these blanks unless they're on the list. Why? Because these fields, called *foreign keys*, are linked to fields called *primary keys* in other tables.

For example, the Household Inventory database has a form for entering a record of each item you own for insurance purposes. The Categories field lets you categorize your possessions as furniture, collectible, appliance, and so on. The entries in this field come from another table, the Categories table. If you want to enter some other category in the Home Inventory table, you should first enter it into the Categories table so you can keep track of all the categories in your database.

Key field supplies data to the foreign field.   Foreign field

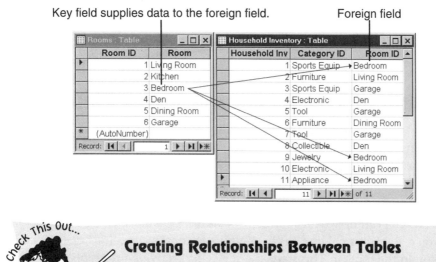

Access relates data in two or more tables by using matching fields.

Creating Relationships Between Tables

Check This Out...

The easiest way to create relationships between tables is to use the Database Wizard to set up your tables. If you need another table, use the Table Wizard to create the new table. The wizard prompts you to create relationships between the new table and existing tables. You can set up, edit, and delete relationships manually by selecting **Tools**, **Relationships**, but that process is beyond the scope of this book.

Speeding Up Data Entry with AutoCorrect

Although AutoCorrect was designed more for automatically fixing typographical errors and spelling mistakes, you can use it in Access to streamline data entry. For example, if you have an entry you must type frequently, such as "Hillary Rodham Clinton," you can create a shorthand AutoCorrect entry (such as "hil") and have Access insert the full entry for you.

To create an AutoCorrect entry, open the **Tools** menu and select **AutoCorrect**. Click in the **Replace** text box and type the abbreviated version of the entry. Click in the **With** text box and type the full version of the entry. Then click the **Add** button. Repeat the process to create additional AutoCorrect entries. When you're done, click **OK**. Whenever you type an abbreviated entry followed by a space or punctuation mark, AutoCorrect inserts the full entry.

You can turn AutoCorrect on and off via the AutoCorrect dialog box. Open the **Tools** menu, select **AutoCorrect**, and select **Replace Text As You Type** to turn the feature on or off.

Checking Spelling in Text Boxes and Memo Fields

Of course there's no way you want to check the spelling of an entire database. Databases contain so many weird entries that the spell checker would probably question ninety percent of them. However, if you have any lengthy text boxes that contain memos or descriptions of products, you might want to check the spelling in that field.

To check the spelling of text in a particular field on a form, first select the field. In Datasheet view, you can drag over a range of fields to check the spelling in all the field entries, or you can select a column to check all the entries in a specific field. Click the **Spelling** button in the toolbar. This starts the spell checker, which stops on the first questionable spelling. You then have the following options:

➤ If the word is incorrectly spelled and the Suggestions list displays the correct spelling, click the correct spelling and click **Change** to replace only this occurrence of the word.

➤ To replace this misspelled word and all other occurrences of the word in this document, click the correct spelling in the Suggestions list and click **Change All**.

➤ Backspace over the word (assuming it is misspelled) and type the correction.

➤ Click **Ignore** if the word is spelled correctly and you want to skip it just this once. The spell checker will stop on the next occurrence of the word.

➤ Click **Ignore All** if the word is spelled correctly and you want to skip any other occurrences of this word in this document.

➤ Click **Add** to add the word to the dictionary so the spell checker will never question it again in any of your databases.

➤ Create an AutoCorrect entry for the misspelling so the spell checker will correct it whenever you type the misspelling. Click the **AutoCorrect** button to create an AutoCorrect entry.

➤ Click **Ignore "_____" Field** to have the spell checker skip over any questionable spellings in this field in your tables or forms.

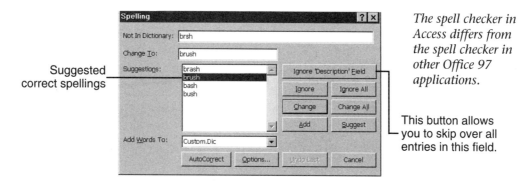

Suggested correct spellings

The spell checker in Access differs from the spell checker in other Office 97 applications.

This button allows you to skip over all entries in this field.

The Least You Need to Know

Once you have all the tables and forms set up, data entry is a breeze. However, there are a couple of issues that might confuse you:

➤ Before you type any entries, decide whether you want to type the entries in a form or in a table.

➤ A form might contain fields that are linked to more than one table.

➤ In Datasheet view, a form looks like a table, but it still acts as a form.

➤ To create a new record in a form, click the button that has the asterisk on it.

➤ To create a new record in a table (or in a form that's displayed in Datasheet view), type the record in the last row.

➤ You can create AutoCorrect entries that act as shorthand for longer text entries.

Chapter 23

Finding, Sorting, and Selecting Records

In This Chapter

➤ Flipping through records one at a time

➤ Sorting records by name, date, and other criteria

➤ Pulling selected records out of the database with queries

➤ Making it easy with the Query Wizard

Now that you have this oversized filing cabinet sitting in your computer, how do you go about getting at those records? You have at least three options. You can browse through the records one at a time. You can list the information in every record according to field name. Or you can create a query that pulls records that match certain criteria out of the database. In this chapter, you'll learn how to use these three methods to work with your records.

Flipping Through Records in Tables and Forms

If you don't know what you're looking for, the only way to find it is to flip through your records. You can flip through records in either Form view or Datasheet view. In Form view, you see one record at a time. Datasheet view lists the records in rows, allowing you to easily skim through a screenful of records.

To display a form, open the Database window, click the **Forms** tab and double-click the form you want to use. Use the controls at the bottom of the window to flip to the next or previous record, or to jump to a specific record (if you know its number).

You can flip through records one at a time in Forms view.

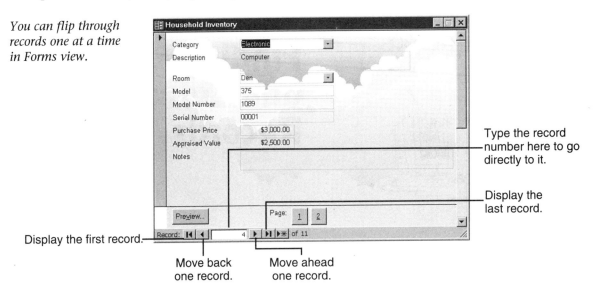

Type the record number here to go directly to it.

Display the last record.

Display the first record.

Move back one record.

Move ahead one record.

In Datasheet view, Access displays each record in a row of its own, just as if you entered the records in an Excel worksheet. To change to Datasheet view, open the **View** menu and click **Datasheet View**. To flip through the records, simply use the scroll bar on the right side of the screen, or use the Page Up and Page Down keys on your keyboard.

Keep in mind that you can view tables or forms in Datasheet view. If you select a table, it automatically appears in Datasheet view. If you select a form, you can display the form in Datasheet view by selecting **View**, **Datasheet View**. If your forms have the same fields as your tables, it really doesn't matter whether you use forms or tables to look for records.

Sorting Your Records by Number, Name, or Date

Suppose your boss comes in with a stack of paper forms you have to enter into the database. They're wrinkled, mixed up, upside down, and generally a big mess. You mindlessly flip through the stack, entering the information into the database. Later, your boss asks you to arrange the forms in alphabetical order and print them out. Is this a problem? Not with Access!

Access can sort the records based on any field entry in the records. For example, you could sort a list of invoices by date, company name, the amount of the order, the time the payment is overdue, or even the ZIP codes. Access offers two sort options: Sort

Ascending and Sort Descending, which you can find on the Records, Sort submenu, or as buttons in the toolbar. Sort Ascending sorts from A to Z or 1 to 10. Sort Descending sorts from Z to A or 10 to 1.

You can sort records in either Datasheet view or Form view, although Datasheet view displays the results of the sorting operation more clearly. Take one of the following steps:

➤ In Form view, click inside the field you want to use to sort the records, and then click the **Sort Ascending** or **Sort Descending** button in the toolbar.

➤ In Datasheet view, click the field name at the top of the column whose entries you want to use to sort the records. Click the **Sort Ascending** or **Sort Descending** button in the toolbar.

Records sorted in Ascending order based
on the entries in the Room column

Category	Description	Room	Mod
Appliance	Shoe shine brus	Bedroom	
Jewelry	Pearl neclace	Bedroom	
Sports Equipment	Exercise Bike	Bedroom	Deluxe
Collectible	Baseball card c	Den	
Electronic	Computer	Den	375
Furniture	Ebony inlaid tal	Dining Room	
Tool	Table saw	Garage	
Tool	Cordless drill	Garage	Deluxe
Sports Equipment	Mountain Bike	Garage	
Electronic	Audio-Visual Re	Living Room	
Furniture	Gray three-cusl	Living Room	70" sleeper

Datasheet view clearly displays the results of the sorting operation.

Filtering Records to Lighten the Load

Sometimes you'll want to work with a distinct group of records. Maybe you work in a doctor's office, and the health department wants a list of all your patients who have had hepatitis in the last two years. Or maybe you work for a collection agency and you need to prioritize a list of people who owe money to one of your clients, and you need to know who has owed the most money for the longest period of time. To extract a select group of records you can *filter* the records, as explained in the following sections.

Filtering the Easy Way

The easiest way to filter records in Access is to use a technique called *filter by selection*. To use this technique, select the entry on a form that you want to use as the filter. For example, open a record that has New York in the City field (in Form or Datasheet view) and click in the **City** field. Then click the **Filter By Selection** button.

293

Access displays only those records that have the specified entry in the selected field (in the example, only those records that have New York in the City field).

If the list of records is still too long, you can filter the list again using another field entry. Repeat the steps using an entry in another field. To remove the filter and return a complete list of records, click the **Apply Filter** button.

When Your Filtering Needs Become More Complex

Filtering by selection is great if you have a specific entry in your record that you can use for the filter. But that rarely happens. Usually, you'll have to select a range of records. For example, you might want a list of clients whom you haven't called for over a month, or you might need a list of records for people whose last name begins with A through K. Filter by selection can't handle anything this complicated.

To create a more complex filter, you should use the *filter by form* technique. With this technique, you type filter criteria into various fields on a blank form to tell Access which records to pull up. For example, in a billing database, you might type <=#2/25/97# (less than or equal to 2/25/97) in the Date field to find all bills dated 2/25/97 or earlier. You might also type the expression >0 (greater than zero) in the Balance Due field to find out which bills dated 2/25/97 or earlier haven't been paid yet. The following table shows some sample expressions.

Filter Criteria Expressions in Action

Field	Sample Expression	Filter Displays
City	"Chicago"	Only those records that have "Chicago" in the City field
City	"Chicago" or "New York"	Records that have "Chicago" or "New York" in the City field
DueDate	Between #12/1/96# and #7/10/97#	Records that have an entry in the DueDate field between the dates listed
LastName	>="K"	All records with a last name entry starting with K or a letter after K in the alphabet
LastName	<="J"	All records with a last name entry starting with J or a letter before J in the alphabet
State	Not "IN"	Only records that have a State entry other than IN
Customer	Like "L*"	Records for companies whose names start with L

To filter by form, open the table that contains the records you want to filter, and then click the **Filter By Form** button. A single-row datasheet appears, displaying the names of all the fields in the table or form. Type a filter criteria expression in each field you want to use to filter the records.

If you type a criteria expression in more than one field, you further limit the group of records that the filter will display. For example, if you typed **Not "IN"** in the State field, you would end up with records from all other states. But if you added the expression **Like "L*"** to the Customer field, the list would be narrowed to only those customers outside Indiana whose names begin with L.

To broaden the filter, you can click one or more **Or** tabs and enter expressions in the fields. For example, you might want a list of customers who owe you money and customers to whom you owe money.

After you've typed your filter criteria expressions, click the **Apply Filter** button. Access filters the records and displays a list of only those records that match the specified criteria.

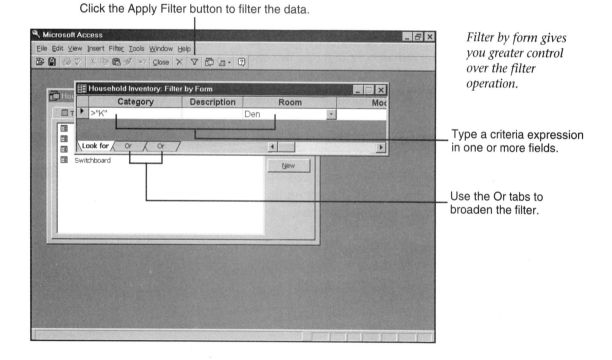

Click the Apply Filter button to filter the data.

Filter by form gives you greater control over the filter operation.

Type a criteria expression in one or more fields.

Use the Or tabs to broaden the filter.

Using Queries to Sort, Select, and Calculate

Although filters are powerful tools for extracting records from individual tables, they are somewhat limited. Filters don't really do anything with the records; they don't allow you to combine information from different tables; and they can't extract only selected fields—they display entire records.

Access provides a more powerful data management tool called a *query*, which can do everything a filter can do and much more. A query can pull pieces of information from various tables and assemble it in a separate datasheet, sort the resulting list, and even perform calculations on the data.

The following sections explain two ways to create and use queries in your database.

Using the Query Wizards

Like all wizards, the Query Wizards are designed to simplify your life. Instead of having to design your own query from scratch, you can use the Query Wizards to lead you step-by-step through the process of creating the following four types of queries:

➤ **Simple** queries pull data from fields in various tables, place it in a query table, and (optionally) sort the records. (This is the most common type of query.)

➤ **Crosstab** queries pull data from fields, assemble it in a table that's structured like an Excel worksheet, and (optionally) perform calculations using the data. The crosstab query is excellent for determining totals and subtotals.

➤ **Find Duplicates** queries select all records that have the same entry in a specified field. For example, in the Home Inventory database, you could use a find duplicates query to find all possessions located in the living room.

➤ **Find Unmatched** queries select all records that have no related records in another table. This type of query is useful for finding records with missing entries. After the query is done, you can enter the missing data.

The following steps lead you through the process of creating a simple query. The steps for creating other types of queries may differ.

1. Open the database you want to query.

2. Open the **Insert** menu and select **Query**. The New Query dialog box appears, listing the Query Wizards.

3. Click the **Simple Query Wizard** and click **OK**. The first Simple Query Wizard dialog box appears, prompting you to select the fields you want included in the query.

4. Open the **Tables/Queries** drop-down list and select one of the tables whose field you want to include in the query. The Available Fields list displays the names of all the fields in the selected table. (You can select fields from more than one table.)

5. In the Available Fields list, double-click a field name to move it to the Selected Fields list to include the field in the query. (You can move all the fields from the Available Fields list to the Selected Fields list by clicking the double-headed arrow.)

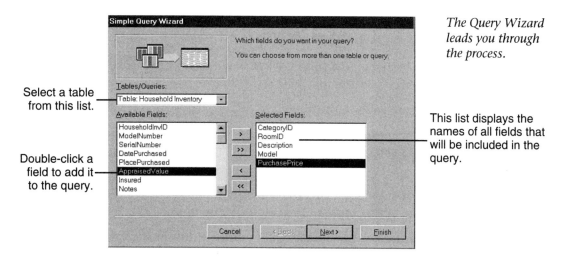

Select a table from this list.

Double-click a field to add it to the query.

The Query Wizard leads you through the process.

This list displays the names of all fields that will be included in the query.

6. Repeat steps 4 and 5 to add more fields to the query. When you're done adding fields, click the **Next>** button. The next dialog box asks if you want a detailed query or a summary.

7. Select **Detail** to display the complete information for each field. (If you want only summary information, such as an average or sum, click **Summary** and enter your summary preferences.)

8. Click the **Next>** button. The next dialog box asks you to type a title for the query or accept the suggested title.

9. If desired, type a title for the query. Then click the **Finish** button. The Simple Query Wizard creates the query and displays it in its own window.

The query appears in Datasheet view. You can click a column heading to select a column and then drag the column to move it. You can also sort the query or filter it as explained earlier in this chapter.

Sorting a Query in Design View

Instead of using the Sort Ascending or Sort Descending buttons to sort the records in a query, change to Design view. Click in the **Sort** box for the field you want to use to sort the records, open the drop-down list, and select **Ascending** or **Descending**.

Creating a Query Without a Wizard

Although the Query Wizards are helpful, they may not create the type of query you need. To make a custom query, take the following steps:

1. Open the database you want to query.

2. Open the Database window, click the **Queries** tab, and click the **New** button. The New Query dialog box appears. (This is the same dialog box you used to run the Query Wizard.)

3. Click **Design View** and click **OK**. The Show Table dialog box appears, prompting you to select the tables you want to get information from.

4. Double-click the name of each table you want to get information from. When you double-click the name of a table, the table is added to the **Query#: Select Query** window.

5. Click the **Close** button. The Query window shows the names of all the tables you added, as well as a list of fields in each table.

6. For each field you want to add to your query, click inside the field box at the bottom of the window, and double-click the field name in one of the tables at the top of the window. The field names are added to the Field boxes. Table names appear directly below the field names.

7. To sort the records in the query based on the entries in one of the fields, click in the **Sort** box for that field, open the drop-down list, and select **Ascending** or **Descending**.

8. To filter the records based on the entries in one field, click inside the **Criteria** box in that field and type a filter criteria expression. See "Filtering Records to Lighten the Load," earlier in this chapter for details.

9. The **Show** check boxes let you hide or display a field in a query. Remove the check from the box to hide the field if desired.

10. To run the query, click the **Run** button (the button with the exclamation point) in the toolbar. Access runs the query and displays the results in Datasheet view.

2. Double-click a field name. ——— 3. Click here to run the query.

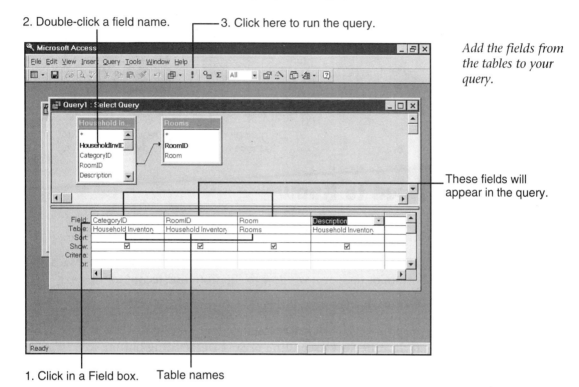

Add the fields from the tables to your query.

These fields will appear in the query.

1. Click in a Field box.　　Table names

Saving, Opening, and Editing Queries

Access does not automatically save queries. To save a query, open the **File** menu and select **Save**. The Save As dialog box appears, prompting you to name the query. Type a name for the query and click **OK**. Queries are saved with the database. To open a query you saved, first open the database file. In the Database window, click the **Queries** tab, and double-click the name of the query you want to open.

Whenever you open a query, Access displays it in Datasheet view. To edit it, you must change to Design view. Open the **View** menu and select **Design View**, or open the **View** drop-down list (on the left end of the toolbar) and click **Design View**. Then you can add or delete fields, hide fields, move fields, or sort and filter your records.

Display your query in design view to edit it.

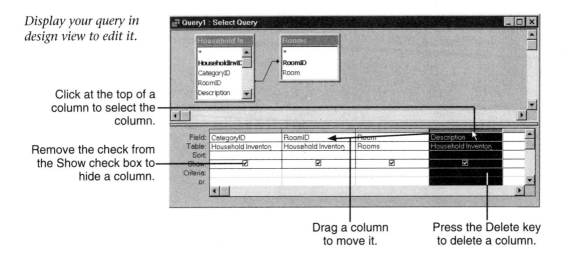

Click at the top of a column to select the column.

Remove the check from the Show check box to hide a column.

Drag a column to move it.

Press the Delete key to delete a column.

The Least You Need to Know

Once you've entered the data that makes up your database, you can sort, filter, and extract that data in various ways:

➤ To manually flip through your records, open the desired form and use the page controls at the bottom of the Form window to flip from one record to the next.

➤ You can change to Datasheet view to display your records in a table.

➤ To sort records in Form view, click inside the field you want to use to sort the records, and then click the **Sort Ascending** or **Sort Descending** button.

➤ To sort records in Datasheet view, click the field name at the top of the column whose entries you want to use to sort the records, and then click the **Sort Ascending** or **Sort Descending** button.

➤ To quickly sort records, click inside the field that has the entry you want all the other records to match, and then click the **Filter By Selection** button.

➤ Create a query to extract data from various tables. To create a query, open the **Insert** menu and select **Query**.

Giving Data Meaning with Reports

Data is like money: If you don't do something with it, it's useless. Reports do something with your data. You can use a report to transform a membership directory into sheets of mailing labels or a phone list. You might also use a report to pull together a list of contributors, the amount each person contributed to the annual fund drive, and the total amount that the fund drive pulled in. Reports can even pull data from one or more tables and graph it.

In this chapter, you will learn various ways to create and customize reports, and you'll learn how to print reports once you've created them.

The Report You Need May Already Exist!

You can save yourself some time and effort by checking to see if your database already has the report you need. If you used one of the Database Wizards to create your database, you might be in luck. The wizards make several reports you can use immediately.

If the Main Switchboard is displayed, you can take a look at these predesigned reports by clicking the **Preview Reports** button. This displays the Reports Switchboard. Click the button next to the report you want to look at, and Access opens the selected report in its own window. If the report has more than one page, you can use the page controls at the bottom of the window to flip pages.

You can also view reports from the Database window. Click the **Reports** tab to view a list of reports. Then click the name of the report you want to view and click the **Preview** button.

You can preview existing reports.

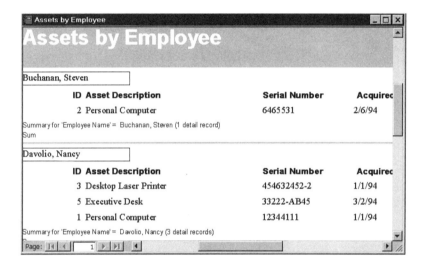

Customize an Existing Report

Even if an existing report doesn't have all the data you need arranged just the way you want it, you might be able to save time by customizing one of the existing reports instead of starting from scratch. See "Customizing the Look and Content of Your Report" later in this chapter for details.

Making Reports with the Report Wizard

No matter which task you want to perform in Access, you can be fairly certain that there's some philanthropic wizard waiting in the wings to lend a hand. This is true with reports, as well. However, the wizards that Access offers for creating reports are kind of strange. There's only one wizard called "Report Wizard," but several other wizards—using other names—can create specialized reports that you might find more useful.

To view a list of the wizards and non-wizards, display the Database window, click the **Reports** tab, and click the **New** button. Here's a list of the wizards (and pseudo-wizards) and their specialties:

➤ **Design View** is no wizard. This is the worst option to select because it displays a blank window on which *you* have to do the work. You don't want this one.

➤ **Report Wizard** is the official "Report Wizard." This wizard leads you through the process of creating a report. A series of dialog boxes prompt you to select data, tell the wizard how to arrange it on the form, and add subheadings to help group the data. Refer to the steps following this list for instructions on how to use the Report Wizard.

➤ **AutoReport: Columnar** creates a report that looks very similar to a form. Field names are printed on the left, and field entries appear on the right. Before you can use this wizard, you must select the table or query for which you want to create the report.

➤ **AutoReport: Tabular** creates a report that looks like a table. Field names appear across the top of the report, and field entries are listed below the field names. Why they don't call this one "columnar," I don't know.

➤ **Chart Wizard** grabs the specified data and charts it for you.

➤ **Label Wizard** transforms a list of names and addresses into mailing labels. You'll have to supply information, such as the size and type of the labels on which you intend to print.

Assuming you didn't luck out and find the perfect report sitting on the Reports tab, and you don't want to use an AutoReport or create a chart or mailing labels, you'll have to create a custom report. Don't panic yet—the process may be fairly easy with the help of the Report Wizard.

The following steps walk you through creating a report with the wizard:

1. Open the database file that has the data you want to include in the report.

2. Open the Database window, click the **Reports** tab, and click **New**. The New Report dialog box appears, showing a list of tools for creating reports.

3. Click **Report Wizard** and click **OK**. The first Report Wizard dialog box appears, prompting you to select the fields you want included in the query.

4. Open the **Tables/Queries** drop-down list and select one of the tables or queries that contains a field you want to include in the report. The Available Fields list displays the names of all the fields in the selected table. (You can select fields from more than one table.)

5. In the **Available Fields** list, double-click a field name to include the field in the report. The field moves to the Selected Fields list. (You can move all the fields from the Available Fields list to the Selected Fields list by clicking the double-headed arrow.)

Select the fields you want to include in the report.

Select a table or query.

Double-click a field to add it to the report.

These fields will appear in the report.

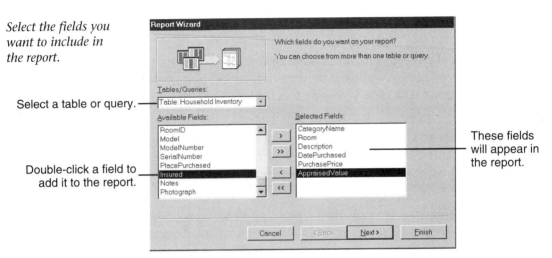

6. Repeat steps 4 and 5 to add more fields to the report. When you finish adding fields, click the **Next>** button. The next dialog box asks if you want to group any records in the report by adding headings.

7. Double-click a field if you want to use it to group records. For example, if you're creating an inventory of your possessions, you might want to group them by rooms. (You can insert additional fields as group headings by double-clicking their names.) Click **Next>**. The next dialog box asks if you want to sort records using any of the fields.

8. Use the drop-down lists as shown in the following figure to select the fields that contain the entries you want to use to sort the records. (For example, you might sort by LastName.) Click the sort button to the right of the drop-down list to change from ascending to descending or vice versa. Click the **Next>** button, and you are asked to pick a layout for the report.

9. Click the desired layout and print orientation. If you have a bunch of columns to fit across the page, you might want to turn off the **Adjust the Field Width** option; otherwise, the type might be too small to read. Click the **Next>** button, and the wizard asks you to pick a type style for the report.

10. Click the desired style and click **Next>**. The final dialog box lets you give the report a title or change its design.

11. Type a title for the report and click **Finish**. Don't worry about the Preview option or the option for changing the report design; you can do all that later. The wizard creates the report and displays it on-screen.

Select the field you want to use to sort the records.

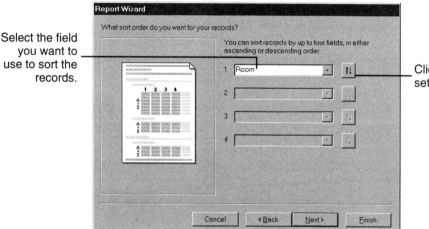

You can sort the records using one or more fields.

Click this button to set the sort order.

Customizing the Look and Content of Your Report

If the Report Wizard just dropped the perfect report in your lap (fat chance), click the **Print** button in the toolbar—and you're done. It's more likely, however, that your report needs a little tweaking before it's ready to present to the general public. The report may need something minor, such as a font change, or some major reconstruction that requires you to move columns, for example.

To make any of these changes, display the report (select the Report from the Reports tab in the Database dialog box), and then open the **View** menu and select **Design View**. Access displays the structure behind the report. In the next few sections, you'll learn how to work in Design view to change the report's look and layout.

Working with a Report in Design View

If this is your first time to work with an Access report in Design view, this view won't make much sense, and it sure doesn't look anything like the report you just created. For one thing, your report doesn't have those gray bars separating it into sections. The following list explains the various sections in your report and what you'll find in each section:

➤ **Headers** print on every page of the report. The report header appears only at the top of the first page. The page header and any additional headers appear at the top of every page. In addition, most reports use a header that contains the field names from one or more tables as column headings.

➤ **Detail** is used for the data you pull from the various tables in your database. The controls in the Detail section are usually fields that pull data from one or more tables and list it under the column headings.

➤ **Footers** appear at the bottom of every page of the report. The report footer appears on the last page of the report; you can use it to calculate grand totals. The Page footer is useful for including a date or page number on every page. The footer just below the Detail section is useful for subtotals.

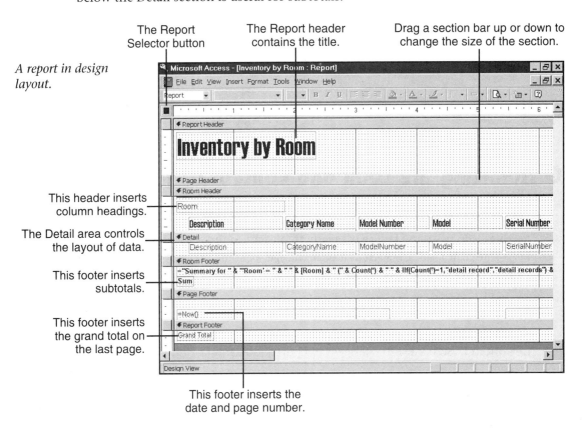

The Report
Selector button

The Report header
contains the title.

Drag a section bar up or down to
change the size of the section.

*A report in design
layout.*

This header inserts
column headings.

The Detail area controls
the layout of data.

This footer inserts
subtotals.

This footer inserts
the grand total on
the last page.

This footer inserts the
date and page number.

You can increase the space used for a particular section of the report by dragging the top of the bar for that section up or down. (Keep in mind that this *will* affect the page breaks in your report.) If there is no space below a section bar, double-click the bar, click the **Format** tab, and type a measurement in the **Height** box (for instance, type 1 to give the section 1 inch of space).

You can change the properties of a section by double-clicking the bar and then entering your preferences. To select the entire report, click the **Report Selector** button, which appears at the intersection of the two rulers.

Changing the Overall Look of the Report

The easiest way to change the overall look of the report is to use AutoFormat. Click the **Report Selector** button in the upper-left corner of the window (where the horizontal and vertical rulers intersect). A black square appears on the button indicating that it is active.

Open the **Format** menu and select **AutoFormat**. The AutoFormat dialog box appears, prompting you to select a style for your report. Click the desired style and click **OK**.

> **AutoFormatting Individual Objects** You can use AutoFormat to change the look of individual objects (controls) on the form by selecting the object before running AutoFormat. However, this might give your report an undesirable patchwork look.

Selecting, Moving, and Aligning Controls

Design view reveals that your report is no more than a collection of text boxes and other controls. Working with these controls is very much like working with objects in a drawing program. To select a control, click it. **Shift**+click on additional controls to work on more than one at a time. When you click a control, a box and a set of handles appear around the control. You can then move, resize, or delete the control, as described here:

➤ To move the control, slide the mouse pointer over the outline of the box that defines the control. When the mouse pointer turns into a hand, drag the box.

➤ To change the size of the control, drag one of its handles.

➤ To delete the selected control, press the **Delete** key.

When moving controls, you may want to align one control with another. Access can do this for you. First, select the controls you want to align. Then open the **Format** menu, point to **Align**, and select the desired alignment option: **Left**, **Right**, **Top**, **Bottom**, or **To Grid** (which aligns one edge of the control with an invisible grid line).

Changing Type Styles and Sizes

You learned earlier how to change type styles for the entire report. You can also change type styles and sizes for individual controls. To do so, first select the controls that have the text you want to format. Then use the tools in the Formatting toolbar to set the font and font size, add attributes such as bold and italic, and change the text and background color. You can also add a border, drop shadow, or other special effect to give the control another dimension.

Change the font.   Pick a font size.   Change the text color.

Use the Formatting toolbar to change the look of individual controls.

Add a special effect.

Add text attributes.   Add a border.

Adding Controls to the Report

In Design view, Access displays a toolbox containing buttons for adding such controls as labels, text boxes, check boxes, and lines to your report. The easiest way to add a control is to use a Control Wizard. These steps tell you how.

1. Click the **Control Wizards** button to turn it on. (The button should appear to be pressed in.)

2. Click the button for the control you want to create.

3. Move the mouse pointer over the report where you want to insert the control. Drag the mouse to create a box that defines the size and location of the control. When you release the mouse button, the control appears, and the Control Wizard dialog box appears, providing instructions on how to proceed.

4. Follow the Control Wizard's instructions to create the control. In most cases, you need to supply a name for the control and tell the Wizard which field to link the control to.

Inserting Fields

If you simply want to insert a field on your report, there's an easier way to do it than by using the Control Toolbox. Open the **View** menu and select **Field List**. This displays a list of the available fields. Drag a field from the field list to the desired location on the report, and Access inserts a label box and a text box for the field.

Adding Totals, Subtotals, and Averages

Some reports simply present data in some easily digestible format, such as a phone list or address list. Other reports are designed to help you draw conclusions or determine final results. For example, you may have a report that lists income and expenses to determine profit. If the report simply lists the numbers, it won't do you much good. You need to know a final number—the profit.

To perform such a task, you need to enter a formula into your report. The formula performs calculations using the data that the report extracts from various tables. You typically enter a formula inside a text box in a section below the section that contains the numbers you want to total (in other words, below the Detail section). Before you start typing formulas, figure out which section you want the formula to appear in:

➤ To insert a calculation at the end of a row, type the formula at the end of the row that contains the numbers you want to calculate. For example, a record might include the number of items ordered and the price of each item. You could insert a formula at the end of the row that multiplies the number of items times the price to determine the total cost.

➤ If the report has more than one Detail section, you can enter formulas to perform subtotals on a column of numbers in the section just below the Detail section.

➤ To determine a grand total that appears at the bottom of the last page of the report, add the formula to the Report Footer section.

➤ The Page Footer section is typically reserved for page numbers and dates. Don't type the formula in this footer area unless you have some special, strange reason for doing so.

To enter a formula in a text box, click the **Text Box** button in the Toolbox and drag the box where you want to insert the formula. In the **Text** box, type the name of the result (for example, Total, Grand Total, or Average). Then click inside the **Unbound** text box and type your formula. For example, type =SUM ([Income]) to total all the values from the Income fields. The following are some other examples of formulas you might use:

=SUM([Income])–SUM([Expenses]) determines the total profit.

=[Quantity]*[Price] determines the total cost of a number of items times the price of each item.

=AVG ([Grades]) determines the average of a series of grades.

=[Qtr1]+[Qtr2]+[Qtr3]+[Qtr4] calculates the total profit over the last four quarters.

=[Subtotal]*.05 multiplies the subtotal by .05 to determine a 5% tax on an order.

=[Subtotal]+[Tax] determines the total due by adding the subtotal of the order and the amount of tax due.

The formulas you see here are very similar to formulas you might use in Excel worksheets. The only difference is that instead of using cell address in the formulas, you use field names to specify values. For details on using formulas in Excel worksheets, see Chapter 13, "Doing Math with Formulas."

Sample formulas in Design view.

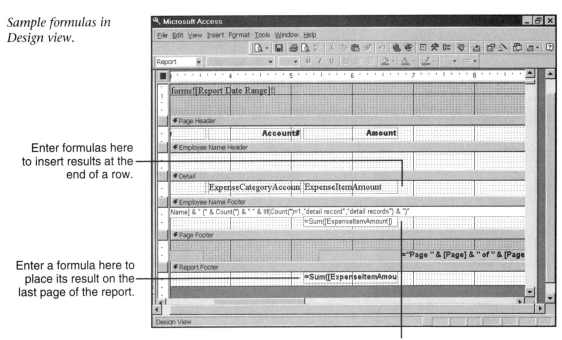

Enter formulas here to insert results at the end of a row.

Enter a formula here to place its result on the last page of the report.

Enter formulas here to insert results at the bottom of each column.

After you enter a formula in a text box, you should format the text box. For example, if the formula enters a dollar amount, you should change the **Format** property of the text box to **Currency**. To change the property of a control on a report, double-click the control, and then enter your preferences in the Format dialog box.

Web Work!

You might want to place your report on the Web so you can boast about your company's profits and attract investors. To save your report as an HTML (Web) document or publish it on the Web, open the **File** menu and select **Save to HTML**. This starts the Publish to the Web Wizard. Follow the wizard's instructions to transform your report into a Web page.

Saving, Opening, and Printing Reports

After you've spent a good part of your day designing a report, you don't want to lose it when you shut down, so be sure to save it. Open the **File** menu and select **Save**, or click the **Save** button in the toolbar. The names of all the reports you save are added to the Reports tab in the Database window. Click the name of the report, and then click **Preview** (to view the report as it will appear in print) or click **Design** (to display the report in Design view).

To quickly print one copy of the report, make sure your printer is turned on, and then click the **Print** button. If you want to print more than one copy of the report or if you want to change other printer settings, open the **File** menu and select **Print**. Enter your preferences and click **OK**.

The Least You Need to Know

Just when you think you're done with a database, you realize that you have to do something with the data you've entered—you have to create a report. Fortunately, Access has some report tools that can make your job easy.

➤ If you used a wizard to create your database, the wizard may have created the report you need. Open the **Database** window and check the **Reports** tab for a list of reports.

➤ You can use a Report Wizard to create a new report. On the Reports tab, click **New**, and then follow the wizard's instructions.

➤ You usually work with reports in Design view and look at them in Print Preview. To change views, open the **View** menu and select the desired view.

➤ In Design view, you can select the entire report by clicking the **Report Selector** button, which is located where the two rulers intersect.

➤ To change the look of the entire report, click the **Report Selector** button, open the **Format** menu, and select **AutoFormat**.

➤ To change the look of individual controls on the form, click the control and use the options in the Formatting toolbar.

Part 6
Looking After Your Life with Outlook

You've always wanted your own personal secretary to inform you of upcoming meetings, remind you of important dates (like Secretary's Day), prioritize your list of things to do, filter your mail and memos…and basically run the office while you're out playing golf with prospective clients.

Office 97 provides you with your own tireless secretary called Microsoft Outlook. Sure, Outlook can't arrange a business trip, drive deposits to the bank, or tuck you into bed when your spouse is out of town, but it can help you keep track of appointments and dates, organize your e-mail, and even remind you of the brilliant ideas that popped into your head during the course of a day. In this section, you'll learn how to use Outlook to do all this and more!

Whoa! Outlook Does All This?!

In 1995, Microsoft added a personal information manager by the name of Schedule+ to its Office suite. It was as though Office 95 had a position to fill, and it hired the first guy who walked through the door. Although fairly competent at keeping track of appointments and important dates, Schedule+ offered a clunky interface, a convoluted address book, and no e-mail support!

For Office 97, Microsoft found a replacement for Schedule+ called Outlook. Outlook provides a smooth interface that lets you shift from your calendar to an address book, inbox, task list, journal, or notes with a single click. It offers e-mail support, allowing you to manage your e-mail from one solitary mailbox. And it gives you access to all the other folders and files on your system (and the network, if you're on a network).

In this chapter, you'll learn how to move around in Outlook and take advantage of its many features.

Schedule+ Plus Microsoft Exchange

Outlook is no great breakthrough. It is basically a combination of Schedule+ (from Office 95) and Microsoft Exchange (from Windows 95). From Schedule+, Outlook took the Calendar, To Do list, and list of Contacts. Microsoft Exchange contributed the e-mail features. If you used Microsoft Exchange for managing your e-mail, you'll see the similarities in Outlook.

Getting Started with Outlook

Before you can take advantage of Outlook, you have to run it. Open the **Start** menu, point to **Programs**, and click **Microsoft Outlook**. The first thing you see is the Office Assistant, welcoming you to Microsoft Office and offering help for some of the tasks you are likely to perform. To get rid of the Assistant and start working, click **OK** in the Assistant's help box.

After you get rid of the Assistant, the Microsoft Outlook window appears, as shown in the figure that follows. The Outlook Bar (on the left) is your key to the various features of Outlook. Here, you can switch to your Inbox, Calendar, Contacts, Tasks, Journal, Notes, or list of items you deleted. Just click the icon for the desired folder in the Outlook Bar. The Information Viewer (on the right) displays the contents of the folder. You can change the relative dimensions of the Outlook Bar and Information Viewer by dragging the bar that separates them.

At the bottom of the Outlook Bar are short gray bars that represent other (hidden) shortcut groups. To see the shortcut icons in any of these groups, click the group (such as Mail or Other). Also notice that just above the Information Viewer is a folder banner that displays the name of the current folder. Click that name to display a list of folders. You can then select a folder from the list (instead of from the Outlook Bar) to view its contents.

Click to display a list of folders.

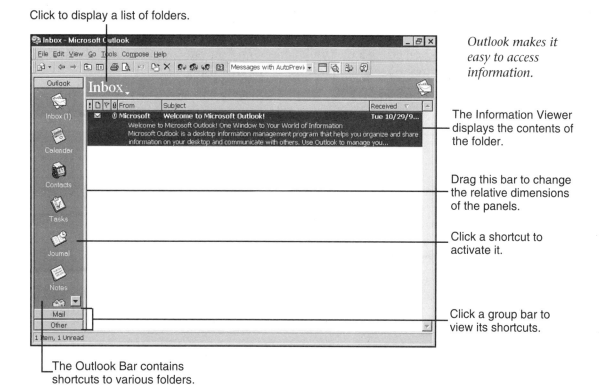

Outlook makes it easy to access information.

The Information Viewer displays the contents of the folder.

Drag this bar to change the relative dimensions of the panels.

Click a shortcut to activate it.

Click a group bar to view its shortcuts.

The Outlook Bar contains shortcuts to various folders.

Using the Standard Toolbar

Like every other Windows application, Outlook has a toolbar you can use to bypass the menu system for commands you enter frequently. The trouble is that I can't really tell you how to use the toolbar because it changes depending on what you're doing. For example, when you're working with the Calendar, the toolbar offers buttons for changing from daily to weekly view and for setting an appointment. If you're using the Inbox to check your e-mail, you'll find a toolbar that offers buttons for deleting and replying to messages.

Although the toolbar keeps changing, you can count on a couple of things. First, as with all toolbars, Outlook's Standard toolbar displays a ScreenTip whenever you rest the mouse pointer on a button. The ScreenTip shows the name of the button so you have some idea of what it does. Second, the left half of the toolbar contains the same buttons no matter which view you're in:

New allows you to create a new mail message, new note, new appointment, or another new item depending on the current view. For example, in the Inbox, this button lets you create a new e-mail message. You can click the arrow to the right of the button to see a complete list of the new things you can create.

Back moves back to the previous screen. For example, if you changed from the Inbox to Notes and then clicked the Back button, Outlook would display the Inbox.

For More Help with Buttons...
If you need additional information about a button, press **Shift+F1** and click the button. A text box appears, displaying a description of the button.

Forward displays the next screen again if you've backed up to a previous screen.

Up One Level displays the contents of the next higher folder. For now, it displays the contents of the Personal Folders folder, which contains subfolders for the Calendar, Contacts, Inbox, and so on.

Folder List displays or hides a panel to the right of the Outlook Bar that displays a list of the available folders. This is similar to the list of folders you might see in the left panel in Windows Explorer.

Print prints the currently displayed item. For example, if you're working with your calendar and you click the Print button, Outlook prints the calendar.

Print Preview shows the currently displayed item as it will print so that you can decide whether you want to print it or format it before printing.

Delete lets you quickly delete a message, note, or other item.

Configuring the Outlook Bar

Outlook is designed to offer you an alternative to the Windows desktop. In addition to keeping track of appointments, dates, and e-mail, Outlook can help you organize your files and run applications. For example, if you click the **Other** group in the Outlook Bar, Outlook displays an icon for My Computer. Click the **My Computer** icon to display a list of icons for disk drives and folders. You can use the Outlook window just like the Windows Explorer window to copy, delete, move, and open files.

Outlook uses this folder system to organize files, notes, e-mail messages, journal entries, contacts, and tasks. You can add folders to the Outlook Bar, in existing groups or in new groups, to give yourself quick access to other resources on your computer or on the network. You can also delete or rename existing groups. To do that, take the following steps:

➤ To create a new group in the Outlook Bar, right-click a blank area of the Bar, select **Add New Group** and type a name for the group.

➤ To remove a group, right-click it and click **Remove Group**.

➤ To rename a group, right-click it, select **Rename Group**, and type a new name for the group.

➤ To add a folder to a group on the Outlook Bar, first click the group. Right-click a blank area inside the group bar and click **Add to Outlook Bar**. Open the **Look In** drop-down list and select Outlook (to add an Outlook folder to the group) or File System (to add a folder from your hard drive or network). Use the folder name list to select the desired folder, and then click **OK**.

➤ To remove a folder from a group, right-click it and select **Remove from Outlook Bar**.

➤ To rename a folder, right-click it and select **Rename Shortcut**. Then type a new name for the folder.

Click Other to view file
management icons.

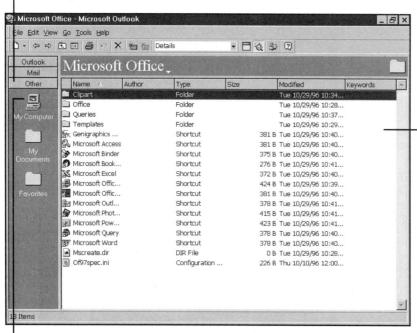

The Outlook Bar contains various folders for organizing your work.

You can use this window to run applications or to copy, delete, move, rename, and open files.

Click My Computer to view
disk, folder, and file icons.

The Calendar: An Electronic Day Planner

In the '60s and '70s, you could hang out at the local tavern and wing it through life. There were only a couple of TV shows that mattered, and a few memorable movies. Kids played together without little leagues, organized football camps, or even the informal intervention of a parent. One person worked while the other person handled the details of owning and keeping up a home. People knew how to kick back and relax.

Check This Out...

Importing Data from Schedule+
If you used Schedule+ to keep track of appointments and contacts, you don't want to type all this information into Outlook—and you don't have to. Open the **File** menu and select **Import and Export**. Then follow the on-screen instructions to import your Schedule+ entries.

In the '90s, we're supposed to keep up on our kids' schoolwork, coach a little league sports team, learn the latest technology, and stay abreast of the current Hollywood offerings, all while trying to hold down a full-time job. Because of this, we're all popping Prozac and toting around day planners.

The solution? Slow down! If you don't like that approach, Outlook's calendar might help you get a handle on this mess we call reality. Click **Outlook** in the Outlook Bar and click **Calendar**. The Calendar appears, showing monthly calendars for this month and next month, a list of things to do, and an hourly list that you can use to enter appointments. In Chapter 26, "Keeping Track of Dates, Mates, and Things to Do," you'll learn more about using the calendar.

The calendar lets you keep track of appointments and things to do.

Today, one hour at a time

Click here to see the previous month.

Click a day to view your hourly schedule.

The task list

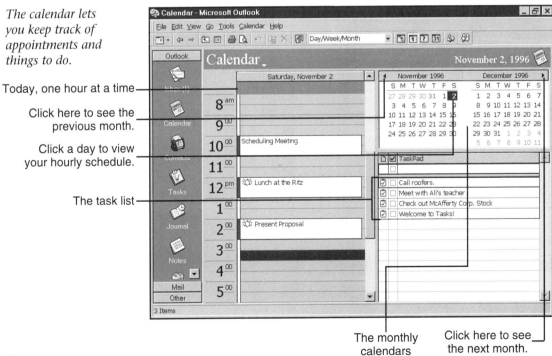

The monthly calendars

Click here to see the next month.

There's a Rolodex on Your Screen!

In my humble opinion, one of the most improved features of Outlook (next to e-mail support) is the Contacts feature. In Schedule+, you had to flip through an address book page-by-page to find a person's name and address. Outlook provides you with a full screen of "index cards" that show abbreviated information about each person.

If your computer has a modem and your phone is connected to it, you can quickly place a call to a person. You can send the person an e-mail message. You can even check out the person's Web page. And you can do this all from Outlook. See Chapter 26 for details on how to enter information for a contact and use that information.

Making a List, Checking It Twice

Working on a computer is sort of like chanting a mantra. Eventually, your eyes glaze over and you start to think about more important things, such as transferring money to your checking account to cover your mortgage payment or making an appointment to see the dentist. While you're thinking of it, you should write down these things you have to do so you won't forget them.

Outlook provides an easy way for you to keep track of the tasks you need to perform. Click the **Tasks** shortcut in the Outlook Bar. In the task list, you can type the various tasks you need to perform and (optionally) the date on which each task needs to be finished. You'll learn more about adding and removing items from the task list in Chapter 26.

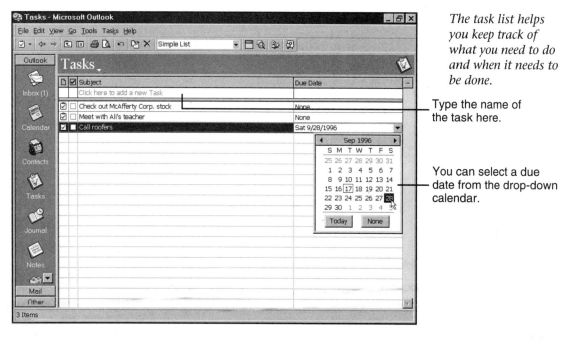

The task list helps you keep track of what you need to do and when it needs to be done.

Type the name of the task here.

You can select a due date from the drop-down calendar.

Doing Away with Paper Post-It Notes

I don't care how advanced the computer is, I will never give up my yellow Post-It notes. They're stuck to my monitor, my checkbook, and even to the pages of my magazines. And at the end of the day, I usually have a couple stuck to the bottom of my shoes.

Outlook now offers an electronic version of these paper notes. You can use notes to jot down ideas or reminders, to store bits of text you would like to use in e-mail messages or documents, or in place of the task list. To create a note, first click the **Notes** icon in the Outlook Bar. Click the **New Note** button, type the text you want to appear on the note, and click the **Close** button.

You can change the color of a note by right-clicking it in the Notes window, pointing to **Color**, and selecting the desired color. To open a note, double-click it. When you open a note, it appears in its own "yellow sticky" window on top of all the other windows on the desktop. If you change to another window, the note is placed in the background, but you can switch back to it by selecting it from the Windows taskbar.

One-Stop E-Mail Delivery

In addition to helping you organize your life, Outlook can help you organize your electronic mail (e-mail, for short). Whenever you start Outlook, it displays the Inbox, showing a list of messages. You can use the Inbox to check for messages, reply to messages you received, and send your own messages.

Microsoft Outlook helps you manage incoming e-mail and send e-mail messages.

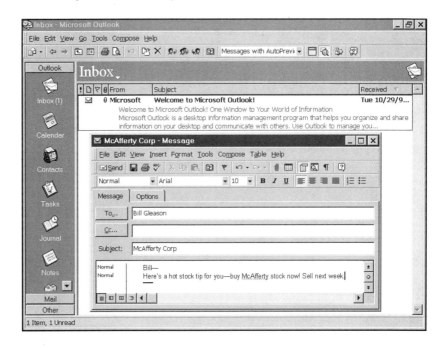

Outlook also offers e-mail support for other features, such as the Calendar. For example, if you're on a network and you need to schedule a meeting with other people on the network, you can send invitations via e-mail specifying the proposed time of the meeting. When the people you invited respond, their replies are stored in your Inbox.

In Chapter 27, "Managing Your E-Mail," you will learn how to use Microsoft Outlook's e-mail folder and tools.

Keeping a Journal (for Future Self-Incrimination)

Outlook's Journal provides another way for you to organize your life (your past life, anyway). The Journal can automatically record such events as the creation of a Word document or Excel worksheet, and can keep track of e-mail messages you send to certain people. For events that the Journal cannot record, the Journal allows you to record the events yourself.

To display the Journal, click **Journal** in the Outlook Bar. The Journal initially displays a week; to display the journal entries for a single day or a month, open the **View** menu and select your preference. To type a Journal entry manually, click the **New Journal** button in the toolbar, complete the Journal Entry dialog box, and click the **Save and Close** button.

To have the Journal automatically record events, open the **Tools** menu, select **Options**, and make sure the **Journal** tab is up front. This tab has options for tracking e-mail messages, meeting cancellations and requests, and task requests and responses. It also offers options for tracking files created in Word, Excel, PowerPoint, Access, and Binder. Click each item you want the Journal to track, placing a check mark next to the items. Click **OK** to save your changes.

As the Journal records events, and as you enter events manually, they appear as shortcut icons on the timeline. You can view an event or open a file that the shortcut points to by double-clicking the shortcut.

The Least You Need to Know

Although Microsoft Outlook sports a fairly intuitive interface, you still have to know the basics in order to find your way around:

➤ The Outlook Bar contains shortcuts to the Inbox (e-mail), Calendar, Contacts, Tasks, Journal, and Notes.

➤ Click a group button in the Outlook Bar to see more shortcuts.

➤ To add something to the Outlook Bar, right-click a blank area of the bar. To delete or change a shortcut in the Outlook Bar, right-click the shortcut.

➤ The Calendar is an electronic day planner that helps you keep track of appointments and important dates.

➤ The Contacts folder is an address book that stores information, such as names, addresses, phone numbers, and e-mail addresses of friends, relatives, colleagues, and customers.

➤ Outlook supports e-mail, providing you with a single e-mail interface for all your e-mail message services.

Keeping Track of Dates, Mates, and Things to Do

A handful of overachievers are ruling our lives. There's the mother who takes her lunch break to help with craft time at school. The father who comes home from a full day's work to organize a soccer league. The old lady down the street who starts a membership drive for her philanthropic organization. Through their examples, they make us feel inferior when we try to relax. Without a word, they make us volunteer when we have no time for ourselves. They quietly force us to pack our calendars with appointments, to sell coupon books and candy, to do more than any person has ever done before, driving us to an early grave with hypertension.

The answer? Slow down. When your kid asks if she can play on the basketball team, hand her a ball and tell her to go to the park. If your boss asks you to work overtime, say no. Don't invest any money. Don't buy anything you can't pay for right now. When a realtor says you can afford more house, fire him. Pare down your life and your schedule, and you won't need Outlook or any other day planner.

Admittedly, slowing down is a challenge, and you don't want to anger too many people by resigning from every organization at once. So in the meantime, use Outlook to manage your life. In this chapter, you'll learn how to use Outlook to keep track of your appointments, contacts, and things you're supposed to do.

Keeping Appointments with the Calendar

Outlook offers a Calendar that enables you to keep track of appointments and plan your days and weeks. Outlook's calendar can even notify you of upcoming appointments ahead of time so you won't be late. In the following sections, you'll learn how to work with the calendar in various views (by day, week, or month), how to add and delete appointments, and how to set advanced appointment options.

Techno Talk

blah blah
blah blah
bl bl
b

Appointments, Meetings, and Events

Before you get immersed in the world of Outlook, brush up on your terminology. Outlook draws a distinction between appointments, meetings, and events. An *appointment* is something you do on your time, which does not demand the time of another person you work with. A *meeting* is something you do with other people at your work; it requires that you coordinate a time block. An *event* is an activity that takes one or more days as opposed to a block of time during one day. An *annual event* (such as a birthday or anniversary) recurs each year.

Daily, Weekly, and Monthly View

To open the Calendar, click the **Outlook** group in the Outlook Bar and click the **Calendar** shortcut. When you first open the Calendar, it displays three items: a daily schedule, showing the hours of the day; two calendar months, the current month and next month; and the task list, displaying the names of any tasks you need to accomplish (assuming you've typed them in).

You can change views in Outlook to display different Calendar objects or to display another arrangement. Use the following controls in the Standard toolbar to change the display:

➤ **Current View** lets you select a different appointment display. Your options include: Day/Week/Month (the default setting), Active Appointments, Events, Annual

Events, Recurring Appointments, or By Category. You'll learn how to work in these displays later in this chapter.

➤ **Go To Today** activates today's date as reported by the clock inside your computer. For example, if you move ahead in the calendar to enter an appointment for a future date, you can click the **Go To Today** button to return to the present.

➤ **Day** is the default setting. This option displays an hourly rundown of the current day on the left side of the Calendar window.

➤ **Week** replaces the day list with a list showing the seven days of the current week. This gives you a quick look at what's going on during a given week.

➤ **Month** displays a full-screen view of the currently selected month, showing the names of all appointments scheduled for each day. This is like the monthly calendar you have hanging in your home or office.

Play around with the different views to get a feel for them. When you're done playing, move on to the next section to enter your first appointment.

Current View

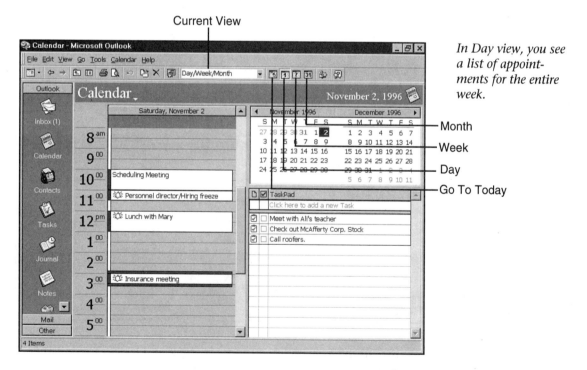

In Day view, you see a list of appointments for the entire week.

327

Setting Appointment Dates and Times

You can quickly enter an appointment in the calendar so the calendar displays the name of the appointment and sounds an alarm to remind you of the appointment 15 minutes ahead of time. To do this, take the following steps:

1. Click the **Day** button to switch back to Day view (if you selected a different view earlier).

2. Drag over the scheduled appointment time. For example, if you have a one-hour appointment that starts at 10:00 a.m., drag over the time blocks for 10:00 and 10:30. The time blocks appear highlighted.

3. Type a description of the appointment (for example, you might type **Meet with Ned about building plans**).

4. Press **Enter**. The appointment description appears on the Day list, and a blue box shows the time blocks that the appointment will take up. A bell appears, indicating that the alarm is on; Outlook will notify you 15 minutes before the appointment.

When you set an appointment, it appears on the daily, weekly, or monthly calendar.

A scheduled appointment ——

This line shows the time you will be at the appointment. ——

The bell indicates that the alarm is on. ——

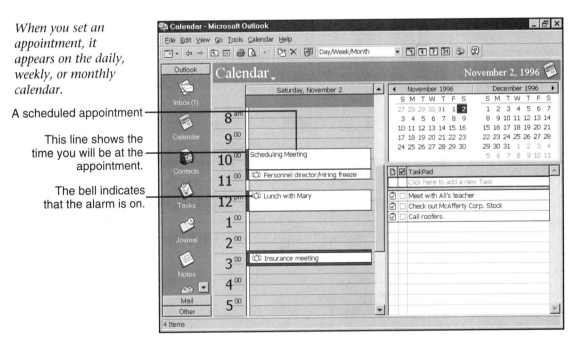

Setting an appointment by dragging and typing is quick, but it does not allow you to enter special settings, such as whether you want the reminder alarm on or off. To enter additional settings, you should use the Appointment dialog box to schedule a new appointment. To display the Appointment dialog box, double-click on a time block on the daily schedule, or click the **New Appointment** button (at the left end of the Standard toolbar). The new Appointment dialog box offers the following options:

➤ **Subject** text box prompts you to enter a description of the appointment.

➤ **Location** lets you specify where the appointment will be held.

➤ **Start Time** provides drop-down lists for entering the starting time and date. If the appointment is going to consume the entire day, check the **All Day Event** check box.

➤ **End Time** provides drop-down lists for entering the scheduled ending time and date (as if appointments ever end on time).

➤ **Reminder** turns the reminder alarm on or off and allows you to specify the number of minutes in advance you want to be reminded of the upcoming appointment.

➤ **Show Time** lets you specify how you want the block of time displayed on your calendar. For example, if you're spending the day at a seminar, you might want to mark the time block as "Out of Office" so your colleagues will know that you can't be reached.

You can type additional information about the appointment in the notes area at the bottom of the dialog box. When you are done entering the appointment, click the **Save and Close** button. The appointment then appears on the daily schedule.

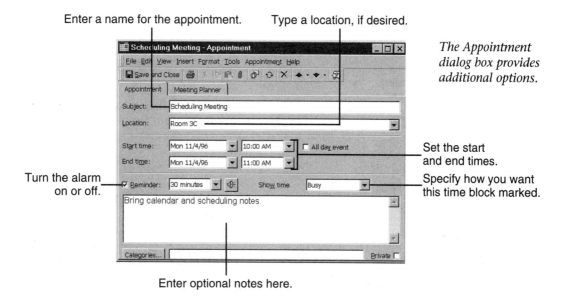

Enter a name for the appointment.

Type a location, if desired.

The Appointment dialog box provides additional options.

Set the start and end times.

Turn the alarm on or off.

Specify how you want this time block marked.

Enter optional notes here.

Editing, Moving, and Deleting Appointments

Unless you have a regularly scheduled appointment, you can count on the fact that your appointment will be rescheduled two or three times before the scheduled date. That's why you need some way to rearrange appointments, delete canceled appointments, and edit the appointment information. The following list provides you with all the instructions you need to perform these tasks.

➤ If the appointment is rescheduled for a time on the same day, you can move it. Position the mouse pointer over the left side of the time block that marks the appointment so the mouse pointer becomes a four-headed arrow. Drag the appointment up or down on the daily schedule to the desired time.

➤ To move an appointment to a different day, change to Week or Month view (by clicking the **Week** button or the **Month** button) and drag the appointment to the desired day.

Check This Out...

My Day Is Divided into 10-Minute Intervals! You can change the default settings for the Calendar to change the times that your day starts and ends, and change the days that comprise your work week. Open the **Tools** menu, select **Options**, and make sure the **Calendar** tab is up front. Enter your preferences and click **OK**. To divide your day into different intervals, right-click inside the area that displays the time intervals and click the desired interval: **60 Minutes, 30 Minutes, 15 Minutes,** etc.

➤ You can increase or decrease the scheduled time for the appointment. Drag the top or bottom line of the time block up or down.

➤ To turn the reminder alarm on or off, right-click the appointment and select **Reminder**.

➤ If your computer is on a network and you don't want other people on the network to know about your appointment, right-click the appointment and select **Private**. A key appears on the appointment, indicating that it is hidden from public view.

➤ You can drag an item from the task list to the calendar to place it on your schedule. When you release the mouse button, the Appointment dialog box appears, prompting you to enter additional details.

➤ If someone cancels the appointment altogether, you can delete it by right-clicking the appointment and selecting **Delete**.

Scheduling a Recurring Weekly or Monthly Appointment

If you have the same appointment at the same time every week or every month, you don't have to enter the appointment into the calendar for each week or month. Have Outlook do it for you, by marking the appointment as a recurring appointment.

First, double-click the recurring appointment to display the Appointment dialog box. Then open the **Appointment** menu and select **Recurrence**. The Appointment Recurrence dialog box appears. Use it to set the frequency of the appointment, its duration, and the number of times you want Outlook to place it on the calendar. Click **OK** after entering your preferences.

Planning a Meeting (Assuming You're Networked)

Here's a feature for all you networkers out there. If you're accustomed to running around trying to figure out a good time for a group of you to meet, you'll be happy to hear that there's a better way. You can use the meeting planner to find out when each person has a free time block, and then one person can schedule the meeting for everyone! Of course, this assumes that everyone involved is using Outlook and is conscientious enough to keep track of blocks of time when they are occupied with other tasks (like work, for instance). It also assumes that you are all connected to the mail server.

To schedule a meeting, use Outlook's Meeting Planner to find out when everyone has a corresponding free block of time and to invite people to the meeting. Take the following steps:

1. Click **Calendar** in the Outlook Bar.

 2. Click the **Plan a Meeting** button in the toolbar. The Plan a Meeting dialog box appears, showing your name as one of the attendees, and displaying any blocks of time marked as a busy time. You can now invite people to the party.

3. Click the **Invite Others** button, and the Select Attendees and Resources dialog box appears. You will use this dialog box to select the names of people you want to attend the meeting from the mail server's post office list or from your personal address book.

4. Open the **Show Names from the** drop-down list and click the resource from which you want to select the names of the people to invite: **Contacts**, **Outlook Address Book**, or **Personal Address Book**. Outlook grabs the names from the selected resource and displays them.

5. To invite a person to the meeting, click the person's name and then click one of the following buttons:

> **Required** is sort of like sending the person a subpoena. The person needs to be at the meeting.

> **Optional** is good if you don't want the person to come to the meeting but you're trying to be nice. Only stupid people go to meetings if attendance isn't required.

Resources lets you reserve a room. The entry in the Resources list will appear in the Location text box when you invite people to the meeting, informing people of the meeting's location. You can leave this list blank for now.

6. Click **OK**. This returns you to the Plan a Meeting dialog box, where the time chart shows each person's free time blocks.

7. Use the scroll bar under the time chart to display a time that is open for all the people you invited. You can click the **AutoPick** button to move to the next time slot that is open for everyone.

8. When you find an open time, drag the vertical bars that mark the start and end times to set the start and end times for the meeting.

Pick a time slot that is open for everyone.

Drag these lines to set the start and end times for the meeting.

Schedules for all the people you invited

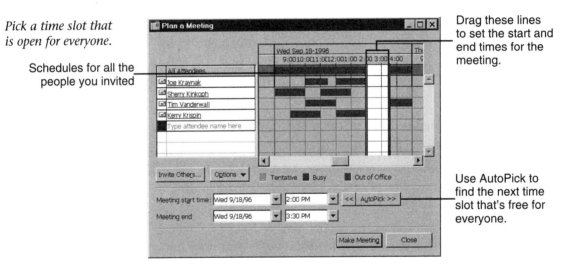

Use AutoPick to find the next time slot that's free for everyone.

9. Click the **Make Meeting** button. The Meeting dialog box appears, showing an invitation message addressed to all the people you chose to invite.

10. In the **Subject** text box, type a brief description or title of the proposed meeting. You can type a lengthy description in the message area at the bottom of the dialog box if you want.

11. If you didn't specify a Resource earlier, click in the **Location** text box and type the place where you will meet (usually a room number).

12. Click the **Send** button. Outlook sends the meeting invitation to all the people on the list. As people respond, their responses appear in your Inbox.

Keeping Track of Birthdays, Anniversaries, and Big Events

Do you have a big family? Have they nearly disowned you because you forget to send out birthday and anniversary cards on time? Does your spouse make jokes about how you always forget your wedding anniversary? Well the Event schedule can help remind you of these big events to help you avoid embarrassment, save your marriage, and reestablish your family ties.

Scheduling an event is no different than scheduling an appointment. First display the Calendar, and then open the **Calendar** menu and select **New Event**. The Event dialog box appears, looking like the Appointment dialog box's identical twin. In the **Subject** text box, type a brief description of the event. To have Outlook remind you before the big day, click the **Reminder** check box. To have Outlook remind you a few days in advance so you have time to buy a present and a card, drag over the entry in the **Reminder** drop-down list and type the number of days warning you want (for example, **5 days**).

If you want Outlook to mark this as an annual event (so Outlook will remind you every year), open the **Appointment** menu and click **Recurrence**. Click **Yearly** and click **OK**. This returns you to the Event dialog box. Click **Save and Close**.

Slapping Together an Online Address Book

Electronic address books used to be only slightly better than their corresponding paper versions. They allowed you to easily edit entries without erasing, and they typically provided search tools to help you find people. The current breed of electronic address books enables you to do much more. For instance, if you have an e-mail connection, you can quickly address e-mail messages from the address book. If you have a modem, the address book can dial phone numbers for you.

In the following sections, you'll learn how to add names, addresses, phone numbers, and other information to your address book and use that information to simplify your life.

Adding Address Cards to the Contacts List

Before you can use the Contacts list, you have to display it. In the Outlook Bar, click **Contacts**. Unless you imported your address list from Schedule+ in the previous chapter, your Contacts list is empty. To start filling it with information about your friends, family, coworkers, customers, and other people, you add address cards. Follow these steps:

1. Click the **New Contact** button in the toolbar (all the way on the left). The New Contact dialog box appears.

2. Click the **Full Name** button and enter the person's title, first name, last name, and any other names the person uses. Click **OK**.

333

3. Type the person's job title and company name (if desired) in the appropriate text boxes.

4. Open the drop-down list below the Address button, and select the type of address you want to enter: **Business** or **Home**.

5. Click the **Address** button and enter the address of the person or business—the street address, city, state, and ZIP code. Click **OK**. (You can repeat steps 4 and 5 to enter other addresses.)

6. Use the Phone number lists and text boxes to enter up to four phone and fax numbers for the person. For example, you might enter the home phone, business phone, cellular phone, and fax numbers.

7. If the person has an e-mail address, type it in the text box next to **E-mail**. You can enter additional e-mail addresses by selecting **E-Mail 2** or **E-Mail 3** from the drop-down list and typing the address.

8. If this person has a personal or business Web page, you can type the Web page address in the **Web Page** text box.

9. If you're on a network, or if you share your computer with others, you can click the **Private** check box to prevent others from viewing this address.

10. Click the **Save and New** button to save this address card and display a new blank card. Repeat these steps to add more address cards to your Contacts list.

Outlook lets you add all sorts of contact information for each person.

Click this button to insert the person's full name.

Click here to insert the person's address.

Enter phone numbers here.

Type an e-mail address here.

If the person has a Web page, type the Web address.

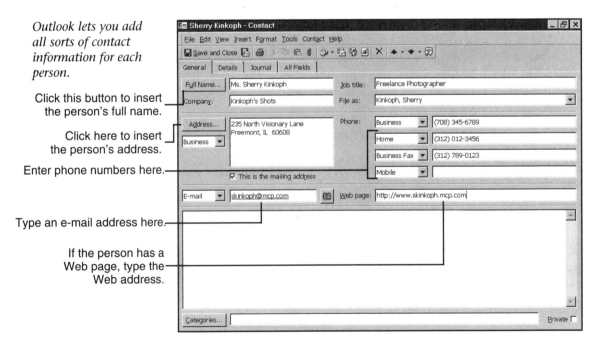

When you switch back to the main Outlook screen, Outlook displays a tiny address card for each contact, arranged alphabetically by last name. If you have gobs of cards, you can click a button on the right side of the screen to display an alphabetical grouping of cards. To select a card, click it. To display all the information a card contains, double-click it.

You can also use the **Current View** drop-down list in the toolbar to display more detailed versions of the cards, to display a phone list, or to group the cards by category, company, or location.

Having Your Modem Dial Phone Numbers

If your computer has a modem, you can use Outlook to transform your three thousand dollar computer into a hundred dollar programmable phone. Your modem should have two phone jacks: one that connects it to the incoming phone line (so it can dial out and talk to other modems), and another one that lets you plug in your phone. First, connect your modem to the phone jack, and then plug your phone into the modem; make sure you have the right wires plugged into the right jacks. Now you're ready to roll.

To dial out, click on the address card for the person you want to call. Then open the **AutoDialer** drop-down list in the toolbar and click the number you want to dial. The New Call dialog box appears. Click the **Start Call** button. Outlook dials the phone number (with the help of your modem) and displays a dialog box telling you to pick up the receiver. Pick up the phone, click the **Talk** button, and start talking.

Using the Speed Dialer

The AutoDialer drop-down list contains a Speed Dial submenu on which you can list the phone numbers of the people you call most often (or emergency numbers). To add a number to the Speed Dial submenu, display the **New Call** dialog box, click **Dialing Options**, and enter the requested information. To dial a number quickly, simply select it from the Speed Dial submenu.

Sending E-Mail Messages to Your Contacts

If you entered an e-mail address for one of your contacts, you can quickly send the person an e-mail message. Click the person's address card, and then click the **New Message to Contact** button in the toolbar. This opens a Message dialog box with a new message addressed to the selected contact. Type a description of the message in the **Subject** text box, type the full message in the large message area at the bottom of the dialog box, and click the **Send** button. For more information about sending e-mail messages, see Chapter 27, "Managing Your E-Mail."

What Do You Have to Do Today?

If you like to be constantly reminded of what you have to do, get married. Short of that, you can use Outlook's task list. Click the **Tasks** shortcut in the Outlook Bar. In the task list, you can type the various tasks you need to perform, and (optionally) the date on which each task needs to be finished (the due date).

Techno Talk

blah blah blah blah bla...

Web Work! If you typed a Web page address for your contact's personal or business Web page, you can quickly pull up the page (assuming you have a Web browser installed) by right-clicking the person's address card and clicking **Explore Web Page**.

To enter this information, click in the **Click Here to Add a New Task** box and type a brief description of the task. Then click in the **Due Date** box next to the Task description, open the drop-down list, and select the date when the task should be done.

If you want to enter additional information about the task, double-click it. This displays a Task dialog box, which allows you to change the name of the task, specify a starting date and due date, and turn on an alarm that sounds when the due date arrives. You can also enter billing information and other notes that provide useful information about the task.

Once you've completed a task, click the check box next to the name of the task. A check mark appears inside the box, and Outlook draws a line through the task title to indicate that you've completed it. This is for management types who need to reward themselves for their minor accomplishments. For the rest of us, there's a **Delete** button. Click it to remove the task from the list.

The Least You Need to Know

This chapter was packed as tight as your schedule with information about how to organize your life with Outlook. Chances are, you're too busy to remember all of it, so just remember the following highlights:

➤ Appointments are for you alone. Meetings are for you and one or more people. Events last an entire day.

➤ Use the Calendar to keep track of appointments, meetings, and events.

➤ To set an appointment, drag over the time block that the appointment will consume, and then type a description of the appointment.

➤ To set a meeting with others on the same network, click the **Plan a Meeting** button.

➤ To insert an address card in the Contacts list, click the **New Contact** button and enter the requested information.

➤ To enter an item on the task list, display the task list, click in the **Click Here to Add a New Task** box, and type a brief description of the task.

Managing Your E-Mail

When you are scheduling appointments, keeping track of contacts, and honing your other life management skills, you don't want to have to switch to some other program to manage your e-mail. You need something more convenient. You need Outlook's Inbox.

In this chapter, you will learn how to use the Inbox to check for incoming mail and manage the messages in the Inbox. You'll also learn how to reply to messages and create and send your own electronic missives.

Nickel Tour of the Inbox

Initially, the Inbox contains a single message from Microsoft, welcoming you to Outlook. To view the title and the first few lines of the message, click the **Inbox** shortcut in the Outlook Bar. Outlook displays several columns above the viewing area:

➤ **Importance** displays an icon that shows whether the sender marked the message as high importance or low importance.

➤ **Icon** shows a picture of a sealed envelope. After you double-click a message to read it, the envelope appears opened.

➤ **Flag Status** displays a flag if you choose to flag a message. You can use flags to mark messages that you might want to reread or respond to later.

➤ **Attachment** shows whether the sender attached a file to the message. If a file is attached, you can open it or save it to your disk.

➤ **From** displays the name of the sender.

➤ **Subject** displays a brief description of the message.

➤ **Received** shows the date and time the message was received.

To sort the messages by the entries in one of the columns, click that column's heading. For example, you can sort the messages by the date and time they were received by clicking **Received**.

Check This Out...

Customizing Your Columns
You can rearrange the columns in the Inbox by dragging them. You can remove a column (such as that useless Importance column) by dragging it off the bar. To further customize the columns, open the **View** menu and select **Show Fields** (to add or remove columns) or **Format Columns** (to change the look of the columns).

When you display the Inbox, notice that the toolbar changes to provide e-mail buttons and controls. You can use these buttons to reply to messages, turn AutoPreview on or off, or change the view. The Current View drop-down list is especially useful. It allows you to filter the list of messages so the list displays only flagged messages, only messages from the last seven days, or only messages you haven't yet read. You can also choose to sort the messages by conversation topic or by sender.

For additional e-mail folders and options, click the **Mail** group in the Outlook Bar. The Outlook Bar changes to display shortcuts for the Inbox, Sent Items (messages you have already sent), Outbox (messages that you will send in the future), and Deleted Items.

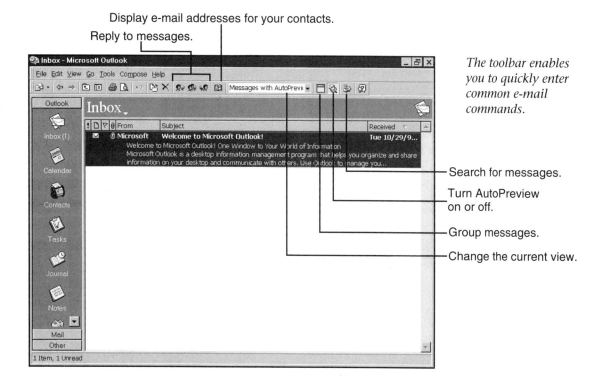

Display e-mail addresses for your contacts.

Reply to messages.

The toolbar enables you to quickly enter common e-mail commands.

Search for messages.

Turn AutoPreview on or off.

Group messages.

Change the current view.

Adding Information Services

In order to check for mail and send mail, Outlook needs to know which types of e-mail services (*information services*) you will be using. Outlook provides support for many information services, including Microsoft Mail, Microsoft Fax, cc:Mail, the Microsoft Exchange Server, and Internet Mail. To use Outlook with one of these services, first install the appropriate software. For example, Microsoft Exchange and Microsoft Fax come with Windows 95, but you may not have installed these components when you installed Windows. Run the Windows Setup program again to see if these components are installed on your system.

Once you have installed the appropriate software for the message service, take the following steps to add it to the list of information services Outlook can use:

1. Open the **Tools** menu and click **Services**. The Services dialog box appears, showing the names of the information services the Outlook is set up to use.

2. Click the **Add** button, and the Add Service to Profile dialog box appears, displaying a list of all the available information services.

3. If the information service you want to add is listed, click its name and click **OK**.

If the name of the information service is not on the list, you must have a disk with the information software on it. Assuming you have the disk, click **Have Disk** and follow the on-screen instructions to set up the service. Then select the information service from the list.

4. Depending on the type of information service you added, Outlook may prompt you to enter additional information. For example, if you are adding Microsoft Fax, a dialog box appears, telling you that you must enter your name and fax number, and you must select the fax modem you will use. Enter the requested information and click **OK**. This returns you to the Services dialog box, which should display the name of the new service.

5. Click **OK**. Outlook is now set up to use the new information service.

You must add an information service to the list before Outlook can use it.

Information services that Outlook is set up to use

All installed information services

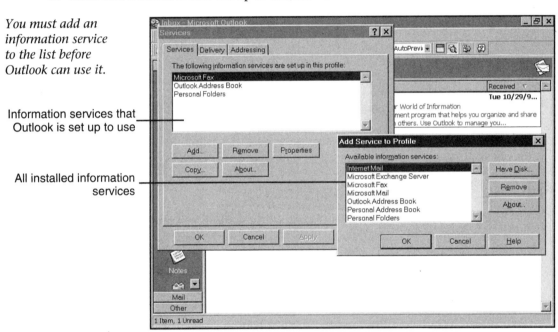

Creating a New E-Mail Message

Once you've set up your e-mail services, sending messages is fairly simple. Click the **New Mail Message** button (at the left end of the toolbar), and Outlook displays the Message dialog box. In the **To** text box, type the e-mail address of the person to whom you want to send the message. If you entered the e-mail address on the Address card in Contacts, click the **To** button to select the person's name from a list instead of typing it. You can send a copy of the message to other people by entering their e-mail addresses in the **Cc** (courtesy copy) text box. If you type more than one address in a text box, separate the addresses with semicolons.

Click in the **Subject** text box and type a brief description of the message. Then click in the message area at the bottom of the window and type your message. If you want to send only a text message, you're done; click the **Send** button. If you want to attach a file, set the importance of the message, or do some other fancy feat, use the appropriate technique described here:

➤ To attach a file to the message, click the **Insert File** button and select the file from the drive and folder in which it is stored.

➤ You can format the body of your message. Drag over the text you want to format, and then use the toolbar buttons to select a font and type size and to add attributes such as bold and italic.

➤ If you typed e-mail addresses in the To or Cc box, you can check the addresses against the addresses in the Contacts list by clicking the **Check Names** button.

➤ You can flag a message to indicate that the recipient needs to perform some action on the message. Click the **Message Flag** button, and the Flag Message dialog box appears, in which you can specify an action (such as Follow Up or Call), and a due date (in the By box). This information will appear at the top of the message when the person receives it.

➤ You can set the importance level of the message by clicking the **Importance:High** or **Importance:Low** button.

➤ You can set other preferences by clicking the **Options** tab and entering your preferences. For example, you can include voting buttons that allow the recipient to reply simply by clicking a Yes/No or Accept/Reject button. And you can have Outlook notify you when a message has been received and read.

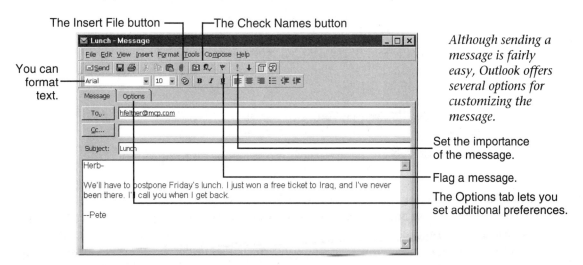

Although sending a message is fairly easy, Outlook offers several options for customizing the message.

The Insert File button ⎯⎯ ⎯The Check Names button

You can format text.

Set the importance of the message.

Flag a message.

The Options tab lets you set additional preferences.

Retrieving and Reading Incoming Messages

Whenever someone sends you an e-mail message, it sits in a special area on the mail server waiting for you to fetch it. To retrieve your messages, open the **Tools** menu and select **Check for New Mail**, or press the **F5** key. Outlook connects to each mail server you set up earlier, retrieves the messages, and displays a list of the messages in the Inbox. If you have AutoPreview on, you can see the first few lines of the message in the Inbox.

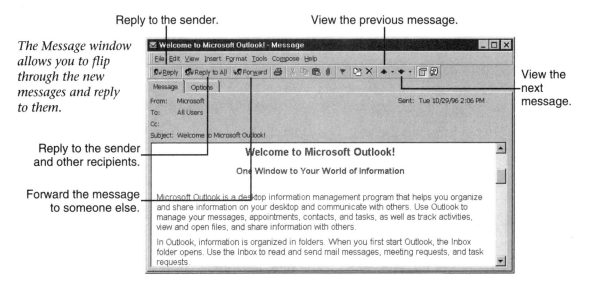

Reply to the sender.

View the previous message.

The Message window allows you to flip through the new messages and reply to them.

View the next message.

Reply to the sender and other recipients.

Forward the message to someone else.

To read the entire message, double-click anywhere on the message. Outlook displays the message in a special Message window, where you can use the following toolbar buttons:

➤ The **Reply** button lets you reply to the person who sent you the message. If you click this button, a Message window appears, addressing your reply to the sender. Outlook inserts the text of the original message to remind the sender what your reply is referring to. You should delete most of the original message so your reply won't be too long.

➤ Click **Reply to All** to send a reply to the sender and to any people other than yourself listed in the To or Cc boxes of the original message.

➤ Click **Forward** to send the message on to someone else, without necessarily adding a reply.

➤ Click the **Previous Item** or **Next Item** button to view the previous message or the next one. These buttons double as drop-down lists providing additional options; for example, you can view the next or previous message sent by the same person, or view the next or previous message concerning this topic.

Organizing Messages in Folders

One e-mailbox is enough for most people. If it gets too cluttered with messages, you can select and delete the old messages to clean it up. However, if you're starting your own e-mail fan club, you may need additional mailboxes (or folders) to keep your mail organized.

To create another mailbox, first click the **Folder List** button. Outlook displays the Personal Folder with its subfolders: Calendar, Contacts, Inbox, and so forth. Open the **File** menu, point to **Folder**, and click **Create Subfolder**. The Create New Folder dialog box appears, prompting you to name the folder. Type a name for the folder in the **Name** text box, and then select the folder below which you want the new subfolder created. Click **OK**. Outlook creates the new folder and displays a shortcut icon for it in the Mail group of the Outlook Bar.

You can move messages to the new folder by dragging them from one folder (probably the Inbox folder) to your new folder in the folder list.

Sending Faxes with Microsoft Fax

If you installed Microsoft Fax (it's part of Windows 95), you can send faxes from Outlook. That's right, you can have your Word documents, Excel worksheets, and just about anything else you've created transformed into a fax and sent through the phone lines, just as if you had a bona fide fax machine sitting on your desk. Here's what you do:

1. Open the **Compose** menu and select **New Fax**. This starts the Fax Wizard, which will lead you through the process of creating and sending a fax. (If New Fax does not appear on the menu, you may need to set up Outlook to use Microsoft Fax. See "Adding Information Services," earlier in this chapter, for details.)

2. The first dialog box you see asks if you're dialing from some location other than where you usually work or live (so the Fax Wizard will know whether it needs to dial an area code). If you don't move around with this computer, click the **I'm Not Using a Portable Computer** option to prevent this annoying dialog box from appearing again. Click the **Next>** button.

3. The wizard asks you to enter information about the recipient. Enter the recipient's name and fax number, or click the **Address Book** button and select a recipient from the list of Contacts. Click the **Next>** button.

4. The next dialog box asks if you want to send a cover page. Click **Yes**, and then select the cover page you want to use.

5. To enter additional preferences, such as the time of day to send the fax, click the **Options** button, enter your preferences, and click **OK**. Click the **Next>** button.

6. You finally get a dialog box that lets you type your message. Type your message and click the **Next>** button.

7. The next dialog box asks if you want to attach a file to your fax. For example, you can transform a Word document into fax pages and send it. To attach a file, click the **Add File** button, pick the file you want to attach, and click **Open**. Repeat this step to attach additional files. Click the **Next** button.

8. The final dialog box tells you that the wizard is ready to send the fax. Click the **Finish** button. The wizard dials the fax number, establishes a connection with the remote fax machine, and transmits the fax.

Sending Faxes from Other Office Applications

There's an easier way to fax a document you created in Word or Excel. Open the document you want to fax, and then open the **File** menu, point to **Send To**, and click **Fax Recipient**. This starts the Fax Wizard, which leads you through the process of faxing the document. By using this method, you don't have to worry about attaching files to the fax.

The Least You Need to Know

Once you've set up Outlook to work with your e-mail services, sending and receiving e-mail messages is easy:

➤ To check for incoming messages, open the **Tools** menu and select **Check for New Messages**.

➤ Click the **Mail** group in the Outlook Bar to view a list of e-mail shortcuts.

➤ Click the **Inbox** shortcut to view a list of messages. To read a message, double-click it.

➤ To reply to an e-mail message, select the message, and then click the **Reply** or **Reply to All** button.

➤ To send a new message, click the **New Mail Message** button. Type the recipient's e-mail message, a brief description of the message, and the message itself. Click **Send**.

➤ If you installed Microsoft Fax, you can fax from Outlook. Open the **Compose** menu and select **New Fax**.

Part 7
Tapping the Office Synergy

As individuals, the Office 97 applications are pretty amazing. But they really show their power when you start using them together and working with them in the shared environment of a network. Only in this type of environment can you see firsthand how seamlessly integrated the office applications are.

In this part, you'll use the Office applications together, on a network, and on the Web to get the most out of Office. You will learn how to cut and paste data between applications, combine documents in binders, share files with coworkers, and even publish your documents electronically on the World Wide Web.

Sharing Data Dynamically

If you flip through newspapers or magazines, or if your financial advisor sends you quarterly reports about your mutual funds, you begin to see that most documents contain more than one type of information. Next to a block of text that explains or describes, you'll find pictures, charts, or numerical data intended to present the information in a format that makes it easier to understand.

As you create your own documents or presentations, send e-mail, or analyze data, you will start to see a need to share data between documents. For example, you may need to insert a chart from Excel into a PowerPoint presentation or insert a portion of an Excel worksheet into a report. This chapter shows you various techniques for using the Office applications together in this way to create more dynamic documents and save yourself some time.

Dynamic Data Sharing with OLE

You can usually share data simply by copying it from a document you've created in one application to a document you've created in another. But just how is the data between the two documents related? If you change the data in one document, will it automatically be changed in the other one? The answer is, "That depends." It depends on how the two applications are set up to share data, and it depends on how you inserted the copied data. You can share data in any of the following three ways:

Link: If you're using Office 97 applications or any other applications that support OLE (pronounced "Oh-lay," and short for Object Linking and Embedding), you can share data by creating a *link*. With a link, the file into which you pasted the data does not actually contain the linked data; the link is stored in a separate file on the disk. Whenever you edit the linked file, any changes you make to it appear in all other documents that are linked to the file. For example, say you insert an Excel graph into a Word document as a link. Whenever you change the graph in Excel, those changes will appear in the Word document.

Embed: With OLE, you can also embed data from one file into another file. With embedding, the pasted data becomes a part of the file into which you pasted it. If you edit the file that contains the copied data, your changes will not appear inside the document that contains the pasted data. However, the pasted data retains a connection with the program that you used to create it. So if you double-click the embedded data, Windows automatically runs the associated application, and you can edit the data.

Paste: You can paste data in any number of ways (including pasting the data as an embedded or linked object). However, not all applications support OLE. For those applications that do not support OLE, you can still share data between programs by copying and pasting the data. However, the pasted data will have no connection with the application that you used to create it.

Sharing Data with Scraps

When you're working with the Office 97 applications, don't forget one of the great data sharing features built right into Windows 95—*scraps*. If you select data in a document and then drag it to a blank area on the Windows desktop, Windows creates a shortcut for the data and marks it as a scrap. You can then drag this scrap into another document to insert it.

Embedding an Object with Copy and Paste

Think of embedding as using a photocopier to make a copy. With a photocopy, the original remains intact in the original location, and you have the copy. You can manipulate the copy in any way that you want. You can edit it, delete part of it, highlight it, and so on, all without affecting the original. This method of sharing information works best when you want to use the same information in another document. Here's all you need to know about embedding objects:

➤ Use the Edit, Copy and Edit, Paste commands to embed a selected object in another document. If you copy and paste between two applications that support OLE (every Office 97 application supports OLE), the object is embedded in the destination document. If one of the applications does not support OLE, the data is pasted, but any link between it and the application used to create it is broken.

➤ You can copy and paste from one document to another or from one application to another. You can paste to other Office programs and any other type of program that supports copy and paste (for example, a WordPerfect document).

➤ The application will try to paste the data into a suitable format in the receiving document. For example, when you paste an Excel worksheet into Word, the information is formatted as a table. In some cases (when you cannot edit the information in the receiving application), the information is pasted as an object; you can double-click the object to edit it in the program you used to create it.

Check This Out...

Drag and Drop You don't need the clunky Cut and Paste commands to embed objects. Display the source document in one window right next to the destination document. Select the data you want to copy in the source document, and then hold down the **Ctrl** key and drag it to the destination document.

➤ To edit an embedded object, double-click it. The toolbars and menus will change to provide options for editing and manipulating the object. For example, if you double-click an Excel chart that's embedded in a Word document, the Excel toolbar and menus appear inside the Word window.

Creating a Link Between Two Files

In many cases, you may be creating a document with data from several sources. You could wait until each document is absolutely, completely finished and then copy the appropriate data, but things can—and usually do—seem to change up to the last minute. To avoid including outdated information in your final document, you can create a link between the two documents. Then when copied data in the original document (called the *source* document) is changed, the pasted data in the other document (called the *destination* document) is updated, too. Here are the key points to remember about linking data:

➤ You can link data between Excel, Word, PowerPoint, and any other application that supports OLE, by using the **Paste Special** command on the **Edit** menu. If a program does not support OLE, the Paste Special command will not be available.

➤ When you link data, you have two separate documents, stored in two separate files. If you send someone a file that contains a link, you should also send the linked file.

➤ Linking works best when you use the same data in several documents. You can maintain the one source document without having to worry about updating the documents that use information from the source.

➤ You can link data in several formats, including RTF (rich text file), as a picture, as an object, or as unformatted text. The format you select controls how you can edit the data. For example, in picture format, you can edit the link only by double-clicking it to run the application used to create the linked data. In RTF format, you can edit individual entries in the destination file, but if you close the file and reopen it, any edited entries revert back to the entries used in the original file.

Creating a link is almost as easy as copying and pasting. First, you copy the data you want to paste as a link (using the application's **Edit**, **Copy** command). Then you change to the document into which you want to paste the data, open the **Edit** menu, and select **Paste Special**. This opens the Paste Special dialog box (shown in the next figure). Make sure **Paste Link** is selected, and then pick the format in which you want the link pasted (for example, Formatted Text or Picture). You can also choose to have the linked data displayed as an icon or floating over the text. After you enter all your preferences, click **OK**.

If you decide later to break the link between the pasted data and its original file, or if you want to change the way the links are updated, open the **Edit** menu and select **Links**.

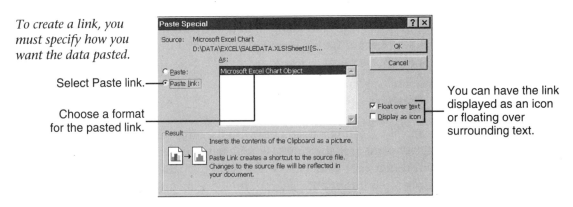

To create a link, you must specify how you want the data pasted.

Select Paste link.

Choose a format for the pasted link.

You can have the link displayed as an icon or floating over surrounding text.

Be Careful When Moving Files

Because a link points to another file in a folder on your hard drive or on the network, you must be careful when moving or deleting files. If you move or delete a file that is supplying data to another file, that other file won't be able to find the data it needs.

Embedding a New Object with Insert Object

You can also link or embed with the Insert Object command. You use this command when you know you want to link or embed something, but you have not yet created the object in the source application. You can also use this command when you want to treat an entire document as an object.

To use this command, open the **Insert** menu and select **Object**. The Object dialog box appears. You'll notice two tabs in the Object dialog box. Use the Create New tab when you need to create an object to link or embed (and haven't done so yet). The Create from File tab offers options for linking or embedding an entire file.

To create a new object, select the type of object you want to insert (for example, an Excel worksheet or a PowerPoint slide). Enter any additional preferences and click **OK**. Windows inserts a placeholder for the selected object and runs the application needed to create the object. By looking at the title bar, you may not realize that Windows has changed applications on you; but if you check out the toolbars and menus, you'll see that you now have options for creating and manipulating the new object. When you finish creating the object, click anywhere outside of it to return to your document.

Select the application you want to use to create the new object.

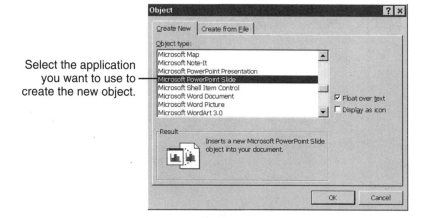

You can create a new object and embed it in your document.

You can also embed or link an entire file created in another application. To do this, click the **Create from File** tab in the Object dialog box. Click the **Browse** button, use the Browse dialog box to select the file you want to insert, and click **OK**. Select any other options (such as Link to file, Float over Text, or Display As Icon) and click **OK**.

Display As Icon?

The Display As Icon option can come in handy if you are working with shared files on a network. Instead of pasting lengthy inserts into a document, you can insert an icon that the reader can click to display additional information.

Transforming Word Documents into Presentations and Vice Versa

Although your marketing department and sales force want you to think that presentations are some sort of magical multimedia event, most presentations are nothing more than an outline on slides. Sure, the outline might contain a few graphical decorations and some sound recordings, but it's still an outline. And knowing it's an outline, you might find some need to transform it into a full-fledged Word document.

Do you have to retype the outline in Word? No way. Just open the presentation in PowerPoint, open the **File** menu, point to **Send To**, and click **Microsoft Word**. The Write-Up dialog box appears, asking how you want the slides and text laid out on Word pages (or if you just want the outline). Click the desired option and click **OK**.

Specify how you want the slides and text to appear in the Word document.

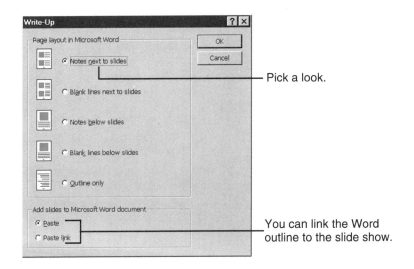

Pick a look.

You can link the Word outline to the slide show.

You can also transform an outline you typed in Word into a PowerPoint presentation. In Word, open the outline you created. Open the **File** menu, point to **Send To**, and click **Microsoft PowerPoint**. Respond to the Write-Up dialog box to pick a layout for the slides, and then click **OK**.

Publishing Access Reports in Word

Access is a great tool for storing and managing data, but it's page layout features are grossly inadequate. Access can slap a title on the report and arrange the data in columns, but that's about it. For more control over the look and layout of your reports, consider transforming the report into a Word document.

To convert an Access report to Word format, first open the report in Access. Then open the **Tools** menu, point to **Office Links**, and click **Publish It with MS Word**. Access exports the report to Word, creating a new document. You can now format the document using Word's advanced formatting tools, and you can add graphics and other objects to enhance the document.

> **Check This Out...**
>
> **Merging Data with Word Documents** You can also use Access and Word together by inserting field codes in your Word document that pull data from an Access database. See Chapter 10, "Creating Mailing Labels and Form Letters," for details on how to merge from Word.

Analyzing Your Access Database in Excel

Although Access is the best tool to use for storing and extracting data, Excel provides superior tools for performing calculations and for analyzing data. If you tried entering formulas in your Access report (as explained in Chapter 24, "Giving Data Meaning with Reports"), you know how difficult it can be to enter the correct formula using the right field codes. It's much easier to do it in Excel with cell addresses and the point-and-click method (as explained in Chapter 13, "Doing Math with Formulas").

In addition, Excel offers scenarios, which allow you to play "What if?" with a set of values. You can change one or more values to see how the changes will affect the net result. And you can create several scenarios to see how they compare.

To send a table, form, query, or report to Excel, first open it in Access. Then open the **Tools** menu, point to **Office Links**, and click **Analyze It with MS Excel**. Access sends the data to Excel and creates a new worksheet for the data. You can now add formulas, format the data, create graphs, and do anything else you normally do with an Excel worksheet.

Sending Office Documents Via E-Mail and Fax

If you're on a network or your computer has a modem, you can send documents to others via e-mail. In Chapter 27, "Managing Your E-Mail," you learned how to attach files to an e-mail message in Outlook to send the file to the e-mail recipient. However, if you're working on the document in Word or Excel, you don't have to switch to Outlook in order to e-mail the document. Instead, you can e-mail it directly from the application in which you created it.

To e-mail a document, open it in the application you used to create it. Open the **File** menu, point to **Send To**, and click **Mail Recipient**. An e-mail window appears, displaying an icon for the attached file in the message area. Type the recipient's e-mail address in the **To** text box, and then type a brief description of the message in the **Subject** text box. Click in the message area—not on the file icon—and type your message. Click the **Send** button.

If your computer has a fax modem and you've installed Microsoft Fax (it comes with Windows 95), you can fax a Word document right from Word. Open the document in Word. Then open the **File** menu, point to **Send To**, and click **Fax Recipient**. This starts the Fax Wizard, which leads you through the process. Follow the on-screen instructions.

The Least You Need to Know

The key to making the most of Office 97 is laziness. You should never have to type something in one application that you already entered in another. Once you have the right mindset, you can start using the Office 97 applications together.

➤ If two applications support OLE, you can embed or link data from a document created in one application into a document created in another application.

➤ Embedding places a duplicate of the copied data inside the destination document. The embedded data is still associated with its original application; if you double-click the pasted data, Windows runs the application used to create it.

➤ Linking inserts instructions that pull data from another (source) file into the current (destination) file. Because the linked data is in a separate file, whenever you edit that file, the link is automatically updated.

➤ To paste copied or cut data as a link (instead of embedding it), open the **Edit** menu, select **Paste Special**, and make sure **Paste Link** is selected.

➤ Many Office 97 applications contain commands that allow you to quickly transform data into a format that can be used in another Office application.

➤ To send a document via e-mail or fax, open the **File** menu, select **Send To**, and select **Mail Recipient** or **Fax Recipient**.

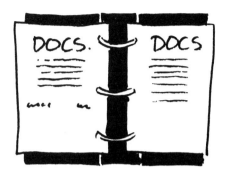

Chapter 29

Combining Documents in Binders

In This Chapter

➤ Combining documents from different applications in a binder

➤ Numbering pages in the bound document

➤ Sectioning off your binder

➤ Sharing binders with your office mates

Way back in Chapter 11, you learned how to combine two or more Word documents in a master document so you could treat the documents as chapters or sections in a "book." This made it easy to perform bookish tasks, such as numbering the pages, finding and replacing text, and creating an index or table of contents.

That's all fine and dandy for Word documents, but what if you want to combine other documents? Say you need to create a report that combines a Word document with an Excel workbook and a PowerPoint slide show. Can you do it? With the help of the Office Binder, yes. You can combine any of these documents and treat them as a unit. In this chapter, you'll learn how.

What Is a Binder?

Microsoft Binder is a document management tool that lets you "clip" related documents together. For example, if you have a report that consists of a cover letter, one or more Excel worksheets, and a PowerPoint slide show, you can add all these files to a binder in order to work with them as a single document.

Once you've bound several documents together, Microsoft Binder enables you to rearrange the documents, number the pages, and perform other tasks to give your bound documents a consistent look and feel. You can even print all the documents with a single Print command. However, there are some limitations to what you can do in Binder. For example, you can't check the spelling in all the documents with a single command; you must run the spell checker on each document individually.

Running Microsoft Binder

Techno Talk

Web Work!
Binder can also be used to manage files on the Internet, a network, or an intranet. Use paths or URLs to specify where the various documents are stored. You can also use the options on Binder's Go menu to open Web pages, navigate the Web, and add Web pages to a Binder file.

Before you start using the Microsoft Office Binder, you have to find it. In Chapter 2, I recommended that you customize your Office Shortcut bar. One of the buttons you can add to the bar is the Binder button. That's what I did. So all I have to do to open the Binder is click the **Binder** button on my Shortcut bar. (Turn back to Chapter 2 for instructions on customizing your Shortcut bar.)

Another way to open the Binder is to use the traditional route: Click the **Start** button, point to **Programs**, and click **Microsoft Binder**. The Binder appears, as shown in the following figure. There's not much to look at the first time you open the Binder; it doesn't even fill up the screen. You'll have to add documents of your own to create a binder.

The Binder isn't much to look at until you add documents to it.

Menu bar

Icons for documents will appear here.

This big empty space is used to display the contents of the selected document.

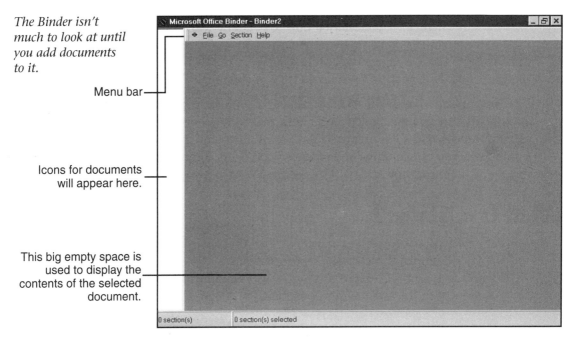

Using the Binder Templates

If you're not quite sure how to go about combining documents in Binder, you might be able to get some help from one of the several Binder templates. Binder offers templates for billing customers, organizing meetings, creating a proposal or marketing plan, and publishing a report. These templates take care of the overall organization for you. All you have to do is come up with the content.

To create a binder using a template, open the **File** menu and select **New Binder**. Click the **Binders** tab, click the desired template, and click **OK**. Binder inserts icons for the various documents that make up the template. You can then edit these documents individually, delete documents you won't use, insert additional documents, and rearrange the documents. Keep reading for details.

Adding Documents to a Binder

By default, a blank binder appears every time you run Binder. To add files to it, use one of the following methods:

➤ Open **My Computer** or **Windows Explorer**, and drag the icons for the files you want to add to your binder into the left pane of the Binder window.

➤ Open the **Section** menu and select **Add from File**. This displays the Add from File dialog box, which allows you to select the file from the folder in which it is stored. When you add a file, Binder runs the associated application and displays its toolbars and menus so you can edit the file.

➤ To add a new document (one you have not yet created), open the **Section** menu and select **Add**. The Add Section dialog box appears, allowing you to create a document from scratch or by using one of the many Office 97 templates. The blank document will be opened in the Binder window, and Binder will display the toolbars and menus of the specified application so you can create the document.

> **Check This Out...**
>
> **Documents or Sections?**
> When you insert a *section* into a binder, you are actually inserting a *document*. Document, section, who cares? Just remember that when you click a section icon, Binder is going to display that document's content.

Repeat these steps to add more files to the binder. When you add a file to the binder, an icon representing the file appears in the left pane. The right pane displays the contents of the document along with a menu bar and toolbar for editing the document. To view a file in the Binder window, click its icon in the left pane. If you're having trouble seeing a file's entire name on the left side of the screen, just hover you mouse pointer over the file icon for a minute; the name appears in full.

You can insert existing document files.

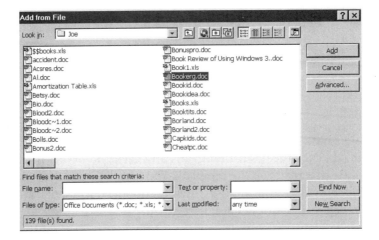

Working with Binders

Once you've added a few sections to your binder, you can start rearranging and renaming your sections and performing other fancy stunts. However, before you start the hands-on activities, scan the following list to learn how documents behave in binders and how to change views to provide yourself with an efficient work area:

➤ When you click an icon for a document, the toolbars and menus for the application you used to create the document appear, along with Binder's menus and toolbar. You may have to search a little to find the commands you need.

➤ To work with a document in the application you used to create it (instead of in the Binder window), click its icon, and then open the **Section** menu and select **View Outside**. After editing the document, open the **File** menu and select the **Update** option. To return to the Binder, open the **File** menu and select **Close & Return to Binder**.

➤ To increase the space where the document's contents are displayed, you can hide the left pane (which contains the document icons) by clicking the double-headed arrow button to the left of the File menu. To reopen the left pane, click the double-headed arrow button again.

➤ To select several documents in a row, click the icon for the first document, hold down the **Shift** key, and click the icon for the last document.

➤ To select non-neighboring document icons, hold down the **Ctrl** key and click each icon.

➤ To select all the documents in a binder, open the **Section** menu and choose **Select All**.

➤ To hide a section in the binder window, click inside the document's icon, open the **Section** menu, and select **Hide**. To redisplay the section, open the **Section** menu and select **Unhide Section**.

Document (section) icons   Toolbars of application used to create document

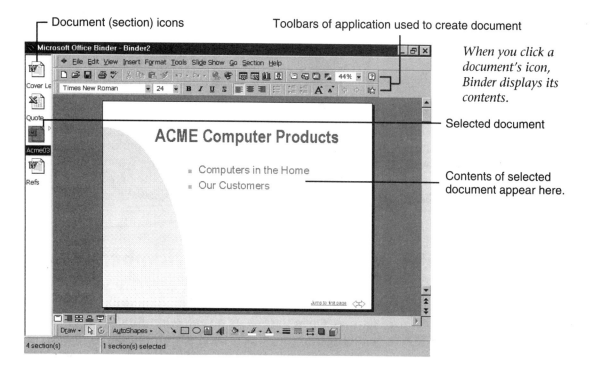

When you click a document's icon, Binder displays its contents.

Selected document

Contents of selected document appear here.

Moving, Deleting, and Renaming Sections in the Binder

Whenever you insert a section (document) into a binder, the section is inserted after the currently selected section. Later, you may decide to rearrange the sections in the binder, or you may find that you need to rename or delete documents.

Rearranging the documents is easy. Simply click the icon for the document you want to move, and then drag it up or down in the list. As you drag, a tiny arrow shows where the document will be moved. When you release the mouse button, Binder inserts the document in its new position. You can also rearrange the sections by opening the **Section** menu and selecting **Rearrange**. This displays a dialog box showing the names of all the documents. Click the document you want to move, and then click the **Move Up** or **Move Down** button to move it.

You can also rename sections without changing the name of the original file. Click the section name just below its icon, and the name should appear highlighted. Type the new name, and then click anywhere outside the icon.

To delete a section (without deleting the file), click the icon for the section, open the **Section** menu, and select **Delete**. A dialog box appears, asking for your confirmation. Click **OK**.

Don't Forget the Right Mouse Button

You can quickly add, rename, and delete sections by right-clicking with your mouse. Right-click a section icon you want to rename or delete, and then pick the appropriate command from the pop-up menu. To add a section, right-click the icon below which you want the new section added and click **Add** or **Add from File**.

Adding a Header or Footer and Page Numbers

Once you have assembled the documents you want to work with, you may want to pull them all together and number their pages as if they were a single document. You can do this by entering Binder page settings. Open the **File** menu and select **Binder Page Setup**. To insert a header or footer on all pages in the binder, select **All Supported Sections**. If you want to add a header or footer only to selected sections, click **Only Sections Selected Below** and select the sections on which you want to print headers or footers.

In the previous version of Binder, you had to create a header or footer for each document (section) in the Binder. However, Binder 97 allows you to add a header or footer that appears in every document in the Binder. To add a header (text that appears at the top of every page), open the **Header** drop-down list and select the header you want to use. If you don't see the perfect header, select one that's close to perfect. If you prefer to have text printed at the bottom of every page, select the desired option from the **Footer** drop-down list.

You can customize the header or footer by clicking the **Custom** button. This displays the Custom Header or Custom Footer dialog box, which contains three windows for entering text (see the next figure). Any text you type inside a window will appear in that area on every page in the binder. You may see codes, such as &[Page], which insert specific text (page numbers, section names, etc.) on the page. You can insert these codes by clicking the appropriate button at the top of the dialog box. Click **OK** to return to the Binder Page Setup dialog box.

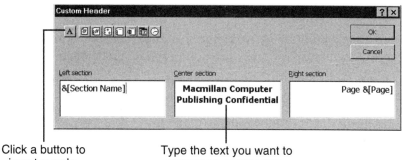

Binder can print headers and footers on every page.

Click a button to insert a code.

Type the text you want to appear on every page.

To control the way Binder prints the documents and numbers pages, click the **Print Settings** tab. Under Print What, you can choose to print all visible sections (excluding any sections you chose to hide) or to print only the sections you selected. Under Page numbering, you can choose to number pages consecutively throughout the binder or to number each section separately. You can also choose to start numbering pages with a number other than 1 (if, for instance, you have a cover page you don't want numbered).

Printing and Saving Binders

After you've filled a binder with all the necessary documents, you'll want to save it. Follow these steps:

1. Open the **File** menu and select **Save Binder** or **Save Binder As**. This opens the typical Save As dialog box for saving files.

2. Type a name for the binder, and select the drive and folder in which you want to store it.

3. Click the **Save** button to save the binder and exit the dialog box. When you save your binder, it's automatically given an .OBD extension to distinguish it as a binder file.

You can also print your binder sections. Open the **File** menu and select **Print Binder**. Make any necessary adjustments in the Print Binder dialog box, and click **OK** to print. Under the Print What area in the dialog box, you can choose to print all of the Binder sections (all the files you've collected in the binder) or just selected sections.

Once you create a binder file, you can easily zip in and out of the files you've stored there without having to reopen applications. You can also pass along the binder file to other Office 97 users, and they can access the files as well.

The Least You Need to Know

The Binder is a relatively simple tool that lets you combine unlike documents and treat them as a single document. When using binder, you don't need to know much.

➤ Use binders to combine related files into a kind of electronic three-ring notebook.

➤ The easiest way to add files to a binder is to drag them from Windows Explorer or My Computer into the left pane of the Binder window.

➤ You can rearrange sections in a binder by dragging their icons up or down.

➤ When you click the icon for a section, Binder displays the contents of the section in the right pane and displays the menus and toolbars of the application in which the document was created.

➤ You can add a header or footer to all the sections in a binder or to only selected sections. Open the **File** menu and select **Binder Page Setup**.

Using Office on a Network or Intranet

Companies have been networked for years—long before the desktop PC was popular. However, new networks are far superior to the networks of old. Not only can we share hard drives and printers, but with the new data sharing technologies, we can link files that automatically update each other, access information from various departments, and even pull up pages stored on other computers anywhere in the world!

This new network technology has challenged Microsoft Office to come up with tools that tap into this power. And throughout its history, Office has responded by providing features designed to take advantage of the shared environment. In this chapter, you learn how to use these tools.

A Quick Look at Networks and Intranets

You probably have some general idea of what a network is. In a typical *client/server* network, some big powerful computer called the *server* acts as the centerpiece. Other computers called *clients* connect to the server and run programs from it, store files on it, and use it to exchange e-mail and other resources with the other client computers.

Currently, networks are undergoing a major transformation, inspired by the Internet. Seeing how easy it is to distribute information and share resources on the Web, network administrators and developers have started introducing Internet technologies to the internal networks of corporations, universities, and other institutions. Networks that take advantage of these Internet technologies are called *intranets*. These intranets offer three major advantages over typical networks:

➤ Intranets are fairly easy to set up, and they provide a quick way to distribute information. Users can use a browser to click links to find the information they need.

➤ Intranets allow any type of computer running any operating system to connect and use the available resources. This is called *platform independence*.

➤ Intranets enable users to quickly access all types of media, including sound, video, and interactive applications.

Now, you're probably wondering what this has to do with Microsoft Office. Office 97 offers tools that you can use on both typical networks and intranets. Its file sharing tools enable users in a network to share files and work more closely as a team. The Office applications also provide Web tools that enable you to link documents to other documents on an intranet or on the Internet, and tools for sending and receiving e-mail. (For more information on using the Office 97 Web tools, see Chapter 31, "Creating Your Own Web Pages.")

Restricting Access to Critical Files

When you are sharing files on a network, one of your major concerns is to preserve the content of the file. You may want to give some people access to only view the file, yet give other people access to view it and edit it. And you may want to prevent some people from even seeing the file. You can control the access to a file by using passwords. The following sections explain how to enter passwords in the various Office applications.

Password Protecting Word and Excel Documents

The procedure for password-protecting documents in Word and Excel is pretty much the same. Open the file you want to protect, and then open the **File** menu and select **Save As**.

In the Save As dialog box, click the **Options** button. In Word, you get a Save dialog box that offers a bunch of options; the password options are at the bottom. In Excel, you should see a dialog box with just a few options, including the password options.

To prevent users from accessing the file without your permission, type a password in the **Password to Open** text box. To allow users to open the file but prevent them from changing its contents without your permission, leave the Password to Open option blank and type a password in the **Password to Modify** text box. Click **OK** to return to the Save As dialog box, and then save the file. (Keep a list of your document names and the passwords you use to protect them. Without these passwords, you won't be able to open or edit your files.)

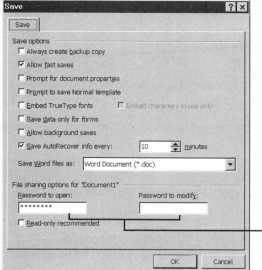

Word offers several options for saving documents.

Type a password in one of these boxes.

Read-Only Recommended

You can informally protect your documents by omitting the passwords and turning on the Read-Only Recommended option. When a user opens the document, a dialog box appears, recommending that the user open the document as a read-only file. If the user chooses to open the file as a read-only file, the user must give the file a different name when saving it. This protects the original file.

Password Protecting Access Databases

Because databases may contain important and confidential information, you don't want just anyone poking around in the database and pulling up sensitive information. To help you protect your database against unauthorized use, Access offers several security options. The easiest way to protect a database is to protect it with a password. The following steps tell you how:

1. Close the database, and have all other people on the network close it.

2. Open the **File** menu and select **Open Database.** The Open dialog box appears, prompting you to specify which database you want to open.

3. Select the database file you want to open and click **Exclusive** to place a check in the box. This tells Access to prevent anyone else on the network from opening the file while you have it open.

4. Click the **Open** button, and Access opens the database.

5. Open the **Tools** menu, point to **Security**, and click **Set Database Password**. The Set Database Password dialog box appears, prompting you to enter the password.

6. Type the same password in both the **Password** and **Verify** text boxes, and click **OK**.

To remove a password later, open the database (check the **Exclusive** check box again), and then open the **Tools** menu, point to **Security**, and click **Unset Database Password**. Type the password and click **OK**.

You can also choose to define groups of users who can log on to the database and perform only specified actions. For example, you might create a group of users called Data Entry, who can open the database and enter records, but who are not allowed to modify the design of the database or run queries. The procedure for setting different levels of database access for various groups of users is far more complicated than setting a database password, and it is way beyond the scope of this book. Call your network administrator for help with this one.

Following the Edit Trail on Team Projects

When you work on a document with other people, you need to keep track of the changes each person is making. This serves two purposes. First, it allows you to determine who made a change, in case you need to discuss the change with that person. Second, it allows you to see what was deleted and what was added so everyone on the team can determine if the change was an improvement or a step back.

To keep track of changes, you have several options: you can turn on the **Track Changes** option (formerly known as Revision Marks) to mark each person's changes in a different color, you can highlight questionable text with the highlighter button, or you can add comments that appear outside the text. The following sections explain these techniques in detail.

You Don't Even Have to Be Networked!

You don't have to be networked to use the Comments or Track Changes features. Even if you share files by passing them back and forth on floppy disks or by sending them via e-mail, these features can come in handy to help you quickly see changes that others have made to your text.

Tracking Changes with Revision Marks

The easiest way to keep track of changes to a document is to turn on the Track Changes feature. As you edit the document, Word displays your changes in color, using a different color for each person's changes. Any text you insert is underlined, and text you delete is displayed with a line through it.

To turn on the Track Changes feature, open the **Tools** menu, point to **Track Changes**, and click **Highlight Changes**. The Highlight Changes dialog box appears. Click **Track Changes While Editing** to turn the option on. The other two options specify whether you want changes to be displayed on-screen, in the printed document, or both. The Options button displays a dialog box that lets you change the color and style used for your changes. Enter the desired preferences and click **OK**.

As you type, Word displays your changes on-screen (assuming you left the Highlight Changes On Screen option on). It's a good idea to type your name at the top of the document. That way, anyone else who needs to edit the document can immediately see which color Word is using for your changes.

A Word About Revision Colors If you click the Options button in the Highlight Changes dialog box, you get a dialog box that lets you change the color Word uses for highlighting. You'd think that if you pick a color, only your changes will appear in that color. Not so. When you select a color, that color is used for changes anyone has made. The only way to view different colors for the changes made by different people is to use the default setting: By Author.

Adding Your Two Cents with Editorial Comments

A less intrusive way to edit a document is to add comments. The comments don't actually affect the document text or change it in any way. When you (or another reviewer) comments on some document text, the text in question appears highlighted. When you move the mouse pointer over the highlighted text, a box pops up displaying your (or the other reviewer's) comment.

To comment on text, first drag over the text you want to comment on. Then open the **Insert** menu and click **Comment**. The selected text appears highlighted in yellow, and a comment area appears at the bottom of the screen. Type your comment. If you have a sound card with a microphone attached, you can record a voice comment by clicking the little tape icon in the bar that divides the window, clicking the **Record** button (the button to the far right), and speaking into your microphone.

When you add a comment, Word inserts a code in the document, such as **[JK1]**. This code indicates the reviewer's initials and the number of the comment. If you add a voice comment, a speaker icon appears in the comment area at the bottom of the screen. Double-click the speaker icon to play the recording.

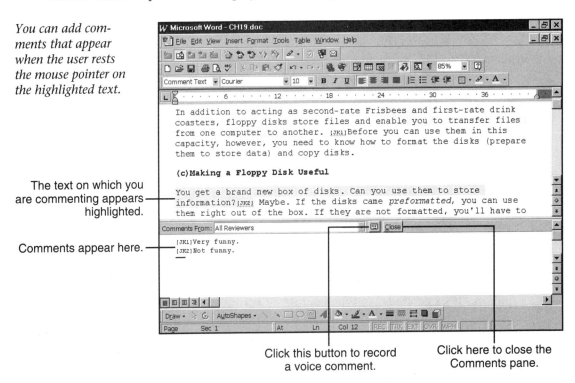

You can add comments that appear when the user rests the mouse pointer on the highlighted text.

The text on which you are commenting appears highlighted.

Comments appear here.

Click this button to record a voice comment.

Click here to close the Comments pane.

Reviewing, Accepting, and Rejecting Changes

After everyone has peppered your document with changes, questions, and snide remarks, you will have to review the changes and accept or reject them.

To review actual changes (where a person added or deleted text), open the **Tools** menu, point to **Track Changes**, and click **Accept or Reject Changes**. (Ignore the **View** buttons for now.) Then click the forward pointing **Find** button. Word highlights the first change it finds and displays the name of the person who made the change. You can then click one of the following buttons in response to the change:

➤ **Accept** makes the change and moves on to the next change. Inserted text (underlined) is added, the underline is removed, and the text is returned to its normal color. Deleted text (displayed with a line through it) is removed. If you accept a comment, it is kept in the document, and the text in question remains highlighted.

➤ **Reject** returns the text to its original form before the change was made. Inserted text is removed, and deleted text is inserted. If you reject a comment, it is removed from the document.

➤ **Accept All** executes all the changes in the document.

➤ **Reject All** returns the document to its original form.

➤ **Undo** undoes the previous Accept or Reject command.

A quick way to add or edit comments or to review the changes made to a document is to use the Reviewing toolbar. To turn it on, right-click any toolbar and select **Reviewing**.

Saving Different Versions of a Document

If you like a particular version of a file, you can save it before you start entering changes or before you review the changes that someone else has made. Just open the **File** menu and select **Versions**. Click the **Save Now** button, type a brief description of the version, and click **OK**. Whenever you open the Versions dialog box for this file, it displays a list of the saved versions. You can then click the version you want and click **Open**. To have Word automatically create a new version whenever you close the document, display the Versions dialog box and click **Automatically Save a Version on Close**.

Routing a Document Through the Proper Channels

You can share your documents with others in various ways. You can place the document in a folder that other users can access, you can send the document as an e-mail attachment to everyone who needs to see it, or you can route the document to users on a routing list via e-mail. If you want feedback on your document, routing is preferred because after everyone has reviewed the document, it is automatically returned to you with the changes.

To route your document, take the following steps:

1. Open the document you want to route.

2. Open the **File** menu, point to **Send To**, and click **Routing Recipient**.

3. Click the **Address** button.

4. Click in the **Type Name or Select from List** box, type the recipient's name, and click **To**.

5. Repeat step 4 to insert the names of additional recipients, if necessary. Then click **OK**.

6. Enter any other routing preferences.

7. To route the document now, click the **Route** button. To route the document later, click **Add Slip**; then whenever you decide to route the document, open the **File** menu, point to **Send To**, and click **Next Routing Recipient**.

Using Word As Your E-Mail Editor

After working with an award-winning word processor, typing messages in a second rate e-mail program is a big step down. E-mail programs are designed for typing brief messages without a lot of fancy formatting. And you're lucky if you can even spell check your message before sending it. Well if you've put up with the shortcomings of your e-mail program long enough, it's time to move up to Word.

With Word as your e-mail program, you'll be able to use all of Word's advanced word processing tools to compose, format, and check your e-mail messages. Just imagine a Word table in an e-mail message! Highlighted text! Automatic spell checking! Word even offers ten e-mail templates to help you automatically format your e-mail messages.

To use Word as your e-mail program, you first must install Microsoft Outlook (which comes with Office 97). In Outlook, open the **Tools** menu, select **Options**, and click the **E-Mail** tab. Select **Use Microsoft Word As the E-Mail Editor** to place a check in the box and click **OK**. Word should now have a Compose menu, which you can use to enter e-mail commands such as **Create New Message**. You can also turn on the e-mail toolbar, which offers buttons for quickly entering e-mail commands.

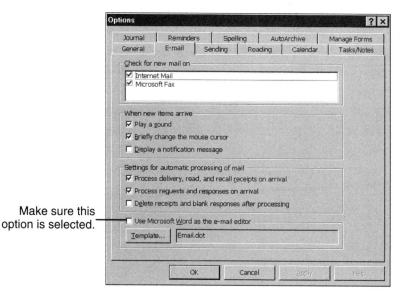

In Outlook, you can set up Word as your e-mail editor.

Make sure this option is selected.

The Least You Need to Know

To get the most out of your Office 97 investment, you should take advantage of the network and intranet features that it offers. When you first start exploring these features, keep the following information handy:

➤ A network allows your computer to share files and resources with other computers.

➤ An intranet is a network that takes advantage of Internet technologies that make it easier to share files and transmit data.

➤ Before you share your documents on the network, consider restricting access to them by adding passwords.

➤ In Word and Excel, you can password protect documents by clicking the **Options** button in the Save As dialog box.

➤ In Word, you can use the **Tools, Track Changes** feature to highlight changes as you edit a document.

Chapter 31

Creating Your Own Web Pages

In This Chapter

➤ Churning out Web pages with templates

➤ Saving existing documents as Web pages

➤ Inserting links to other Internet and intranet resources

➤ Inserting links that connect to files on your hard drive

➤ Opening Web pages from Word, Excel, PowerPoint, and Access

Nowadays, if you're not on the Web, you're out of the mainstream. Corporations, universities, towns, churches, and individuals are flocking to the Web to express themselves and reach out to customers, members, citizens, and anyone else who might be wandering the Web. Using Web authoring tools, these companies and individuals are beginning to move away from paper publications to more interactive electronic publications on the Web.

As you can imagine, the Microsoft Office applications have also been forced to make the transition from printing on paper to publishing electronically on the Web. Office 97 now offers several tools that work together with Microsoft's award-winning Web browser, Internet Explorer, to help you create your own Web pages and help you navigate the Web. In this chapter, you learn how to use these tools.

What the Heck Is "the Web?"

If you need an explanation of the Web, you're in the wrong chapter. Buy a good beginner's guide to the Internet, such as Peter Kent's *The Complete Idiot's Guide to the Internet*, and read that first. This chapter assumes you have used a Web browser to explore the Web, and that you have an Internet connection and a copy of Microsoft Internet Explorer.

Internet Explorer comes on the Microsoft Office CD. When you installed Office, the installation program placed an Internet setup icon on the Windows desktop. If you have a modem or a network connection to the Internet, you can install Internet Explorer and get connected to the Internet right now. To install, insert the CD, double-click the setup icon, and follow the on-screen instructions.

Creating Web Pages in Word

For years, we have used desktop publishing programs and word processors to publish on paper. However, when we need to make the transition to publishing on the Web, we have no idea which program to use. We need to learn a whole new set of tools for coding and outputting pages.

Fortunately, Microsoft has added some Web page creation tools to Microsoft Word. With these tools, we can easily make the transition to Webtop publishing without having to learn a new program. Word offers two ways to create Web pages; you can use the Web Page Wizard to create a page from scratch, or you can transform an existing document into a Web page. These techniques are discussed in the following sections.

Making Web Pages from Scratch with a Wizard

The easiest way to make a Web page in Word is to use the Web Page Wizard. Like all wizards, this wizard displays a series of dialog boxes that lead you through the process of creating a custom Web page.

To run the Web Page Wizard, open Word's **File** menu and select **New**. In the New dialog box, click the **Web Pages** tab and double-click **Web Page Wizard**. The wizard creates a simple Web page and opens it in a new document window. In front of the page, the first wizard dialog box pops up, asking you to specify the type of page you want to create: survey, calendar, personal home page, table of contents, etc. Make your selection and click the **Next** button.

The second dialog box (there are only two) asks you to pick an overall design: contemporary, professional, elegant, and so on. Pick the design you want, and the wizard applies the selected design immediately so you can see how it will affect your page. Click the

Finish button. The wizard disappears, leaving you with a fill-in-the-blanks Web page. The following figure shows a personal home page created with the Jazzy design.

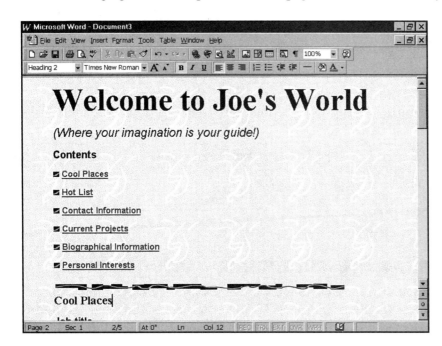

The personal home page jazzed up.

To modify the page, follow the instructions on the page itself. For example, to add a title to the page, click **[Insert Heading Here]** and type the title. Inserting links that connect your page to other Web pages is a little more difficult. Skip ahead to the section called "Connecting Your Page to Other Pages with Hyperlinks," later in this chapter for details.

Transforming Existing Documents into Web Pages

As a society, we work far too much. So if you have a document that already contains most of the text you want on your Web page, don't re-create it, just transform it. To transform a Word document into a Web page, first save the document as a normal Word document so you don't mess up the original. Then open the **File** menu and select **Save As HTML**. The Save as HTML dialog box appears. Type a name for the document, and then select the folder in which you want it stored. Word will automatically give the document the HTML extension. Click **Save**.

When Word saves the document, it automatically converts any Word formatting codes into HTML codes.

HTML: The Codes Behind the Document

HTML stands for HyperText Markup Language, which is a coding system used to format documents on the Web. For example, in HTML, you can make text bold by adding the <b> code (start bold) before the text and the </b> code (end bold) after it. Of course, when you're creating the Web page in Word, all you have to do is drag over the text and click the **Bold** button in the formatting toolbar. Word automatically inserts the HTML codes for you. For more details about formatting Web pages, see "Formatting Documents to Publish on the Web," later in this chapter.

If you are interested in viewing the codes, or if you need to edit the codes directly yourself, you can view the coded document. Open the **View** menu and select **HTML Source**. When you finish working with the codes, click the **Exit HTML Source** button in the toolbar.

Creating an Online Presentation in PowerPoint

Although Word seems like the most obvious choice for publishing pages on the Web, PowerPoint offers a more graphical approach, allowing you to transform a slide show into individual linked pages. Visitors to your Web page can advance through the slide show by clicking buttons or other types of hyperlinks. PowerPoint offers various ways to create Internet presentations:

➤ If you have already created the presentation you want to use, save it as an HTML file. Open the presentation in PowerPoint, and then open the **File** menu and select **Save As HTML**. Type a name for the file, select a folder in which to store it, and click **Save**.

➤ You can create a new Web presentation using one of PowerPoint's many Online templates. Open the **File** menu and select **New**. In the New dialog box, click the **Presentations** tab to view a list of templates. The templates that have "(Online)" in their names are designed for the Web. Click one of the Online templates and click **OK**.

➤ Use the AutoContent Wizard when you start PowerPoint (as explained in Chapter 17, "Slapping Together a Basic Slide Show"). In the second AutoContent Wizard dialog box, the wizard provides three output options for the slide show. Select **Internet, Kiosk**.

After you create your Web presentation, you can insert links to other files in the presentation using the Animation Settings option. Select the object or text you want the user to click to move to another slide (the next slide or any slide in the presentation). Right-click the selected text or object and click **Action Settings**. The Action Settings dialog box appears. Click the **Mouse Click** tab if it is not already in front.

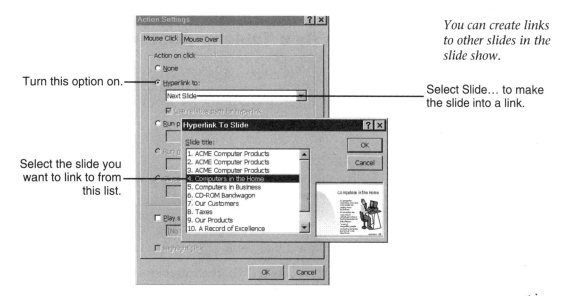

You can create links to other slides in the slide show.

Turn this option on.

Select Slide... to make the slide into a link.

Select the slide you want to link to from this list.

Click the **Hyperlink To** option to turn it on. Open the **Hyperlink To** drop-down list and select the slide to which you want this object or text to point. You can select the first or last slide, the next or previous slide, or click on **Slide...** and pick the specific slide you want this link to point to. (You can also choose to point a link to another file, a page on the Web, or another PowerPoint presentation.) Click **OK**.

To learn more about inserting hyperlinks that point to other pages on the Web, see "Connecting Your Page to Other Pages with Hyperlinks," later in this chapter.

Editing Links in Predesigned Templates
If you used one of PowerPoint's Online templates to create a presentation, it already has links that connect the slides in the presentation. To override any of these links, use the Animation Settings option as explained here.

Placing Excel Worksheets on the Web

You don't see many worksheets or spreadsheets on the Web. They're just not the type of thing that grabs the attention of an audience. You are more likely to see worksheets on an intranet, where colleagues might post sales information and other data that people from the same company need to access.

To place an Excel worksheet on the Web, you must run the Internet Assistant Wizard, which can convert the worksheet into a table. You can have the wizard insert the table into another Web page (for instance, a page created in Word), or create a table that acts as its own, separate Web page.

Inserting Worksheet Data As a Table in Another Web Page

If you choose to insert the table into some other Web page, first create the page into which you want to insert the table. Choose the **View**, **HTML Source** command to view the coded version of the document. Create a new blank line where you want to insert the table, and then type the following line:

<!--##Table##-->

Save the Web page and close the file. You can now transform the worksheet data into a table and insert it into the Web page by following these steps:

1. Open the worksheet that you want to convert into a table.

2. Drag over the data in the worksheet that you want to covert into a table.

3. Open the **File** menu and click **Save As HTML**. The Internet Assistant Wizard Step 1 dialog box appears, showing the range of cells that the wizard is about to transform into a table.

4. To add a range of cells or select a different range of cells, click the **Add** button, drag over the cells you want to transform into a table, and click **OK**. This returns you to the Internet Assistant Wizard Step 1 box. (You can remove a range from the list of selected ranges by clicking it and clicking the **Remove** button.)

5. Click the Next> button. The Step 2 dialog box asks if you want to create a separate Web page, or if you want to insert the data as a table into another Web page.

6. Click **Insert the Converted Table into an Existing HTML File** and click the **Next>** button. The Step 3 dialog box asks you to specify the location and name of the file into which you typed the <!--##Table##--> code.

7. Click the **Browse** button, use the Select Your HTML File dialog box to pick the file, and click the **Open** button. This inserts the path to the file. Click the **Next>** button, and the Step 4 dialog box asks if you want to save the resulting file as an HTML file or save it to your FrontPage Web. (If you have a FrontPage Web, you can save the page to your Web, where it's immediately accessible.)

8. If you have a FrontPage Web, select **Add the Result to My FrontPage Web**. If you don't have FrontPage, select **Save the Result As an HTML File**.

9. Click the **Browse** button, use the **Save** dialog box to select the desired name and folder for the new file, and click **Save**. Then click the **Finish** button. The Internet Assistant Wizard creates a new HTML file that is a combination of the destination Web page and the Excel worksheet data. The original Web page remains unchanged.

What's FrontPage?

Microsoft's FrontPage is a program that enables you to create a Web (a collection of related Web pages), set up a Web server (to make the pages available to visitors), and manage your Web site. If you or someone in your company has set up a FrontPage Web and you have access to it, you can save your page directly to the Web, making it accessible to anyone who wants to view it. If you don't have a FrontPage Web, you must save the file as a Web document and then upload it to your Web site. Check with your Web site administrator for specific instructions on where to save the Web document.

Transforming an Excel Worksheet into a Web Page

The Internet Assistant Wizard can also help you transform an Excel worksheet into a separate Web page, instead of using the data as a table in another Web page. Take the following steps to turn an Excel worksheet out on the Web:

1. Open the worksheet that you want to convert into a Web page, and drag over all the data that you want to place on the page.

2. Open the **File menu** and select **Save As HTML**. The Internet Assistant Wizard Step 1 dialog box appears, showing the range of cells that the wizard is about to transform into a table.

3. Click the **Next>** button. The Step 2 dialog box asks if you want to create a separate Web page or insert the data as a table in another Web page.

4. Click **Create an Independent, Ready-to-View HTML Document** and click the **Next>** button. The Step 3 dialog box asks you to type a title, header, description, and footer information for the new page.

5. In the **Title** text box, type a title for your page. Type any other entries as necessary in the remaining text boxes, and set any additional preferences. Click the **Next>** button. The Step 4 dialog box asks if you want to save the result as an HTML file or save it to your FrontPage Web.

6. If you have a FrontPage Web, select **Add the Result to My FrontPage Web**. If you don't have FrontPage, select **Save the Result As an HTML File**.

Type any additional text that you want on the page with the table.

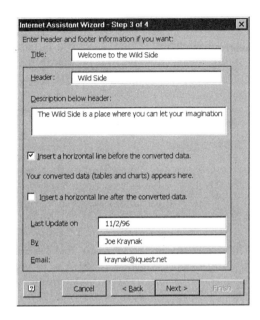

7. Click the **Browse** button, use the **Save** dialog box to select the desired name and folder for the new file, and click **Save**. Then click the **Finish** button. The Internet Assistant Wizard creates a new HTML file including the title and any other information you chose to include on the page.

Preparing a Database for Life on the Web

Manually coding a database to convert it into a series of Web pages would be a monumental task. However, Access provides a command (File, Save As HTML) that can insert all the codes for you. The easiest way to convert a database for Web use is to use the Publish to the Web Wizard. The wizard can convert an entire database or only selected objects (such as a table or report) into Web pages. To run the wizard, follow these steps:

1. Open the database file that contains the objects you want to convert for Web use.

2. Open the **File** menu, point to **Save As HTML**. The Publish to the Web dialog box simply tells you what the wizard will do.

3. Click the **Next>** button. The second dialog box provides tabs for all the objects in the database: Tables, Queries, Forms, and Reports.

4. Click a tab, and then click the check box for each object that you want to transform into a Web page. Each datasheet, table, or page of a report will be a separate Web page. Click the **Next>** button, and the next dialog box lets you choose an HTML file to use as a template for the design of your Web pages.

5. If you have an HTML file you want to use as a template, click the **Browse** button, use the Select an HTML Template dialog box to select the file, and click the **Select** button. Click **Next>**. The next dialog box asks if you want to create static or dynamic Web pages. *Static* pages contain data that does not change; *dynamic* pages pull information from your database using queries, so that the information is up-to-date.

6. Select the type of Web pages you want to create: **Static HTML, Dynamic HTX/IDC (Microsoft Internet Server)**, or **Dynamic ASP (ActiveX Server) Publications**. Click the **Next>** button. The next dialog box asks where you want to save the pages.

7. Click the **Browse** button, select the folder in which you want the Web pages placed, and click **Select**. If you want to run WebPost, a wizard that automatically sends your Web pages to a Web server, click one of the WebPost options. Click the **Next>** button, and the wizard asks if you want to create a home page.

8. Click **Yes, I Want to Create a Home Page** and type a name for the Web page file in the text box. Click the **Next>** button. The final dialog box appears.

9. Click **Yes, I Want to Save Wizard Answers to a Web Publication Profile** and enter a name for the profile. This saves your settings, so you can quickly adjust the settings the next time you run the wizard. Click the **Finish** button. The wizard converts the selected objects and places the new Web pages in the specified folder.

Formatting Web Documents in Word

Whenever you open a Web document in Word, the Web toolbar appears, Word makes the Web page styles available, and the Formatting toolbar changes slightly to provide formatting options for your Web page text. In most cases, you can format your text just as you would if you were working on a Word document (see Chapter 5, "Giving Your Text a Makeover"). When you apply formatting to selected text, Word inserts the proper HTML codes for you. The following list provides a quick rundown of your formatting options:

➤ Use the **Style** drop-down list in the Formatting toolbar to apply common Web page styles. For example, apply the **Heading 1** style to the page's title.

➤ Don't forget to use tables to align text. You can create and edit tables on a Web page just as you can in any Word document. Word handles all the complicated HTML table codes for you.

➤ The **Format, Text Colors** command displays a dialog box that lets you set the text color for body text, unfollowed hyperlinks, and followed hyperlinks. To apply a special color to selected text, use the **Font Color** drop-down list in the Formatting toolbar.

381

➤ Use the **Format**, **Background** options to give your Web page a cool background color and design. To create a textured background, click **Fill Effects**.

➤ Check out the **Insert** menu; it looks much different when you're working on a Web page. The Insert menu offers commands for inserting a background recording (which plays whenever a person opens the page), adding form controls, inserting pictures from a Web Art page, and inserting video clips.

Viewing Your Page in Your Web Browser

Assuming you have a Web browser installed on your computer, you can preview your Web page to see how it will look in a browser. (This is sort of like Print Preview for Web pages.) Open the **File** menu and click **Web Page Preview**. This preview is especially useful for tables, which have a lot more room to spread out on a Web page than they do on a typical 8.5-by-11-inch piece of paper.

Connecting Your Page to Other Pages with Hyperlinks

No Web page is complete without a few links that kick you out to another part of the page or to another page on the Web. All of the Office 97 applications have the Insert Hyperlink feature, which allows you to quickly insert links to other documents, files, or pages.

Unlinking a Link If you decide to remove the link from your page, highlight the link, click the **Insert Hyperlink** button, and click **Remove Link**.

To quickly transform normal text into a link, drag over the text you want to use as the link and click the **Insert Hyperlink** button (the button with the globe and chain on it) in the Standard toolbar. The Hyperlink dialog box appears, prompting you to specify the URL of the page you want the link to point to. In the **Link to File or URL** text box, type the page's URL. When you click **OK**, the selected text is transformed into a link and appears blue (or whatever color you chose for displaying links).

If you have a long page that uses several subheadings, you may want to include a table of contents at the beginning of the page that contains links to the various sections of the page. To do this, you use *bookmarks* and links. You mark each section or destination as a bookmark. Then when you transform your table of contents entries into links, you point each link to one of the bookmarks.

The address of the page you want to link to should be displayed here.

This text box allows you to link to text on the same page.

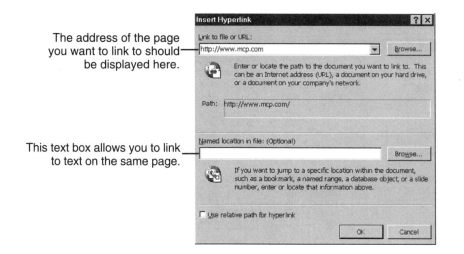

You can create links that point to different areas on the same page or to different pages.

To designate text as a bookmark, drag over the text, open the **Insert** menu, and select **Bookmark**. The Bookmark dialog box appears. Type a name for the bookmark and click the **Add** button. The name is added to the list of bookmarks in this document.

You can now create a link that points to the bookmark. Drag over the text you want to use as the link and click the **Insert Hyperlink** button. The Hyperlink dialog box appears. Click the **Browse** button next to **Named Location in File**, select the bookmark to which you want this link to point, and click **OK**.

Opening Web Pages from the Office 97 Applications

Assuming you have an Internet connection and you are using Microsoft Internet Explorer as your Web browser, you can open Web pages directly from the Office 97 applications and use the Web toolbar to navigate the Web. To turn on the Web toolbar, click the **Web Toolbar** button in the Standard toolbar. The toolbar appears, as shown in the figure below.

To start browsing the Web, you can type the address of the page you want to go to in the **Address** text box. Or, if you added pages to the Favorites list in Internet Explorer, you can open the **Favorites** list and select the page you want to pull up. In either case, the application loads the page with the help of Internet Explorer.

Some Office applications offer additional Web commands. For example, in Word, you can open the **Help** menu and point to **Microsoft on the Web** to view a list of Microsoft Web pages that you can open for additional information.

The Web toolbar lets you navigate the Web from within the Office applications.

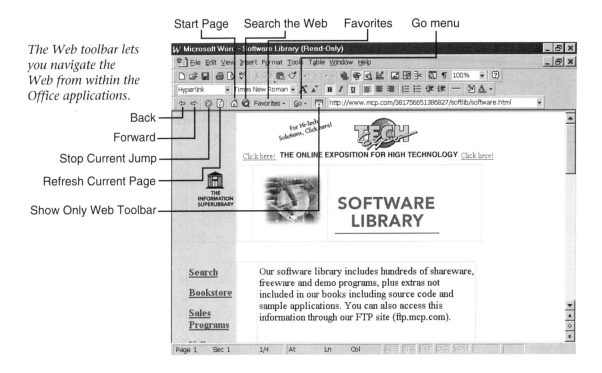

Start Page   Search the Web   Favorites   Go menu

Back

Forward

Stop Current Jump

Refresh Current Page

Show Only Web Toolbar

The Least You Need to Know

This chapter provided the least you need to know about using Office 97's Web page authoring tools. These tools are too powerful to cover completely in a single chapter. However, we did manage to cover the following important points:

➤ To create a new Web page in Word, run the Web Page Wizard. It's in the New dialog box.

➤ To transform an existing Word document, Excel worksheet, or Access database into a Web page, open the document and use the **File**, **Save As HTML** command to save it.

➤ PowerPoint has several templates for creating online presentations. When selecting a template, make sure it has "(Online)" in its name.

➤ Use the **Insert Hyperlink** button in the Standard toolbar to insert links that point to other documents, pages, or files.

Speak Like a Geek: The Complete Archive

absolute cell reference   In an Excel worksheet formula, a cell address that does not change when you move or copy the formula. See also *relative cell reference*.

Access   The database application included with Microsoft Office 97 Professional. Access allows you to create forms, use the forms to enter data, and create reports with stored data.

action button   On a PowerPoint slide, a button that appears at the bottom of the slide and enables the person viewing the slide show to perform some action, such as advancing to the next slide.

add-in   A small program that adds a feature or capability to an application. You can obtain add-ins from Microsoft and other companies and install them to use in your Office 97 applications.

address   A combination of a column letter and row number that specifies the location of a cell in an Excel worksheet. For example, the address of the cell in the upper-left corner of a worksheet is A1. Addresses are commonly used in formulas to pull values into the calculation.

argument   The part of a function statement in an Excel worksheet that tells the function which values to use in the calculations. For example, in =AVG(A1..K15), AVG is the function, and (A1..K15) is the argument.

AutoCorrect   A feature that automatically corrects typos and misspellings as you type.

AutoText   A feature that enables you to create shorthand entries for text you commonly type. For example, you can create an AutoText entry that inserts "Microsoft Office Shortcut Bar" anytime you type MOS and press the F3 key.

Binder   An Office 97 document management tool that enables you to electronically staple together documents of different types, such as Word documents, Excel worksheets, and PowerPoint slides.

border   A box around text, a picture, or some other object. You can change the color, thickness, and style of borders to give them a different look.

browser   See *Web browser*.

build   An animated effect in a slide show that introduces elements on a slide one at a time. For example, you can create a build that assembles a bulleted list one bullet at a time.

cell   The rectangle formed by the intersection of a column and a row in an Excel worksheet. You type text labels, values, and formulas in cells to create a worksheet.

chart   Another name for a graph. In Excel, Word, and PowerPoint, you can insert charts to graphically display the relationships between sets of data.

client   A program that receives copied, linked, or embedded data from other programs. The term "client" is also used to describe your computer when you are connecting to a server computer on a network or on the Internet.

clip art   A collection of predrawn images that you can use to decorate your documents; great for those who have no artistic talent.

Clipboard   A temporary storage area in which data is temporarily stored when you cut or copy it. The Clipboard stores only the most recently cut or copied chunk of data. When you cut or copy another chunk, the new chunk bounces the previous chunk off the Clipboard.

command   An instruction that tells the computer what to do.

concordance file   In Word, a table that contains the text entries you want to index in a chapter or book. Word uses a concordance file to match the entries in the file with the entries in a document. It then marks any matching entries in the document as index entries. When you create an index, Word inserts the index entry into the index along with the page numbers specifying where that entry appears.

conditional formatting   A new cell formatting option in Excel that changes the way a cell looks based on the value in that cell. For example, you can format a cell so that it displays the value in black when the value is positive or in red when the value is negative.

control   A graphical object on an Access form or report, which enables a user to enter data, execute a command, or display data. Common controls include text boxes, option buttons, check boxes, and drop-down lists.

control source   The field from which a control on a form or report obtains data entries. For example, if you place a Product Name field on your report, it has no data of its own. The

Product Name field on the report extracts this data from a source, such as the Product Name field in the Products table.

cursor   Another name for the vertical line that indicates where text will be inserted when you start typing. The preferred name is *insertion point*.

data   Information a computer stores and works with.

database   A computer program used for storing, organizing, and retrieving information. The term is also used to describe the collection of data.

desktop   The area on your Windows 95 computer screen from which you can run applications, open files, remove files with the Recycle Bin, and manage other resources.

destination document   The file into which you paste data that has been cut or copied from another document.

dialog box   A typically small window that an application displays when it needs more information to perform a required task.

document   The file you create when you work in any of the Office 97 applications. These files include Word documents, Excel workbooks, PowerPoint presentations, and Access databases.

Document Map   A new Word feature that displays your document as an outline, allowing you to quickly reorganize it by dragging sections of the document.

drag and drop   To copy or move data simply by selecting it and dragging it from one place to another in the same document or in different documents.

e-mail   Short for electronic mail, a system that enables users to exchange messages and files over network connections or via modem.

embed   To copy data from a document in one application and paste it into a document created with another application while retaining a link to the application in which the data was created. For example, if you embed an Excel worksheet into a Word document, you can double-click the worksheet in the Word document to run Excel and edit the worksheet.

Excel   A spreadsheet program made by Microsoft. You can use Excel to organize numbers and other data, perform complex mathematical operations, and much more.

field   On a fill-in-the-blank form, the blank. In a database, you create forms for entering data. Each form has one or more fields into which you type data. A collection of field entries makes up a record.

file   A collection of data saved to disk under a specific name. Whenever you save a document, the application stores it in a file on your computer's hard disk or on a network drive.

fill handle   A little black box that appears just outside the lower-right corner of a selected Excel worksheet cell. You can drag the fill handle to copy the entry from the selected cell into a string of neighboring cells.

fill series   A string of related values that you can quickly insert into neighboring cells in an Excel worksheet. For example, Excel has a fill series that consists of the names of the week. To insert the names into a series of cells, all you have to do is type **Monday** in the first cell and then drag the cell's fill handle over six neighboring cells. When you release the mouse button, Excel inserts the names of the remaining six days of the week.

filter   To extract related records from a database. For example, if you had a phone book full of names and addresses, you could use a filter to pull out the records Smith through Smythe.

font   A set of characters sharing the same design.

foreign key   In an Access table, a field that obtains its entries from a corresponding field (the primary key) in another table. See also *primary key*.

formatting   Changing the appearance or layout of text on a page. Formatting includes changing margins, picking different type styles, and adding headers and footers.

form   In Access, a tool used to enter data into a database. Forms are sort of like dialog boxes that request information. Each form contains one or more fields into which you type entries.

formula   A mathematical statement in a table or worksheet that tells the application how to perform calculations on a set of values. Formulas typically consist of cell addresses that pull values from specific cells, and mathematical operators that specify which operations to perform. For example, (C1+C2+C3)/3 determines the average of the values in cells C1 to C3.

frame   A light gray box that appears around a text box in PowerPoint or Word to keep any text and graphics together.

function   A ready-made formula that performs a mathematical operation on a set of values. For example, the simple function SUM determines the total of a set of values. A more complicated function might determine a payment on a loan given the loan amount, the term, and the interest rate.

grammar checker   An editing tool built into most word processors and rarely used by anyone for any real good. Microsoft Word has a grammar checker; you can see firsthand what I mean.

graph   See *chart*. Although most people call them graphs, Microsoft insists on calling them *charts*.

graphical user interface (GUI; pronounced "GOO-ey")   A picture-oriented work surface that allows a person (like you) to communicate with an operating system (such as Windows 95) or an application (such as Excel). Graphical user interfaces commonly use icons, dialog boxes, and pull-down menus so you don't have to type commands.

graphics   Electronic art and pictures. A graphic can be a drawing created on the computer, an image scanned in for digital manipulation (clip art), or various shapes, lines, and boxes created with the computer.

handles   Tiny squares that surround a selected graphic object or text box. You can easily change the size or dimensions of an object by dragging one of its handles.

hyperlink   Text, graphics, icons, or other items in a document that link to other areas in the document or to pages, files, and other resources outside a document. Hyperlinks are commonly used on Web pages to link one Web page to another.

icon   A graphic image that represents a command, a program, or a feature.

insertion point   A blinking vertical line that indicates where text will appear when you start typing or where an object will be inserted.

integration   The process of uniting different applications and resources and making them work together.

IntelliMouse   A new three-button pointing device from Microsoft. The middle button on the IntelliMouse is a little gray wheel you can spin to scroll through a document. You can use this button for other tasks, as explained in Chapter 1.

Internet   A global system of interconnected networks that makes it possible for anyone with a computer and an Internet connection to tap its resources and communicate with anyone else connected to the Internet.

intranet   An internal network (in a corporation, university, or other institution) that uses Internet technologies to simplify data transfer and communications.

labels   Entries in an Excel worksheet that are typically used to indicate the meaning of other entries, such as values. Labels usually appear at the tops of columns and to the left of rows.

leader   A string of characters that lead up to the text at the tab stop, like this:

Chapter 14 157

link   To copy data from a source document and paste it into a destination document while retaining a live connection between the two documents. Whenever you edit the data in the source document, the changes appear automatically in the destination document. For example, if you paste an Excel worksheet as a link into a PowerPoint presentation, whenever you edit the worksheet, the changes appear in your presentation.

master document   A Word file into which you can insert other documents and treat them as a single document. For example, you might use a master document to store several chapters of a book. You could then number the pages consecutively throughout the book, create an index or table of contents, and create headers and footers for the entire book.

maximize To enlarge your window to fill the entire screen (the computer equivalent of paying 69 cents extra to move up to a large order of fries and a Biggie Coke).

memory The computer's electronic storage area. Memory used to be measured in kilobytes, but with the advances in operating systems and applications, it is now measured in megabytes. Your computer had better have at least 16 megabytes if you want to use Office 97.

menu A list of commands you can choose by clicking on them with your mouse. Menus can drop down from a menu bar or pop up on your screen when you click the right mouse button. You can usually get a menu to disappear by clicking something outside of the menu.

minimize To reduce your window to a button on the taskbar (or to OD on Redux).

network A group of computers connected with high-speed data cables for the purpose of sharing hardware, software, and data, and for simplifying communications.

newspaper columns A formatting option for text that causes it to display two or more columns of text on a page. The text runs from the top of the first column to the bottom, and continues at the top of the next column, as in a newspaper or magazine.

Office Assistant An animated character that pops up on your screen and offers help whenever you start an Office 97 application or try to perform a somewhat complex task. Office Assistants are a new Help feature in Office 97.

OLE Short for object linking and embedding, OLE is a technology that allows different types of documents to freely share data. When two applications support OLE, you can copy and paste data between the documents in the two applications. See also *embed* and *link*.

online To be connected to another computer or network of computers.

order of operations The sequence in which Excel performs a series of calculations. Excel performs all operations enclosed in parentheses first; then it performs exponential equations, multiplication and division, and addition and subtraction.

Outlook The new personal information manager/e-mail application that comes with Office 97. With Outlook, you can keep track of appointments and special dates, prioritize your list of things to do, manage your e-mail, keep an address book and journal, and even write yourself personal reminder notes.

PowerPoint The Office 97 slide show program. With PowerPoint, you can create on-screen presentations, transfer your presentation to 35mm slides, or print it out on paper or overhead transparencies. You can even create talkies by recording a voice narration.

primary key In an Access table, a field that supplies entries to a corresponding field in another table. For example, if you have one table that contains information about customers and another table that contains order information, the Customer Name field in the Customers table would supply customer names to the Customer Name field in the Orders table.

program A special set of instructions written for the computer, telling it how to perform some useful task. You'll hear the words *program*, *software*, and *application* used interchangeably; they all mean the same thing.

query A set of instructions that tells Access which data to extract from a database, how to sort the data, and how to arrange it. You use queries to pull data from one or more tables or from various databases and to combine that data.

range In an Excel worksheet, a group of neighboring cells or a set of cell blocks.

record A collection of fields making one complete entry in a database. Think of a Rolodex as a database: each card on that Rolodex is a record.

relative cell reference In an Excel worksheet formula, a cell address that changes when you paste the formula into a different cell. Unless you specify otherwise, Excel makes all cell references in formulas relative, so that when you copy a formula into a different cell, the addresses automatically adjust to perform the calculations on a different set of data. If you don't want a cell address to change, you must mark it as an *absolute cell reference.*

report In Access, a tool that extracts data from one or more tables, arranges the data attractively on a page, and (optionally) performs calculations on the data. You typically use reports to analyze data and present it in some meaningful format.

scenario In Excel, a set of values that you can plug into a worksheet to see how these values will affect the end result. When you play with sets of values in this way, you are said to be playing *What-if?*

Schedule+ The old personal information management program that shipped with Office 95, and which has subsequently been replaced by a more competent information manager, Microsoft Outlook.

scrap Selected text, graphic, or other object that you dragged from a document and placed on the Windows desktop. Scraps enables you to quickly move and copy data from one document to another.

ScreenTip Formerly known as ToolTips, a ScreenTip is a brief description or explanation of an object that appears whenever you rest the mouse pointer on the object (usually a button in a toolbar).

section In a Word document, a part of a document that has the same format settings for headers, footers, and columns. By default, every document has one section. If you change the section formatting for part of the document, you create a new section.

selection box An outline that appears around a cell or block of cells in an Excel worksheet when the cell(s) are selected.

server On a network or on the Internet, the computer that your computer (the client) connects to and uses to access information, use applications, or share resources.

Shortcut bar   A strip of buttons that make it easy to access the Office 97 applications and perform specific tasks, such as creating a new document or recording an appointment. After you install Office, the Shortcut bar appears whenever you start your computer.

shortcut keys   Key combinations designed to let you bypass a menu or command sequence.

source document   The file from which you copy or cut data to insert into another document. If you copy data from a source document and paste it as a link into another (destination) document, whenever you edit the source document, your changes appear in the destination document.

Spike   A feature in Word that enables you to add two or more cut or pasted chunks of text to a temporary storage area and paste them as a whole into another document.

spreadsheet   A program made to imitate a ledger's rows and columns, which you use to organize and display data. You can use spreadsheets to arrange data in rows and columns, to perform calculations on numerical entries, and to analyze data through charts.

style   A collection of format settings that you can apply to a paragraph or to selected text. If you change one or more format settings in a style, the changes affect all the text you formatted with that style.

subdocument   A document inside a master document. See also *master document.*

Switchboard   In Access, a control panel that lets you quickly perform various tasks, such as viewing your data or viewing reports.

table   A structure that organizes data in rows and columns. Tables are commonly used in Word documents to help align text without having to enter awkward tab settings.

taskbar   The bar at the bottom of your Windows 95 desktop that lets you switch back and forth between applications or launch new programs with the Start button.

template   A pattern for a document that controls fonts, sizes, and other format settings.

text file   A type of file that contains no special formatting, just plain text.

toolbar   A strip of buttons that usually appears at the top of an application's window just below the menu bar. With a toolbar, you can bypass the pull-down menu commands by clicking a button.

ToolTip   See *ScreenTip.*

values   Numerical entries in a worksheet, as opposed to *labels*, which are text entries.

Web   Short for the World Wide Web, a collection of pages that are stored on computers all over the world and are linked to one another with hyperlinks. Office 97 applications offer many new features that help you create your own pages for publication on the Web.

Web browser   An application that opens and displays pages on the World Wide Web. In addition to displaying the text that makes up those pages, most Web browsers can display graphics and play audio clips.

Windows   Microsoft's grand invention, designed to make the computer easier to use by enabling people to select commands from menus and click pictures instead of having to type commands.

wizard   A series of dialog boxes that leads you through the process of performing a complicated task. Office 97 applications offer wizards as a quick way of creating documents. For example, the Letter Wizard in Word can help you create a properly formatted business letter.

Word   The Office 97 word processor. In Office 97, Word allows you to create not only printed pages but also electronic pages suitable for Web publishing.

word processor   An application that allows you to slice, dice, and mince your words and phrases, add graphics to your pages, and perform all other tasks required to create a printed publication.

WordMail   A new Office 97 feature that allows you to use Word's advanced word processing tools to create, edit, and format your e-mail messages.

workbook   A collection of Excel worksheets. Each file you create in Excel is a workbook.

worksheet   A page in an Excel workbook on which you enter data.

Windows 95 and Windows NT Primer

Windows 95 and Windows NT are graphical operating systems that make your computer easy to use by providing menus and pictures from which you select. Before you can take advantage of either operating system, however, you need to learn some basics that apply to both of them.

Fortunately, Windows 95 and Windows NT operate very much alike. (In fact, they're so similar I'll refer to them both just as Windows throughout the remainder of this appendix.) If the figures you see in this primer don't look exactly like what's on your screen, don't sweat it. Some slight variation may occur depending on your setup, the applications you use, and whether you're on a network. Rest assured, however, that the basic information presented here applies no matter what your setup may be.

A First Look at Windows

You don't really have to start Windows because it starts automatically when you turn on your PC. After the initial startup screens, you arrive at a screen something like the one shown in the following figure.

Parts of the Screen

As you can see, the Windows screen contains a lot of special elements and controls. Here's a brief summary:

> ➤ The Desktop consists of the background and icons that represent programs, tools, and other elements.

The Windows screen.

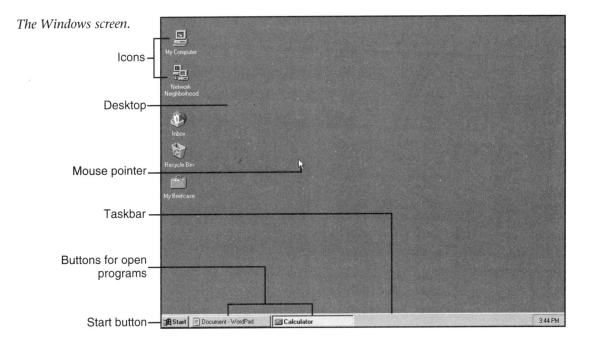

Icons

Desktop

Mouse pointer

Taskbar

Buttons for open
programs

Start button

➤ The Taskbar shows a button for each open window and program. You can switch
between open windows and programs by clicking the taskbar button that represents
the program you want. (The program you are currently working in is highlighted in
the taskbar.)

➤ The Start button opens a menu from which you can start programs, get help, and
find files. To use it, you click the **Start** button, and then you point or click to make a
selection from each successive menu that appears. (When you point to a selection
that has a right-pointing arrow beside it, a secondary—or cascading—menu
appears.)

➤ The icons that appear on your desktop give you access to certain programs and
computer components. You open an icon by double-clicking it. (An open icon
displays a window containing programs, files, or other items.)

➤ The mouse pointer moves around the screen in relation to your movement of the
mouse. You use the mouse pointer to select what you want to work with.

You'll learn more about these elements as you work through the rest of this Windows
primer.

Also Appearing: Microsoft Office

If your computer has Microsoft Office installed on it, the Office Short-cuts toolbar also appears on-screen. It's a series of little pictures strung together horizontally that represent Office programs. Hold the mouse over a picture (icon) to see what it does; click it to launch the program. See your Microsoft Office documentation to learn more.

You may have some other icons on your desktop (representing networks, folders, printers, files, and so on) depending upon what options you chose during initial setup. Double-click an icon to view the items it contains.

Using a Mouse

To work most efficiently in Windows, you need a mouse. You will perform the following mouse actions as you work:

➤ **Point**   To position the mouse so that the on-screen pointer touches an item.

➤ **Click**   To press and release the left mouse button once. Clicking an item usually selects it. Except when you're told to do otherwise (i.e. to right-click), you always use the left mouse button.

➤ **Double-click**   To press and release the left mouse button twice quickly. Double-clicking usually activates an item or opens a window, folder, or program. (Double-clicking may take some practice because the speed needs to be just right. To change the speed so it better matches your "clicking style," choose **Start**, **Settings**, **Control Panel**, and **Mouse**. Then click the **Buttons** tab of the Mouse Properties dialog box and adjust the double-clicking speed so that it's just right for you.)

➤ **Drag**   To place the mouse pointer over the element you want to move, press and hold down the left mouse button, and then move the mouse to a new location. You might drag to move a window, dialog box, or file from one location to another. Except when you're told to do otherwise (i.e. to right-drag), you drag with the left mouse button.

➤ **Right-click**   To click with the right mouse button. Right-clicking usually displays a shortcut (or pop-up) menu from which you can choose common commands.

Southpaw Strategy   You can reverse these mouse button actions if you want to use the mouse left-handed. To do so, click **Start**, **Settings**, **Control Panel**, and **Mouse**. Then click the **Buttons** tab of the Control Panel dialog box and choose **Left-handed**.

Controlling a Window with the Mouse

Ever wonder why the program is called "Windows"? Well, Windows operating systems section off the desktop into rectangular work areas called "windows." These windows are used for particular purposes, such as running a program, displaying options or lists, and so on. Each window has common features used to manipulate the window. The following figure shows how you can use the mouse to control your windows.

Use your mouse to control and manipulate windows.

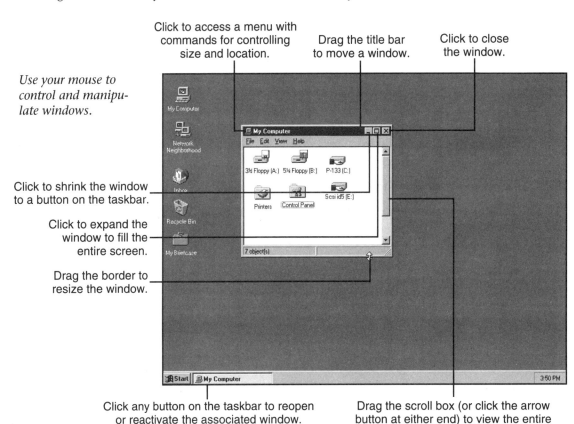

Click to access a menu with commands for controlling size and location.

Drag the title bar to move a window.

Click to close the window.

Click to shrink the window to a button on the taskbar.

Click to expand the window to fill the entire screen.

Drag the border to resize the window.

Click any button on the taskbar to reopen or reactivate the associated window.

Drag the scroll box (or click the arrow button at either end) to view the entire contents of the window.

Check This Out...

Scrolling for Information

If your window contains more information than it can display at once, scroll bars appear on the bottom and/or right edges of the window. To move through the window's contents, click an arrow button at either end of a scroll bar to move in that direction, or drag the scroll box in the direction you want to move. If you're using the professional version of Office 97, you'll also have enhanced scrolling available to you via your "Intellimouse"—a new mouse by Microsoft that includes a scrolling wheel.

Getting Help

Windows comes with a great online Help system. To access it, click the **Start** button and then click **Help**.

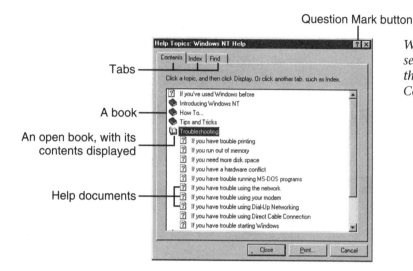

Question Mark button

Tabs

A book

An open book, with its contents displayed

Help documents

Windows offers several kinds of help; this figure shows the Contents tab.

As you can see here, the Help box contains three tabs (Contents, Index, and Find), each of which provides you with a different type of help. To move to a tab, just click it.

Here's how to use each tab:

➤ **Contents** Double-click any book to open it and see its sub-books and documents. Double-click a sub-book or document to open it and read the Help topic.

➤ **Index** When you click this tab, Windows asks you for more information on what you're looking for. Type the word you want to look up, and the Index list scrolls to that part of the alphabetical listing. When you see the topic that you want to read in the list, double-click it.

➤ **Find** The first time you click this tab, Windows tells you it needs to create a list. Click **Next** and then **Finish** to allow this. When Windows finishes, it asks you to type the word you want to find in the top text box. Then click a word in the middle box to narrow the search. And finally, review the list of Help topics at the bottom and double-click the one you want to read.

When you finish reading about a document, click **Help Topics** to return to the main Help screen, or click **Back** to return to the previous Help topic. When you finish with the Help system itself, click the window's **Close** (X) button to exit.

Another Way to Get Help

In the upper-right corner of the Help window, you should see a question mark next to the Close button. This is (surprise!) the Question Mark button. Whenever you see this button (it appears in other windows besides the Help window), you can click it to change your mouse pointer to a combined arrow-and-question mark. You can then point at any element in the window for a quick "pop-up" description of that element.

Some applications or application suites (such as Microsoft Office 97) may also offer online help. You can learn more about using online help by reading the application's documentation or any Que book that covers the application.

Starting a Program

Of the many possible ways to start a program, this is the simplest:

1. Click the **Start** button.

2. Point to **Programs**.

3. Click the group that contains the program you want to start (such as **Accessories**).

4. Click the program you want to start (such as **Notepad**).

Here are a few more ways you can start a program in Windows:

➤ Open a document that you created in that program. The program automatically opens when the document opens. For example, double-click the **My Computer** icon on the desktop, find the icon of the document you want to open, and then double-click a document file.

➤ (Optional) Open a document you created in that program by clicking the **Start** button, pointing to **Programs**, and then clicking **Windows Explorer**. The Windows Explorer window opens; it looks very similar to the File Manager window you've worked with in Windows 3.1. Locate the directory (or "folder" in Windows 95/NT 4.0 terminology) and double-click the file name. The document opens in the program in which it was created.

➤ Click the **Start** button, point to **Documents**, and select a recently used document from the Documents submenu. Windows immediately starts the program in which you created the file and opens the file.

➤ If you created a shortcut to the program, you can start the program by double-clicking its shortcut icon on the desktop.

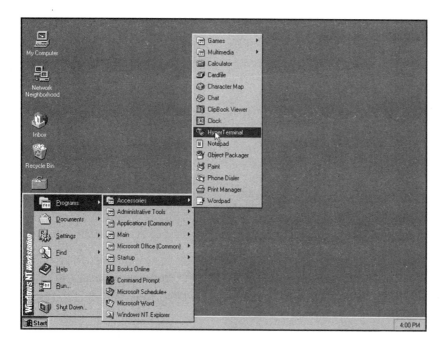

Work through the Start menu and its successive submenus until you find the program you want to start.

What's a Shortcut?

Shortcut icons are links to other files. When you use a shortcut, Windows simply follows the link back to the original file. If you find that you use any document or program frequently, you might consider creating a desktop shortcut for it. To do so, just use the right mouse button to drag an object out of Windows Explorer or My Computer and onto the desktop. In the shortcut menu that appears, select **Create Shortcut(s) Here**.

Using Menus

Almost every Windows program has a menu bar that contains menus. The menu names appear in a row across the top of the screen. To open a menu, click its name (after you click anywhere in the menu bar, you need only point to a menu name to produce the drop-down menu). The menu drops down, displaying its commands (as shown in the next figure). To select a command, you simply click it.

A menu lists various commands you can perform.

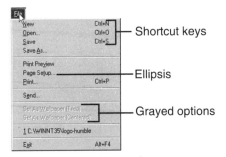

Usually, when you select a command, Windows executes the command immediately. But you need to keep the following exceptions to that rule in mind:

➤ If the command name is gray (instead of black), the command is unavailable at the moment, and you cannot choose it.

➤ If the command name is followed by an arrow (as the selections on the Start menu are), selecting the command causes another menu to appear, from which you must make another selection.

➤ If the command is followed by an ellipsis (…), selecting it will cause a dialog box to appear. You'll learn about dialog boxes later in this primer.

Shortcut Keys

Key names appear after some command names (for example, Ctrl+O appears to the right of the Open command, and Ctrl+S appears next to the Save command). These are shortcut keys, and you can use them to perform the command without opening the menu. You should also note that some menu names and commands have one letter underlined. By pressing Alt+the underlined letter in a menu name, you can open the menu; by pressing the underlined letter in a command name, you can select that command from the open menu.

Using Shortcut Menus

A fairly new feature in Windows is the shortcut or pop-up menu. Right-click any object (any icon, screen element, file, or folder), and a shortcut menu like the one shown in the next figure appears. The shortcut menu contains commands that apply only to the selected object. Click any command to select it, or click outside the menu to cancel it.

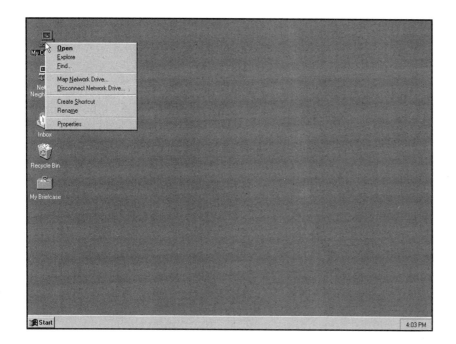

Shortcut menus are new in Windows 95 and WindowsNT 4.0.

Navigating Dialog Boxes

A dialog box is Windows way of requesting additional information or giving you information. For example, if you choose Print from the File menu of the WordPad application, you see a dialog box something like the one shown in the figure below. (The options it displays will vary from system to system.)

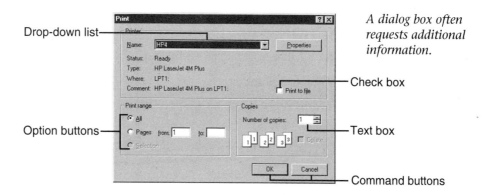

A dialog box often requests additional information.

Drop-down list

Option buttons

Check box

Text box

Command buttons

Each dialog box contains one or more of the following elements:

➤ List boxes display available choices. Click any item in the list to select it. If the entire list is not visible, use the scroll bar to see additional choices.

➤ Drop-down lists are similar to list boxes, but only one item in the list is shown. To see the rest of the list, click the drop-down arrow (to the right of the list box), and then click an item to select it.

➤ Text boxes allow you to type an entry. Just click inside the text box and type. Text boxes that are designed to hold numbers usually have up and down arrow buttons (called increment buttons) that let you bump the number up and down.

➤ Check boxes enable you to turn individual options on or off by clicking them. (A check mark or "X" appears when an option is on.) Each check box is an independent unit that doesn't affect other check boxes.

➤ Option buttons are like check boxes, except that option buttons appear in groups and you can select only one. When you select an option button, the program automatically deselects whichever one was previously selected. Click a button to activate it, and a black bullet appears inside of the white option circle.

➤ Command buttons perform an action, such as executing the options you set (OK), canceling the options (Cancel), closing the dialog box, or opening another dialog box. To select a command button, click it.

➤ Tabs bring up additional "pages" of options you can choose. Click a tab to activate it. (See the section on online help for more information on tabs.)

From Here

If you need more help with Windows, you may want to pick up one of these books:

The Complete Idiot's Guide to Windows 95 by Paul McFedries

Easy Windows 95 by Sue Plumley

The Big Basics Book of Windows 95 by Shelley O'Hara, Jennifer Fulton, and Ed Guilford

Using Windows 95 by Ed Bott

The Complete Idiot's Guide to Windows NT 4.0 Workstation by Paul McFedries

Using Windows NT 4.0 Workstation by Ed Bott

Index

G

415

417

QUE'S
MICROSOFT® OFFICE 97
RESOURCE CENTER

For the most up-to-date information about all the Microsoft Office 97
products, visit Que's Web Resource Center at

http://www.mcp.com/que/msoffice

The web site extends the reach of this Que book by offering you
a rich selection of supplementary content.

You'll find information about Que books as well as additional content
about these new **Office 97 topics**:

- **Word**
- **Excel**
- **PowerPoint®**
- **Visual Basic® for Applications**
- **Access**
- **Outlook™**
- **FrontPage™**

Visit Que's web site regularly for a variety of new
and updated Office 97 information.

The best resources and tips for getting things done with Office 97!